THE CATHOLIC BI QUARTERLY

MONOGRAPH SERIES

8

PESHARIM:

QUMRAN INTERPRETATIONS OF BIBLICAL BOOKS

by

Maurya P. Horgan

PESHARIM:
QUMRAN INTERPRETATIONS OF BIBLICAL BOOKS

By

MAURYA P. HORGAN

The Catholic Biblical Association of America
Washington, DC 20064
1979

PESHARIM:
QUMRAN INTERPRETATIONS OF BIBLICAL BOOKS
by Maurya P. Horgan

Washington, DC 20064

PRODUCED IN THE UNITED STATES

Library of Congress Cataloging in Publication Data

Horgan, Maurya P. 1947-
Pesharim.

(The Catholic Biblical Quarterly: Monograph series; 8)
Bibliography: p.
Includes index.
1. Dead Sea scrolls — Criticism, intrepretation, etc.
2. Bible. O. T. — Criticism, interpretation, etc., Jewish.
I. Title. II. Series.
BM487.H62 221.6 78-12910
ISBN 0-915170-07-8

For my mother

Contents

ABBREVIATIONS

In addition to the abbreviations listed in Instructions to Contributors to the *CBQ* and the CBQMS, the following abbreviations and sigla are used.

Bauer and Leander	Bauer, Hans and Pontus Leander, *Historische Grammatik der hebräischen Sprache des Alten Testaments, Erster Band: Einleitung, Schriftlehre, Laut- und Formenlehre* (Halle: Max Niemeyer, 1922).
Beer-Meyer	Beer, Georg, *Hebräische Grammatik,* 3 vols. (2nd ed. revised by Rudolf Meyer; Sammlung Göschen 763/763a, 764/764a, 769/769a; Berlin: de Gruyter, 1952, 1955, 1960).
[ ]	a hole in the skin, which may or may not have contained a portion of the text.
{ }	an editorial deletion by the present writer
{{ }}	deletion marked in the text itself, presumably by the original scribe or by a corrector
‹ ›	an editorial addition by the present writer
. . .	visible but illegible traces of one or more letters
( )	words added in translations for the sake of English style

ACKNOWLEDGMENTS

The present work is a slightly revised version of a doctoral dissertation presented to the Department of Theology at Fordham University, Bronx, New York, in December, 1976. At this time I am happy to be able to record my continuing gratitude to Prof. Joseph A. Fitzmyer, S.J., who directed the dissertation closely through all of its stages and whose personal interest in me and my work has always been a source of encouragement and inspiration. The late Prof. George S. Glanzman, S.J., first reader of the dissertation, worked through each draft of this study with great care. Under his direction I first studied the Dead Sea scrolls in Hebrew, and I shall always be indebted to him. My thanks are warmly expressed to Prof. Francis T. Gignac, S.J., my Greek professor at Fordham and second reader of the dissertation, who offered, throughout my years of graduate study, the example of his exacting scholarship and the enrichment of his friendship.

I should also like to thank Rev. Daniel J. Harrington, S.J., the general editor of *New Testament Abstracts,* with whom I worked during the years of completing the dissertation in Cambridge, Massachusetts, for his support, advice, and example. During my time in Cambridge, I also benefited from many discussions with Prof. John Strugnell of Harvard Divinity School.

Finally, I am grateful to Prof. Bruce Vawter, C.M., and the associate editors of CBQMS for accepting this volume for publication and for seeing it through production.

INTRODUCTION

Among the Hebrew documents recovered from the Qumran caves are eighteen texts distinguished by the fact that each is a continuous commentary on or an interpretation of a single biblical book. These texts are called pesharim because each section of interpretation following a biblical citation is introduced by one of several formulas using the word *pēšer*, "interpretation" (plural: *pĕšārîm*).[1] Thus far the following texts have been identified as pesharim: four from Cave 1: 1QpHab (formerly designated DSH), 1QpMic (=1Q*14*), 1QpZeph (=1Q*15*), and 1QpPs (=1Q*16*); one from Cave 3: 3QpIsa (=3Q*4*); and the rest from Cave 4: 4QpIsa$^{a\text{-}e}$ (=4Q *161-165*), 4QpHos^{a,b} (=4Q*166, 167*), 4QpMic (=4Q*168*), 4QpNah (=4Q *169*), 4QpZeph (=4Q*170*), 4QpPs^{a,b} (=4Q*171, 173*), 4QpUnid (=4Q*172*, unidentified fragments presumed to be of pesharim).

Of these eighteen texts, only fifteen (1QpHab, 1QpMic, 1QpZeph, 1QpPs, 4QpIsa$^{a\text{-}e}$, 4QpHos^{a,b}, 4QpNah, 4QpZeph, 4QpPs^{a}, and 4QpPs^{b} [excluding fragment 5]) can be identified with certainty as pesharim. In two of the remaining three texts (3QpIsa and 4QpMic) there are no conclusive indications that these documents belong to the literary genre of the pesher, and 4QpUnid is too fragmentary to be of substantive use in this study. These three texts, along with 4QpPs^{b} fragment 5, which is clearly from a later time than the other fragments of that document, are presented in an appendix.

Among all the Qumran documents, these fifteen are neither the only texts in which the key word "pesher" occurs, nor are they the only texts that reflect aspects of biblical interpretation and study among the members of the Qumran community.[2] Virtually the whole of Qumran literature

[1]Since it has been generally accepted, I use the roman spelling "pesher" (singular) and "pesharim" (plural), except in the word-study section in Part II, where the exact transliteration of the Hebrew word is used.

[2]The activity of interpretation of the Scriptures was not restricted to the Qumran sect but was also a focal point of Pharisaic Judaism—and, as will be seen in Part II, can also be paralleled outside Judaism. See below, pp. 249-59, and see also, e.g., M. Gertner, "Terms of Scriptural Interpretation: A Study in Hebrew Semantics," *BSO(A)S* 25 (1962) 2-4; G. Vermes, "The Qumran Interpretation of Scripture in Its Historical Setting," ALUOS 6 (1966-1968) (ed. J. Macdonald; Leiden: Brill, 1969) 85-97; also in *Post-Biblical Jewish Studies* (SJLA 8; Leiden: Brill, 1975) 37-49; D. Patte, *Early Jewish Hermeneutic in Palestine* (SBLDS 22; Missoula: Scholars Press, 1975).

springs from and testifies to the dedication of the Qumran sect to the study of Scripture, a community activity described in 1QS 6:6-8:

> In a place where the ten are, there must not cease to be one who studies the Law (*ʾyš dwrš btwrh*) day and night continuously, according to the arrangement, one after another. The Many will watch together the third part of every night of the year, reciting from the book, studying commandment(s) (*mšpṭ*) and saying benedictions together.

Considering themselves to be the people of the New Covenant, the true remnant of Israel living in the end-time, the members of the Qumran community believed that they were the guardians of the purity and authenticity of the true priesthood and of the correct interpretation of Scripture, an interpretation revealed to the Teacher of Righteousness,[3] "to whom God made known all the mysteries of his servants the prophets" (1QpHab 7:4-5).[4]

Though this special kind of interpretation assumes its most systematic form in the biblical commentaries, it appears in other types of texts, several of which even use the word "pesher" to introduce interpretative statements, e.g., 4Q*159* 5:1, 5; 4QFlor 1-2 i 14, [19]; 11QMelch 12, 17; 4QCatena[a] (4Q*177*) 1-4:6; 4QAges of Creation (4Q*180*)[5] 1:1, 7. Because of the

[3]In the translation of the texts and in the discussions, I refer to the figure called *mwrh hṣdq* as "the Teacher of Righteousness," because this is the most familiar translation of the epithet for this early leader of the Qumran community. The noun *ṣdq* is frequent in biblical Hebrew, meaning "righteousness," "justice," and also "what is right, normal, or true." The construct relationship of the nouns *mwrh* and *ṣdq* could indicate an objective genitive, i.e., "the teacher of righteousness," "the teacher of truth," or a subjective genitive, i.e., "the righteous teacher," "the true teacher," or "the legitimate teacher." Although the different translations of the epithet may have some bearing on the attempts to identify this person historically, it is not necessary to go into that question in this study.

[4]For more on the self-identification of the Qumran sect and its attitude to the Scriptures, see especially O. Betz, *Offenbarung und Schriftforschung in der Qumransekte* (WUNT 6; Tübingen: Mohr-Siebeck, 1960), and see also, e.g., J. T. Milik, *Ten Years of Discovery in the Wilderness of Judaea* (tr. by J. Strugnell; SBT 26; London: SCM, 1959) 103-105, 113-18; W. H. Brownlee, *The Meaning of the Qumran Scrolls for the Bible* (New York: Oxford University, 1964) 62-109; J. C. Trever, "The Qumran Covenanters and Their Use of Scripture," *The Personalist* 31 (1958) 127-38; M. Burrows, "Prophecy and the Prophets at Qumran," *Israel's Prophetic Heritage: Essays in Honor of James Muilenberg* (ed. B. W. Anderson and W. Harrelson; New York: Harper & Brothers, 1962) 224-27; F. M. Cross, *The Ancient Library of Qumran and Modern Biblical Studies* (rev. ed.; Anchor Books; Garden City, NY: Doubleday, 1961) 109-20.

[5]Possibly also 4Q*181,* though the word "pesher" does not occur in this text. See J. T. Milik ("Milkî-ṣedeq et Milkî-rešaʿ," *JJS* 23 [1972] 110), who thinks that 4Q*180* and *181* preserve parts of two copies of the same work, a commentary on the periods of history. In addition he proposes that 11QMelch is part of the same work (pp. 109-10, 122-24), and he suggests that 4Q*183* might be part of a pesher on Ps 110:1b-2a (pp. 138-39).

use of the word "pesher," these texts are sometimes described as pesharim and are frequently grouped with the biblical commentaries. For this study, however, I separate them from the texts presented here. A workable distinction is that of Jean Carmignac, who differentiates between the "continuous pesher" (*pesher continu*), in which a single biblical book is methodically interpreted section by section, and the "thematic pesher" (*pesher thématique*), in which certain citations to be interpreted are chosen from various biblical books and grouped artificially around a central idea, e.g., 11QMelchizedek and 4QFlorilegium.[6] This study, then, is devoted to the "continuous pesharim" of Qumran literature.

These commentaries purport to preserve a special revealed interpretation of the biblical texts, which was probably transmitted orally from the early days of the community until it was written down during the Herodian period, if not before.[7] J. T. Milik speculates that the commentaries may have arisen in the context of the daily watch, the continuous study of the Scriptures (1QS 6:6-8), during which a group probably read a text and commented on it phrase by phrase.[8] Another possibility that he has proposed is that the commentaries "are to be connected with the expositions of the Bible that were given in the sect's meetings for worship."[9]

Each of the pesharim is a unique hand-written work; no copies of any of them have thus far been discovered. It has therefore been suggested that these texts are autographs.[10] But there is evidence that calls this into question, e.g., 1QpHab 2:5, where a space between the words *wkn* and *pšr,* which must go together syntactically, may be best explained as a mistake made by a copyist who was accustomed to leaving a space before the word *pšr* (similarly 1QpHab 3:7); 4QpIsa^{e} 5:5a-5, where the interlinear addition (line 5a) seems to be correcting a copying error of homoioteleuton (similarly 4QpPs^{a} 1-10 iii 5a-5); see also 1QpHab 5:3-6. There are also places pointed out in the notes below, where textual variants in the biblical material might be explained as copying mistakes. It is true that these could have

[6] "Le document de Qumran sur Melkisédeq," *RevQ* 7 (1969-71) 360-61.

[7] F. M. Cross, *Ancient Library,* 113-14; *Scrolls from Qumran Cave I: The Great Isaiah Scroll, The Order of the Community, The* Pesher *to Habakkuk* (From the photographs by John C. Trever; ed. under the direction of the Dead Sea Scroll Committee, ASOR, by F. M. Cross, D. N. Freedman, J. A. Sanders; Jerusalem: The Albright Institute of Archaeological Research and the Shrine of the Book, 1972) 5. See also J. van der Ploeg, *Bijbelverklarung te Qumrân* (Mededelingen der Koninklijke Nederlandse Akademie van Wetenschappen, afd. Letterkunde Nieuwe Reeks, Deel 23, No. 8; Amsterdam: North-Holland, 1960) 210-11.

[8] "Fragments d'un midrash de Michée dans les manuscrits de Qumrân," *RB* 59 (1952) 418.

[9] *Ten Years,* 41.

[10] J. T. Milik, *Ten Years,* 41; so also F. M. Cross, *Ancient Library,* 114-15; *Scrolls from Cave I,* 5.

arisen at some earlier point in the transmission of the biblical texts themselves, but when they are taken together with the other instances, they lead me to conclude that at least some of the manuscripts containing pesharim are not autographs.

All of these texts have been edited and published with photographs, transcriptions of the Hebrew texts, and translations, but they have not yet been presented as a group and studied together as documents of one literary genre, which is the purpose of this study.

The transcription of the Hebrew text of each document is presented in the insert that is enclosed. Part I of the body of the work contains the English translation and notes on the text and translation of each of the fifteen texts that have been identified with certainty as pesharim. The *editio princeps,* preliminary publications, secondary transcriptions and translations, and other secondary works on specific topics are listed at the beginning of the presentation of each text. References to works that are cited repeatedly are abbreviated in these lists, and the general bibliography should be consulted for the additional publication information.

All of the pesharim have been transcribed and translated as part of the work of publishing the individual texts, but there is room for correction and improvement in many cases. The present transcription has been prepared from the published photographs of the documents. Where fragments have been properly matched and identified this does not offer serious problems in reading the texts, since infra-red photography has often produced pictures that are clearer than the manuscripts in their present state of preservation. However, for what cannot be read from the photographs, one must rely on the competence and professional judgment of the original editors and subsequent commentators who have seen the manuscripts themselves.

In the transcription doubtful or mutilated letters are not marked with a circle or a dot. The photographs of the original publications should be consulted when there is doubt about the reading. Words or letters that have been added above the lines in the original documents are transcribed on the line, but the fact that they are supralinear in the manuscripts is indicated in the notes. In the transcription the relative spacing of the words is preserved insofar as it is possible.

A number of lacunas in the texts both in the biblical citations and in the interpretation-sections are restored here. The biblical text is restored following the text of the *Biblia Hebraica Stuttgartensia,*[11] unless there is evi-

[11]K. Elliger and W. Rudolph, general editors (Stuttgart: Württembergische Bibelanstalt, 1968—), hereafter referred to as *BHS.*

dence in the text that suggests an alternative reading, or where a different Qumran spelling would be expected. It is not, however, assumed that the MT as restored in the various pesharim was the text known to the Qumran authors. These biblical passages are restored mainly for the purpose of continuity in order to give a sense of the content and movement of the documents, prescinding from the problems that pertain to the MT alone. The task of studying the pesharim in the light of the history of the text of the Hebrew Bible must be left to experts in that field. In restoring lacunas in the interpretation-sections, I have in some places followed the reconstructions proposed by others, and in other passages I have been able to offer new suggestions. Some of these restorations are incomplete and suggested with hesitation, and others are probable; but all reconstructions are tentative.

The words in parentheses in the translations have been added for the sake of the English sense of a passage. Where only a few letters of a word that cannot be reconstructed with ease are legible, these Hebrew letters have been transliterated in italics in the translation, and where traces of one or more letters are visible but illegible, this is indicated—as in the transcription—by one or more dots on the line. In translating difficult passages of the biblical texts that have been restored, I have often followed the RSV, again prescinding from the internal problems of the MT.

Following the Hebrew text and English translation of each document are notes. These comments are not an exhaustive treatment of any one aspect of the pesharim. Variants from the MT, excluding purely orthographic variants, are noted but not usually discussed in detail. Historical allusions to persons and events in the history of the Qumran community are treated briefly where it is necessary for understanding a particular passage. Similarly, comments on and evaluations of the opinions and suggestions of others are included on important and disputed points. However, the focus of the notes, beyond those demanded by details of transcription and translation, is to call attention to elements in each text that come to light when the pesharim are studied as a group.

In Part II, the description of the literary genre, the chief characteristics of the pesharim are summarized, with observations on the word *pēšer,* the structure of the texts, the formulaic expressions used to introduce the lemmas and the interpretations, the modes of interpretation, and the content of the interpretation-sections. Finally, the pesharim are compared with some other interpretative writings.

At this point a brief overview of the persons and events that are the subject of the interpretations is appropriate. Surveys of the historical events alluded to in the pesharim can be found in most general introductions to and collections of the Dead Sea scrolls. Several of these are listed in the general bibliography, and works on specific problems are noted in connection with individual texts. Any discussion about the historical allusions contained in these documents must be prefaced by a warning: the history recounted in the pesharim, like the history recounted in the biblical books, is an interpreted history. As J. T. Milik describes it, "the apocalyptic Essene mind, especially when obliged to give a continuous exposition of a prophetic text, cannot be expected either to confine itself to the events of one period, or to separate out different events into clear groups."[12] The Qumran community viewed history in terms of its own identity and destiny, and when the authors referred to events in their past or present, they moved freely from one time period to another and frequently telescoped several events into one interpretation. The problem of pinpointing the persons or events about which a Qumran document is speaking is further complicated by the fact that the authors regularly referred to specific figures or groups by epithets or figurative descriptive phrases. Finally, it cannot be assumed that any of the Qumran texts is a "homogeneous block of material."[13] As with biblical material, one section in these texts may be the product of different stages of tradition.[14]

In the pesharim there are a number of isolated clues about events in different periods in the history of the Qumran community. About the early days of the sect, the texts tell that God chose the Teacher of Righteousness to build a congregation (4QpPs^{a} 1-10 iii 15-17), and that he made known to him all the mysteries of his servants the prophets (1QpHab 7:4-5). The Teacher of Righteousness came into conflict with the Man of the Lie (*ʾyš hkzb*), and at a confrontation between these two the House of Absalom (*byt ʾbšlwm*) and its partisans did not support the Teacher (1QpHab 5:9-12). The Man of the Lie was in league with traitors (*bwgdym,* 1QpHab 2:1-3) and led many astray by deceit (4QpPs^{a} 1-10 i 26-27). The arch-enemy of the Teacher of Righteousness was the Wicked Priest (*hkwhn hršʿ*), who was trustworthy at first but subsequently abandoned God when he ruled over Israel, betraying the statutes for the sake of wealth (1QpHab 8:8-13). He defiled the sanctuary (1QpHab 12-7:10), lived in drunkenness (1QpHab 11:12-15), and practiced thievery and abomination (1QpHab 8:8-13). He lay in ambush for the Teacher of Righteousness (4QpPs^{a} 1-10 iv 8-10), and on one occasion pursued him to his place of exile at the feast of the Day

[12] *Ten Years,* 65.

[13] J. Murphy-O'Connor warns against this presupposition in "The Essenes and their History," *RB* 81 (1974) 216.

[14] This point cannot be pursued here, but there are places in the texts where layers of tradition might possibly be isolated, e.g., the three-part pesher in 1QpHab 2:1-10 or the complex interpretation in 1QpHab 12:2-6.

of Atonement "to make him stumble" (1QpHab 11:4-8). But the Wicked Priest was given into the hands of his enemies (1QpHab 9:9-12) and was punished with horrors of evil diseases (1QpHab 9:1-2) to the point of annihilation in despair (1QpHab 9:9-12).

There have been numerous attempts to identify these figures and to situate these events historically. The opinions can be divided into three groups:[15] (1) There are those who place the events involving the Teacher of Righteousness and the Wicked Priest during the reigns of Antiochus IV Epiphanes and Demetrius I Soter (ca. 175-150 B.C.), but this position has few advocates today. (2) Some others place these events in the period of the later Hasmoneans, identifying the Wicked Priest as Alexander Jannaeus (103-76 B.C., e.g., J. M. Allegro) or Hyrcanus II (67 B.C., e.g., A. Dupont-Sommer). This time period seems to me to be too late. From the texts it is clear that the Wicked Priest was a contemporary of the Teacher of Righteousness, and the burden of proof must be on those who would place the appearance of the Teacher of Righteousness this late in the history of the community. (3) The position that has come to be widely accepted is the Maccabean theory, which identifies the Wicked Priest with Jonathan (160-143 B.C.) and/or Simon (142-134 B.C.), the brothers of Judas Maccabaeus.[16] A thorough examination of the clues in the pesharim may well provide still better support for the Maccabean position, but that will have to be the subject of future work. For now, this theory is accepted here as that most in accord with the evidence in these texts.

The next time period reflected in the Qumran texts presented here, especially in 4QpNah, is the period of the Lion of Wrath (*kpyr hḥrwn*) and the Seekers-After-Smooth-Things (*dwršy hḥlqwt*). In 4QpNah it is related that the Seekers-After-Smooth-Things advised Demetrius, the king of

[15]See G. Vermes, *The Dead Sea Scrolls in English* (Baltimore: Penguin Books, 1970) 57-58, and see also the recent summary and discussion by H. Bardtke ("Literaturbericht über Qumrān. X. Teil: Der Lehrer der Gerechtigkeit und die Geschichte der Qumrāngemeinde," *TRu* 41 [1976] 97-140.

[16]This was the first suggested by G. Vermes (see *Dead Sea Scrolls in English,* 57) and is now followed by many, e.g., J. T. Milik, who favors identifying the Wicked Priest as Jonathan (*Ten Years,* 85-87), while F. M. Cross argues for Simon as the Wicked Priest (*Ancient Library,* 127-60; see also G. W. E. Nickelsburg, Jr., "Simon—A Priest With a Reputation for Faithfulness," *BASOR* 223 [1976] 67-68). J. Murphy-O'Connor feels that the identification of the Wicked Priest as Jonathan has been established ("The Essenes and their History," 229-33), and in this he is following H. Stegemann, who made a detailed study of the history of the Qumran community in his 1965 Bonn dissertation, *Die Entstehung der Qumrangemeinde,* which was privately published in 1971 (see the review by J. Carmignac, *RevQ* 8 [1973] 277-81, and also the lengthy summary of Stegemann's study by H. Bardtke, "Literaturbericht über Qumrān," 100-19). Following Stegemann, Murphy-O'Connor suggests that the Teacher of Righteousness was Jonathan's predecessor as High Priest (Jonathan was named High Priest

Greece, to invade Jerusalem (3-4 i 2-4) and make war against the Lion of Wrath (3-4 i 5-6). The attempt was unsuccessful, and the Lion of Wrath retaliated against the Seekers-After-Smooth-Things by crucifying many of them (3-4 i 6-8). The Seekers-After-Smooth-Things, also called Ephraim (3-4 ii 2), are pictured as those who lead people astray with false teaching (3-4 ii 8-10). Another adversary of the Qumran community during this period, frequently mentioned in connection with Ephraim, was Manasseh (3-4 iii 9; 3-4 iv 1, 3-4). There is now almost complete agreement among modern authors that these passages refer to the reigns of Alexander Jannaeus (103-76 B.C.), Salome Alexandra (76-67 B.C.), and Hyrcanus II and Aristobolus II (67-63 B.C.). For further detail about the events that are alluded to in 4QpNah, see the introductory remarks to that text, pp. 159-62.

Finally, there are references to the events of the end-time, in which the Qumran authors believed they were living. Among these texts, some refer to concrete historical events that are imminently anticipated or already upon the community, while others refer in general to the ultimate triumph of the righteous over the wicked at the eschatological judgment.

The passages that refer to historical events deal mainly with the Kittim, who are described as swift and vigorous in battle (1QpHab 2:12-15), who come by the level plain to smite and loot the cities of the land (1QpHab 3:1-2), who are cunning and deceitful, angry and furious (1QpHab 3:4-13). They are mocking and arrogant, and their rulers ridicule and despise the people (1QpHab 4:1-9). They sacrifice to their standards and revere their military arms; they divide up their forced service upon all year by year (1QpHab 6:1-8). Again, it is almost unanimously agreed that the period being referred to is the Roman conquest in 63 B.C., and that the Kittim are the Roman armies.

by Alexander Balas in 152 B.C.), an interim figure following Alcimus (High Priest, 161-159 B.C.), who functioned as High Priest without official appointment for seven years and whose name therefore was not recorded. Murphy-O'Connor suggests that the Teacher of Righteousness was dismissed by Jonathan and took refuge with the Essenes at Qumran, where he easily gained a position of authority ("The Essenes and their History," 233). There he came into conflict with the Man of the Lie. Although most have assumed that the Man of the Lie was the same person as the Wicked Priest (e.g., F. M. Cross, *Ancient Library,* 154; G. Vermes, *Dead Sea Scrolls in English,* 59), Murphy-O'Connor believes, again following Stegemann, that he was a leader in the Essene movement before the Teacher came to the group and that he subsequently led a rival faction of the group in opposition to the adherents of the Teacher of Righteousness ("The Essenes and their History," 233-38; but cf. H. Burgmann, "Gerichtsherr and Generalankläger: Jonathan und Simon," *RevQ* 9 [1977] 3-72, who argues that the Wicked Priest is Jonathan and that the Man of the Lie is Simon). See also J. Murphy-O'Connor, "Demetrius I and the Teacher of Righteousness," *RB* 83 (1976) 400-20.

These, then, are the main time periods alluded to in the pesharim, and the preceding outline has set the general context for understanding the content of the Qumran interpretations of the biblical texts.

PART I

THE TEXTS

1QpHab

Editio princeps: "The Habakkuk Commentary," *The Dead Sea Scrolls of St. Mark's Monastery,* Vol. I (W. H. Brownlee), pp. xix-xxi and pls. lv-lxi. See also two separate publications of photographs under the same title, *Scrolls from Qumran Cave I: The Great Isaiah Scroll, The Order of the Community, The* Pesher *to Habakkuk* (1972, color photographs, pp. [149]-[163]; 1974, black-and-white photographs, pp. [75]-[82]).

Preliminary publications: W. H. Brownlee, "The Jerusalem Habakkuk Scroll," *BASOR* 112 (1948) 8-18 (including a transcription of cols. 1 and 2 and a translation of all thirteen cols.); "Further Light on Habakkuk," *BASOR* 114 (1949) 9-10; "Further Corrections of the Translation of the Habakkuk Scroll," *BASOR* 116 (1949) 14-16.

Secondary transcriptions and translations:* M. Burrows, *Dead Sea Scrolls,* 365-70; J. Carmignac, *Les Textes,* 2. 93-117; A. Dupont-Sommer, "Le 'Commentaire d'Habacuc' découvert près de la Mer Morte: Traduction et notes," *RHR* 137 (1950) 129-71; *Essene Writings,* 258-68; K. Elliger, *Studien zum Habakuk-Kommentar,* [insert] 1-15 and 165-225; T. H. Gaster, *Dead Sea Scriptures*, 244-52; A. M. Habermann, *Megilloth,* 43-49; E. Lohse, *Die Texte,* 227-43; J. Maier, *Die Texte,* 1. 149-56, 2. 137-42; G. Vermes, *Dead Sea Scrolls in English,* 235-43; A. S. van der Woude, *Bijbelcommentaren,* 29-45.

Secondary literature: W. H. Brownlee, "The Placarded Revelation of Habakkuk," *JBL* 82 (1963) 319-25; M. Burrows, "The Meaning of *ʾšr ʾmr* in DSH," *VT* 2 (1952) 255-60; J. Carmignac, "Notes sur les Peshârîm," *RevQ* 3 (1961-62) 505-10; A. Dupont-Sommer, "Encore sur le mot *ʾbwt* dans DSH XI 6," *VT* 2 (1952) 276-78; "Résumé des cours de 1970-71: Hébreu et Araméen," *Annuaire du Collège de France* 71 (1971-72) 391-95; D. N. Freedman, "The House of Absalom in the Habakkuk Scroll," *BASOR* 114 (1949) 11-12; I. Rabinowitz, "The Second and Third Columns of the Habakkuk Interpretation Scroll," *JBL* 69 (1950) 31-49; Y. Ratzaby, "Remarks Concerning the

*Secondary literature on 1QpHab is very extensive. Listed under this heading and the following are a selected number of studies that are especially important for those aspects of the Habakkuk commentary treated here. Many other works are incorporated into the general bibliography.

Distinction Between Waw and Yod in the Habakkuk Scroll," *JQR* 41 (1950-51) 155-57; S. Segert, "Zur Habakuk-Rolle aus dem Funde vom Toten Meer," *ArOr* 21 (1953) 218-39; 22 (1954) 99-113, 444-59; 23 (1955) 178-83, 364-73, 575-619; E. Sjöberg, "The Restoration of Col. II of the Habakkuk Commentary of the Dead Sea Scrolls," *ST* 4 (1950) 120-28; S. M. Stern, "Notes on the New Manuscript Find," *JBL* 69 (1950) 18-30; H. G. M. Williamson, "The translation of 1QpHab. V, 10," *RevQ* 9 (1977) 263-65.

The commentary on Habakkuk, designated 1QpHab, was one of the first documents from among the Dead Sea scrolls to be published, and up to the present it is the most complete of the biblical commentaries. Much has been written already about this text, and the works listed above should be consulted for details about the scroll's physical appearance and distinctive features. One of the most important works, which treats almost every aspect of this document in great detail, is the study by Karl Elliger that is named above. It is to this volume that one should turn first for information on those elements of 1QpHab not covered here, since this presentation must be limited to those features of the Habakkuk commentary that are useful in studying the biblical commentaries as a group.

There are thirteen cols. preserved virtually intact, giving the biblical text of and commentary on the first two chaps. of Habakkuk. The fact that col. 13 is only four lines long (with the rest of the col. blank) almost certainly indicates that the commentary included only the first two chaps. of the prophetic book. Of the first col. only the ends of the lines remain, and the bottom of the scroll has deteriorated, so that the last two or three lines of every col. are lost.

The commentary comes mainly from two hands: 1:1—12:13 from one hand, and 12:13 (*ʾšr*)—13:4 from another (see Elliger, *Studien*, 72-74). The script of both is Herodian, and the time of the copying of the scroll can probably be placed in the second half of the first century B.C.

The structure of the commentary is fairly regular, with citations of the biblical text (from one-half to two verses) followed by brief interpretations introduced by the formulas *pšr hdbr ʿl, pšr hdbr ʾšr, pšrw ʿl, pšrw ʾšr,* and *pšrw*. In a number of places in the document there are repetitions of portions of the preceding lemma. These "second citations" are introduced either by *kyʾ hwʾ ʾšr ʾmr* or *wʾšr ʾmr* and are followed either by another lemma or by a commentary. See further Part II, p. 243.

The content of the interpretation-sections deals both with the history of the community and with the events of the end of days. Figuring in the history of the community are the Teacher of Righteousness (1:13; 2:2; 5:9-12; 7:4-5; 8:3; 9:9-12; 11:4-8), the Man of the Lie (2:1-2); the House of Absalom (5:9-12), the Wicked Priest (8:8-13; 8:16—9:2; 9:9-12; 11:4-8,

12-15; 12:2-6, 7-10), and the One who Spouts the Lie (10:9-13). Among the eschatological events mentioned in the document are the coming of the Kittim (2:12-15; 2:17—3:1; 3:4-6, 9-13; 4:1-3, 5-9, 10-13; 6:1-2, 6-8, 10-12; 9:6-7), the final judgment (5:3-6; 8:1-3; 10:3-5; 12:12-14; 13:1-4), and the downfall of the last priest of Jerusalem (9:4-7). The importance of these historical allusions and the main attempts at their identification have been summarized above in the Introduction. For detailed studies of the historical background of 1QpHab, see the general bibliography.

1QpHab: Translation

Column 1

1. [THE BURDEN THAT HABAKKUK THE PROPHET SAW: HOW LONG, YAHWEH,] HAVE I CRIED OUT FOR HELP, BUT YOU DO NOT — Hab 1:1-2a
2. [HEAR? The interpretation of the passage concerns everything that Habakkuk prophesied concerning the expec]tation of the generation of
3. [the visitation in the last days all the things that are going to co]me upon them.
4. [I CRY OUT TO YOU "VIOLENCE!" BUT YOU DO NOT SAVE. The interpretation of it is that] they [c]ry out against — 1:2b
5. [men of violence who WHY DO YOU MAKE ME SEE EVIL, AND] DO YOU GAZE AT [TR]IBULATION? — 1:3a
6. [The interpretation of it concerns who rebelled against] God with oppression and unfaithfulness.
7. [DESTRUCTION AND VIOLENCE ARE BEFORE ME; THERE IS STRIFE, AND CONTENTION ARISES.] — 1:3b
8. [The interpretation of it] *wg*. [ ]*ly h*[ ]. and strife
9. [qu]arrel, and *ḥ*[ ]*h* is
10. [ ]THEREFORE THE LAW IS NUMBED, — 1:4a
11. [AND JUDGMENT DOES NOT GO FORTH TO VICTORY. The interpretation of it is] that they rejected the law of God
12. [FOR THE WICKED SURROU]ND THE RIGHTEOUS. — 1:4bα
13. [The interpretation of it: the wicked one is the Wicked Priest, and the righteous one] is the Teacher of Righteousness.
14. [TH]EREFORE THE JUDGMENT GOES FORTH — 1:4b β
15. [PERVERTED. The interpretation of it] and not *m*[ ]
16. [LOOK, O TRAITORS, AND] S[EE;] — 1:5
17. [WONDER AND BE AMAZED, FOR I AM DOING A DEED IN YOUR DAYS THAT YOU WOULD NOT BELIEVE IF]

Column 2

1. IT WERE TOLD. [The interpretation of the passage concerns] the traitors together with the Man of
2. the Lie, for [they did] not [believe the words of] the Teacher of Righteousness (which were) from the mouth of
3. God. And it concerns the trai[tors to] the new [covenant,] f[o]r they were not
4. faithful to the covenant of God, [but they profaned] his holy name.
5. Likewise, the interpretation of the passage [concerns the trai]tors at the end of
6. days. They are the ruthless [ones of the coven]ant who will not believe
7. when they hear all that is going to co[me up]on the last generation from the mouth of
8. the priest into [whose heart] God put [understandi]ng to interpret all
9. the words of his servants the prophets by [whose] hand God enumerated
10. all that is going to come upon his people and up[on his congregation.] FOR BEHOLD I AM RAISING UP 1:6a
11. THE CHALDEANS, THAT BITTER [AND HA]STY NATION.
12. The interpretation of it concerns the Kittim, wh[o ar]e swift and vigorous
13. in battle, so as to destroy many [by the sword and by famine] in the dominion of
14. the Kittim, and the wick[ed ones will betray the covena]nt, and they will not be faithful
15. to the statutes of [Go]d [ ]
16. ^{c}l[WHO GO THROUGH THE BREADTH OF THE LAND] 1:6b
17. [TO TAKE POSSESSION OF DWELLING PLACES THAT ARE NOT THEIRS. The interpretation of it concerns the Kittim]

Column 3

1. and by (way of) the level plain they come to smite and to loot the cities of the land,
2. for this is what it says: TO TAKE POSSESSION OF DWELLING PLACES NOT THEIR OWN. FEARFUL 1:6bβ-7
3. AND TERRIBLE ARE THEY. A CLAIM TO DIGNITY GOES OUT FROM THEM.
4. The interpretation of it concerns the Kittim, fear and dread of whom are upon all
5. the nations. By design all their plans are to do evil, and with cunning and deceit
6. they associate with all the peoples. THEIR HORSES ARE SWIFTER THAN LEOPARDS AND MORE FIERCE 1:8-9a
7. THAN THE WOLVES OF THE NIGHT. THEY PAW THE

GROUND, AND THEIR RIDERS SPREAD OUT FROM A DISTANCE.

8. THEY FLY LIKE THE EAGLE, (WHICH) HASTENS TO DEVOUR ALL. THEY COME FOR VIOLENCE. THE HORROR
9. OF THEIR FACES IS AN EAST WIND. The in[terpretation] of it concerns the Kittim, who
10. trample the earth with [their] horses and with their beasts. And from a distance
11. they come, from the islands of the sea, to devour all the peoples like an eagle,
12. and there is no satiety. With rage [they] gr[ow hot, and with] burning anger and fury
13. they speak with all [the peoples, fo]r this is what it
14. says: THE HORR[OR OF THEIR FACES IS AN EAST WIND. THEY GATHER CAPTIVES LIKE SA]ND. 1:9aβ-9b
15. [The interpreta]tion of it [concerns the Kittim, who]
16. [ ]
17. [AND AT KINGS] 1:10a

Column 4

1. THEY SCOFF, AND PRINCES ARE TO THEM A LAUGHING MATTER. The interpretation of it is that
2. they mock great ones, and they despise honored ones; kings
3. and princes they mock, and they scoff at a great people. AND THEY 1:10b
4. LAUGH AT EVERY FORTRESS, AND THEY HEAP UP EARTHEN MOUNDS TO CAPTURE IT.
5. The interpretation of it concerns the rulers of the Kittim, who despise
6. the fortifications of the peoples and laugh with derision at them;
7. and with many people they (i.e., the rulers of the Kittim) surround them (i.e., the fortifications) to capture them. And with terror and dread
8. they (i.e., the fortifications) are given into their hand, and they tear them down, because of the guilt of those who dwell
9. in them. THEN THEY CHANGED, A WIND, AND THEY PASSED BY, AND THESE MADE THEIR POWER 1:11
10. THEIR GOD. The interpretation of it [con]cerns the rulers of the Kittim,
11. who, according to the decision of [their] guilty house, pass one
12. before the other. [Their] rulers come [on]e after another
13. to ruin the l[and. AND] THESE [MADE] THEIR POWER THEIR GOD. 1:11b
14. The interpretation of it [al]l the people
15. /[ ]/
16. [ARE YOU NOT FROM OF OLD,] 1:12

17. [YAHWEH, MY HOLY GOD? WE SHALL NOT DIE. YAHWEH,]

Column 5

1. FOR JUDGMENT YOU HAVE SET HIM UP, AND A ROCK AS HIS REPROVER YOU HAVE ESTABLISHED. (YOU ARE) TOO PURE OF EYES 1:12b-13a
2. TO LOOK ON EVIL, AND TO GAZE AT TRIBULATION YOU ARE NOT ABLE.
3. The interpretation of the passage is that God will not destroy his people by the hand of the nations,
4. but into the hand of his chosen ones God will give the judgment of all the nations. And by means of their rebuke
5. all the wicked ones of his people will be convicted (by those) who have kept his commandments
6. in their distress. For this is what it says: (YOU ARE) TOO PURE OF EYES TO LOOK 1:13aα
7. ON EVIL. The interpretation of it is that they were not unfaithful, whoring after their own eyes in the time of
8. wickedness. WHY DO YOU HEED TRAITORS, BUT ARE SILENT WHEN 1:13b
9. A WICKED ONE SWALLOWS UP ONE MORE RIGHTEOUS THAN HE? The interpretation of it concerns the House of Absalom
10. and their partisans, who were silent at the rebuke of the Teacher of Righteousness
11. and did not support him against the Man of the Lie—who rejected
12. the Law in the midst of all their council. AND YOU MAKE HUMANITY LIKE THE FISH OF THE SEA, 1:14-16
13. LIKE CREEPING THINGS TO RULE OVER IT. HE BRINGS EVERYTHI[NG] UP [WITH THE FISH]HOOK AND DRAGS IT INTO HIS NET.
14. AND HE GATHERS IT IN [HIS] SE[INE. THEREFORE HE SACRI]FICES TO HIS NET; THEREFORE HE IS GLAD
15. [AND SHOUTS FOR JO]Y, [AND HE BURNS INCENSE TO HIS FISHING NET, FOR ON ACCOUNT OF THEM] HIS LOT IS LUXURIOUS
16. [AND HIS FOOD IS RICH. The interpretation of it]
17. [ ]

Column 6

1. the Kittim, and they increase their wealth with all their booty
2. like the fish of the sea. And when it says, THEREFORE HE SACRIFICES TO HIS NET 1:16a
3. AND BURNS INCENSE TO HIS SEINE, the interpretation of it is that they

4. sacrifice to their standards, and their military arms are
5. the objects of their reverence. FOR ON ACCOUNT OF THEM HIS LOT IS LUXURIOUS AND HIS FOOD IS RICH. 1:16b
6. The interpretation of it is that they divide up their yoke and
7. their forced service—their food—upon all the peoples year by year
8. to lay waste many lands. THEREFORE HE DRAWS HIS SWORD CONTINUALLY 1:17
9. TO SLAUGHTER NATIONS, AND HE HAS NO COMPASSION.
10. The interpretation of it concerns the Kittim, who destroy many with the sword
11. —young men, strong men and old men, women and toddlers—and on the fruit of
12. the womb they have no compassion. AT MY STATION SHALL I STAND, 2:1-2
13. AND I SHALL POST MYSELF AT MY FORTIFICATION, AND I SHALL WATCH TO SEE WHAT HE SAYS
14. TO ME AND WHAT [HE ANSWERS RE]GARDING MY OBJECTION. AND YAHWEH DID ANSWER ME,
15. [AND HE SAID: WRITE THE VISION AND MAKE IT PL]AIN UPON THE TABLETS SO THAT HE CAN RUN
16. [WHO READS IT. The interpretation of it]*t*.[ ]
17. [ ]

Column 7

1. and God told Habakkuk to write down the things that are going to come upon
2. the last generation, but the fulfillment of the end-time he did not make known to him.
3. And when it says, SO THAT HE CAN RUN WHO READS IT, 2:2-bβ
4. the interpretation of it concerns the Teacher of Righteousness, to whom God made known
5. all the mysteries of the words of his servants the prophets. FOR THERE IS YET A VISION 2:3a
6. CONCERNING THE APPOINTED TIME. IT TESTIFIES TO THE END-TIME, AND IT WILL NOT DECEIVE.
7. The interpretation of it is that the last end-time will be prolonged, and it will be greater than anything
8. of which the prophets spoke, for the mysteries of God are awesome.
9. IF IT TARRIES, WAIT FOR IT, FOR IT WILL SURELY COME, AND IT WILL NOT 2:3b
10. BE LATE. The interpretation of it concerns the men of truth,
11. those who observe the Law, whose hands do not grow slack in the service of
12. the truth, when the last end-time is drawn out for them, for

13. all of God's end-times will come according to their fixed order, as he decreed
14. for them in the mysteries of his prudence. BEHOLD [HIS SOUL] IS HEEDLESS, NOT UPRIGHT 2:4a
15. [WITHIN HIM.] The interpretation of it is that they double upon them
16. [but] they will not find favor at their judgment .[ ]*l* [ ]
17. [THE RIGHTEOUS MAN WILL LIVE BY HIS FAITHFULNESS.] 2:4b

Column 8

1. The interpretation of it concerns all those who observe the Law in the House of Judah, whom
2. God will save from the house of judgment on account of their tribulation and their fidelity
3. to the Teacher of Righteousness. AND MOREOVER, WEALTH BETRAYS A HAUGHTY MAN, AND HE 2:5-6
4. IS UNSEEMLY (?), WHO OPENS HIS THROAT WIDE LIKE SHEOL; LIKE DEATH, HE CANNOT BE SATED.
5. ALL THE NATIONS ARE GATHERED ABOUT HIM, AND ALL THE PEOPLES ARE ASSEMBLED TO HIM.
6. AND DO NOT ALL OF THEM RAISE A TAUNT AGAINST HIM AND INTERPRETERS OF RIDDLES ABOUT HIM,
7. WHO SAY: "WOE TO THE ONE WHO MULTIPLIES WHAT IS NOT HIS OWN! HOW LONG WILL HE WEIGH HIMSELF DOWN WITH
8. DEBT?" The interpretation of it concerns the Wicked Priest, who
9. was called by the true name at the beginning of his course, but when he ruled
10. in Israel, he became arrogant, abandoned God, and betrayed the statutes for the sake of
11. wealth. He stole and amassed the wealth of the men of violence who had rebelled against God,
12. and he took the wealth of peoples to add to himself guilty sin. And the abominable ways
13. he pursued with every sort of unclean impurity. AND WILL IT NOT BE *pt.*[ ]*ʾwm,* THAT YOUR CRE[DI]TORS WILL ARISE? 2:7-8a
14. WILL THOSE WHO MAKE YOU TREMBLE AWAKE, AND WILL YOU BECOME THEIR PLUNDER?
15. FOR YOU HAVE PLUNDERED MANY NATIONS, BUT ALL THE REST OF PEOPLES WILL PLUNDER YOU.
16. The in[terpretation of the passage] concerns the priest, who rebelled

17. [and trans]gressed the statutes of [God, plundering many peoples, but they will pl]under him *l* [ ]

Column 9

1. his injury (?) on account of wicked judgments. And horrors of evil diseases
2. were at work in him, and acts of vengeance on his decaying flesh. And when
3. it says, FOR YOU HAVE PLUNDERED MANY NATIONS, BUT ALL THE REST OF PEOPLES WILL PLUNDER YOU, 2:8a
4. the interpretation of it concerns the last priests of Jerusalem,
5. who amass wealth and profit from the plunder of the peoples;
6. but at the end of days their wealth together with their booty will be given into the hand of
7. the army of the Kittim. For they are the rest of the peoples.
8. ON ACCOUNT OF HUMAN BLOODSHED AND VIOLENCE DONE TO THE LAND, THE CITY, AND ALL ITS INHABITANTS. 2:8b
9. The interpretation of it concerns the [W]icked Priest, whom—because of wrong done to the Teacher of
10. Righteousness and his partisans—God gave into the hand of his enemies to humble him
11. with disease for annihilation in despair, beca[u]se he had acted wickedly
12. against his chosen ones. WOE TO THE ONE WHO MAKES AN EVIL PROFIT FOR HIS HOUSE, SETTING 2:9-11
13. HIS NEST ON HIGH TO BE DELIVERED FROM THE REACH OF EVIL. YOU HAVE PLANNED SHAME
14. FOR YOUR HOUSE, THE ENDS OF (?) MANY PEOPLES AND (EVEN) THE THREADS OF YOUR OWN [LI]FE. FOR
15. A STO[NE] WILL CRY OUT FROM THE WALL, [AND] STUCCO FROM THE FRAMEWORK WILL GIVE AN[SWER.]
16. [The interpretation of the passa]ge concerns the pr[iest,] who .[ ]ṣ
17. [ ]..[ ]

Column 10

1. so that its stones are (built up) by oppression and the stucco of its framework by robbery. And when
2. it says CUTTING OFF MANY PEOPLES AND (EVEN) THE THREADS OF YOUR OWN LIFE, 2:10b
3. the interpretation of it: This is the house of judgment. God will give
4. his judgment in the midst of many peoples, and from there he will bring him up for judgment,
5. and in their midst he will condemn him as guilty and with a fire of

brimstone he will punish him. WOE 2:12-13

6. TO THE ONE WHO BUILDS A TOWN WITH BLOOD AND FOUNDS A CITY ON INIQUITY. ARE NOT
7. THESE FROM YAHWEH OF HOSTS? PEOPLE TOIL FOR FIRE
8. AND NATIONS GROW WEARY FOR NOTHING.
9. The interpretation of the passage concerns the One who Spouts the Lie, who caused many to err,
10. building a city of vanity with bloodshed and establishing a congregation with deceit,
11. for the sake of its glory making many toil in the service of vanity and saturating (?) them
12. with w[o]rks of falsehood, with the result that their labor is for nothing; so that they will come
13. to the judgments of fire, because they reviled and reproached the elect of God.
14. FOR THE EARTH WILL BE FILLED WITH THE KNOWLEDGE OF THE GLORY OF YAHWEH, AS THE WATERS 2:14
15. COVER THE SEA. [(*vacat*)] The interpretation of the passage [is that,]
16. when they return. [ ]/[ ]
17. [the One who Spouts]

Column 11

1. the Lie, and afterwards knowledge will be revealed to them in abundance, like the waters of
2. the sea. WOE TO HIM WHO GIVES HIS NEIGHBORS TO DRINK MIXING IN 2:15
3. HIS POISON, INDEED, MAKING (THEM) DRUNK IN ORDER THAT HE MIGHT LOOK UPON THEIR FEASTS.
4. The interpretation of it concerns the Wicked Priest, who
5. pursued the Teacher of Righteousness—to swallow him up with his poisonous vexation—
6. to his place of exile. And at the end of the feast, (during) the repose of
7. the Day of Atonement, he appeared to them to swallow them up
8. and to make them stumble on the fast day, their restful sabbath. YOU WILL BE SATED
9. WITH DISHONOR RATHER THAN GLORY. DRINK THEN, YOU YOURSELF, AND TOTTER. 2:16
10. THE CUP OF YAHWEH'S RIGHT HAND WILL COME AROUND TO YOU, AND DISGRACE (WILL COME)
11. UPON YOUR GLORY.
12. The interpretation of it concerns the priest whose shame prevailed over his glory,

13. for he did not circumcise the foreskin of his heart, but he walked in the ways of
14. inebriety in order that the thirst might be consumed, but the cup of the wrath of
15. [Go]d will swallow him up, adding [t]o [all] his [sha]m[e] and a wound
16. [ ]/[ ]/[ ]/[ ]
17. [FOR THE VIOLENCE TO LEBANON WILL COVER YOU AND THE ASSAULT OF BEASTS] 2:17

Column 12

1. WILL DESTROY. ON ACCOUNT OF HUMAN BLOODSHED AND VIOLENCE (DONE TO) THE LAND, THE TOWN AND ALL WHO INHABIT IT.
2. The interpretation of the passage concerns the Wicked Priest—to pay him
3. his due inasmuch as he dealt wickedly with the poor ones; for "Lebanon" is
4. the council of the community, and the "beasts" are the simple ones of Judah, those who observe
5. the Law—(he it is) whom God will sentence to complete destruction
6. because he plotted to destroy completely the poor ones. And when it says ON ACCOUNT OF THE BLOODSHED OF 2:17b
7. THE TOWN AND VIOLENCE (DONE TO) THE LAND, the interpretation of it: the "town" is Jerusalem,
8. where the Wicked Priest committed abominable deeds and defiled
9. God's sanctuary. And "violence (done to) the land" (refers to) the cities of Judah, where
10. he stole the wealth of the poor ones. WHAT PROFIT DOES AN IDOL BRING, WHEN ITS MAKER HAS HEWED (IT), 2:18
11. A MOLTEN STATUE AND AN IMAGE (?) OF FALSEHOOD? FOR THE ARTISAN RELIES UPON THE THINGS HE MAKES,
12. FASHIONING DUMB IDOLS. The interpretation of the passage concerns all
13. the idols of the nations, which they have made so that they may serve them and bow down
14. before them, but they will not save them on the day of judgment. WOE, 2:19-20
15. WO[E TO THE ONE WHO SAYS] TO THE WOOD, "WAKE UP!" "A[RISE!"] TO DUMB [ST]ONE.
16. [IS THIS A TEACHER? BEHOLD, IT IS OVERLAID WITH GOLD AND SILVER, YET NO]
17. [BREATH IS IN IT. BUT YAHWEH IS IN HIS HOLY TEMPLE;]

Column 13

1. ALL THE EARTH KEEPS SILENT BEFORE HIM. The interpretation of it concerns all the nations
2. who have served stone and wood, but on the day of
3. judgment God will wipe out completely all who serve the idols
4. and the evil ones from the earth.

1QpHab: Notes

Column 1

Only the left side of col. 1 remains. The determination of the width of the col. is based on the probable restoration of lines 11 and 13. If the restoration of these lines is correct, then the width of the col. is about 144 mm., i.e., room for about forty-eight spaces with an average of 3 mm. per space. This would be by far the widest of the thirteen cols. of the commentary, but if this width is not accepted, it must be concluded that some of the text of Hab 1:1-5 was omitted from the commentary.

1:1 The full title of the prophetic work is restored here according to the MT of Hab 1:1, followed by a short pesher. Compare 4QpPs[a] 1-10 iv 23, where, after the commentary on Psalm 37, a commentary on Psalm 45 begins with the title of the work followed by a short pesher.

Yhwh would have been written in paleo-Hebrew script as it is below in 6:14; 10:7, 14; 11:10. This special treatment of the sacred tetragrammaton appears also in 1QpMic 1-5:1, 2; 1QpZeph 3, 4; 4QpIsa[a] 7-10 iii 17 (Allegro's 8-10:13); 4QpPs[a] 1-10 ii 4, 13, 25; 1-10 iii 14; 1-10 iv 7, 10. But cf. 4QpIsa[b] 2:3, 7, 8; 4QpIsa[c] 6-7 ii 19; 8-10:6; 21:9; 23 ii 3, 9; 4QpNah 3-4 ii 10; 4QpZeph 1-2:1; 4QpPs[a] 1-10 iii 5a; 4QpPs[b] 4:2; 4QpMic 1, 3:4, where it is written in regular script. In one instance (4QpIsa[e] 6:4) a space is left for the tetragrammaton. For a study of some of the implications of the treatment of the tetragrammaton in ancient manuscripts, see G. Howard, "The Tetragram and the New Testament," *JBL* 96 (1977) 63-83.

1:2 Here some authors (e.g., Brownlee, Carmignac, Dupont-Sommer, Elliger) continue the citation through the end of Hab 1:2 and then begin the pesher. While this is possible, it leaves no room for a space between the citation and the pesher. Elsewhere in the document, when the end of a citation occurs in the middle of a line, there is a space before the beginning of the pesher (2:1; 3:9; 4:10; 5:7, 9; 6:3; 7:10, 15; 8:8, 9:4; 10:15). Only in two instances, 12:12 and 13:1, the latter of which is certainly by a different hand, does the pesher follow the citation immediately without an intervening space.

expectation or "hope" ([*tw*]*ḥlt*). Suggested by the context, this is restored by Carmignac, Dupont-Sommer (*Essene Writings*), Elliger, and van der Woude, but other possibilities include *mḥlt*, "affliction" (Habermann) or *tḥlt*, "beginning" (Dupont-Sommer ["Résumé 1970-71," 392] Vermes).

1:2-3 *the generation of the visitation* (*dwr* [*hpqwdh*]); see 4QpHos^{a} 1:10. Also possible is *dwr ʾḥrwn,* "a later generation" (so Habermann), cf. *bdwr ʾḥrwn* in CD 1:12 and *hdwr hʾḥrwn*, "the last generation," in 1QpHab 2:7; 7:2; 1QpMic 17-18:[5]. The "last generation" is restored here by Dupont-Sommer ("Résumé 1970-71," 392), van der Woude, and Vermes, but it is unclear what Hebrew words they are suggesting.

all the things that are going to come upon them ([*kwl hbʾ*]*wt ʿlyhm*), i.e., upon the generation of the visitation, cf. 1QpHab 2:[7], 10; 7:1-2.

1:4 Here Hab 1:2b is restored, thus leaving enough room for a space between the end of the lemma and the beginning of the pesher.

1:5-6 *men of violence* ([*ʾnšy ḥms*]); see 1QpHab 8:11. This phrase is similarly restored by Dupont-Sommer ("Résumé 1970-71," 392) and Vermes.

Restoration of Hab 1:3a fits the letters and traces at the end of line 5, but it is impossible to tell whether the Qumran commentator read *tbyṭ,* "do you gaze," as in the MT or *ʾbyṭ*, "must I gaze," as suggested in *BHS*.

Some continue the citation of Hab 1:3a (line 5), restoring 1:3bα at the beginning of line 6 followed by a pesher (e.g., Dupont-Sommer ["Le 'Commentaire,'" 131]), but I prefer to restore Hab 1:3a in line 5, a pesher in line 6, and Hab 1:3b in line 7. However, there are problems with the Hebrew text of Hab 1:3b, and there is no way of determining the exact wording of the Qumran citation.

As it is restored here, the pesher in line 6 probably focused on enemies of the Qumran sect; Dupont-Sommer restores ". . . ceux qui persécutent les élus de Dieu . . ." ("Résumé 1970-71," 392).

1:8 At the end of the line, three words are partially preserved. Restoration and syntax of the first word are uncertain owing to the lack of context and the difficulty of distinguishing *w* and *y*. There are parts of five letters of the first word preserved: *w/y, g,* a trace of a letter, *l*, and *w/y*. If the first letter is read as *y* and the last as *w*, the word could be a verb in the 3rd pers. pl. impf., e.g., *ygzlw*, "they rob" (Dupont-Sommer ["Résumé 1970-71," 392], Vermes), *ygʿlw*, "they loathe" (Dupont-Sommer [*Essene Writings*]), or *ygdlw*, "they are great." Brownlee's suggestion of *ygmlw*, "they will recompense" ("Jerusalem Habakkuk Scroll," 8-9) does not fit the visible traces of letters. If both the first and the last letters are read as *w*, the word could be a verb in the 3rd pers. pl. perf. with the copula. Or if the first letter is read as *w* and the last as *y*, the word could be a masc. pl. noun in the construct state with the copula, e.g., *wgdwly*, "and the great ones of," or *wgzly*, "and the robberies of." The choice of the best reading of the first word depends partly on how the first letter of the second word is read. It is read here as *h*; the wedge-shaped stroke across the top seems to make *ḥ* unlikely, though it cannot be excluded. If *ḥ* were read, it might be the first letter of a verb or of a noun, and any of the forms noted above for the first word would be possible. However, if *h* is read, it could be the article, and this would indicate that the first word should probably be a masc. pl. noun in the construct state. (If the first word were a verb, apparently followed by a definite object—the noun beginning with the article—the particle *ʾt* might be expected.) It is better, therefore, to look for a masc. pl. noun in the construct state for the first word.

The third word, *wryb*, "and strife," is taken up from the lemma.

1:9 Of the three words partially preserved at the end of the line, the last word seems to be the pronoun *hyʾh* (or *hwʾh*). This spelling is frequent in 1QS, though elsewhere in 1QpHab the personal pronouns are always *hwʾ* and *hyʾ*. The first of the three words is restored as *mrybh*, "quarrel," though it could also be a hiph. part. with a 3rd pers. sing. fem. sf., "the one who reproaches her." The syntax of this and the following words is unclear. Elliger reads the three as *mr]ybh wḥ[šb]w hwʾh,* "Gezänk und sinnen Verderben" but this is not a satisfactory reading of the second word. In that word the first letter could be *w* or *y*, the second letter could be *h* or *ḥ*, but the last letter is better read as *h*. Elliger understands the last of the three words not as the personal pronoun but as the noun *hawwâ*, "destruction," but nowhere in QL is this noun spelled with medial ʾ.

1:11 *to victory* ([*lnṣḥ*]). For this translation of *nēṣaḥ*, see e.g., Job 14:20.

they rejected (*mʾśw*). This is the only place in QL where this verb is spelled *mʾś*; elsewhere it is *mʾs*, e.g., below 5:11; 4QpIsa^b 2:7, cf. Isa 5:24.

1:14 The citation of Hab 1:4bβ presents the following variant from the MT: *hmšpṭ* (MT: *mšpṭ*).

1:16-17 There are traces of letters visible for a sixteenth line, but it is not certain how many additional lines are missing from the bottom of the col. I favor a col. of seventeen lines (so also Brownlee ["The Original Height of the Dead Sea Habakkuk Scroll," *BASOR* 118 (1950) 8], Dupont-Sommer ["Résumé 1970-71," 393], Vermes), but others leave room for eighteen lines (Carmignac, Elliger, van der Woude). In either case, the text of Hab 1:5 is to be restored at the end of the col.; the last word of the verse begins col. 2. In the citation of Hab 1:5 *bwgdym*, "traitors," is restored rather than *bgwym*, "among the nations," as in the MT on the basis of the pesher in 2:1; the Qumran text thus agrees with the emendation suggested in *BHS* on the basis of the Greek οἱ καταφρονηταί.

Column 2

This col. begins with the last word of Hab 1:5 followed by a lengthy three-part pesher (lines 1-10) built around the noun *hbwgdym*, "the traitors," the verb *ʾmn*, "believe" or "be faithful," and the ideas of speaking, relating, or reporting, reflected in the words *spr, bdbry mpyʾ, bšwmʿm, lpšww*. The introductory formula for the first interpretation (line 1) is lost, but it was surely either *pšrw ʿl* or *pšr hdbr ʿl*. The first pesher refers to the enemies in the time of the Teacher of Righteousness, cf. below 5:8-12. The second pesher, introduced simply by the elliptical formula *wʿl*, refers to the enemies of the Qumran congregation during the period after the Teacher of Righteousness. The third pesher is introduced by the unique formula *wkn pšr hdbr* [*ʿl*, and the content of this interpretation is eschatological. For the translation of *wkn* as "and likewise," see M. H. Segal, *A Grammar of Mishnaic Hebrew* (Oxford: Clarendon, 1958) 140.

2:1-2 *the Man of the Lie* (*ʾyš hkzb*). See above, pp. 6-8. This person appears in the pesharim as the enemy of the Teacher of Righteousness (1QpHab 5:10-11), who "led many astray" (4QpPsa 1-10 i 26) and who opposed the elect of God (4QpPsa 1-10 iv 14). The epithet occurs elsewhere in QL, e.g., CD 20:15, cf. the one called the *mṭyp hkzb*, "the One who Spouts the Lie," in 1QpHab 10:9. See further D. Pardee, "A Restudy of the Commentary on Psalm 37 from Qumran Cave 4 (Discoveries in the Judaean Desert of Jordan, vol. V nᵒ 171)," *RevQ* 8 (1973) 172; H. Burgmann, "Gerichtsherr und Generalankläger: Jonathan und Simon," *RevQ* 9 (1977) 3-72.

2:2 *for they did not believe the words of* (*ky lwʾ* [*hʾmynw bdbry*]). Those who restore the lacuna similarly, using a form of the verb *ʾmn*, include Brownlee ("Jerusalem Habakkuk Scroll," 9), Carmignac, Dupont-Sommer ("Le 'Commentaire,'" 132), and Stern. Elliger, van der Woude, Vermes, and Rabinowitz prefer the verb *šmʿ*. However, the fact that *ʾmn* (from Hab 1:5) appears in 2:4 and 2:6 shows that it is a key word in this interpretation and is therefore the better choice.

The first word in the clause, *ky*, is spelled without the final ʾ here and in 8:15 and 9:3 (both of the latter in agreement with the MT; see also 4QpIsac 6-7 ii 13; 4QpIsae 6:3; 4QpHosb 2:2; 11-13:5). It is usually spelled *kyʾ* in the pesher sections, but cf. 4QpNah 1-2 ii 6; 3-4 ii 12, where it appears without the final ʾ in the pesher sections. This anomalous addition of final ʾ has not been satisfactorily explained. See M. H. Goshen-Gottstein, "Linguistic Structure and Tradition in the Qumran Documents," *Aspects of the Dead Sea Scrolls* (ed. C. Rabin and Y. Yadin; Scripta Hierosolymitana 4; Jerusalem: Magnes Press, Hebrew University, 1965) 111-112.

the Teacher of Righteousness (*mwrh hṣdqh*). The article (*h*) is added above the line before *ṣdqh*. The reading is not entirely certain, owing to a large area where the skin is discolored, but it is clearer on the color photograph in *Scrolls from Qumran Cave I.* Elsewhere in QL the title appears as *mwrh hṣdq* or *mwrh ṣdq.*

from the mouth of (*mpy*ʾ). The spelling of *py*ʾ with final ʾ is unique; elsewhere it is *py*, as in *mpy* in line 7. This is another instance of the anomalous addition of final ʾ as in the word *ky*ʾ (see above).

2:5-6 The space between *lkn* and *pšr* is puzzling. The scribe could have left the space deliberately in order to set the word apart from the stereotyped formula *pšr hdbr.* A more likely explanation, however, is that this is a false interspace left by a copyist who was accustomed to leaving a space before the word *pšr* (so Brownlee, "Further Corrections," 15). This presupposes that the manuscript is a copy rather than an autograph; see above, pp. 3-4.

At the end of the line is an ʾ, which could be a scribal error. But compare the "X" signs at the end of lines 3:12, 14; 4:11, 14; 6:4, 12; 8:1; 9:1, 13; 10:3; 12:2. The meaning of these signs is as yet undetermined.

at the end of days (*lʾḥryt hymym*). Carmignac (*Les Textes*, 2. 95, n. 8) translates this phrase "la suite des jours," contending that the phrase indicates not the final age, the end of time, but the period of the domination of Belial and the war preceding the end. Carmignac's distinction may prove to be correct; only a detailed study of the eschatology of the Qumran sect will lead to a satisfactory judgment. My translation is tentative and is intended to convey the obvious eschatological import of the phrase.

the ruthless ones of the covenant (*ʿryṣ*[*y hbr*]*yt*). Parallels in 4QpPsa 1-10 ii 14 and 1-10 iii [12] make this restoration almost certain and exclude earlier suggestions such as *ʿryṣy mʾsy bbryt*, "des violents, contempteurs (?) de l'Alliance" (Dupont-Sommer, "Le 'Commentaire,'" 140), *ʿryṣy mpyry hbryt*, "the ruthless ones, the breakers of the covenant" (Habermann, Vermes), *ʿryṣy hʾwmwt*, "the ruthless ones of the nations" (Rabinowitz). Carmignac's suggestion, *ʿrwly lb*, "the uncircumcised of heart," does not fit the traces. See further the note below on 4QpPsa 1-10 ii 14-16.

they will not believe (*lw*ʾ *yʾmynw*ʾ). The form *yʾmynw*ʾ seems to be written with a final ʾ, as was *myp*ʾ above in line 2, but the ʾ could be a sign added at the end of the line as apparently in line 5.

2:8 *into whose heart God put understanding* (*ʾšr ntn ʾl b*[*lbw byn*]*h*). The words *blbw bynh* are restored here following Habermann and Vermes. Several other reconstructions have been suggested. Authors who take *kwhn* as the object of the verb *ntn* supply an indirect object, e.g., *bbyt yhwdh*, "in the house of Judah" (e.g., Dupont-Sommer, *Essene Writings*, 259), *bny yśrʾl lmwrh*, "(to) the sons of Israel as a teacher" (Brownlee, "Jerusalem Habakkuk Scroll," 9), or an adverbial phrase such as *btwk hʿdh*, "in the midst of the congregation" (Elliger, Stern, van der Woude). In such a construction, however, one would expect a direct object suffix on the verb *ntn*, cf. *pšrw ʿl hkwhn h[r]šʿ ʾšr . . . ntnw ʾl byd*, "the interpretation of it concerns the Wicked Priest, whom . . . God gave into the hand" (1QpHab 9:9). Others supply a direct object for the verb *ntn*, e.g., *blbw ḥkmh*, "into whose heart (God put) wisdom" (Rabinowitz). The latter is possible in terms of context, but with the full writing of *ḥwkmh*, which is the ususal Qumran spelling, it would be too long.

2:10 *and upon his congregation* (*w ʿ[l ʿdtw]*). Other possible restorations include *wʿl hgwʾym*, "and upon the nations" (Dupont-Sommer, "Le 'Commentaire,'" 140), *wʾrṣw*, "and his land" (Sjöberg, Vermes), *yśrʾl*, "(his people) Israel" (Carmignac, van der Woude). Elliger restores *ʿdtw* without the repeated preposition *ʿl*.

2:11 The citation of Hab 1:6a presents the following variant from the MT: *hkśdʾym* (MT: *hkśdym*, the regular spelling in biblical Hebrew). Compare the alternation between *gwym* (in biblical Hebrew and 1QpHab except at 3:5) and *gwʾym* (e.g., 4QpIsa[a] 7-10 iii 8 [Allegro's 8-10:4]; 4QpHos[a] 2:13, 16). This alternation is probably not a purely orthographic variation, according to M. H. Goshen-Gottstein ("Linguistic Structure," 114-115), but is an orthographic change that reflects a phonetic situation.

2:12 *the Kittim* (*hktyʾym*). In biblical Hebrew the spelling alternates between *kittîm* and *kittiyyîm*. In QL both *ktyym* (4QpNah 1-2 ii [3]; 3-4 i 3; regularly in 1QM) and *ktyʾym* (1QpHab 2:14; 3:4, 9; 4:5, 10; 6:1, 10; 9:7; 1QpPs 9:[4]; 4QpIsa[a] 7-10 iii [7], [9], 11, [12] [Allegro's 8-10:3, 5, 7, 8]) occur. The latter alternation is similar to that noted above for *gwʾym* and *gwym*. The Kittim are surely to be identified with the Romans; see above, p. 8.

and vigorous (*wgbwrym*). Appearing here in the pesher on Hab 1:6, the word *gbwrym* could indicate that the Qumran commentator was aware of the textual tradition reflected in the Greek of Hab 1:6, τοὺς χαλδαίους τοὺς μαχητάς (*haggibbôrîm*).

2:13 *so as to destroy many by the sword and by famine* (*lʾbd rbym [bḥrb wbrʿb]*). The present reading of *rbym* is better than *rʿym*, "the wicked ones" (Habermann) or *rznym*, "the officials" (Elliger), which would more likely appear with the full writing, i.e., *rwznym*. The word *rbym* could also be translated "great ones," but cf. *yʾbdw rbym bḥrb*, "(who) destroy many by the sword" (1QpHab 6:10). The restoration is proposed in the light of 1QpHab 6:10 and 4QpPs[a] 1-10 ii 1 (*ywbdw bḥrb wbrʿb*, "they will perish by the sword and by famine," cf. 1-10 iii 3-4). Other suggestions for the restoration of the words following *rbym* include *whyth hʾrṣ*, "and the land will be" (Dupont-Sommer, "Le 'Commentaire,'" 140), *ʾšr yplw*, "who will fall" (Maier, similarly Vermes), *ky ylḥmw*, "should they war (against)" (Rabinowitz), and *wlknyʿm*, "und sie unterwerfen" (Elliger).

2:14 At the end of the line the verb *ʾmn* reappears. With this clue the lacuna is restored along the lines of the three-part pesher in lines 1-10, using the verb *bgd* and the noun *bryt*. For "the wicked ones," *ršʿym*, compare *ršʿy ʾprym wmnšh* (4QpPsa 1-10 ii 18) and *ršʿy yśrʾl* (4QpPsa 1-10 iii [12]). Another possibility is *yršw ʾrṣwt rbwt*, "they take possession of many lands" (Elliger), but this is a little too short; Rabinowitz's suggestion, *wršʿym hm lbṭwḥ bšqr*, "and they are wicked so as to trust in falsehood," does not fit the visible traces of letters.

2:15-17 At the end of the col., probably beginning in line 16, the text of Hab 1:6b is to be restored followed by a pesher that interprets the lemma with reference to the Kittim. The interpretation is continued in col. 3.

that are not theirs ([*lwʾ lw*]), literally, "that are not his." In Hab 1:6-11 the topic is clearly the Chaldeans, but the nation is sometimes referred to by the singular collective and sometimes by the plural. The same variation is also found at times in the interpretation of these verses throughout col. 3.

Column 3

3:1 *and by (way of) the level plain* (*wbmyšwr*). This is probably an interpretation of *lmrḥby ʾrṣ*, "the breadth of the land," in Hab 1:6. The phrase is translated literally by Burrows, Dupont-Sommer, and Elliger, but others, e.g., Carmignac and van der Woude, interpret *bmyšwr* figuratively, translating it something like "unhindered" or "unimpeded." Rabinowitz seems to combine the two ideas, translating "and over easy terrain." Brownlee's translation, "and in uprightness," does not fit the context, which speaks of the Kittim.

to smite (*lkwt*). This form is the hiph. inf. cs. of *nkh*. For similar elision of the *h* in the hiph. inf., see *lšḥyt* (1QpHab 4:13), *lḥryb* (1QpHab 6:8), *lwsyp* (1QpHab 8:12), *wlqym* (1QpHab 10:10), *lwgyʿ* (1QpHab 10:11), *wlkšylm* (1QpHab 11:8), *ltʿwt* (4QpNah 3-4 iii 7), *lpyl* (4QpPsa 1-10 ii 16), and possibly also *lwsp* (1QpMic 10:5).

3:2 *for this is what it says* (*kyʾ hwʾ ʾšr ʾmr*). This formula is found only in 1QpHab among the pesharim (see also 3:[13-14]; 5:6), except that it might be restored in 4QpIsac 1:2. It is used to introduce the repetition of part or all of a biblical text previously cited, which thus supports the suggestion of restoring 1QpHab 1:6b in the last lines of col. 2. See further p. 243.

3:3 *a claim to dignity goes out from them* (*mmnw mšpṭw wśʾtw yṣʾ*), literally, "his claim and his dignity go out from himself," but cf. Rabinowitz's translation, "his justice and his honor depart from him."

3:4 *and dread* (*wʾmtm*). This is restored with the defective orthography as in 4:7. Rabinowitz and others restore the full writing, *wʾymtm*, but this does not fit the visible traces of letters. The final *m* is written above the line.

3:5 *the nations* (*hgwʾym*). This word is added above the line. Only here in 1QpHab is this word spelled with a medial ʾ; elsewhere it is *gwym*, the usual spelling in biblical Hebrew (5:3, 4; 6:9; 8:5, 15; 9:3; 12:13; 13:1). See the note above on 2:11.

all their plans (*kwl mḥšbtm*). The form *mḥšbtm* could be the defectively written pl. or the sing., "their whole plan."

and with cunning (*wbnkl*). The noun *nēkel* occurs in biblical Hebrew only in Num 25:18; it does not occur elsewhere in QL but the restoration here is almost certain.

3:6 *they associate with all the peoples* (*ylkw ʿm kwl hʿmym*), literally, "they walk with all the peoples," cf. e.g., Mal 2:6.

The citation of Hab 1:8a presents the following variant from the MT: *wqwl* (MT: *wqlw*), almost certainly a scribal error.

3:7-9 The MT of Hab 1:8b-9a is corrupt, and the textual difficulties are reflected in problems in the Qumran citation of the passage. (On the problems of the MT, see e.g., M. Bosshard, "Bemerkungen zum Text von Habakuk I,8," *VT* 19 [1969] 480-82; G. R. Driver, "Linguistic and Textual Problems: Minor Prophets III," *JTS* 39 [1938] 394-96).

The first two words of line 7 end the citation of Hab 1:8a. This is followed by a space before the citation of Hab 1:8b. It appears to be a false interspace where the scribe expected an interpretation to begin; the first word of Hab 1:8b, *pšw,* could easily have been mistaken at a glance for *pšr,* and it looks as if *pšr* may even have been written, with the *r* then corrected to a *w.* (On the question of the work being a copy rather than an autograph, see above, pp. 3-4.)

The MT of Hab 1:8bα reads *ûpāšû pārāšā(yw) ûpārāšā(yw) mērāḥôq yābōʾû,* "and his horses paw the ground, and his riders come from a distance (?)." 1QpHab reads *pšw wpršw* (or *wpršw*) *pršw* (or *pršw*) *mrḥwq,* "they paw the ground, and his riders are scattered afar." The following variants from the MT appear:

(1) *pšw* (MT: *wpšw*). The form of 1QpHab is from the verb *pwš,* "paw the ground," as is the form of the MT, rather than from *pśh,* "spread out" (so Brownlee, "Jerusalem Habakkuk Scroll," 10). That the former was understood by the Qumran commentator is supported by the use of the synonym *wdwšw,* "they trample," in the interpretation (line 10).

(2) *wpršw pršw* (MT: *pršyw wpršyw*). The two words *wpršw* (or *wprśw*) and *pršw* (or *prśw*) could be verb forms from either *prš,* "declare distinctly," or *prś,* "spread out," or they could be forms of the noun *pārāš,* "rider," as are the forms of the MT. There are a number of possibilities for reading and translating the phrase *wpršw* (or *wprśw*) *pršw* (or *prśw*) *mrḥwq:*

(a) *wpršw* (noun) *prśw* (verb) *mrḥwq* (or with a different word order: *wprśw* [verb] *pršw* [noun] *mrḥwq*), and his riders spread out from a distance." In the former the subject *wpršw* has the conjunction, and the 3rd pers. pl. form (with the 3rd pers. sing. masc. sf.) is written defectively, as opposed to the MT, which has *pršyw*. In the latter, the word order differs from the MT. The first possibility is the interpretation of the phrase followed here.

(b) *wpršw* (noun) *pršw* (verb) *mrḥwq* (or with a different word order: *wpršw* [verb] *pršw* [noun] *mrḥwq*). The first word order is followed by Elliger, who translates the phrase "und sprengen heran seine Rosse aus der Ferne," but such a meaning for the verb *prš* is unattested in biblical Hebrew.

(c) *wpršw* (noun) *pršw* (noun) *mrḥwq*. The phrase is interpreted this way by Dupont-Sommer ("Le 'Commentaire,' " 133), who translates "et ses cavaliers, ses cavaliers (arrivent) de loin." A similar possibility is *wpršy* (noun) *pršw* (noun) *mrḥwq*, "and the horses of his riders are from a distance," where the first two words form a construct chain, and the whole is a nominal sentence.

(d) *yprśw* (niph. impf. of *prś*) *pršw* (noun) *mrḥwq*, "his riders are scattered from a distance."

(3) The verb *ybʾw* of the MT is omitted in the citation in 1QpHab, which probably indicates that either *wpršw* (or *wprśw*) or *pršw* (or *prśw*) should be read as a verb in 1QpHab.

(4) *qdym*, the absolute "East" or "east wind" (MT: *qdymh*, the locative "toward the East").

from a distance (*mrḥwq*) (= *mn* + *rḥwq*).

the horror (*mgmt*). The derivation and meaning of this word are unknown. Suggested translations include "l'haleine" (Carmignac), "la tension" (Dupont-Sommer, "Le 'Comentaire,'" 133), "abundance" (Rabinowitz), "mutterings" (Brownlee, "Biblical Interpretation Among the Sectaries of the Dead Sea Scrolls," *BA* 14 [1951] 63), "Überfluss" (Elliger). The emendation suggested in *BHS* is *mĕgōrat*, "horror."

of their faces (*pnyhm*). There is a slightly larger than usual space between the *y* and the *h* of *pnyhm*, which has led some authors to think that *pnyhm* was deliberately written as two words. Rabinowitz, for example, translates it "the abundance of my wrath (*pny*) are they to the East." Similarly, Brownlee translates it "as for the mutterings of his face (reading *pnw*) they are the East Wind" ("Biblical Interpretation," 63).

3:10 *and with their beasts* (*wbbhmtm*), the defectively written pl.

3:11 *they come, from the islands of the sea* (*ybwʾw mʾyy hym*). The occurrence of the verb *ybwʾw* here in the pesher may indicate that the Qumran author knew of the textual tradition of Hab 1:8 that is preserved in the MT. In the citation of that verse in 1QpHab the verb *yb*ʾ*w* does not appear; see the note above on 3:7-9. The phrase *m*ʾ*yy hym* could also be translated "from the coastlands of the sea."

3:12 they grow hot (*yk*[*mrw*]). Other suggested restorations include *ykny*ʿ*wm,* "unterwerfen sie" (Elliger), *yk*ʿ*sw,* "they are angry" (Rabinowitz). In my opinion the letter before the break cannot be a *b,* and so the suggestions of Habermann, *wbqṣp,* "and with wrath"; Dupont-Sommer, *wbrgz,* "and with agitation" ("Le 'Commentaire,'" 141); and Stern, *wbk*ʿ*s,* "and with vexation" have to be rejected.

Column 4

In Hab 1:10-11 the Chaldeans are referred to by the 3rd pers. sing. masc. used collectively, which is here translated by the pl. In the interpretations in this col. the 3rd pers. pl. is used to refer to the rulers of the Kittim.

4:1 The citation of Hab 1:10a presents the following variant from the MT: *yqls,* the piel impf. (MT: *ytqls,* the hithpael impf.). In biblical Hebrew the piel of the verb *qls* is used only in Ezek 16:31, but it is frequent in later Hebrew. It may also be that the form in 1QpHab reflects the assimilation of *t* to *q* in the hithpael impf. This phenomenon occurs in Mishnaic Hebrew; see M. H. Segal, *Grammar of Mishnaic Hebrew,* §§ 134-135, p. 65.

4:2 *great ones* (*rbym*). Most authors translate *rbym* as "great ones" parallel with "honored ones," but Lohse and Vermes translate "many." Elsewhere in QL the determinate state *hrbym* is used frequently to designate "the Many," a specific group within the sect, e.g., 1QS 6:1, 7, 8, 9, etc., but this technical use does not appear in the pesharim.

4:3-4 *they mock* (*yt*ʿ*t*ʿ*w*). The form is taken here as the hithpalpel impf. of *t*ʿʿ.

a great people (ʿ*m rb*), cf. *rbym* in 4:2. Most authors prefer to translate this as "many people," e.g., Elliger, Lohse, Dupont-Sommer, Carmignac, and Maier, but in the light of "honored ones" and "kings and princes" in this pesher, I translate it "a great people."

The citation of Hab 1:10b presents the following variants from the MT:

(1) *whw*ʾ (MT: *hw*ʾ)

(2) *wylkdhw* (MT: *wylkdh*). There is a hole in the manuscript, and the second letter of the word is mutilated. It looks as if the letter has been corrected or that something has been added above the line. The form in the MT is vocalized with the fem. sing. sf., while the form in 1QpHab has the masc. sing. sf. Both a masc. and a fem. pl. are attested in biblical Hebrew for *mbṣr,* "fortification," the antecedent of the sf. It is also possible that the form of the MT could have the masc. sing. sf. without the *mater lectionis;* see GKC §§ 58g, 91e.

4:4 *and they heap up* (*wyṣbwr*), literally, "and he heaps up." The *y* is added above the line. There is an inconsistency in the use of tenses in the MT of Hab 1:10-11. In 1:10b there is an impf. followed by two converted impf. forms. It is suggested in the *apparatus criticus* of *BHS* that the two verbs *wyṣbr* and *wylkdh* should be read as impf. forms with simple *w*'s. This difficulty of tenses may have been the source of the correction in the form *wyṣbwr* in 1QpHab, where the *y* was added, since the form would have needed correction if the first letter had been read as *w*.

4:6 *they laugh* (*yśḥ*{ {*w*} }*qw*). There are dots above and below the middle *w* of the form, probably indicating that it is to be deleted. (It is unlikely that the hiph. impf. *yśḥyqw* was intended, since the hiph. of this verb occurs in biblical Hebrew only as a part. in 2 Chr 30:10.) The corrected form could be the qal or piel impf. and the uncorrected form might be an example of the so-called pseudo-pausal form, which reflects a penultimate accent, cf. *yqbwṣw* (1QpHab 9:5), *ykšwlw* (4QpNah 3-4 ii 6), *ypwlw* (4QpNah 3-4 ii 6, 10). See further M. H. Goshen-Gottstein, "Linguistic Structure," 123-25.

4:7 *and with terror* (*wbʾmh*). Here the noun *ʾymh* is written defectively; see the restoration in 3:4.

4:8 *because of the guilt* (*bʿwwn*). This is read by most authors, e.g., Burrows, Carmignac, Dupont-Sommer, Lohse, and Vermes. There are others, however, who read *bʿyyn,* "in ruins," e.g., Elliger and Brownlee ("Jerusalem Habakkuk Scroll," 11). The latter reading, however, is impossible in terms of context and syntax.

4:9 The citation of Hab 1:11 presents the following variant from the MT: *wyśm zh,* "and this one made" (MT: *wʾšm zw,* "and a guilty man, whose"). The text of 1QpHab agrees with the emendation suggested in *BHS,* except that the Qumran text is probably to be understood as a converted impf. form, "and he made." In the interpretation of the verse in line 11, the use of the word *ʾšmh,* "guilt," in the phrase *byt ʾšmtm* could indicate that the commentator was aware of the textual tradition preserved in the MT.

4:11 *their guilty house* (*byt ʾšm*[*tm*]). The restoration of *ʾšmtm* fills the space better than *ʾšmh* (Elliger, Lohse, Maier). Most authors see here a reference to some political institution, possibly the Roman senate.

4:11-12 *one before the other* (*ʾyš mlpny rʿyhw*), literally, "a man before his fellow." The *y* of *rʿyhw* is added above the line.

4:13 *to ruin* (*lšḥyt*), the hiph. inf. cs. with the *h* elided; see the note above on 3:1.

If the restoration of this line is correct, it is an example of a second citation appearing without any introductory formula; see Part II, p. 243.

4:16-17 The citation of Hab 1:12-13a begins at the end of the col. and continues through 5:2.

Column 5

5:1-2 The citation of Hab 1:12-13a presents the following variants from the MT: (1) *lmwkyḥw,* hiph. part. of *ykḥ* with the 3rd pers. sing. masc. sf. (MT: *lhwkyḥ,* hiph. inf. cs. of *ykḥ*); (2) *brᶜ* (MT: *rᶜ*).

eyes (*ᶜynym*). The first *y* is written above the line.

5:3-6 The translation of this pesher section involves two difficulties: (1) the sf. of *wbtwkḥtm in* line 4 is ambiguous; and (2) the antecedent of *ʾšr* in line 5 is unclear.

With regard to the first problem, it must be determined whether the sf. is objective or subjective. If it is an objective sf., the antecedent is "all the nations"; thus, "at/through their rebuke," i.e., when the chosen ones rebuke all the nations. If the sf. is subjective, then the antecedent is the "chosen ones" and the object of the rebuke is implied; thus, "at/through their (i.e., the chosen ones') rebuke (of all the nations)." In both cases the meaning is the same: the chosen ones are rebuking all the nations.

The second difficulty is the antecedent of *ʾšr* in line 5. One might expect that the antecedent would be *kl ršᶜy ᶜmw,* which immediately precedes *ʾšr,* but "all the wicked of his people, who kept his commandments" does not make sense. As the text stands, sense requires that *ʾšr* refer back to *bḥyrw* in line 4. Otherwise the disruption in the logical sequence must be viewed as anacoluthon. It is not impossible, however, that there is a scribal error here. The repetition of words (*ᶜmw* in lines 3, 5; *byd* in lines 3, 4; *hgwym* in lines 3, 4) could easily have given rise to a copying error. In fact, the phrase that is a problem, *ʾšr šmrw ʾt mṣwwtw bṣr lmw,* which now follows *ᶜmw* in line 5, would make much better sense following *ᶜmw* in line 3, i.e., "God will not destroy his people who have kept his commandments in their distress."

5:3 *his people* (*ᶜmw*). The *w* is written above the line.

5:4 *his chosen ones* (*bḥyrw*). This form could be the sing. or the defectively written pl. with the 3rd pers. sing. masc. sf. The latter identification seems more likely, since elsewhere the word is used in the pl. as a designation for the community, e.g., *bḥyry ʾl* (1QpHab 10:13; 1QpMic 10:[5-6] [Milik's 8-10:7-8]; 4QpPs^a 1-10 iv [14]), *bḥyry yśrʾl* (4QpIsa^e 6:[1]; 4QpPs^a 11:[2]). Similar defective writing occurs in *ᶜdt bḥyrw* (4QpIsa^d 1:3; 4QpPs^a 1-10 ii 5; 1-10 iii 5) and *wᶜm bḥyrw* (4QpPs^a 1-10 iv [11-12]).

5:5 *will be convicted* (*yʾšmw*), literally, "will be held guilty," but other translations have been suggested, such as "shall expiate their guilt" (Vermes), "qu'expieront" (Dupont-Sommer, "Le 'Commentaire,'" 134), "werden Büssen" (Elliger). The meanings "to expiate" and "to atone" are unattested for the verb *ʾšm,* but these translations are imposed upon the text by authors who connect the following *ʾšr*-clause with "all the wicked ones of his people," i.e., "they shall expiate their guilt, insofar as they keep the commandments." But see the remarks above on the antecedent of *ʾšr*.

all (*kl*). Elsewhere in this document this word is spelled *kwl*.

5:7 The repetition of the citation of Hab 1:13aα has the same variant as the first citation in line 2: *brʿ* (MT: *rʿ*).

This second citation is followed by a pesher, but compare the second citations above in 3:2, 13-14, which are followed immediately by new quotations from the biblical text. See Part II, p. 243.

5:7-8 *the time of wickedness* (*bqṣ hršʿh*). In biblical Hebrew the noun *qēṣ* means "limit" or "end." In QL it frequently has the eschatological connotations of the end-time, e.g., *gmr hqṣ*, "the fulfillment of the end-time" (1QpHab 7:2), *hqṣ hʾḥrwn*, "the last end-time" (1QpHab 7:7, 12), but the word is also used at times without an eschatological nuance, e.g., 4QpNah 3-4 ii 6.

5:8-9 The citation of Hab 1:13b presents the following variants from the MT:

(1) *tbyṭw* (MT: *tbyṭ*). The form in 1QpHab has the 2nd pers. pl. ending, which is probably an error since this verb is coordinated with a verb that has the 2nd pers. sing. ending, i.e., *wtḥryš*.

(2) *wtḥryš* (MT: *tḥryš*).

the House of Absalom (*byt ʾbšlwm*). In the opinion of many commentators this phrase indicates an actual group contemporary with the Teacher of Righteousness, a certain Absalom and his family or followers. For possible identifications, see D. N. Freedman, "The House of Absalom in the Habakkuk Scroll," *BASOR* 114 (1949) 11-12.

5:10 *and their partisans* (*wʾnšy ʿṣtm*), literally, "the men of their counsel," i.e., those who hold the same opinions. In biblical Hebrew the noun *ʿēṣâ* means "counsel," "plan," or "design." In the Qumran documents the word seems to be used with this meaning in the phrase *ʾnšy ʿṣtm* here and in the similar phrase *ʾnšy ʿṣtw*, "his partisans," e.g., in 1QpHab 9:10 referring to the partisans of the Teacher of Righteousness, in 4QpNah 1-2 ii [8] probably referring to the partisans of the Seekers-After-Smooth-Things, in 4QpNah 3-4 i 5 referring to the partisans of the Lion of Wrath, and in 4QpPs^a 1-10 ii 19 referring to the partisans of "the Priest." The word also occurs in the phrase *ʿṣt hyḥd*, which is usually translated "the council of the community." See the note below on 1QpHab 12:4, and see further J. Worrell, "*ʿṣh:* 'Counsel' or 'council' at Qumran?" *VT* 20 (1970) 65-74.

at the rebuke of the Teacher of Righteousness (*btwkḥt mwrh hṣdq*). The word *twkḥt* is variously translated: "chastisement" (Vermes, and similarly Dupont-Sommer, "Le 'Commentaire,'" 134) "reproof"

(Brownlee, "Jerusalem Habakkuk Scroll," 11), "Zurechtweisung" (Lohse, Maier), "Anklage" (Elliger). I agree with all of these authors that the reprimand was levelled against the Teacher of Righteousness by the Man of the Lie. Carmignac ("Notes," 507-10), however, thinks that it is the rebuke of the Man of the Lie by the Teacher of Righteousness. He suggests that the Man of the Lie held an interpretation of the Law that the Teacher of Righteousness considered as treachery and that the House of Absalom refused to intervene in support of the Qumran Teacher's interpretation. See also H. G. M. Williamson ("The translation of 1QpHab. V, 10," *RevQ* 9 [1977] 263-65), who believes that it was the House of Absalom and its partisans who were the objects of the Teacher's reprimand. He would translate the phrase ". . . who were reduced to silence by the reprimand of the Teacher of Righteousness and (so) did not help him . . . ."

5:11 *the Man of the Lie* (*ʾyš hkzb*). See the note above on 2:1-2. At the end of this line is a clause beginning with *ʾšr,* separated from the preceding commentary by an unusually large space. The verb *mʾs* is singular and must refer to the Man of the Lie. There seems to be no interruption in logic or snytax, but the space is puzzling.

5:12 *their council* (*ʿṣtm*). The two middle letters of this word are mutilated; other suggested readings include *ʿdtm,* "their congregation" (Carmignac, Lohse, van der Woude) and *ʿmym,* "the peoples" (Brownlee, "Jerusalem Habakkuk Scroll," 11). The visible traces of letters seem to fit the present reading better than the others.

5:12-16 The citation of Hab 1:14-16 presents the following variants from the MT:

(1) *wtʿś* (MT: *wtʿśh*).

(2) *lmšl* (MT: *lʾ mšl*). The MT gives the negative particle with the part., "there is none to rule over him." The variant in 1QpHab could be a scribal error, but the form appears to be the defectively written inf. cs. "to rule over it." If the inf. cs. was intended, however, both the subject of the inf. and the antecedent of *bô* are unclear. Is it God or humanity who is "to rule," and does *bô* refer to humanity or to the sea? Another possibility is that suggested by Carmignac, who reads the Qumran text as *lĕ-māšāl bô,* "en allégorie pour lui," but he does not explain how this fits into the context of Hab 1:14-16. Unfortunately, the pesher on these verses is lost, so there is no way of knowing how the Qumran author understood this form.

(3) *yʿlh* (MT: *hʿlh*). In the form in 1QpHab the *y* appears to have a dot over it. The hiph. perf. of the MT breaks the sequence of tenses, which is restored by the use of the hiph. impf. in 1QpHab.

(4) *wygrhw* (MT: *ygrhw*).

(5) *wysphw* (MT: *wyʾsphw*). The form in 1QpHab could be an ortho-

graphic variant, but it is more likely that it is from *ysp,* "to increase," rather than from *ʾsp*, "to gather," as is the form of the MT. This is supported by the commentary on these verses in 6:1, where the form *wywsypw* occurs, which is probably also from *ysp*. See the note below on 6:1.

(6) The form *bhm* is restored in line 15 and the form *bry* in line 16 rather than *bhmh* and *brʾh* as in the MT in the light of the second citation of Hab 1:16b below in 6:5.

his lot is luxurious and his food is rich (*šmn ḥlqw* [*wmʾklw bry*]), literally, "his lot is fat and his food is fatty."

5:14-17 From the visible traces of letters in this citation of Hab 1:15b-16, there seems to be a problem in the order of the phrases. There might be a scribal error here arising from the similarity of words in the short clauses, especially from the repetition of *ʿl kn*.

Column 6

6:1 The col. begins with the continuation of the pesher on Hab 1:14-16, which began in the last lines of the preceding col.

they increase (*wywsypw*). The form is here taken to be the hiph. impf. 3rd pers. pl. of *ysp*. However, some authors connect this form with *ʾsp,* which occurs in the citation of Hab 1:15b (e.g., Vermes, Dupont-Sommer, Brownlee, van der Woude). Since the preceding verb is not preserved, the tense of this form must be determined from the context. Elsewhere the Kittim are referred to in the present or future time (e.g., 1QpHab 3:4-6, 9-13; 4:5-9, 10-13; 6:10-12; 4QpIsa[a] 7-10 iii 12 [Allegro's 8-10:8]), and so this form should be understood as the impf. with the simple *w* rather than *w* conversive.

6:2 *like the fish of the sea* (*kdgt hym*). This phrase is picked up from Hab 1:14a. In 1QpHab the form is from the fem. *dgh*, while in the citation above in 5:12 and in the MT the masc. *dg* is used.

and when it says (*wʾšr ʾmr*). This is the first occurrence in 1QpHab of this formula, which introduces a second citation of the biblical text. See further Part II, p. 243.

6:3-4 *they sacrifice to their standards* (*hmh zbḥym lʾwtwtm*). The verb *zbḥ* is picked up from Hab 1:16; in the pesher the form is the qal part., while the MT has the piel. Part of the early debate over the historical situation reflected in 1QpHab focused on this phrase. Some authors argued that worship of military standards was a practice of the Seleucid army (e.g., E. Stauffer and especially H. H. Rowley), but most now hold that the phrase can be applied equally well to the Roman forces.

6:5 The second citation of Hab 1:16b has no introductory formula, cf. 4:[13]; it presents the following variants from the MT:

(1) *bhm* (MT: *bhmh*).

(2) *bry* (MT: *brʾh*). Apparently the form in 1QpHab is masc., while the MT has a fem. form. It is noted in the *apparatus criticus* of *BHS,* however, that the final *h* of the form *brʾh* might be an error of dittography. If this is the case, the forms of 1QpHab and the MT would be the same, and the orthography of 1QpHab could reflect the lack of stability of ʾ as a vowel letter in the final position; see M. H. Goshen-Gottstein, "Linguistic Structure," 111-12.

6:8 *to lay waste many lands* (*lḥryb ʾrṣwt rbwt*). The form *lḥryb* is the hiph. inf. cs. with the *h* elided; see the note above on 3:1.

6:8-9 The citation of Hab 1:17 presents the following variants from the MT:

(1) *ʿl* (MT: *hʿl*)

(2) *ḥrbw*, "sword" (MT: *ḥrmw*, "net"). The context of the biblical verse and the usage of the verb *ryq* with *ḥrb*, e.g., Exod 15:9; Ezek 5:12 perhaps favor the reading of 1QpHab. M. H. Goshen-Gottstein ("Linguistic Structure," 115) notes this variant as a possible instance of the interchange of labials.

(3) *tmyd* (MT: *wtmyd*). The *w* of the form in the MT may be an error of dittography.

(4) *wlʾw* (MT: *lʾ*).

6:11 *strong men* (*ʾšyšym*). The word *ʾšyšym* is unattested with any meaning that would fit this context; in biblical Hebrew in Hos 3:1 and Isa 16:7 the word is translated "raisin cakes." The biconsonantal stem *ʾš* has not been satisfactorily explained, but one line of conjecture is that it is related to *ʾyš*, "man," and means "be firm," "be strong." Such a meaning fits the context here, where the word apparently designates a group between young men and old men. Most authors adopt similar translations, e.g., "adultes" (Dupont-Sommer, "Le 'Commentaire,'" 135; similarly Vermes and Carmignac); "Männer" (Elliger; similarly Maier and van der Woude). W. Baumgartner suggests that this is the meaning of the word in biblical Hebrew (*HALAT,* under the conjectured form *ʾāšîš*). Others, however, take the word as an attributive modifying *nʿrym*. Lohse, for example, reads *ʾšwšym*, "wehrlose Knaben," apparently deriving the word from *yšš*, "be weak," but Brownlee translates it "sturdy youths" ("Jerusalem Habakkuk Scroll," 12). M. H. Goshen-Gottstein ("Linguistic Structure," 114) mentions the possibility that *ʾšyšym* might be a ghost word formed by the occurrence of an otiose ʾ at a word juncture, but he does not explain what the meaning would be. Another possible explanation is that *ʾšyšym* is a dittographical spelling of the irregular pl. of *ʾyš* (*ʾ{š}yšym*), see Ps 141:4; Prov 8:4; Isa 53:3 (1QIsa^{a} XLIV:7).

6:12-16 The citation of Hab 2:1-2 presents the following variants from the MT:

(1) *mṣwry* (MT: *mṣwr*).

(2) According to the emendation suggested in *BHS, yšyb*, "he will answer," is restored in line 14 (Hab 2:1) rather than *ʾšyb*, "I shall answer," as in the MT. Also possible, however, is reading *ʾšyb . . . twkḥtw*, "how I shall answer . . . his charge."

(3) The verb *wywmr* is restored in line 15 according to the orthography in 1QpHab 8:7, *wywmrw* (for *wyʾmr* of Hab 2:6), rather than *wyʾmr* as in the MT.

(4) In the light of the second citation in 7:3, *hqwrʾ* is restored in line 16 rather than *qwrʾ* as in the MT.

my objection (*twkḥty*). It looks as if the *w* has been partially erased.

Column 7

7:1 The col. begins with the continuation of the pesher on Hab 2:1-2.

and God told Habakkuk (*wydbr ʾl ʾl ḥbqwq*). One *ʾl* is written above the line. It might have been added as a gloss for clarification, or it might be a correction for an earlier haplography.

7:2 The first word in the line, the preposition *ʿl*, is an error of dittography, since this is also the last word in line 1. There may be dots over it to indicate deletion, but this is not certain.

the fulfillment of the end-time (*gmr hqṣ*). Other translations that have been suggested include "the final phase of the end" (Brownlee, "Jerusalem Habakkuk Scroll," 12), "the end of time" (Vermes), "die Vollendung der Zeit" (Elliger, similarly van der Woude), "l'époque de l'accomplissement" (Carmignac), "la consommation du temps" (Dupont-Sommer, "Le 'Commentaire,'" 135). In biblical Hebrew the root *gmr* occurs only as a verb meaning "to come to an end." In Mishnaic Hebrew a noun form *gāmār* is attested meaning "consummation."

he did not make known to him (*lwʾ hwdʿw*). The hiph. perf. form *hwdʿw* is written defectively; compare the full writing in 7:4.

7:3 The beginning of this line is indented, and the second citation of Hab 2:2bβ is introduced by the formula *wʾšr ʾmr*. Elsewhere in 1QpHab, regardless of whether the citation appears for the first or second time, and regardless of whether an introductory formula is used or not, there is no space preceding the citation.

he can run (*yrwṣ*). This word is written above the line.

The second citation of Hab 2:2bβ presents the following variant from the MT: *hqwrʾ* (MT: *qwrʾ*)

7:4 *to whom God made known* (*ʾšr hwdyʿw ʾl*). Here the hiph. perf. appears with the full writing; cf. the defective writing above in 7:2.

7:5 *all the mysteries* (*kwl rzy*). The word *rāz*, "secret," or "mystery," does not occur in biblical Hebrew but is found in biblical Aramaic and in later Hebrew. For the significance of the word in the context of the Qumran pesharim, see Part II, p. 237.

the prophets (*hnbʾym*). The word is spelled defectively here, but cf. the full writing in line 8.

7:6 *it testifies to the end-time* (*ypyḥ lqṣ*). This phrase in 1QpHab differs from the MT of Hab 2:3a, which has *wĕyāpēaḥ laqqēṣ*. The MT is difficult, since the derivation of the form *wĕyāpēaḥ* is open to question. Emendations suggested in *BHS* are (*wĕ*)*yipraḥ*, "it breaks forth," cf. the Greek καὶ ἀνατελεῖ; *ûpētaḥ*, "and the disclosure"; and *wypyḥ*, which would agree with the form in 1QpHab except for the copula. The most probable derivation of the form in 1QpHab is from *pwḥ*, which in biblical Hebrew means "breathe," "gasp," or "launch forth." The same root, however, also appears in Ugaritic, where it means "testify," a meaning that fits this context very well. (See further M. Dahood, *Psalms II: 51-100* [AB 17; Garden City, NY: Doubleday, 1968] 169.) Cf. 1QS 7:14, where the root appears in a context in which none of these meanings seems to fit.

7:7 *will be prolonged* (*yʾrwk*). This form is taken as the qal impf. 3rd pers. sing. masc. of *ʾrk*. Also possible, however, is *yʾryk*, the hiph. impf., "will last a long time," which is read by Habermann and Y. Ratzaby ("Remarks," 157).

and it will be greater (*wytr*). This form could be either the niph. or the hiph. impf. spelled defectively. Elsewhere in QL the very *ytr* is used in the niph. It is unlikely that *ywtr* should be read (so Ratzaby, "Remarks," 157), since the copula would be lacking. The only possible examples in 1QpHab of independent clauses without the copula are in 2:6 and 4:12, but both are uncertain owing to lacunas in the text.

7:8 *awesome* (*lhplh*). This form is taken as the niph. inf. cs. of *plʾ*, "be extraordinary," "be marvellous," but cf. the niph. inf. cs. *lnṣl* with the *h* elided, in 9:13. The root *plʾ* is frequently connected with *rāz* in QL, e.g., 1QS 11:5; 1QH 1:21; 2:13, but this is the only instance of the spelling with final *h* instead of ʾ (it looks as though the final *h* may have been corrected from another letter). The substitution of *h* for ʾ is known from other Qumran texts; see E. Y. Kutscher, *The Language and Linguistic Background of the Isaiah Scroll* (*1Q Isa^a*) (STDJ 6; Leiden: Brill, 1974) 164.

7:9 The citation of Hab 2:3b presents the following variant from the MT: *wlwʾ* (MT: *lʾ*).

7:10-11 *the men of truth, those who observe the Law* (*ʾnšy hʾmt ʿwśy htwrh*). The phrase *ʾnšy hʾmt* does not occur elsewhere in the Qumran documents published thus far, but for the phrase *ʿwśy htwrh*, see below 8:1; 4QpPs^a 1-10 ii 15; and cf. *ʿwśh htwrh* below in 12:4-5; 4QpPs^a 1-10 ii 23.

7:11 *whose hands do not grow slack* (*ʾšr lwʾ yrpw ydyhm*), i.e., "who do not lose heart," see 2 Sam 4:1; Isa 13:7.

7:13 *all of God's end-times* (*kwl qyṣy ʾl*). The form *qyṣy* is the pl. cs. of *qṣ*, "end-time." Brownlee's early translation "summer fruits of" ("Jerusalem Habakkuk Scroll," 13, taking the form as the pl. cs. of *qyṣ*), which he thought was an allusion to Amos 8:1-2, has been abandoned. The form is an example of a *y* used to represent a short *i*-vowel, a phenomenon that is sometimes overlooked in the Qumran documents because of the confusion of *w* and *y*. It occurs e.g., in the form *ryqmh* in 1QM 5:6, 9, 14; 7:11; see further E. Y. Kutscher, *Isaiah Scroll*, 156-59.

according to their fixed order (*ltkwnm*). In biblical Hebrew a fem. substantive *tkwnh*, "fixed place," "arrangement," is attested in Job 23:3; Ezek 43:11; Nah 2:10. In 1QpHab, however, the substantive is masc. in form, as elsewhere in QL, e.g., 1QS 9:12; 1QH 12:5, 8. See further M. Kaddari, "The Root *tkn* in the Qumran Texts," *RevQ* 5 (1964-66) 219-24. In this text the word is variously translated according to the nuance given to the preposition *l*, e.g., "nach ihrer Ordnung" (Maier, Lohse), "to their appointed end" (Vermes), "à point nommé" (Carmignac), "zu ihrer Bestimmung" (Elliger). S. M. Stern ("Notes," 27) reads *qyṣw*, the defectively written pl. of *qṣ* with the 3rd pers. sing. masc. sf., and he translates the line "all His appointed times God will bring to their fulfillment." The verb *ybwʾw*, however, is pl., and *qyṣy ʾl* must be the subject.

7:14-15 These lines seem to cite the text of Hab 2:4a in agreement with the MT except for orthographic variations, but there are problems with the text; see further P. J. M. Southwell, "A Note on Habakkuk ii 4," *JTS* 19 (1968) 614-17. Both *ʿwplh* and *ywšrh* are fem. and therefore must refer to *npšw*, but the syntactical relationship is unclear. Either form may be a finite verb or a participle. Moreover, there seems to be no antecedent for *bw*.

7:15-17 A few words of the pesher on Hab 2:4a are preserved in these lines; at the end of line 17, Hab 2:4b is restored.

they double upon them (*ykplw ʿlyhm*). The form *ykplw* in line 15 is probably an interpretation of *ʿwplh* in Hab 2:4a. The form is here taken to be the qal impf. "they double," in which case the subject is either "they," referring to a group not specifically named, or it is to be restored in line 16, e.g., "[the wicked] shall double" (Vermes), cf. above 7:7, where the subject follows the verb. It is unlikely that the form is the niph. impf. "they are doubled," since that would leave *ʿlyhm* without an antecedent.

At the beginning of line 16 some authors restore a subject for *ykplw*, e.g., *hršʿym*, "the wicked" (Elliger, Dupont-Sommer [*Essene Writings*], and Vermes as noted above). Others restore a direct object, e.g., *ḥṭʾtyhm*, "their sins" (Lohse).

Column 8

8:1 The col. opens with the pesher on Hab 2:4b, which is restored at the end of col. 7.

all those who observe the Law (*kwl* ᶜ*wśy htwrh*), see the note above on 7:10-11.

in the house of Judah (*bbyt yhwdh*), see the note below on 4QpPsa 1-10 ii 14-16.

8:2 *from the house of judgment* (*mbyt hmšpṭ*). This phrase, parallel to *byt yhwdh* in line 1, probably does not refer to an actual place or tribunal of judgment but rather to the judgment that God will execute in the eschaton, see below 10:3-5.

and their fidelity (*w*ʾ*mntm*). This form could be vocalized as ʾ*ĕmûnātām* from ʾ*ĕmûnâ,* "trust," "fidelity" (which appears elsewhere in QL with the full writing) or possibly as ʾ*amnātām* from ʾ*ămānâ,* which appears in biblical Hebrew meaning "trustworthy arrangement," e.g., Neh 10:1, and in Mishnaic Hebrew meaning "trust" or "fidelity." In 1QpHab the word is an allusion to Hab 2:4b *b*ʾ*mwntw,* "by his faithfulness," and the 3rd pers. pl. sf. in 1QpHab might support the MT against the Greek πίστεώς μου, cf. Gal 3:11; Rom 1:17; Heb 10:38.

8:3 The citation of Hab 2:5a presents the following variants from the MT:

(1) *hwn,* "wealth" (MT: *hyyn,* "wine").

(2) *ybgwd* (MT: *bwgd*). The syntax of the MT is a problem; 1QpHab is only slightly smoother with *ybgwd* as a finite verb. See further C. Rabin, "Notes on the Habakkuk Scroll and the Zadokite Documents," *VT* 5 (1955) 152-53.

8:4 *he is unseemly* (*ynwh*). The derivation and meaning of the form *ynwh* are uncertain. The form is here taken from the root *n*ʾ*h,* which occurs infrequently in biblical Hebrew, e.g., Isa 52:7; Ps 93:5, meaning "be comely" or "be lovely." Most translators connect this form with the root *nwh*, which appears in biblical Hebrew in substantive formations meaning "pasture," "abode," and so they translate *ynwh* "he will not abide" or "he will not rest." Other definitions that have been suggested for the root *nwh* are "to reach one's goal" (see G. R. Driver, "Linguistic and Textual Problems," 395, who translates "a boastful man and he performs not [what he boasts]") or "to praise" (see P. J. M. Southwell, "A Note," 617, who translates "the insolent man will not be exalted").

who opens (ʾ*šr hrḥyb*). This translation, which connects the ʾ*šr*-clause with what precedes it, is possible for the text as it stands in 1QpHab, but in the MT the vocalization calls for a full stop after *ynwh.*

8:4-8 The citation of Hab 2:5b-6 presents the following variants from the

MT:

(1) *lw*ʾ, line 4 (MT: *wl*ʾ).

(2) *wyʾspw,* line 5 (MT: *wyʾsp*); *wyqbṣw,* line 5 (MT: *wyqbṣ).* While in the MT both verbs are the qal impf. 3rd pers. sing. masc., in 1QpHab they are both pl. forms and therefore should be read as niph. impfs.

(3) *hlwʾ kwlm mšl ʿlyw yśʾw,* line 6 (MT: *hlwʾ ʾlh klm ʿlyw mšl yśʾw*). 1QpHab omits *ʾlh* of the MT and reverses the order of *ʿlyw mšl.*

(4) *wmlyṣy ḥydwt,* line 6 (MT: *wmlyṣh ḥydwt*). The text of the MT is difficult; there are two nouns in the absolute state, "a jeering saying, sneers about him." In 1QpHab, however, there is a construct chain in which *wmlyṣy* is the hiph. part. of *lyṣ,* "to interpret" or "to slander," rather than a form of the substantive *mlyṣh* as in the MT. This part. appears frequently in 1QH meaning "interpreter," e.g., 1QH 2:13, 14, 31; 4:7, 9; 6:13; 18:11; cf. *mlyṣ dʿt* in 4QpPs^{a} 1-10 i 27. On the significance of this term in QL, see further G. Dautzenberg, *Urchristliche Prophetie: Ihre Erforschung, ihre Voraussetzungen im Judentum und ihre Struktur im ersten Korintherbrief* (BWANT 104; Stuttgart: Kohlhammer, 1975) 64-75. For the translation of Hab 2:6a, see M. Dahood, "Hebrew Lexicography: A Review of W. Baumgartner's *Lexikon,* Volume II," *Or* 45 (1976) 352.

(5) *wywmrw,* line 7 (MT: *wyʾmr*). Similar spelling is seen in *ywbdw* (4QpNah 3-4 ii 9; 4QpPs^{a} 1-10 ii 1; 1-10 iii 3, 4), *twbd* (4QpNah 3-4 iii 7).

(6) *wlw*ʾ, line 7 (MT: *l*ʾ*).*

(7) *ykbyd,* line 7 (MT: *wmkbyd*).

8:7 *How long?* (*ʿd mty*). This phrase is an exclamatory question that is part of the vocabulary of laments, e.g., Jer 4:14, 21; Isa 6:11; Ps 90:13. It may originally have been a gloss in the Hebrew text here, since it does not fit syntactically as the verse stands in the MT but is interjected between two coordinated participles, *hmrbh* and *mkbyd.* But in 1QpHab it is a real question, introducing a new clause in which the predicate is the finite verb *ykbyd.*

8:8 *the Wicked Priest* (*hkwhn hršʿ*). See above, pp. 6-8. This is the first mention in 1QpHab of the Wicked Priest; see also 9:[9]; 11:4; 12:2, 8; 4QpIsa^{c} 30:[3]; 4QpPs^{a} 1-10 iv [8]. This is presumably the same figure as the one designated simply as *hkwhn,* "the priest" in 8:16; 11:12.

8:9 *was called by the true name* (*nqrʾ ʿl šm hʾmt*), i.e., was a legitimate priest. The phrase might also be translated "was summoned in the name of the truth," i.e., to serve the cause of the truth.

his course (*ʿwmdw*), literally, "his standing," i.e., his term of service as priest.

8:10 *he became arrogant* (*rm lbw*), literally, "his heart became high," see Deut 8:14; Ezek 31:10.

8:12 *to add* (*lwsyp*), the hiph. inf. cs. of *ysp* with the *h* elided; see the note above on 3:1.

8:13-15 The citation of Hab 2:7-8a presents the following variants from the MT:

(1) *pt.*[ ]*ʾwm* (MT: *ptʿ*). The reading is not certain, since there is a hole in the skin, and only a trace of a letter is visible after the *t*. Most modern commentators read *ptʿʾwm* and explain the form as a conflation of *ptʿ* and *ptʾwm,* both of which mean "sudden" or "suddenly." It seems to me more likely, however, that this is a scribal error: either the scribe intended *ptʾwm* and made an error of dittography, or the scribe intended to write both words *ptʿ ptʾwm* and made an error of haplography, see 1QH 17:5 where both forms are used together, *ptʿ ptʾwm*. If the text were so emended, the translation would be "and will it not be sudden that your creditors will arise?"

(2) *wyqmw* (MT: *yqwmw*). In 1QpHab this word is written with a final *m,* even though the *m* is apparently followed by a *w* (the last letter is not certain). The presence of the copula creates a syntax different from that in the MT, where *hlwʾ ptʿ yqwmw nškyk* is one clause, "Will not your creditors suddenly arise?" In 1QpHab, however, there are two clauses (regardless of how one reads *pt.*[ ]*ʾwm*): "Will it not (be) [sudden], that your creditors will arise?"

(3) {{*w*}}*n*[*š*]*kyk* (MT: *nškyk*). At the beginning of line 14 there are dots or strokes above and below the *w*, probably indicating that it is to be deleted. The corrected text conforms to the MT. This is the only place in 1QpHab where the 2nd pers. sing. masc. sf. is spelled as in the MT without the final vowel letter *h*. Elsewhere it appears as *kh*, e.g., 8:14, 15; 9:3, 14 (twice); 10:2; 11:10, 11.

(4) *wyqyṣw* (MT: *wyqṣw*). The form in the MT is the qal impf. of *yqṣ,* while the form in 1QpHab is the hiph. impf. of *qyṣ*. Both stems are derived from the same biconsonantal root (*qṣ*) and have the same meaning, "to awake."

(5) *mzʿzyʿykh* (MT: *mzʿzʿyk*). This is an orthographic variant. Both forms are the pilpel part. from *zwʿ*, but the form in 1QpHab appears with the full writing and with the vowel letter *h* in the 2nd pers. sing. masc. sf.

(6) *wyšlwkh* (MT: *yšlwk*).

plunder (lmšyswt). There is a hole in the manuscript, but it is certain that either a *w* or a *y* should be restored between the *š* and the *s*. The form *lmšyswt* would be the same as that of the MT but with the full writing, but cf. *lmšwsh* in 4QpZeph [3].

Column 9

9:1-2. The beginning of the col. is the continuation of the pesher on Hab

2:7-8a, which began in line 16 of col. 8. Since the end of col. 8 is lost, the first two lines of this col. are without context; it is therefore difficult to identify some of the forms and to translate these lines.

his injury (ngw^{c}w ?). The first word in line 1 is a problem. The form is here taken to be a substantive with the 3rd pers. sing. masc. sf., but this is not certain. In biblical Hebrew there is a segolate noun *nega^{c}*, a qatl noun-type; in QL two substantive forms occur, *ng^{c}* (e.g., 1QpHab 9:11; 1QH 1:32; 4:36; 9:12) and *ngy^{c}* (e.g., 1QS 3:14; 4:12). Since *w* and *y* are not clearly differentiated in 1QpHab, it would be possible to read *ngy^{c}w* here; such a formation would have to have a passive meaning. If *ngw^{c}w* is the correct reading, it is probably to be explained as an example of the fluctuation of segolate noun forms in Qumran Hebrew (see T. Muraoka, "Segolate Nouns in Biblical and Other Aramaic Dialects," *JAOS* 96 [1976] 226-235). Other explanations of the form have been suggested: (1) B. Jongeling thinks that *ngw^{c}w* is best understood as a *qittûl* noun-type or as the pass. part. with the 3rd pers. sing. masc. sf. (see "Les forms qṭwl dans l'hébreu des manuscrits de Qumrân," *RevQ* 1 [1958-59] 483). (2) Some authors (e.g., Elliger, Carmignac, Lohse, and van der Woude) take the form as the qal inf. cs. with the 3rd pers. sing. masc. sf., but such an inf. cs. form with a sf. is unattested in biblical Hebrew and in Mishnaic Hebrew. Another possibility that should not be overlooked is that the *w* that is assumed to be the sf. might go with the next word. The first two words in the line are written very closely together, and it is not easy to decide where the division should be. If the *w* were to go with the next word as the copula, *ngw^{c}* could be a substantive or a qal pass. part., "an injured one (?)," but it is difficult to determine what the syntax would be. But if the *w* is taken as the 3rd pers. sing. masc. sf., the most logical antecedent is the Wicked Priest, who is the subject of preceding (8:8-13; 8:16-?) and following (9:9-12; 9:16-?) interpretations.

on account of wicked judgments (*bmšpṭy rš^{c}h*), or possibly "false judgments." The meaning of the phrase cannot be determined, since the immediate context is lost.

and horrors of evil diseases were at work in him (*wš^{c}rwrywt mḥlym r^{c}ym ^{c}św*). The phrase *wš^{c}rwrywt mḥlym* is taken as the subject of *^{c}św*, but Dupont-Sommer ("Le 'Commentaire,'" 137) understands *mḥlym* as the hiph. part. of *ḥll* and translates the clause "et d'odieux profanateurs ont commis des horreurs sur lui."

his decaying flesh (*bgwyt bśrw*) literally, "the corpse of his flesh." Cf. 4QpNah 3-4 ii 6, where the phrase *bgwyt bśrm* apparently refers to corpses.

9:3 The citation of Hab 2:8a presents the following variant from the MT: *wyšlwkh* (MT: *yšlwk*).

9:4 *Jerusalem* (*yrwšlm*). Here, in 1QpHab 12:7, and in 4QpIsa^{e} 1-2:2, the spelling of the name "Jerusalem" is *yrwšlm,* which is the *kĕtîb* of the MT. Elsewhere in QL, however, the name is usually spelled *yrwšlym,* e.g., 1QpPs 9:2; 4QpIsa^{a} 2-6 ii 25, 29 (Allegro's 5-6:9, 13); 4QpIsa^{b} 2:7, 10; 4QpIsa^{c} 23 ii 11; 4QpNah 3-4 i 2, 11.

9:4-5 *the last priests of Jerusalem* (*kwhny yrwšlm hʾḥrwnym*), cf. *kwhn hʾḥrwn* in 4QpHos^{b} 2:3; *kwhn lʾḥryt hqṣ* in 4QpPs^{b} 1:[5]; and *kwhny yrwšlym* in 4QpNah 3-4 i [11].

9:5 *who amass* (*yqbwṣw*). See the note above on 4:6.

9:7 Following the phrase *ḥyl hktyʾym,* "the army of the Kittim," at the beginning of the line, there is a large space. This is followed by the phrase *kyʾ hmh ytr hʿmym,* "for they are the remainder of the peoples," in which *hmh* apparently designates the Kittim. The phrase picks up the words *ytr hʿmym* (MT: *ytr ʿmym*) from Hab 2:8a, and the phrase is treated by some modern authors almost as a third citation with *kyʾ hmh* as an introductory formula (e.g., Dupont-Sommer, Carmignac, Vermes, van der Woude). This does not account for the space, which would not normally follow a pesher section, but there are other puzzling spaces in this document, e.g., in 3:7; 5:11; 10:10; 11:9.

9:8 *and all its inhabitants* (*wywšby bh*). The word *ywšby* is added above the line.

9:9-10 *wrong done to the Teacher of Righteousness* (*bʿwwn mwrh ḥṣdq*). Brownlee reads *bʿyyn,* "in the sight of," but does not explain the unusual spelling ("Jerusalem Habakkuk Scroll," 14).

into the hand of (*byd*). There might be enough space to restore the pl. cs. *byd*[*y*], "into the hands of."

to humble him (*lʿnwtw*). The first *w* of the form is added above the line.

9:12 *against his chosen ones* (*ʿl bḥyrw*). This form is taken as the defectively written pl. with the 3rd pers. sing. masc. sf., referring to the Teacher of Righteousness and his partisans. See the note above on 5:4.

9:12-15 The citation of Hab 2:9-11 presents the following variants from the MT:

(1) *hbwṣʿ* (MT: *bṣʿ*).

(2) *lnṣl* (MT: *lhnṣl*). Both forms are the niph. inf. cs., but in 1QpHab the *h* is elided; similar elision occurs in *llḥm* (4QpIsa^{a} 2-6 ii 27 [Allegro's 5-6:11], and possibly *lwsp* (1QpMic 10:5) and *lʾsp* (4QpHos^{a} 1:[12]). Cf. the niph. inf. cs. *lhplh* above in 7:8, where the *h* is not elided. Elision of the *h* also occurs at times in Qumran Hebrew in the hiph. inf. cs.; see the note above on 3:1.

(3) *qṣwwt* (MT: *qṣwt*). The form in the MT of Hab 2:10b is a problem. It is vocalized *qĕṣôt,* the pl. cs. of *qāṣâ,* which means "end," "border," or "extremity," but it is suggested in *BHS* that either *qaṣṣôtā* (the qal perf.

2nd pers. sing. masc. of *qṣṣ*), "you have cut off," or *qaṣṣôt* (the piel inf. of *qṣh*), "cutting off," be read. Another possibility is *qĕṣāwōt,* the pl. of the noun *qĕṣāt*, "end," which is termed an Aramaic loanword by KB. The piel inf. from *qṣh* seems to make the best sense of the phrase, "cutting off many peoples."

The form in 1QpHab, *qṣwwt,* might be the pl. cs. of *qāṣâ* or *qĕṣāt,* cf. the phrase *qṣwwt tbl,* "the ends of the earth," in 1QM 1:8. No such pl. cs. form is attested in biblical Hebrew, but there are two places (Exod 37:8 and 39:4) where the suffixal form *qṣwwtw* is the *kĕtîb* of the MT. In the second citation of Hab 2:10b in 10:2, the form *is qṣwt,* which conforms to the consonants in the MT and might be read as the piel inf. of *qṣh.* Are the two forms *qṣwt* and *qṣwwt* the same, or do they perhaps indicate that the Qumran author was aware of differing textual traditions? The interpretation of the first citation is almost entirely lost, and the pesher on the second citation gives no clue as to how the forms should be understood.

(4) *wḥwṭy,* "and the threads of" (MT: *wḥwṭʾ,* "and a sinner" ?). The reading of 1QpHab in line 14 is not entirely certain, but the second citation in 10:2 clearly has *ḥwṭy.*

9:15 *stucco from the framework* (*kpys mʿṣ*). The translation is uncertain; the word *kpys,* which seems to be connected with stucco-work, occurs only here in biblical Hebrew.

9:16-17 The col. ends with a pesher on Hab 2:9-11, which continues into col. 10. The subject of the interpretation is apparently the Wicked Priest.

Column 10

10:1 *its stones . . . its framework* (*ʾbnyh . . . ʿyṣh*). The pronominal suffixes of these two words are fem.; thus, the antecedent in the last lines of col. 9 would have been fem., perhaps *ʿyr*, "city," in anticipation of Hab 2:12 (lines 5-6) or *ʾrṣ,* "land" (a final *ṣ* is probably to be read at the end of 9:16).

The *y* of *ʿyṣh* is added above the line.

10:2 See the note above on the first citation of this text in 9:13-15.

10:3 *this is the house of judgment: God will give his judgment* (*hwʾ byt hmšpṭ ʾšr ytn ʾl ʾt mšpṭw*). Some translate the relative sign *ʾšr*, which connects these clauses, either adjectivally, e.g., "the condemned House whose judgement God will pronounce" (Vermes) or adverbially, e.g., "inasmuch as God will give his judgment" (similarly Elliger, van der Woude). The *ʾšr* might be better left untranslated; it can be interpreted almost as a colon, with the following phrases as explications of the metaphorical "house of judgment." See Part II, p. 240, n. 31.

he will bring him up . . . he will condemn him as guilty . . . he will punish him (*yʿlnw . . . yršyʿnw . . . yšpṭnw*). The antecedent of the 3rd pers. sing. masc. sfs. of these verbs is probably again the Wicked Priest, who is the focus of the interpretations in 9:9-12 and 9:16—10:1.

10:6-8 The citation of Hab 2:12-13 presents the following variants from the MT: (1) *wykwnn* (MT: *wkwnn*); (2) *mʿm* (MT: *mʾt*); (3) *ygʿw* (MT: *wyygʿw*).

are not these (*hlwʾ hnh*). According to the emendation suggested in *BHS, hnh* is taken as the fem. pl. pronoun *hēnâ,* rather than as the expletive *hinnēh,* "behold!" Since it is fem., it must refer to *ʿyr* and *qryh.*

10:9-13 The pesher on Hab 2:12-13 is one long grammatical unit with a main clause (the introductory nominal sentence, *pšr hdbr ʿl mṭyp hkzb*), followed by a dependent clause modifying *mṭyp hkzb* (*ʾšr htʿh rbym*), to which are subordinated the following: (1) two inf. phrases explaining how *mṭyp hkzb* led many astray (*lbnwt . . . wlqym*); (2) two additional inf. phrases (with an inverted word order in the first), each specifying further one of the preceding infs. (*lwgyʿ . . . wlhrwtm*); (3) an inf. phrase expressing the result of the four preceding infs. (*lhywt*); (4) an adverbial clause introduced by *bʿbwr,* expressing the purpose or perhaps the result of the verb *htʿh,* i.e., "he caused many to err . . . so that they will come" (this clause might also be subordinated to the preceding inf.); (5) an *ʾšr*-clause that could be interpreted either causally, e.g., "they will come to judgment . . . because they reviled," or as an explanation of the unexpressed subject of the verb *ybw'w,* i.e., "they will come to judgment . . . who reviled." This grammatical unit can be visually represented as follows:

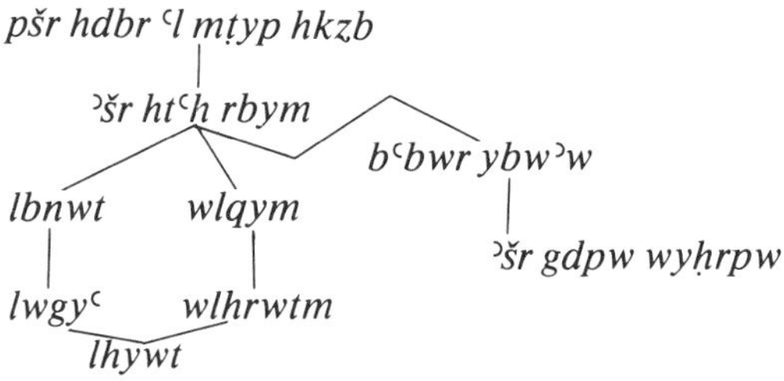

10:9 *the One who Spouts the Lie* (*mṭyp hkzb*). This figure does not appear elsewhere in the pesharim, unless the title is to be restored below in 10:17 —11:1 (I reject the doubtful reading of *mṭyp hkzb* in 1QpMic 10:2; see the note below on that text). This epithet might refer to the same person who is called "the Man of the Lie" (*ʾyš hkzb*) in 1QpHab 2:1-2; 5:11; 4QpPsa 1-10 i 26 (Allegro's 1-2 i 18); 1-10 iv [14]. Cf. *ʾyš hlṣwn ʾšr hṭyp lyśrʾl mymy kzb,* "the man of boasting who spouted over Israel waters of a lie" (CD 1:14); *wmṭyp kzb* (CD 8:13) and *wmṭyp ʾdm lkzb* (CD 19:25-26).

10:10 *vanity* (*šww*), or "deception." In biblical Hebrew the word appears as *šwʾ;* it is found once as *šw* in Job 15:31. In the form in 1QpHab the doubled *w* indicates a consonantal *w;* this should not be read as a suffixal form (*pace* Dupont-Sommer ["Le 'Commentaire,'" 138], Vermes).

and to establish (*wlqym*), the hiph. inf. cs. with the *h* elided. See the note above on 3:1.

The space between ʿ*dh* and *bšqr* is larger than usual, but it should probably not be interpreted as a break in the commentary.

10:11 *for the sake of its glory* (*bʿbwr kbwdh*). In the *editio princeps*, the first of the two words was read as *bʿbwd*, "working for its glory," but the *r* is certain. The form *kbwdh* is here taken to be the substantive *kbwd* with the 3rd pers. sing. fem. sf. referring to ʿ*yr* (or possibly to ʿ*dh*). The form is so understood by Brownlee ("Further Light," 9) and Vermes. Elliger, however, translates "seiner Ehre," taking the *h* as the 3rd pers. sing. masc. sf., apparently referring to *mṭyp hkzb* (see *Studien*, 64-65, 209). The use of *h* as a vowel letter in the 3rd pers. sing. masc. sf. is attested in biblical Hebrew in pre-exilic writings (see GKC §91e), but Elliger offers no examples from QL to support his interpretation.

making many toil (*lwgyʿ*), the hiph. inf. cs. with the *h* elided. See the note above on 3:1.

and saturating (*?*) *them* (*wlhrwtm*). This form has not been satisfactorily explained. There is an irregularity in the skin, and the reading is not absolutely certain. What appears to be the left side of the wedge-shaped stroke across the top of the *h* is separated slightly from the rest of the stroke, and the possibility that this is actually another letter (a *w* or a *y*?) between the *h* and the *r* cannot be entirely excluded. However, I read the form as *lhrwtm* and tentatively identify it as the hiph. inf. cs. of *rwh*, "to saturate" (so Vermes, *Discovery in the Judean Desert* [New York: Desclee, 1956] 130). This fits the grammatical scheme and the logical context and is perhaps supported by the fact that the same root appears in a substantive form below in 11:14 (*hrwyh*). But there are problems with this identification of the form: (1) The form would be expected to appear as *lhrwwtm*. (2) Elsewhere in this document in hiph. infs. the *h* is elided; see the note above on 3:1. (3) In biblical Hebrew the hiph. of the verb *rwh* is construed with one or two accusatives but not with the preposition *b*, e.g., Lam 3:15; Isa 43:24.

Some authors identify the form as the hiph. inf. cs. of *yrh*, "to teach" (Brownlee ["Jerusalem Habakkuk Scroll," 14], Maier). This, too, fits the grammatical scheme and the logical context, but similar difficulties arise: (1) the form would be expected to appear as *lhwrwtm*; and (2) in the hiph. inf. the *h* would probably be elided.

Most commentators take the form as the qal inf. cs. of *hrh*, "to conceive," "to be pregnant" (Dupont-Sommer ["Le 'Commentaire,'" 138, 148], Vermes [*Dead Sea Scrolls in English*], Carmignac, Elliger). This is a satisfactory identification of the form as it stands, but there are problems with its use here: (1) The grammatical scheme seems to demand a causative inf. parallel to *lwgyᶜ*, but the verb *hrh* is unattested with a causative meaning such as "to impregnate." (2) If the inf. expressed result, i.e., "making them toil . . . so that they become pregnant," how would the *w* be explained? (3) In biblical Hebrew the verb *hrh* is not construed with *b.*

10:13 *the elect of God* (*bḥyry ʾl*). See the note above on 5:4.

10:15 The citation of Hab 2:14 presents the following variant from the MT: *hym* (MT: *ym*).

10:17 The last word in the col. may have been either *ʾyš* or *mṭyp.* The first word in col. 11 is *hkzb,* and the pesher is probably speaking either of the Man of the Lie (*ʾyš hkzb*) or the One who Spouts the Lie (*mṭyp hkzb*). See the notes above on 2:1-2 and 10:9.

Column 11

11:1 The col. opens with the last words of the pesher on Hab 2:15.

11:2 *the sea* (*hyym*), cf. the spelling of this word (*ym*) in the citation of the biblical text above (10:15). If this is interpreted as a scribal error of dittography, it should be transcribed *hy{y}m,* but it may be that the doubled *y* here indicates a consonantal *y,* cf. *šww* above in 10:10, 11. See further E. Y. Kutscher, *Isaiah Scroll*, 159-60.

11:2-3 The citation of Hab 2:15 presents the following variants from the MT:

(1) *rᶜyhw* (MT: *rᶜhw*). The form of the MT, vocalized *rēᶜēhû,* could be the sing. noun or the defectively written pl. with the 3rd pers. sing. masc. sf. The form in 1QpHab is probably the pl. with the sf., but it might also be the sing. with the full writing. Thus, this could be an orthographic variant.

(2) *ḥmtw* (MT: *ḥmtk*).

(3) *ʾp* (MT: *wʾp*).

(4) *mwᶜdyhm,* "their feasts" (MT: *mᶜwryhm,* "their nakedness"). This variant could have arisen at some point through the confusion of *d* and *r* in a defectively written text.

Compare the allusion to Hab 2:15 in 1QH 4:11-12: *wyᶜṣwrw mšqh dᶜt mṣmʾym wlṣmʾm yšqwm hwmṣ lmᶜ‹n› hbṭ ʾl tᶜwtm lhthwll bmwᶜdyhm lhtpś bmṣwdwtm,* "and they withhold the drink of knowledge from the thirsty, and for their thirst they give them vinegar to drink in order that they might look at their confusion in that they are madmen in their feasts and are caught in their nets."

mixing in his poison (*msph ḥmtw*), or possibly "his wrath." The form *msph* is here taken to be the piel part. (*mĕsappēaḥ*) from the root *spḥ* (I), "to add" (so also Elliger, Maier, van der Woude). Other commentators (e.g., Dupont-Sommer ["Le 'Commentaire,'" 138], Brownlee ["Jerusalem

Habakkuk Scroll," 15], Carmignac, Lohse) derive the word from the root *spḥ* (III), "to pour out," and they translate the phrase "pouring out his wrath." This root, however, is unattested in biblical Hebrew in any verbal form, although it seemingly appears in the substantive form *sāpîaḥ* "outpouring," in Job 14:19.

making (them) drunk in order that he might look (*šqr lmʿn hbṭ*). The form *šqr* is here taken to be the piel inf. abs. (continuing the piel part. *msph*), and the form *hbṭ* is taken as the defectively written hiph. inf. cs.

11:6 *to his place of exile* (*ʾbyt glwtw*), literally, "to the house of his exile." Early interpretations of this phrase such as "intending him to go into exile" (Brownlee ["Jerusalem Habakkuk Scroll," 15], reading *ʾbwt* as the qal inf. of *ʾbh,* "to want," and *glwtw* as the qal inf. of *glh*) or "wishing to uncover him" (Brownlee ["Further Light," 9], taking *glwtw* as the piel inf. of *glh*) have been abandoned by most in favor of treating the form *ʾbyt* as a contraction of *ʾl byt,* "to the house of." The same contracted form appears in a text from Murabbaʿat, where it has been similarly interpreted. See P. Benoit, J. T. Milik, and R. de Vaux, *Les grottes de Murabbaʿât* (DJD 2; Oxford: Clarendon, 1961), p. 156, No. 42, line 4 (J. T. Milik).

and at the end (*wbqṣ*). In this instance the word *qṣ*, which frequently has eschatological connotations in QL, simply means "termination"; see the note above on 5:7-8.

11:7 *he appeared to them* (*hwpyʿ*). The subject of the verb *hwpyʿ* is ambiguous. Is it the Wicked Priest or the Teacher of Righteousness who appeared? In biblical Hebrew the verb *hwpyʿ* is used in the hiph. to refer to light shining forth (Job 3:4; 37:15) and especially to the appearance of God in a theophany (Deut 33:2; Ps 50:2; 80:2; 94:1). For this reason, Dupont-Sommer (*Essene Writings,* 266, n. 4) argues that the word would never have been used of the Wicked Priest. In QL the verb is used in the hiph. frequently in connection with theophany-like descriptions, e.g., 1QS 10:2; 1QM 1:16; 12:13; 1QH 4:6, 23: 7:24; 9:26, 31; 11:26; 18:6; CD 20:25-26. In other texts, however, the verb is used in a more neutral sense meaning "to appear," "to be manifest," or "to be seen," e.g., *whywm hwpyʿ lnw,* "and today it [the appointed time] has appeared to us" (1QM 18:10-11), [ ]*lbm wyṣrm hwpyʿ ly lmrwrym,* "[of] their heart and their [evil ?] inclination appears as bitterness to me" (1QH 5:31-32), *bhwpʿ mʿśyw,* "when his deeds are manifest" (CD 20:3; similarly 20:6). Of special importance is 1QH 7:3, where Belial is the subject of the verb: *ky blyʿl ʿm hwpʿ yṣr hwwtm,* "for Belial shows forth with their inclination of destruction (?)." In terms of the usage of the verb in QL, then, either the Wicked Priest or the Teacher of Righteousness could be the subject, and the context favors the Wicked Priest. Not only is he the subject of the preceding verb *rdp*, but also the biblical citation being interpreted is a "woe" to the aggressor. It is logical to assume that the woe falls upon the Wicked Priest and that he is the aggressor—pursuing the Teacher of Righteousness to swallow him up.

the Day of Atonement (*ywm hkpwrym*). This reference to the aggression of the Wicked Priest against the Teacher of Righteousness on the Day of Atonement brings up the problem of the Qumran calendar. It can be inferred from this text that the Wicked Priest followed a different calendar—probably the luni-solar calendar used in the Jerusalem Temple—from that of the Qumran sect, which followed a solar calendar of 364 days. See further J. A. Fitzmyer, *The Dead Sea Scrolls: Major Publications and Tools for Study* (2nd ed.; SBLSBS 8; Missoula: Scholars Press, 1977) 131-37.

11:8 *to make them stumble (wlkšlym),* the hiph. inf. cs. with the *h* elided. See the note above on 3:1.

11:9 *rather than glory* (*m‹k›bwd*). The text as it stands in 1 QpHab (*mbwd*) is probably a scribal error.

The citation of Hab 2:16 presents the following variant from the MT: *whrᶜl,* "totter" (MT: *whᶜrl,* "be uncircumcised"); see the note below on 11:13.

11:13 *the foreskin of* (*ᶜwrlt*). In this form the *w* represents a short *o*-vowel. There is a small space between the *r* and the *l*, but this should not be interpreted as a division of the word (*pace* Brownlee, "Biblical Exegesis," 68-69). The appearance of this word in the commentary on Hab 2:16 could indicate that the Qumran author was aware of the textual tradition reflected in the form *whᶜrl* in the MT.

11:14 *in order that the thirst might be consumed* (*lmᶜn spwt hṣmʾh*). The form *spwt* is here taken as the qal inf. cs. of *sph*, perhaps an allusion to Deut 29:18, cf. 1QS 2:14. Brownlee interprets *spwt* as the qal inf. cs. of *ysp,* and he translates the phrase "only to add to his thirst" ("Jerusalem Habakkuk Scroll," 14).

11:15 In this line Elliger restores *lwsy[p ᶜ]l[yw ʾt q]l[wn]w,* "zu vermehren bei ihm] seine [Schande]," but this is a little too long for the space. Moreover, the syntax is not entirely satisfactory, with the preposition with a suffix (*ᶜlyw*) followed by the noun with a suffix (*qlwnw*), "to add upon him his shame (?)," cf. above 8:12 *lwsyp ᶜlyw ᶜwn ʾšmh* (no suffix), "to add to him guilty sin."

11:17 At the end of the col. the first words of the citation of Hab 2:17 are restored.

Column 12

12:1 The citation of Hab 2:17 presents the following variant from the MT: *yḥth* (MT: *yḥytn*). The form of the MT, which is vocalized *yĕḥîtan* has been questionably identified as the hiph. impf. of *ḥtt,* "to be terrified" (see

KB under the root *ḥtt*) with what appears to be a 3rd pers. pl. fem. sf. This suffix may have arisen at some point through confusion of final *k* and final *n*; it is suggested in *BHS* that the form be emended to *yĕḥittekā,* parallel to *yĕkassekā* in 2:17a. The variant in 1QpHab is explained by some (e.g., Habermann, Carmignac, Elliger, Lohse, Maier, Vermes) as a scribal error for *yḥtkh,* which would correspond to the emended form of the MT. S. Talmon ("Notes on the Habakkuk Scroll," *VT* 1 [1951] 36-37) reads *wĕḥattâ,* which he apparently identifies as the qal perf. 2nd pers. sing. masc. of *ḥtt* with the *w* conversive, "and you will be afraid." Not only is this reading syntactically difficult, since it leaves the preceding phrase *wšwd bhmwt* (as restored according to the MT) without a verb, but also the form would be expected to be *wĕḥattôtā.* If the first letter is read as *w,* the form could be the qal perf. 3rd pers. sing. fem. of *ḥtt,* but a fem. verb form does not fit the context. Again, reading the first letter as *w*, the form could be the noun *ḥittâ,* "terror," but this too is snytactically awkward. Dupont-Sommer ("Le 'Commentaire,'" 139) apparently takes the form from *ḥth* (II), "to rake together (the coals of a fire)"; he translates it "attisera (le feu)." The form is here taken tentatively as the qal impf. 3rd pers. sing. masc. of *ḥth* (I), which is attested in biblical Hebrew only in Ps 52:7 meaning "to knock down" or "to destroy." This meaning is perhaps supported by the commentary on this section, which speaks of God's decision for "complete destruction" (*lklh*) of the Wicked Priest (line 5) because he plotted "to destroy completely" (*lklwt*) the poor ones (line 6).

12:2-6 The structure and syntax of this pesher are complicated and may reflect different levels of interpretation. Six grammatical units can be isolated: (1) the introductory nominal sentence (*pšr hdbr ʿl hkwhn hršʿ,* "the interpretation of the passage concerns the Wicked Priest"); (2) an inf. phrase (*lšlm lw ʾt gmwlw,* "to pay him his due"), which is separated from the preceding word by a space that is slightly larger than the usual space between words; (3) an *ʾšr*-clause that seems to qualify the preceding inf. phrase (*ʾšr gml ʿl ʾbywnym,* "inasmuch as he dealt wickedly with the poor ones"); (4) the metaphorical identification of "Lebanon" and the "beasts," which seems to be a pesher within the pesher (*kyʾ hlbnwn hwʾ ʿṣt hyḥd whbhmwt hmh ptʾy yhwdh ʿwśh htwrh,* "for 'Lebanon' is the council of the community, and the 'beasts' are the simple ones of Judah, those who observe the Law"); (5) an *ʾšr*-clause after which the rest of the line is left blank (*ʾšr yšwpṭnw ʾl lklh,* "whom God will sentence to complete destruction"), which seems to refer back to the Wicked Priest, who is the subject of the original nominal sentence; (6) a final clause that begins a new line following the large space at the end of line 5, but which seems to continue logically and syntactically from the preceding clause (*kʾšr zmm lklwt ʾbywnym,* "because he plotted to destroy completely the poor ones").

Thus, the basic interpretation seems to be *pšr hdbr ʿl hkwhn hršʿ . . . ʾšr yšwpṭnw ʾl klh kʾšr zmm lklwt ʾbywnym,* "The interpretation of the passage concerns the Wicked Priest . . . whom God will sentence to complete destruction because he plotted to destroy completely the poor ones." This structure is interrupted by explanatory remarks about the Wicked Priest and by the figurative identifications of "Lebanon" and the "beasts."

12:2 At the end of this line an "X" appears; see the note above on 2:5-6.

12:3 *the poor ones* (*ʾbywnym*). This word appears three times in this col. (lines 3, 6, 10), each time without the article, but cf. *ʿdt hʾbywnym,* "the congregation of the poor ones," in 4QpPs^{a} 1-10 ii 10 (Allegro's 1-2 ii 9); 1-10 iii 10. It is not entirely certain what specific group or type of people is designated by this term, but the term seems here to refer to the members of the Qumran community, with whom the Wicked Priest dealt wickedly and whom he robbed and plotted to destroy. In 4QpPs^{a}, where the term is used with the article, the group is described as a "congregation" (*ʿdh*), whose inheritance is all the earth (1-10 iii 10). See further L. E. Keck, "The Poor among the Saints in the New Testament," *ZNW* 56 (1965) 100-29; "The Poor among the Saints in Jewish Christianity and Qumran," *ZNW* 57 (1966) 54-78; J. A. Fitzmyer, "Jewish Christianity in Acts in the Light of the Qumran Scrolls," *Essays,* 287-88.

Lebanon (*hlbnwn*). Lebanon is here figuratively identified with the council of the community, cf. 4QpIsa^{a} 7-10 iii 6-7 (Allegro's 8-10.2-3), where Lebanon is identified with the Kittim, and 4QpNah 1-2 ii 7-9, where Lebanon seems to be given another figurative identification, but the text is fragmentary. For other interpretations of "Lebanon" in Jewish exegetical tradition, see G. Vermes, "'Car le Liban, c'est le conseil de la communauté': Note sur Pésher d'Habacuc 12,3-4," *Mélanges bibliques rédigés en l'honneur d'André Robert* (Travaux de l'Institut Catholique de Paris 4; Paris: Bloud & Gay, n.d.), 316-25; "The Symbolical Interpretation of *Lebanon* in the Targums: The Origin and Development of an Exegetical Tradition," *JTS* 9 (1958) 1-12, reprinted in *Scripture and Tradition in Judaism: Haggadic Studies* (SPB 4; Leiden: Brill, 1961) 26-39; B. Gärtner, *The Temple and the Community in Qumran and the New Testament: A Comparative Study in the Temple Symbolism of the Qumran Texts and the New Testament* (SNTSMS 1; Cambridge University Press, 1965) 43-44.

12:4 *the council of the community* (*ʿṣt hyḥd*). Among the pesharim, this phrase is found in 1QpMic 10:6; 4QpIsa^{d} 1:2; 4QpPs^{a} 1-10 ii 15 (Allegro's 1-2 ii 14). The phrase also occurs frequently in 1QS (e.g., 5:7; 6:10, 12-13, 14, 16), where it seems to designate a specific group having authority within the community. In this context, therefore, I translate the word *ʿṣh* as "council," but the meaning "counsel" cannot be fully excluded; see the note above on 5:10. Other translations reflect the ambiguity of the Hebrew word *ʿṣh:* "le parti" (Dupont-Sommer, "Le 'Commentaire,'" 139), "der Rat" (Elliger, Lohse, and similarly van der Woude), "le counseil" (Carmignac). See further J. Worrell, "*ʿṣh:* 'Counsel' or 'council' at Qumran?" *VT* 20 (1970) 65-74.

the simple ones of Judah (*ptʾy yhwdh*). The "simple ones" are described here as "those who observe the Law" (see the following note). The term *ptʾym* also occurs in 1QpMic 7:[3]; 10:[3]; 20-21:[1], but these texts are fragmentary and the contexts are lost. In 4QpNah 3-4 iii [7], the "simple ones" (*pt*[*ʾym*]) appear as those who "will no longer support" the policy of the Seekers-After-Smooth-Things (i.e., probably the Pharisees; see the note on 4QpNah 3-4 i 2), when the perversity of the latter is revealed at the end of time. In 4QpNah 3-4 iii 5, it is said that "the simple ones of Ephraim" (*ptʾy ʾprym*), who had been led astray by the Seekers-After-Smooth-Things, will flee from them. Thus, those described as the "simple ones" seem to be those who, though they observed the Law, were intellectually vulnerable and could be led astray. See further J. Dupont, "Les 'simples' (*petâyim*) dans la Bible et à Qumran: A propos des νήπιοι de Mt. 11,25; Lc. 10,21," *Studi sull' Oriente e la Bibbia offerti al P. Giovanni Rinaldi nel 60° compleanno da allievi, colleghi, amici* (Genoa: Editrice Studio e Vita, 1967) 329-36; A. Dupont-Sommer, "Le Commentaire de Nahum découvert près de la Mer Morte (4QpNah): Traduction et notes," *Sem* 13 (1963) 79.

12:4-5 *those who observe the Law* (*ʿwśh htwrh*), cf. *ʿwśy htwrh* above in 7:10-11; 8:1. The form *ʿwśh* looks like the sing. part., where the masc. pl. part. *ʿwśy* would be expected, if it refers to *ptʾym,* "the simple ones." Most authors translate the part. as if it were pl. and explain the form either as a scribal error or as an orthographic variant for *ʿwśy*. A scribal error seems more likely, and on the photograph it looks as though the right side of the *h* has been written over to alter it to a *y*. If the sing. were to be kept, then the phrase could modify *yhwdh,* "the simple ones of Judah, who observes the Law."

whom God will sentence (*ʾšr yšwpṭnw*). If the spelling of *yšwpṭnw* does not involve a metathesis of *w* and *p,* then the form would be an impf. that preserves a long vowel after the first radical, reflecting a recession of accent to that syllable. The usual biblical Hebrew form would be *yišpĕṭennû*. The impf. form with the long vowel after the first radical is infrequent in QL, but it does occur in some cases even when a pronominal sf. is added to a sing. verb, e.g., *ydwršyhw* in 1QS 6:14; *ydwršhw* in 1QS 6:17. See further M. H. Goshen-Gottstein, "Linguistic Structure," 123-28.

12:6-7 Following the introductory phrase *wʾšr ʾmr* there seems to be a second citation of Hab 2:17b, but the text corresponds neither to that of the

MT nor to the first citation above in 12:1. The *ʾdm* is replaced by *qryh*, and the last phrase, *wkwl ywšby bh,* is left out.

12:7 *Jerusalem* (*yrwšlm*); see the note above on 9:4.

12:8 *the Wicked Priest* (*hkwhn hršʿ*). The word *hršʿ* is added above the line.

12:10-11 The citation of Hab 2:18 presents the following variants from the MT:

(1) *psl* (second) (MT: *pslw*).

(2) *msykh* (MT: *mskh*). The *y* of the form in 1QpHab is mutilated and may have been partially erased.

(3) *wmry,* "image?" (MT: *wmwrh,* "teacher?"). Some commentators (e.g., Elliger, Lohse, van der Woude) believe that this is an orthographic variant from the MT, but C. Rabin ("Notes on the Habakkuk Scroll," 153) is probably correct: if the Qumran interpreter had read the text as a form of *mwrh,* "teacher," the Teacher of Falsehood would surely have been the focal point of the pesher. If another noun is intended in the text of 1QpHab, possibilities include: *mārê* (pl. cs. of *mar*), "the bitter things of falsehood" (so apparently Brownlee ["Jerusalem Habakkuk Scroll," 15], who translates it "bitterness"); *mĕrî,* "a rebellion of falsehood" (Vermes, *Discovery*, 132); *mōrê* (qal part. masc. pl. cs. of *mrh*), "rebels of falsehood," though the full writing *môrê* would be expected; an orthographic variant of *mĕrî,* "fatling of falsehood" (Vermes [*Dead Sea Scrolls in English*]). I follow Rabin ("Notes on the Habakkuk Scroll," 153) and Carmignac, who treat this form as an orthographic variant of *marʾeh,* "sight," "image," or "appearance of falsehood." The brief interpretation of this citation in 12:12-14 gives no clue as to how the Qumran author understood the form.

(4) *yṣryw* (MT: *yṣrw*).

(5) *ʿlyhw* (MT: *ʿlyw*).

12:14 *before them* (*lhmh*). The *m* is written in the final form.

12:15 Hab 2:19a is certainly to be restored in this line, but the text as in the MT seems too short for the beginning of the line. Habermann may be correct in restoring a second *hwy,* "Woe!" at the beginning of the line: *hw*[*y ʾwmr*]*lʿṣ* (so also Dupont-Sommer, "Le 'Commentaire,'" 139). Elliger, however, restores *h*[*ʾwmr*] for the *ʾmr* of the MT.

In the word *lʿṣ,* the *ṣ* is written in the nonfinal form.

The last word in the line is certainly *dwmm* as in the MT, rather than *dwmh* (so Habermann, Elliger, Lohse) or *rwmh* (so Talmon, "Notes on the Habakkuk Scroll," 37).

12:16-17 At the end of the col. the text of Hab 2:19b-20a is restored.

Column 13

13:1 The citation of Hab 2:20 presents the following variants from the MT:

(1) *mlpnyw* (MT: *mpnyw*).

(2) *hrṣ* (MT: *hʾrṣ*). This is probably best explained as a scribal error, and so it is transcribed *h* ‹ʾ› *rṣ*.

13:2-3 *but on the day of judgment* (*wbywm hmšpṭ*). The *m* of *wbywm* is written in the nonfinal form.

1QpMic (1Q*14*)

Editio princeps: "Commentaire de Michée" (J. T. Milik), *Qumran Cave I,* pp. 77-80 and pl. XV.

Preliminary publication: J. T. Milik, "Fragments d'un midrash de Michée dans les manuscrits de Qumrân," *RB* 59 (1952) 412-18.

Secondary transcriptions and translations: H. Bardtke, *Die Handschriftenfunde,* 293-94; J. Carmignac, *Les Textes,* 2. 82-84 [under the incorrect title 4QpMic]; T. H. Gaster, *Dead Sea Scriptures,* 239-40; A. M. Habermann, *Megilloth,* 151-53; J. Maier, *Die Texte,* 1. 166-67, 2. 153; G. Molin, *Die Söhne,* 17-18; L. Moraldi, *I manoscritti,* 541-43; E. F. Sutcliffe, *The Monks,* 179; G. Vermes, *Dead Sea Scrolls in English,* 230-31; A. Vincent, *Les manuscrits,* 105-107; A. S. van der Woude, *Bijbelcommentaren,* 47-51.

Secondary literature: J. Carmignac, "Notes," 515-19.

The document entitled 1QpMic consists of twenty-three frgs. Transcriptions of twelve of the frgs. are given in the preliminary publication, where J. T. Milik tentatively arranges ten of the frgs. into four groups: (1) frgs. 1-5, 9; (2) frg. 10; (3) frg. 11; (4) frgs. 17, 19 (the numbers are those assigned to the frgs. in the *editio princeps*). In *Qumran Cave I* Milik revises the first two groups to frgs. 1-5 (acknowledging that the placement of frg. 5 is only probable) and frgs. 8-10. These first two groups give the biblical text and interpretation of Mic 1:2-6, and it is likely that they belonged to the first col. of the commentary, as Milik suggests ("Fragments," 414). In frgs. 1-5, the text of Mic 1:2b-5a can be restored with satisfactory alignment and spacing. I differ with Milik, however, on the arrangement and restoration of frgs. 8-10. Placing frgs. 8 and 9 at the upper left hand side of frg. 10, Milik restores a second citation of Mic 1:5a (cf. 1-5:4-5) and continues the lemma through Mic 1:6a. According to his arrangement, the further citations of 1:5c (10:3) and possibly 1:6a (10:8) would have to be second citations, apparently without any introductory formulas. This arrangement of the biblical text with at least three second citations in a space of eight lines is awkward. Moreover, Milik's reading of frg. 9 has been challenged by J. Carmignac ("Notes," 516; see the note below on frg. 9). I agree with Carmignac on this point and so transcribe frgs. 8, 9, and 10 separately. The lines, therefore, must be renumbered: Milik's 8-10:3-11 = my 10:1-9. According to the present arrangement of the frgs. then, frgs. 1-5 end with the citation of Mic 1:5a and the beginning of a commentary that probably continued to 10:1, followed in 10:2 by a citation of Mic 1:5b.

Frgs. 6 and 7, according to Milik, are part of the pesher on Mic 1:2-6. Either both are to be placed between frgs. 1-5 and frg. 10, or perhaps frg. 6 belongs with frgs. 1-5, and frg. 7 should be placed after frg. 10 (*hlwʾ* appears in 7:2 and is restored in 10:2, 4 [= Mic 1:5b,c]). Unless the two frgs. are to be placed side by side it is unlikely that both should follow frgs. 1-5, since this arrangement would give a commentary section of at least nine lines.

Both in the preliminary publication and in the *editio princeps* Milik takes frgs. 17 and 19 as part of a group and relates them to Mic 6:14-16. However, he acknowledges the uncertainty of the grouping, not knowing exactly where to place frg. 19. Frg. 19 is transcribed separately here.

Though the text is fragmentary, it is apparent from the phrases that are partially or completely preserved that the text of Micah was interpreted both eschatologically ("at the end of days" 6:[2]; "day of judgment" 10:[6-7]; "the last generation" 17-18:[5]) and in terms of the history of the sect ("the simple ones" 7:[3]; 10:[3]; "the Teacher of Righteousness" 10:[4]; "the elect of God" 10:[5-6]; "the council of the community" 10:6). There are also phrases that reveal an atmosphere of conflict, possibly the conflict between the Teacher of Righteousness and the Wicked Priest ("against him" 7:4; "who lead astray" 11:[1]; "his enemies" 11:2; "will betray" 11:5). Cf. 1QpHab 2:2-10; 5:9-12; 9:9-12; 4QpPs^{a} 1-10 iv 8-10.

1QpMic: Translation

Fragments 1-5

1. [YA]HWEH [THE LORD WILL] BE AGAINST YOU Mic 1:2b-5a
2. [AS A WITNESS, THE LORD FROM HIS HOLY TEMPLE, FOR BEHOL]D, YAH[WEH GOES FORTH FROM] HIS PLACE
3. [AND WILL DESCEND UPON THE HIGH] PLACES OF THE EAR[TH. THE MOUNTAIN]S [WILL MELT] BENEA[TH HIM, AND THE VALLEYS WILL BE] RENT,
4. [LIKE W]AX BEFOR[E THE FI]RE, LIKE [WATERS POURED

DOWN A SLOPE. ON ACCOUNT OF THE TRANSGRESSION OF JACO]B (IS) ALL
5. [THI]S, AND ON ACCOUNT OF THE SIN[S OF THE HOUSE OF ISRAEL. The interpretation of it concerns]

Fragment 10

1. [ ]*š*[ ]
2. [WHAT IS THE TRANSGRESSION OF JACOB? IS IT NOT SAMARIA?] The interpretation of it concerns *m* . .[ ] . . 1:5b
3. [the sim]ple ones. AND WHAT ARE THE HIGH PLACES OF JUDAH? 1:5c
4. [IS IT NOT JERUSALEM? The interpretation of it concerns] the Tea[ch]er of Righteousness, who is the one
5. [ ]*w* and to a[l]l those who volunteer to be added to the chosen ones of
6. [God, those who observe the Law] in the council of the community, who will be saved from the day of
7. [judgment]*l*.[ ] . . [ ].
8. [AND I SHALL MAKE SAMARIA A] PILE OF STONES IN THE FIELD. 1:6a
9. [ ]*l*[ ]*l*[ ]

Fragment 6

1.].[
2. at] the end of [days
3.] . .*h* glory [
4. wh]o transgressed [

Fragment 7

1.]*m* [
2.]is it not.[
3.]. the simple one[s
4.]*ṣh* against him[
5.]. *l*[

Fragment 8

1.] . .[
2.] . .[

Fragment 9

1.] . .ʿ[
2.].*l*ʾ[

Fragment 11

1.].[ ]*m* who lead astray[
2.]his enemies. Barefoot and na[ked
3. IT HAS REACHED T]O THE GATE OF MY PEOPLE, T[O JERUSALEM 1:9b
4. he] will judge [his] enemies
5.]. will betray[ ].*w*.[
6.] . . [

Fragment 12

1.].[ ] . .[
2.]. his glory from Seir[

Fragment 13

]*wnym*[

3. fo]r God goes forth from[
4.]. .[

Fragment 14

1.]and the Lord of [
2.]*yw* .[

Fragment 15

1.]*mḥ*.[
2. ʾ]*šr* [

Fragment 16

1.].[
2.].*ḥ*[

Fragments 17-18

1. [ ]*h* [ ]
2. [YOU WILL SOW, BUT YOU WILL NOT] REAP; YO[U WILL TREAD OLIVES,] 6:15-16
3. [BUT YOU WILL NOT ANOINT YOURSELF WITH OIL. AND YOU WILL TREAD (GRAPES), BUT YOU WILL N]OT DRINK [W]INE, FOR [THE STATUTES OF OMRI ARE KEPT,]
4. [AND EVERY DEED OF THE HOUSE OF AHAB, AND YOU HAVE WAL]KED IN THEIR COUNSELS SO [THAT I MUST MAKE OF YOU A HORROR]
5. [AND ITS INHABITANTS INTO AN OBJECT TO HISS AT. The interpretation of it] concerns the [l]as[t] generation
6. [ ]*ym* and their house[ ]

Fragment 19

]*hm* [

Fragments 20-21

1.]. . [the sim]ple ones[
2.] the men [of] his [hou]se

Fragment 22

1.]*ṭty* .*šr*[
2.]and the light[
3.].*m ṣ.b.*[
4.]*bl y* . .[

Fragment 23

1.].[
2.]. and the creeping things of [the earth, they are

1QpMic: Notes

1-5:1-2 The text of Mic 1:2bα which Milik restores here, differs from the MT (*wyhy ʾdny yhwh bkm lʿd*) in its word order, the use of a non-apocopated verb form, and the absence of the copula with the verb form.

The tetragrammaton is written in line 1 and in line 2 in paleo-Hebrew script; see the note above on 1QpHab 1:1.

1-5:3 According to Milik's arrangement of the frgs., there is not enough room to restore the text of Mic 1:3b as it appears in the MT; Milik suggests that *wdrk* was omitted, a variant from the MT that is supported by the Lucianic recension of the LXX.

Another variant that appears in the apparent citation of Mic 1:3b is *hʾrṣ* (MT: *ʾrṣ*), cf. the Greek τῆς γῆς.

1-5:4-5 In the preliminary publication Milik placed frg. 9 here on a level with frgs. 1 and 5, but see the remarks above on the arrangement of frgs. 1-10.

For the orthography of *mwgrym*, which is restored in line 4, compare the allusion to Mic 1:4 in 1QH 4:34, *kmym mwgrym bmwrd.*

6:2 The phrase *ʾḥryt hymym,* "the end of days," might be preceded by *b* as is suggested here (see 1QSa 1:1; 4QpIsa^a 7-10 iii [22]; 4QFlor 1-2 i 19; CD 4:4; 6:11) or *l* (see 1QpHab 2:5-6; 9:6; 4QpIsa^a 2-6 ii 26; 4QpNah 3-4 ii 2).

6:4 In his transcription, Milik did not indicate the space that is visible after *ʿbrw.*

7:4 Milik reads *ʾ*]*šr bw*[; this is rejected by Carmignac ("Notes," 517), who suggests]*ʿh bw*[. The *h* is certain, and it was read by Milik in the preliminary publication (]*šh*). The letter preceding the *h* could be *ʿ*, but *ṣ* seems to fit the visible traces better.

7:5 Milik reads].*w*.[.

8:1 See the comments above on the placement of this frg. The reading of this line is not certain, since only traces of letters remain. Taking the frg. as part of the citation of Mic 1:5b, Milik reads *yʿ*]*qb*, while Habermann, following Milik's arrangement of the frgs., reads *yʿ*]*qwb*.

9:1 See the remarks above on the identification and placement of this frg. In the photograph, the only clear letter in this line is *ʿ*. Milik is able to read]*bpšʿ*[, while Carmignac ("Notes," 516) reads only]*pšʿ*[.

9:2 Carmignac's reading (]*lʾ*[, "Notes," 516) is better than Milik's (]*hlʾ*[), but there is a trace of the letter before the *l*. I further agree with Carmignac that Milik's identification of the frg. is impossible. Here *lʾ* is probably not the negative particle, for which the full writing (*lwʾ*) would be expected. Carmignac may be correct in suggesting that frg. 9 might be part of a citation of Mic 1:13-14 with]*pšʿ*[*y* (=Mic 1:13) in line 1 and]*lʾ*[*kzb* (=Mic 1:14) in line 2.

10:1-2 The introductory word *pšrw*, which is preserved in line 2, must have been preceded by a biblical citation. Since the next lemma that appears is Mic 1:5c (line 3), the text of Mic 1:5b should be restored. Therefore, the *š* in line 1 is probably part of a commentary section rather than part of a biblical citation (Milik reads *yr]wš[lm* as part of Mic 1:5c, but the *š* seems to be followed by a space).

10:2 In the citation of Mic 1:5b *mh* is restored rather than *my* as in the MT in the light of the parallel variant in line 3.

At the end of the line after the formula *pšrw ʿl*, only a *m* can be clearly read from the photograph in *Qumran Cave I*, but Milik reads *mṭyp hkzb*, "le Prophète de mensonge." (In the preliminary publication he read *myṭyp kzb*.) I reject this reading as does Carmignac ("Notes," 516), who points out that the *m* is followed by a vertical stroke of a letter that cannot be a *ṭ* but might be *w, y, h, ḥ,* or *t*.

10:3 Since the reading *mṭyp hkzb* in line 2 is doubtful, Milik's restoration of the beginning of line 3, *ʾšr hwʾh ytʿh ʾt h]ptʾym*, "qui est celui qui égare les] simples," must also be questioned.

the simple ones ([*hp*]*tʾym*). See the note above on 1QpHab 12:4.

The citation of Mic 1:5c presents the following variant from the MT: *wmh* (MT: *wmy*); see the restoration of Mic 1:5b in line 2.

10:4 At the end of the line Milik reads *mwry hṣdq ʾšr hwʾh,* taking this as a reference to the Teacher of Righteousness. He regards *mwry* as an orthographic variant for *mwrh* analogous to *ḥwṭy* in 1QpHab 10:2 for *ḥwṭʾ* of Hab 2:10b. There are problems with the passage in the biblical text of Habakkuk, however, and the form *ḥwṭy* is open to different interpretations (see the note above on 1QpHab 9:14, the first occurrence of Hab 2:10b). Consequently this text does not offer convincing support for Milik's suggestion. In the preliminary publication he went so far as to suggest that *mwry* may be the intensification of the name of the Teacher of Righteousness by the use of the pl. (T. H. Gaster apparently takes the word as a pl. form when he translates "those who expound the Law correctly.") Rejecting Milik's reading, Carmignac reads the interrogative *mh* ("Notes," 516), since he can see only one letter after the *m*. He then reads the next word as *hṣyṣ,* "la fleur," and translates the phrase "Qu'est-ce qu'est la fleur, elle qui?" The suggestion is not at all convincing. Not only does there definitely appear to be more than one letter following the *m*, but also the reading *hṣdq* is almost certain. Moreover, Carmignac does not explain how the phrase would fit into the pesher structure as it is found in this document. I think that Milik is correct in taking this as a reference to the Teacher of Righteousness, but *mwry* is not a good reading. This spelling does not occur elsewhere in the Qumran documents for the name of the Teacher of Righteousness, and the traces that are visible on the photograph do not entirely exclude the usual spelling *mwrh*. The word is vertically aligned with other words that are partially obscured by some damage to the skin; compare the *h* of *hmtndbym* in line 5 and the *h* of *hyḥd* in line 6. Thus, I transcribe *mw*[*r*]*h*.

10:5 At the beginning of the line Milik restores [*ywrh htwrh lʿṣt*]*w*, "enseigne la Loi à son Conseil," describing the Teacher of Righteousness. Though this fits the context, it seems too short for the space. However, if this restoration is accepted, it should be translated in the past tense, since the Teacher of Righteousness is generally referred to in the past tense.

those who volunteer (*hmtndbym*). This word, the hithpael part. of *ndb*, is part of the vocabulary of 1QS (see 5:1, 6, 8, 10, 21, 22, and especially 6:13), cf. 1 Macc 2:42, πᾶς ὁ ἑκουσιαζόμενος τῷ νόμῳ. This word does not occur elsewhere in the pesharim.

to be added to (*lwsp*). This form is taken by Milik to be the niph. inf. cs. with the *h* elided; see the note above on *lnṣl* in 1QpHab 9:13. The form would be vocalized *liwwāsēp* for the biblical Hebrew form *lĕhiwwāsēp*. It is also possible that the form is the defectively written hiph. inf. cs. with the *h* elided; see the note above on *lkwt* in 1QpHab 3:1. In the latter case it would probably be vocalized *lôsip* or *lôsēp* for the biblical Hebrew form *lĕhôsîp*, and it would be translated "to increase (the chosen ones of God)."

10:5-6 *the chosen ones of God, those who observe the Law* (*bḥyry* [*ʾl ʿwśy htwrh*]). This restoration of the beginning of line 6 was suggested by Milik. For parallel phrases, see the notes above on 1QpHab 5:4; 7:10-11. Following *bḥyry* one might also restore at the beginning of line 6 *yśrʾl*, "the chosen ones of Israel"; see 4QpIsa^e 6:[1]; 4QpPs^a 11:[2].

10:6 *in the council of the community* (*bʿṣt hyḥd*). See the note above on 1QpHab 12:4.

10:6-7 *from the day of judgment* (*mywm* [*hmšpṭ*]). The restoration of *hmšpṭ* at the beginning of line 7 is almost certain; the determinate state is preferable to Milik's *mšpṭ*; see 1QpHab 12:14; 13:2-3; 3QpIsa [6].

As the last letter of line 7 Milik reads *h*.

10:7-9 The traces that Milik reads as part of three lines appear on the photograph to be noticeably closer together than the other lines in the frg. It might be that there are only two lines indicated—or perhaps two lines and an interlinear addition—with *śdh* ending line 7 instead of line 8.

10:8-9 The pesher begun in line 4 probably ended at the beginning of line 8, and the biblical text is resumed in the second half of line 8 with Mic 1:6a. In lines 8 and 9 Milik restores a second citation of Mic 1:6 followed by 1:7, but the present arrangement of the frgs. excludes this reconstruction.

The apparent citation of Mic 1:6a in line 8 presents the following variant from the MT: *śdh* (MT: *hśdh*). In the preliminary publication Milik read *śdh*, but in the *editio princeps* he has [*h*]*śdh*. Carmignac ("Notes," 517) sees no room for a *h* and the preceding word he reads as [*m*]*tʿ*. He thus regards the text as a pesher on Mic 1:6 rather than as a lemma.

11:1 Milik's restoration of the line, *kwhny yrw*]*š*[*l*]*m ʾšr ytʿ*[*w*, "prêtres de Jérusalem qui égarent,'' seems to be largely conjecture. Only a trace of the *m* and an unidentifiable dot, which Milik takes as the *š* of *yrwšlm*, are visible on the photograph before *ʾšr*.

11:2 At the end of this line the words *šll wʿ[rwm*, ''barefoot and naked,'' allude to Mic 1:8. The unusually large space before *šll* suggests that this might be a citation; however, there is not room to restore all of Mic 1:8-9a before Mic 1:9b in line 3. It is impossible to tell whether the form *šll* reflects *šîlāl*, the *kĕtîb* of the MT or *šwll*, the *qĕrê*.

11:5 The only letters that can be clearly read from the photograph in the *editio princeps* are *bgwd* before a break in the skin and a *w* or *y* after the break. Milik reads *l*]*bgwd lw* .[, ''en se révoltant contre lui,'' though in the preliminary publication he read *y*]*bgwd*[*w*. Carmignac accepts the reading]*bgwd lw* .[, but questions whether it is two words, as Milik understands it, or one word *bgwdly* (reading *y* for Milik's *w*), ''in the great ones of.''

12:3 Cf. Mic 1:3. The word *ʾl* is written here in paleo-Hebrew script, a singular occurrence in the pesharim. See the note above on 1QpHab 1:1.

Fragments 13-16. Milik tentatively relates these frgs. to Mic 4:13 on the basis of his reading *q*]*rnym*[, ''horns,'' in frg. 13 (see *qarnēk* in Mic 4:13) and *wʾdwn*, ''and the Lord of,'' in frg. 14 (see *laʾădôn* in Mic 4:13). However, in frg. 13 the *r* is very doubtful, and consequently the relation of this frg. to Mic 4:13 is questionable. In the transcription of frg. 14, Milik did not indicate the space following the *n* in *wʾdwn*.

16:2 In the transcription of this line, Milik did not indicate the space after the *ḥ*. Either the letter before the *ḥ* extends below the line, or else the lower mark that is visible on the frg. is the top of a *l* (or another letter), and a third line should be added to the transcription.

17-18:1 On the photograph only the left side of the *h* is clearly visible followed by a discoloration, but Milik is apparently able to see]*h wtšyḥ*[, ''tu méditera(s),'' possibly a pesher on Mic 6:14.

17-18:3 The spacing of the transcription in the *editio princeps* (*wl*] *ʾ tšt h* [*y*]*yn*) does not accurately reflect the letters and traces of letters in the middle of the line as they appear on the photograph.

17-18:4 There is no indication elsewhere in the text that is preserved whether the word *ʾwtk*, ''you,'' should be restored with the vowel letter *h* in the sf. (*ʾwtkh*) or whether the form would conform to the MT.

17-18:5 *the last generation* (*hdwr h*[*ʾ*]*ḥrw*[*n*]), see 1QpHab 2:7.

Fragments 20-21. Milik notes a possible connection with Mic 7:6, where the phrase *ʾnšy bytw*, ''the men of his house,'' occurs.

22:1-2 Milik suggests a possible relation to Mic 7:8-9, where the words *ḥṭʾty*, ''I have sinned,'' and *ʾwr*, ''light,'' occur. In line 1 Milik reads]*ṭty* .*šw*[. In line 2, for Milik's *whʾwr*, Carmignac (''Notes,'' 518) reads *whʾyr*, "et il illuminera," arguing that in QL the substantive *ʾwr* is never found with the definite article.

22:3 Milik reads]*ym ṣrb* .[, while Carmignac suggests [*y*]*wm ṣtk*[*h*] (for *ṣʾtkh*), "le jour de ta sortie," possibly referring to Mic 7:15. But Carmignac's reading of *t* and *k* are not satisfactory. The former letter is unclear, and the latter is better read as *b*.

22:4 Milik reads]*bl* . . . [.

Fragment 23. Milik relates this frg. to Mic 7:17, where the phrase *kzḥly ʾrṣ*, "like the creeping things of the earth," occurs. Carmignac ("Notes," 518) thinks that this frg. could in fact be the citation of Mic 7:17, with *wzwḥly* for the *kzḥly* of the MT, a variant that Carmignac feels is supported by the Greek, which has no preposition, and by the Peshitta, which has the conjunction "and."

1QpZeph (1Q*15*)

Editio princeps: "Commentaire de Sophonie" (J. T. Milik), *Qumran Cave I,* p. 80 and plate XV.

Secondary transcriptions and translations: H. Bardtke, *Die Handschriftenfunde,* 294; J. Carmignac, *Les Textes,* 2. 118; A. M. Habermann, *Megilloth,* 154.

Secondary literature: J. Carmignac, "Notes," 519-20.

This small frg. preserves parts of six lines of a commentary on Zephaniah. The text that remains is difficult to read. Milik explains that the skin is blackened, the script is uneven, and the upper right hand part of the frg. has shrunk because of humidity.

The text of Zeph 1:18b-2:2, which seems to constitute lines 1-4 of the frg., cannot be restored with certainty, since neither side margin is visible to show the beginning or the end of a line. The vertical alignment of the words *qn*] *ʾtw* (line 1 = Zeph 1:18b) and *h*[*ʾ*]*rṣ* (line 2 = Zeph 1:18c) suggests that there are about fifty units in a line, but the script is very uneven and the spacing of words is irregular, e.g., *ḥrwn ʾp* (line 3) and *yhwdh ʾš*[*r* (line 5, if the present restoration is correct). The problem of arranging the lines is further complicated by an apparent scribal omission of uncertain length, which seems to have been subsequently added between lines 2 and 3. Moreover, the internal problems of the MT render any restoration of the biblical text uncertain.

A. M. Habermann and H. Bardtke follow Milik's transcription, while J. Carmignac offers a different arrangement of the lines. Both reconstructions are open to question, since they do not reflect the same vertical alignment of letters as the frg. itself and the lines are of uneven length. The present transcription is not entirely satisfactory, but it has a better vertical alignment than the others and approximately equal lines.

The few words that are preserved are mostly from the biblical lemma; the interpretation of the prophetic text is almost entirely lost. It is safe to suggest, however, that given the eschatological thrust of the biblical passage, the commentary would probably have dealt with the Qumran community in the last days.

1QpZeph: Translation

1. [AND IN THE FIRE OF] HIS [ZE]AL [ALL THE EARTH] WILL BE DEVOU[RED, FOR A COMPLETE—INDEED A TERRIBLE—END] Zeph 1: 18b-2:2
2. [HE WILL MAKE OF ALL THE INHABITA]NTS OF THE [EA]RTH. GA[TH]ER TOGETHER [AND] H[OLD ASSEMBLY, O NATION WITHOUT SHAME]

2a. BEFORE THE BIRTH OF A STATUTE] LIKE A FLOWER [ ] THAT PASSES IN A DAY (?)

3. [BEFORE] Y[AHWEH'S BURNING WRATH [COMES UPON YO]U, [BEFORE]
4. [THE DAY OF] YAHWEH'S [WRA]TH [COMES UPON YOU.] The interpretation of [the passage with regard to the end of days]
5. [concerns all the inhabitants of] the land of Judah, wh[o]
6. [ ] and they are *l* . .[ ] . .[ ]

1QpZeph: Notes

1 According to the present arrangement of lines, there would be room at the beginning of line 1 for one or two words, which might have been from the preceding phrase of Zeph 1:18b or from a commentary section.

2 Milik reads *htqw*[*ššw wqw*]*š*[*w,* but even considering shrinkage there does not seem to be room for seven units between the visible *w* and *š*, especially for two *š*'s, which are wider than the other letters, cf. *pšr* in line 4. Therefore, I suggest *htqw*[*š*]*š*[*w w*]*q*[*wšw*, though the trace that is read as *q* is very doubtful.

2a Between lines 2 and 3 Milik is able to read several letters, which he identifies as part of Zeph 2:2a, *kmwṣ ʿbr* [*y*]*wm*, "like chaff that passes in a day." Milik is probably correct that all of verse 2a was omitted through a scribal error, since 2a, b, and c all begin with the same word. The phrase was then added between the lines. Carmignac ("Notes," 520), however, reads *knṣ ʿbr ywm,* "like a flower that passes in a day," a variant from the MT that is reflected in the Greek ὡς ἄνθος παραπορευόμενον. The traces of letters on the photograph are so faint that it is impossible to verify either suggested reading. I follow Carmignac, whose suggestion seems to be compatible with the visible traces of letters and sheds some light on a difficult passage of the MT. The first phrase of Zeph 2:2a is an equally difficult text; it is restored here according to the MT, *bĕṭerem ledet ḥōq,* "before the birth of a statute," though Carmignac follows the emendation suggested in *BHS, bĕṭerem lōʾ tiddaḥēqû,* before you are driven away."

3 At the beginning of the line the restoration of Zeph 2:2b does not fill the space, but it may be correct in view of the unevenness of the script.

The tetragrammaton would have been written in paleo-Hebrew script as in line 4; see the note above on 1QpHab 1:1. This would take up at least ten units of space.

4-5 In line 4 the interpretation began. No trace of a letter is visible after *pšr*, but there seems to be a space. The formula to be restored, therefore, probably began with *pšr hdbr* rather than *pšrw*. I follow Milik's restoration of the first phrase of the commentary, "concerns all the inhabitants of," but I suggest a longer introductory formula, *pšr hdbr lʾḥryt hymym*, to fill out line 4. Milik comments that the space after *yhwdh* seems to indicate that a citation followed, but if a citation did begin here in line 5, the preceding commentary section would be too short. In view of the apparent irregularity of word spacing in the text, it is probably better to assume that the commentary continued in line 5.

6 The only letters that can be certainly read are *h* and *l*. For the first word, which Milik reads as *whyw*, "and they are," Carmignac suggests *hwy*, "Woe!", commenting that the scribe differentiated here between *w* and *y*. But compare the *w* in *ḥrwn* (line 3). Following this word, Milik is able to read *l . . . t . . . .*

1QpPs (1Q*16*)

Editio princeps: "Commentaire de Psaumes" (J. T. Milik), *Qumran Cave I,* pp. 81-82 and plate XV.

Secondary transcriptions and translations: H. Bardtke, *Die Handschriftenfunde,* 295; J. Carmignac, *Les Textes,* 2. 127-28; A. M. Habermann, *Megilloth,* 156-57.

Secondary literature: J. Carmignac, "Notes," 526.

Grouped as 1QpPs are eighteen frgs. Only six of them (frgs. 1-4, 8, 9) preserve complete words, and of these only three (frgs. 3, 8, 9) contain identifiable portions of the biblical text of Psalms. Only traces of letters are visible on the other frgs.

According to Milik, frg. 1 preserves part of a citation of Ps 57:1, and frg. 2 may be part of a pesher on Ps 57:4. This identification, however, is very doubtful and has been rejected by H. Stegemann ("Der Pešer Psalm 37 aus Höhle 4 von Qumran [4QpPs37]," *RevQ* 4 [1963-64] 242, n. 21). In commenting on frg. 1, Milik makes reference to a frg. from Cave 4 that he describes as part of a commentary on Psalm 57. He suggests that the Cave 4 frg. and frg. 1 of this text from Cave 1 belong to copies of the same work. Thus far, however, no commentary on Psalm 57 is known from Cave 4, and Stegemann thinks that Milik may be referring to a fragment of 4QpIsa^a, which contains the phrase *bbrḥw mlp[ny yś]rʾl,* "when he flees before Israel" (4QpIsa^a 7-10 iii 13). In the preliminary publication of 4QpIsa^a ("Further Messianic References in Qumran Literature," *JBL* 75 [1956] 180, n. 40), J. M. Allegro noted that frg. 8 was at first tentatively identified as part of a pesher on Psalms. It may be just the opposite, however; the frg. from Cave 1 might actually be part of a commentary on Isaiah. In any case, there is insufficient evidence to identify it with Ps 57:1.

Milik identifies frgs. 3-18 as a pesher on Psalm 68. It may be no coincidence that a commentary on this psalm is among the Qumran writings. The Hebrew text of Psalm 68 is filled with problems, and W. F. Albright notes that it "has always been considered with justice as the most difficult of all the Psalms" ("A Catalogue of Early Hebrew Lyric Poems [Psalm LXVIII]," *HUCA* Vol. 23, Part 1 [1950-51] 7). Unfortunately, the small amount of biblical material that is preserved in the Qumran text sheds little light on the many obscurities of the psalm.

Milik treats frgs. 3-7 as a group. Only traces of letters remain on frgs. 5-7, and frg. 3 is especially hard to read, since the surface of the skin appears to be damaged. Milik places frg. 4 in relation to frg. 3 so that 4:1 gives the end of 3:2 and 4:2 gives the end of 3:3. While this arrangement is possible, it seems to make 3:3 too long. Frgs. 3 and 4 are transcribed separately here (so also Carmignac). Again, Milik puts frgs. 9 and 10 together, but only traces of letters remain on frg. 10.

The only clue to the content of the commentary is the mention of the Kittim in 9:4; see the note above on 1QpHab 2:12. This may indicate that the commentary referred to the history of the community in the time of the Romans.

1QpPs: Translation

Fragment 1

when] he flees before [

Fragment 2

1. his [faith]fulness, befo[re
2.]graciousness [

Fragment 3

1.]*tr* [
2.]. . they recognized *b* . . . [
3.].*l*. KINGS OF HOSTS, THEY FL[EE, THEY FLEE, AND AT HOME A WOMAN DIVIDES THE BOOTY (?) The interpretation] Ps 68:13
4.].*h l*[the b]eauty of [
5.]. who divide [
6.] . [

Fragment 4

1.]they guarded[ ]
2.]. The interpretation of it: *b*.[

Fragment 5

1.]. .. .*k*[
2.].*l*... .[

Fragment 6

1.]. . . [
2.] ..[

Fragment 7

1.]..[
2.]...[

Fragment 8

1.]. .[
2.] IN THE MIDST OF YOUNG WOMEN BEATING TAM-BOURIN]ES. IN THE ASSEMBLIES, BLESS GO[D 68:26b-27a
3.].*t* the convo[ca]tion to bless [his holy] na[me

Fragment 9

1. [FROM YOUR TEMPLE AT JERUSALEM, KING]S [BRING] GIFTS [TO YOU.] The interpretation of it concerns all the ru[lers of] 68:30
2. [the Kittim, who]before him in Jerusalem. YOU REBUKED [THE BEASTS OF THE REED THICKET] 68:31
3. [A HERD OF BULLS AMONG CALVES OF PEOPLES, TRAMPLING] SILVER [ORE.] The interpretation of it: the beasts of the r[eed thicket are]
4. [the K]ittim *l*. . [ ]
5. [ ].*h* ..*lt*[ ]
6. [ ].*m b*[ ]
7. [ ]*l* [ ]

Fragment 10

1.].[
2.].[

Fragment 11

1.]*m b*[
2.].*l ʾt* .[

Fragment 12

] *ḥqy*[

Fragment 13

1.].[
2.]*šmy*.[

Fragment 14

1.]*šrw*[
2.]. .[

Fragment 15

]*šrw* [

Fragment 16

] *nšm*[

Fragment 17

1.] .[
2.]*ʿdm*[

Fragment 18

].ʾ.[

1QpPs: Notes

1:1 See the remarks above on the identification of frgs. 1-2.

2:2 Milik reads]*ḥsd*[*w,* but on the photograph there seems to be a space after *ḥsd*, which would exclude restoring a suffixal form.

3:1 Milik reads]*t* .[, but the second letter is almost certainly a *r* and it is followed by a space.

3:2 *they recognized* (*hkyrw)*, or possibly "he recognized him/it."

3:3 The citation of Ps 68:13 is restored according to the MT with hesitation, since the verse is filled with problems. Milik translates, "et la belle de la maison partage le butin." Also possible is " . . . you divide the booty." After minor emendation of the consonantal text, W. F. Albright translates "While the kings of the armies flee headlong, flee headlong, in the meadow they divide the spoil" ("A Catalogue," 13, 21-22, 37).

3:5 *who divide* (*yḥlqw*), or possibly "which they divide" (so Bardtke), alluding to *tḥlq* of the biblical text.

4:2 See the comments above on Milik's arrangement of frgs. 3-7. In 4:2 a commentary begins with the introductory word *pšrw*. The next word is lost, but the first letter is certainly a *b*. This excludes the usual formulas *pšrw ʿl* and *pšrw ʾšr*. The word *pšrw* must have been followed directly by a noun as in 9:3 (see further Part II, pp. 241-42). According to Milik's arrangement of the frgs., this line begins the commentary on Ps 68:13; he restores *pšrw by*[*t hyʾ*, "Explication de ceci: 'la maiso[n' c'est," an interpretation of *byt* in the biblical text.

8:1 There are traces of letters visible above the first line indicated by Milik, and so a third line must be added to the transcription and the other two lines must be renumbered accordingly.

8:2 Milik cites the text of Ps 68:26b-27a. His restoration of the full writing *ʿwlmwt*, "young woman," for the biblical Hebrew form *ʿălāmôt* is puzzling.

in the assemblies (*bmqhlwt*). This is the translation of Albright ("A Catalogue," 15, 30). The form *mqhlwt* is a *hapax legomenon* in the MT.

8:3 This line preserves part of the commentary on Ps 68:26-27. Milik restores the text of the commentary (*br*]*kt hmqw*[*r*] *lbrk ʾt ʿ*[, "la bénédiction de le Source pour bénir le") according to the MT of Ps 68:27b, *yhwh mmqwr yśrʾl*, "Yahweh, from the source of Israel (?)." Carmignac ("Notes," 526) restores *br*]*kt hmqwʾ*, "la bénédiction de l'espérance," noting that *qwh* also appears in 4QpPsa (1-10 ii 4) as a third-aleph verb. In either case, the sense is difficult. It is suggested in *BHS* that the MT be emended to *mmqrʾy*, "from the convocations of." Albright emends the text similarly to *bĕmiqrĕʾê*, "in the meetings of" ("A Catalogue," 15). In the text of 1QpPs 8:3, the letters following *hmq* cannot be read with certainty, but the letter read by Milik as *w* is mutilated and could as well be *r*. Thus, *hmqr*[ʾ], "the convocation," is restored here. This word occurs frequently in 1QM in the phrase *ḥṣwṣrwt mqrʾ*, "the trumpets of convocation," e.g., 1QM 3:2, 3, 7; 7:13; 8:3; 9:3.

The restoration of *br*]*kt* at the beginning of the line seems to be based only on *brkw* of the biblical text and *lbrk* later in line 3. The letter read by Milik as *k* might also be *b* or *h*.

The letter at the end of the line that Milik reads as ʿ is better read as *š*. The absence of the article following *ʾt* indicates that the word to be restored is probably a proper name, a suffixal form, or a noun in the construct state. For the phrase *šm qwdšw*, which is restored here, see 1QpHab 2:4.

9:1 At the beginning of the line the text of Ps 68:30 is restored according to the MT, though the meaning of the verse is unclear. Emending the text, Albright translates "How great is thy triumph over Jerusalem, the kings will bring their offerings to thee" ("A Catalogue," 15, 31-32, 39). In what is preserved of 1QpPs, there is no indication of whether the 2nd pers. sing. masc. sf. was written with the vowel letter *h* or whether the orthography agreed with MT. The spelling of *yrwšlym*, however, is clear from line 2; Milik restores *yrwšlm* agreeing with the MT. See the note above on 1QpHab 9:4.

At the end of the line Milik restores *ml*[*ky ktyʾym*, "les ro[is des Kittiim," but the *l* is unlikely. I suggest *mš*[*ly hktyʾym*, "the rulers of the Kittim," though elsewhere this appears with the full writing of *mwšly*, e.g., 1QpHab 4:5, 10.

9:2-3 The text of Ps 68:31 is restored according to the MT, though again, the verse is filled with problems. See further Albright ("A Catalogue," 15-16, 32-33, 39), who translates "There roared the beasts of the reed thicket, the herd of wild bulls . . ., at the calves wearied by running; peoples lusty for booty. . . ."

The apparent citation of Ps 68:31 may offer the following variant from the MT: *gᶜrt* (MT: *gᶜr*). The reading *gᶜrt* is probable, but the *t* is not entirely certain. The form could be either the substantive *gᶜrh*, "rebuke," "menace" (so Milik) or, more likely, the verb *gᶜr*, "rebuke" (so Carmignac).

The form *ḥyyt* is restored rather than *ḥyt* as in the MT in the light of the commentary in line 3.

silver ore ([*bṣry*] *ksp*). The reading of the MT, *bĕraṣṣê kāsep*, is a problem, and several emendations have been suggested. The text is transcribed here according to the emendation suggested by E. Nestle, *bṣry ksp* (see KB under *beṣer*). Milik restores *brwṣy*] *ksp*, "avec des monceaux] d'argent."

Frgs. 10-18. For Milik's suggestions about possible identification of these small frgs., see *Qumran Cave I*, 82. I differ with Milik's readings as follows:

(1) In frg. 12 there is almost certainly a space before the *ḥ*.

(2) The photograph of frg. 14 that appears in the *editio princeps* must have been taken after a portion of the right side of the frg. had deteriorated; Milik's transcription does not reflect the frg. as it appears in the present photograph.

(3) In frg. 15 there is probably a space after the *w*.

(4) In frg. 16 Milik reads]*tšb*[.

(5) In 17:2 Milik reads] *ᶜd ʾ*[, but there is no space to indicate that parts of two words are preserved.

(6) In frg. 18 Milik reads]*ry y*[, but there is no space between the traces of letters that are visible.

4QpIsaª (4Q*161*)

Editio princeps: "Commentary on Isaiah (A)" (J. M. Allegro), *Qumrân Cave 4,* Vol. I., pp. 11-15 and pls. IV-V.

Preliminary publication: J. M. Allegro, "Further Messianic References in Qumran Literature," *JBL* 75 (1956) 174-87, esp. 177-82 (Document III) and pls. II-III.

Secondary transcriptions and translations: H. Bardtke, *Die Handschriftenfunde,* 299-300; M. Burrows, *More Light,* 403-404; J. Carmignac, *Les Textes,* 2. 68-72; A. Dupont-Sommer, *Essene Writings,* 274-75; T. H. Gaster,

Dead Sea Scriptures, 232-34; A. M. Habermann, *Megilloth,* 150-51; J. Maier, *Die Texte,* 1. 186-87, 2. 166; F. Michelini Tocci, *I manoscritti,* 288-90; L. Moraldi, *I manoscritti,* 528-31; G. Vermes, *Dead Sea Scrolls in English* 226-27; A. S. van der Woude, *Bijbelcommentaren,* 71-77; Y. Yadin, "Recent Developments," 49-52.

Secondary literature: J. M. Allegro, "Addendum to Professor Millar Burrow's [*sic*] Note on the Ascent from Accho in 4QpIsa[a]," *VT* 7 (1957) 183; J. D. Amoussine, "A propos de l'interprétation de 4 Q 161 (Fragments 5-6 et 8)," *RevQ* 8 (1974) 381-92; M. Burrows, "The Ascent from Acco in 4Q p Isa[a]," *VT* 7 (1957) 104-105; J. Carmignac, "Notes," 511-15; J. M. Rosenthal, "Biblical Exegesis of 4QpIs," *JQR* 60 (1969-70) 27-36; J. Strugnell, "Notes," 183-86 and pl. I, frgs. b, c; Y. Yadin, "Some Notes on the Commentaries on Genesis xlix and Isaiah, from Qumran Cave 4," *IEJ* 7 (1957) 66-68.

Under the number 4Q*161* in *Qumrân Cave 4,* J. M. Allegro has grouped ten frgs. of a commentary on Isaiah. The frgs. preserve parts of three cols., containing portions of the biblical text of Isa 10:22—11:5 with an interpretation. J. Strugnell ("Notes," 183) describes the script as "rustic semiformal" according to the categories of F. M. Cross. The script appears to be the same as that of 4QpHos[a] and 4QpPs[a] (Strugnell ["Notes," 183]; Carmignac ["Notes," 511, n. 21]), and these manuscripts may have been produced by the same scribe or by the same scribal school.

In the preliminary publication Allegro presented only four frgs.: those numbered 5, 8, 9, and 10 in *Qumrân Cave 4.* For the *editio princeps* he was able to join other tiny frgs. to give additional letters in the following lines: 1:3, 4; 5-6:2, 3, 11-13; 8-10:18, 19, 23, 24 (Allegro's numbers = my numbers 1 i 28, 29; 2-6 ii 18, 19, 27-29; 7-10 iii 23, 24, 28, 29). Subsequently Strugnell joined two small, previously unidentified frgs., one to the top of Allegro's frg. 2, and one to the right edge of the lower portion of frg. 8 ("Notes," 183-86; pl. I, frgs. b, c).

There are problems with the ordering of the frgs. of this document. Allegro did not attempt to arrange the frgs. according to their cols., though lower margins are clearly visible on frgs. 1, 5, and 10. Frg. 1 preserves the last four lines of a col., and the lines should be renumbered to correspond to the other cols.; see below for a discussion of the number of lines in a col. A second col. is formed by frgs. 2-6, and a third by frgs. 7-10. It is in the arrangement of frgs. 7-10 that the greatest difficulties arise. Frg. 8 is actually three separate pieces, two upper parts and one lower piece. The two upper parts were treated separately in the preliminary publication, but in the *editio princeps* Allegro explains, "Shrinkage and darkening of the skin had disguised their relationship [in the preliminary publication], and the depradation of worms has left an actual contact only possible at one place (1. 5)'' (*Qumrân Cave 4,* 14). Strugnell concurs in this join at line 5, placing the two upper parts of the frg. side by side. J. Carmignac, however, arranged the two upper pieces in such a way that the right hand portion was a little above the left hand part, with line 6 of the right corresponding to line 2 of the left (''Notes,'' 512).

I follow Allegro and Strugnell in arranging frgs. 7-10, but I reconstruct a col. of at least twenty-nine lines. Carmignac (''Notes,'' 511) restores a col. of twenty-eight lines, but I disagree with Carmignac's arrangement of the two upper parts of frg. 8. The present tentative reconstruction is based on this document's structure insofar as it can be discerned from what is preserved of the text. While this commentary does not depart from the general pesher form observed in the other documents, in 4QpIsa[a] both the biblical citations and the pesher sections tend to be longer than in other commentaries, e.g., 2-6 ii 10-15 (Allegro's 2-4:6-10), where four verses of the biblical text can be satisfactorily restored for a total of five and one half lines; 7-10 iii 15-20 (Allegro's 8-10:11-16), where five verses are cited for a total of six lines; 7-10 iii 22-29 (Allegro's 8-10:17-24), which is a commentary of at least eight lines. In addition, either the lemma or the pesher or both are sometimes followed by a blank line, e.g., 2-6 ii 20 (Allegro's 5-6:4); 7-10 iii 14 (Allegro's 8-10:10). In these cases the blank line follows a commentary, but in 7-10 iii 21 (a blank line not numbered by Allegro), the *vacat* follows the lemma. Finally, the first word of the biblical citation is sometimes indented, e.g., *lkn* in 2-6 ii 10 (Allegro's 2-4:6); *bʾ* in 2-6 ii 21 (Allegro's 5-6:5). As will be seen, this structure was not followed without exception, but the basic outline is helpful in arranging the frgs. and restoring the text.

In frg. 1 Allegro restores Isa 10:21 in the first line, but there are only three letters preserved in this line and this restoration is very doubtful. Moreover, the absence of a blank line after the supposed citation could indicate that the words are actually part of a commentary.

In the second col., formed by frgs. 2-6, the bottom margin is visible. The last four lines of the col. can only belong to a commentary section (2-6 ii 26-29 = Allegro's 5-6:10-13), while in the five lines preceding, the biblical text of Isa 10:28-32 can be restored with fair certainty. There is no blank line here between the lemma and the interpretation, an apparent exception to the structure suggested above. The next line up (line 20 = Allegro's 5-6:4) is blank, and it is preceded by three fragmentary lines that appear to belong to a commentary. Above this I restore a blank line (line 16) to precede the pesher. In the next six lines up, the biblical text of Isa 10:24-27 can be restored (lines 10-15 = Allegro's 2-4:6-10). Here I differ with Allegro on the positioning of frg. 4; I place it at the right, at the beginning of the lines, rather than at the left. This gives an additional line in the lemma. The citation is directly preceded by a pesher section without an intervening blank line, another exception to the structure described above. There are parts of five lines of this commentary preserved (lines 5-9 = Allegro's 2-4:1-6), of which two may contain a second citation of Isa 10:22 (lines 6-7) introduced by the phrase *wʾšr ʾmr*. Since this is a second citation of 10:22 and the next citation is 10:24-27 (lines 10-15), it seems that the text of Isa 10:22-23 may have been quoted at the beginning of col. ii, preceding lines 5-9. I restore these verses in lines 1-3, followed by a blank line (line 4), thus making a col. of twenty-nine lines.

In the third col., the bottom eight lines (22-29 = Allegro's 8-10:17-24) belong to a commentary, and they contain a second citation of Isa 11:3b. This pesher section is preceded by a blank line, and in the next six lines up (lines 15-20 = Allegro's 8-10:11-16), the biblical text of Isa 11:1-5 is restored, preceded by a blank line (line 14 = Allegro's 8-10:10). Above this are the two pieces of frg. 8, which if placed side by side preserve parts of nine lines. These lines are probably one long commentary section containing short repetitions of portions of the biblical text. Phrases from the preceding lemma are repeated and then explained briefly with figurative identifications of key words. See further Part II, pp. 244-27. I restore a blank line preceding this interpretation, and before that the biblical text of Isa 10:33-34, making a col. of twenty-nine lines.

The prophetic verses here preserved refer to the Assyrian threat to Israel (Isa 10:24), relating how Yahweh will finally save his people and cause Assyria to fall (10:25-34) and presenting a description of the shoot of Jesse, the messiah of the Davidic line (11:1-5). What is preserved of the commentary on these verses indicates that the author interpreted these verses eschatologically in terms of the Qumran community. There is mention of the end of days (2-6 ii 26 = Allegro's 5-6:10), and there seem to be references to a battle with the Kittim, the eschatological foe of the Qumran community (2-6 ii 27; 7-10 iii 8, 9 = Allegro's 5-6:11; 8-10:4-5). If more of the Qumran author's interpretation of the description of the shoot of Jesse had been preserved, it might have given some information on the messianic expectations of the Qumran community. See further A. S. van der Woude, *Die messianischen Vorstellungen der Gemeinde von Qumrân* (Assen: Van Gorcum; G. A. Hak & Dr. H. J. Prakke, n. d.), 175-82.

4QpIsa^a: Translation

Fragment 1, Column i

26. [ ]. God (?) ʾ[ ]
27. [I]srael is [ ]

28. [ ]*lw* the men of his army *wpw*[ ]
29. [ ]. the priests, for he[ ]

Fragments 2-6, Column ii

1. [FOR IF YOUR PEOPLE, O ISRAEL, WERE AS THE SAND OF THE SEA, ONLY A REMNANT] Isa 10:22-23
2. [OF THEM WOULD RETURN. ANNIHILATION IS DECIDED, AND (IT IS) OVERFLOWING WITH RIGHTEOUSNESS. FOR—IT IS DETERMINED—THE LORD]
3. [YAHWEH OF HOSTS WILL WORK COMPLETE DESTRUCTION IN THE MIDST OF ALL THE LAND.]
4. [(*vacat*)]
5. [The interpretation of it]for[ ]*by* the children of[ ]
6. [ ] his people [and wh]en it says, IF [YOUR PEOPLE, O ISRAEL,] WER[E] 10:22
7. [AS THE SAND OF THE SEA, ONLY A REMNANT OF THEM WOULD RETURN.] A[NNIHILATION IS DECI]DED, AND (IT IS) OVERFLOWING WITH RIGHT[EOUSNESS]
8. [The interpretation of it]*lwt by*. [ ]*gh* and many will per[ish]
9. [but they will not es]cape *lmṭ*[the] land in truth .[ ]
10. (*vacat*) THEREFORE, TH[US SA]YS THE LO[RD, YAHWEH] 10:24-27
11. [OF HOSTS: O MY PEOPLE WHO DWEL]L IN ZIO[N, DO NOT BE AFRAID OF ASSYRIA. THEY WILL STRIKE WITH THE R]OD [AND RAISE THEIR STAFF]
12. [AGAINST YOU, AS THE EGYPTIANS DID. FOR] YET A WHI[LE AND WRATH WILL CUL]MI[NATE, AND MY ANGER (WILL BE DIRECTED) TO]
13. THEIR [DESTRUCTION;] AND [YAHWEH OF HOSTS] WILL WI[ELD AGAINST THEM A WHIP, AS WHEN HE SMOTE MIDIAN AT THE ROCK OF]
14. [O]REB; AND [HIS] ROD [WILL BE OVER THE SEA, AND HE WILL LIFT IT AS (HE DID IN) EGYPT. AND IT WILL HAPPEN ON THAT DAY]
15. [THAT HIS] BUR[DEN] WILL DEPART [FROM YOUR SHOULDERS, AND HIS YOKE FROM YOUR NECK, AND THE YOKE WILL BE BROKEN ON ACCOUNT OF FAT (?)]
16. [(*vacat*)]
17. [The interpretation of it] . . . [ ]
18. [ ]when they return from the wilderness of the p[eopl]es [ ]*b*[ ]
19. [the rod is] the prince of the congregation. And afterward he will de[pa]rt from [them.]

20. [ ] (*vacat*) [ ]
21. [ ] HE HAS COME TO AIATH. HE HAS PASSED [THROUGH MIGRON.] AT MICHMA[SH] 10:28-32
22. [HE STORES HIS BAGGAGE. THEY HAVE CROSSED] OVER THE PASS. GEBA IS A LODGING PLACE FOR THEM. [RAMAH BECOMES] ILL. [GIBEAH OF]
23. [SAUL HAS FLED. CRY] ALOUD, O DAUGHTER OF GALLIM! HEARKEN [O LAISHAH! ANSWER HER, O ANATHOTH!]
24. MADMENAH [IS IN FLIGHT.] THE [IN]HABITANTS OF GEBIM FLEE FOR SAFETY. THIS VERY [DAY HE WILL HALT AT NOB.]
25. [HE WILL SHAKE] HIS FIST AT THE MOUNT OF THE DAUGHTER OF ZION, THE HILL OF JERUSALEM. [ ]
26. [The interpretation of the] matter with regard to the end of days concerns the coming of .[ ]
27. [ ]*rh* when he goes up from the Valley of Acco to fight against Phil[istia]
28. [ ]*dh,* and there is none like it, and among all the cities of *h*.[ ]
29. even up to the boundary of Jerusalem [ ]

Fragments 7-10, Column iii

Fragment 7

1.]*bry l*[
2.]they [will] be brought low[

1. [BEHOLD THE LORD YAHWEH OF HOSTS WILL CUT OFF] 10:33-34
2. [BOUGHS WITH TERROR, AND THOSE WHO ARE LOFTY IN STATURE WILL BE CUT OFF, AND THOSE WHO ARE HAUGHTY WILL BE HUMBLED.]
3. [THE THICKETS OF THE FOREST WILL BE CUT DOWN WITH AN AXE, AND LEBANON TOGETHER WITH A MIGHTY ONE WILL FALL.]
4. [(*vacat*)]
5. [The interpretation].. [ ]*m*[ ]
6. [AND THE TH]ICKETS OF [THE FOREST WILL BE CUT DOWN] WITH AN AXE, AND LEBANON TOGETHER WITH A MIGHTY ONE 10:34
7. [WILL FALL. They are the] Kittim, wh[o] will fa[ll] by the hand of Israel. And the poor ones of
8. [Judah will judge] all the nations, and the warriors will be filled with terror, and [their] cour[age] will dissolve
9. [AND THOSE WHO ARE LOFTY] IN STATURE WILL BE CUT OFF. They are the warriors of the Kitt[im] 10:33b

10. [who]*d* AND THE THICKETS OF [THE] FOREST WILL BE CUT DOWN WITH AN AXE. Th[ey are] 10:34a
11. [ ].*m* for the battle of the Kittim. AND LEBANON TOGETHER WITH A MI[GHTY ONE] 10:34b
12. [WILL FALL. They are the] Kittim, who will be gi[ven] into the hand of his great ones[ ]
13. [ ]*ym* when he flees befo[re Is]rael .[ ]*m*[ ]
14. [ ] (*vacat*) [ ]
15. [THERE WILL COME FORTH A SHOOT FROM THE STU]MP OF JESSE, AND A BRANCH [WILL GROW] OUT OF [HIS] ROO[TS. AND] ON HIM [WILL RE]ST THE SP[IRIT OF] 11:1-5
16. [YAHWEH, A SPIRIT OF] WISDOM AND UNDERSTANDING, A SPIRIT OF COUN[SEL AND MIGHT,] A SPIRIT OF KNOW[LEDGE]
17. [AND FEAR OF YAHWEH. AND HIS DELIGHT WILL BE IN FEAR OF] YAHWEH. [NEITHER WILL HE JUDGE] BY APPEARAN[CES,]
18. [NOR WILL HE DECI]DE [ON HEARSAY,] BUT HE WILL JUDGE [THE LOWLY WITH RIGHTEOUSNESS, AND HE WILL DECIDE]
19. [WITH FAIRNESS FOR THE POOR OF THE EARTH. HE WILL SMITE THE EARTH WITH THE ROD OF HIS MOUTH, AND WITH THE BREATH OF HIS LIPS]
20. [HE WILL SLAY THE WICKED. RIGHTEOUSNESS WILL BE THE BELT AROUND] HIS [W]AIST, AND FAI[THFULNESS, THE BELT AROUND HIS LOINS.]
21. [ ] (*vacat*) [ ]
22. [The interpretation of the matter concerns the scion of] David, who will take his stand at the en[d of days to save]
23. [Israel and to exterminate] his [ene]mies. And God will sustain him with [a mi]ghty [spirit]
24. [And God will give him a th]rone of glory, a h[oly] crown, and garments of variegated stu[ff]
25. [And God will place a scepter] in his hand, and over all the n[ation]s he will rule, and Magog
26. [al]l the peoples will his sword judge, and when it says, NEITHER 11:3b
27. [WILL HE JUDGE BY APPEARANCES] NOR WILL HE DECIDE ON HEARSAY, the interpretation of it is that
28. [ ] and as they teach him, so will he judge, and according to their command
29. [ ] with him. One of the priests of repute will go out, and in his hand the garments of

4QpIsa^a: Notes

Fragment 1, Column i

1 i 26-27 See the comments above on Allegro's restoration of frg. 1 in relation to the structure of the commentary.

1 i 27 Allegro reads *hyʾh,* but it could as well be *hwʾh, since w* and *y* are almost identical in the script of this document. Either form could refer to Israel, which can be either masc. or fem., depending on whether it denotes the people Israel or the country (GKC §122i).

1 i 28-29 At the right edge of frg. 1, Allegro joins a tiny frg. by which he reads in line 28 (his line 3)] *ʾyly ʾnšy ḥylw,* and in line 29 (his line 4) *mw*] *ʿdy hkwhnym.* The phrase *ʾyly ʾnšy ḥylw,* which Allegro translates "the leaders of his warrior band," does not occur elsewhere in QL, though *ʾnšy ḥyl,* "the men of the army," occurs e.g., in 1QM 2:8; 6:13; similarly 1QSa 1:28; cf. *gdwdy ḥylw,* "the detachments of his army," in 4QpNah 3-4 i 10. Allegro translates *mwʿdy hkwhnym* as "assembly places of the priests," but in QL the word *mwʿd* usually means "appointed time" rather than "appointed place," e.g., *mwʿd mnwḥt ywm hkpwrym,* "the appointed time of rest, the Day of Atonement," in 1QpHab 11:6-7. Strugnell is not convinced of this join; in his opinion both the physical appearance and the material content argue against it. For these reasons only the original frg. is transcribed here.

Fragments 2-6, Column ii

2-6 ii 1-2. The citation of Isa 10:22 is restored with the following variants from the MT in the light of the apparent second citation below in lines 6-7: (1) *hyh* (MT and 1QIsa^a: *yhyh*); (2) *wšwṭp* (MT and 1QIsa^a: *šwṭp*).

2-6 ii 3 The tetragrammaton would almost certainly have been written in paleo-Hebrew script, as it is in 7-10 iii 17 (Allegro's 8-10:13). It would be similarly restored below in 2-6 ii 10, 13; 7-10 iii 1, 16, 17 (Allegro's 2-4:6, 9; 8-10:12, 13; my number 7-10 iii 1 is restored). See the note above on 1QpHab 1:1.

2-6 ii 3-4 As the col. is restored here, the citation of Isa 10:23 ends in line 3 and is followed by a blank line. See the comments above on the structure of this pesher.

2-6 ii 5-9 (Allegro's 2-4:1-5) Strugnell has joined a previously unpublished and unidentified frg. to the right side of frg. 2 (see "Notes," 184 and pl. I, frg. b), which gives several letters at the beginning of lines 5-9 as follows: line 5:]*kyʾ*[; line 6:]*ʿmw*[ ]*šr;* line 7:] *k*[; line 8:]*lwt by.*[; line 9:]*lṭw lmṭ*[. These lines would have contained the interpretation of Isa

10:22-23. Only a few words are preserved, but the focus of the commentary seems to have been the destructive rampage of the Kittim, cf. 1QpHab 2:12-14; 6:10-12.

2-6 ii 5 (Allegro's 2-4:1) Allegro reads].*y bny*[. The trace of a letter before the *y*, which is read here as *b*, might also be *k* or *p*.

2-6 ii 6-7 (Allegro's 2-4:2-3) In these lines there is apparently a second citation of Isa 10:22 (with the first word of the verse as in the MT [*ky*] omitted); it is introduced by the formula *wʾšr ʾmr* and seems to have been followed by a short commentary (lines 8-9). See Part II, p. 243.

This second citation of Isa 10:22 presents the following variants from the MT, as noted above for the first citation restored in lines 1-2: (1) *hyh* (MT and 1QIsaª: *yhyh*); (2) *wšwṭp* (MT and 1QIsaª: *šwṭp*).

2-6 ii 8 (Allegro's 2-4:4) On the frg. that he adds, Strugnell can make out *byʾ*[, but the ʾ seems to me very doubtful.

2-6 ii 10-15 (Allegro's 2-4:6-10) In these lines the biblical text of Isa 10:24-27 is restored. The present arrangement of the lines gives a better vertical alignment than that in the *editio princeps.* As noted above in the introductory remarks, frg. 4 is positioned to the right of frg. 2 rather than to the left as Allegro suggests.

2-6 ii 11 (Allegro's 2-4:7) *with the rod* ([*bš*]*bṭ*). The text has been restored according to the MT, but cf. 1QIsaª, which reads *mšbṭ*. Also restored in agreement with the MT is the form *wmṭhw*, "their staff," but 1QIsaª has *wmṭw*.

2-6 ii 12 (Allegro's 2-4:7) *as the Egyptians did* ([*bdrk mṣrym*]), or possibly "on the road to Egypt."

Near the end of this line (line 8 of frg. 3), a trace of a letter is visible, which is probably the top of the *l* of *wklh,* but this was not transcribed by Allegro.

2-6 ii 13 (Allegro's 2-4:8) *will wield* (*wyʿ*[*yr*]). I follow Strugnell in restoring the hiph. impf. of *ʿwr* as in 1QIsaª rather than the polel perf. *wʿwrr* as in the MT. Allegro's restoration of the polel impf. *wyʿwrr* is also possible.

2-6 ii 14 (Allegro's 2-4:9) *as* (*he did in*) *Egypt* ([*bdrk mṣrym*]), or possibly "on the road to Egypt," cf. above line 12.

2-6 ii 17 (Allegro's 5-6:1) The photograph in the preliminary publication shows more of the traces of the three letters in this line than does the photograph in *Qumrân Cave 4,* but they still cannot be read with certainty.

2-6 ii 18-19 (Allegro's 5-6:2-3) For the *editio princeps* Allegro was able to join a small frg. to the upper right edge of frg. 5, which gives the additional letters]*bšw* at the beginning of line 18, and]*nś* at the beginning of line 19.

2-6 ii 18 (Allegro's 5-6:2) *when they return from the wilderness of the peoples* (*bšwbm mmdbr hʿ*[*my*]*m*). The phrase *mdbr hʿmym* also occurs in

1QM 1:3, where it refers to a stopping place of the sons of light on their return from exile before they reach *mdbr yrwšlym,* "the wilderness of Jerusalem." The phrase is restored by Allegro in 4QpIsa[e] 5:6, but the restoration is not at all certain. In Ezek 20:35 the phrase designates an intermediate area through which the Israelites passed on returning from captivity in Babylon. It was a place of judgment, where the unfaithful were weeded out. The phrase may have a figurative significance here, but it may also be a reference to an actual migration of the Qumran community; see the note below on 4QpHos[a] 1:16. See also *The Scroll of the War of the Sons of Light against the Sons of Darkness* (ed. Y. Yadin; Oxford: Oxford University, 1962), 257.

There seems to be a trace of a letter visible at the right edge of 6:1. This was not indicated by Allegro, but it is probably the lower point of the final *m* of *hᶜmym.*

2-6 ii 19 (Allegro's 5-6:3) *the prince of the congregation* (*nśyᵓ hᶜdh*). This designation occurs also in 1QSb 5:20; 1QM 5:1 (*nśyᵓ kwl hᶜdh*); and CD 7:20 (*nśyᵓ kl hᶜdh*). According to Carmignac (*Les Textes,* 2. 69, n. 4), the prince of the congregation was to lead the army in the eschatological battle. In CD 7:20 the title occurs in an interpretation of Num 24:17, and the rod is there identified with the prince of the whole congregation. In the light of this I restore *hšbṭ hwᵓh* preceding *nśyᵓ hᶜdh.*

At the end of the line Allegro reads *mᶜlh*[*m*], "from them," but a *y* is clear, and the form should be read *mᶜly*[*hm*].

2-6 ii 20 (Allegro's 5-6:4) This line was probably blank, and the first word of the citation of 10:28-32 in line 21 was indented as was the first word of 10:24 (*lkn*) above in line 10.

2-6 ii 21 (Allegro's 5-6:5) The citation of Isa 10:28 presents the following variants from the MT: (1) *ᵓl* (MT and 1QIsa[a]: *ᶜl*); (2) *ᶜyth* (MT: *ᶜyt,* but cf. 1QIsa[a], where *ᶜyh* was corrected to *ᶜyth*).

2-6 ii 22-25 (Allegro's 5-6:6-9) In Allegro's transcription in *Qumrân Cave 4,* line 22 is mistakenly numbered 5-6:5; according to his numbering it should be line 6.

The citation of Isa 10:29 presents the following variants from the MT:

(1) *lmw,* "for them" (MT and 1QIsa[a]: *lnw,* "for us"). In the Hebrew text of Isa 10:28-29 there is a change in number from the sing. in v 28 (*bᵓ, ᶜbr, ypqyd*) to the pl. in v 29 (*ᶜbrw*). This problem could have resulted from an error of dittography in a consonantal manuscript. The original text might have been *ᶜbr mᶜbrh gbᶜ mlnw,* "he has crossed over the pass; Geba is his lodging place," which continues the thought of v 28. If the phrase *gbᶜ mlnw* was at some point copied as *gbᶜ mlnlnw* with dittography of *ln,* it would have been translated "Geba is a lodging place for us." The sing. verb *ᶜbr* might then have been altered to the pl. *ᶜbrw* in the

light of the apparently pl. pronominal sf. The text in 4QpIsa^a might represent the additional change of the 1st pers. pl. pronominal sf. (*lnw*) to the 3rd pers. pl. sf. (*lmw*) to agree with the 3rd pers. pl. verb form. Thus, the pl. verb form *ᶜbrw* is restored here in agreement with the MT (1QIsa^a has *ᶜbr bmᶜbrh*), and this is probably supported by the 3rd pers. pl. pronominal suffixal form *lmw*.

(2) *ḥl*[*th*], "(Ramah) becomes ill" (MT and 1QIsa^a: *ḥrdh*, "[Ramah] trembles"). In the *editio princeps*, Allegro reads *ḥr*[*dh hrmh*], "Ramah trembles" in agreement with the MT of Isa 10:29. However, in the photograph in the preliminary publication more of the edge of the frg. is visible, and *ḥl*[seems to be a better reading. I suggest restoring *ḥlth* because of the context, though it is an unattested variant from the MT; cf. Habermann's suggestion *ḥl*[*ḥlh*, "anguish."

(3) *qwlky* (MT and 1QIsa^a: *qwlk*). The form in 4QpIsa^a preserves a variant form of the 2nd pers. sing. fem. sf.; see GKC §91e.

(4) *bt* (MT: *byt*, but cf. 1QIsa^a, which has *bt*). The form in 4QpIsa^a and 1QIsa^a is the *qĕrê* of the MT.

2-6 ii 23 (Allegro's 5-6:7 *O Laishah* ([*lyšh*]). This form is restored in agreement with the MT of Isa 10:30, but cf. 1QIsa^a, which has *lyš*.

2-6 ii 24 (Allegro's 5-6:8) *the inhabitants of* (⌊*y*⌋*wšby*). Allegro reads *yšby*, but I agree with Strugnell that the full writing fits the space better and is consistent with the usual Qumran orthography.

2-6 ii 25 (Allegro's 5-6:9) *he will shake his fist* (⌊*ynwpp*⌋ *ydw*). The verb form is restored in agreement with the MT, but cf. 1QIsa^a, which has *ynwp ydyw*.

2-6 ii 25-29 (Allegro's 5-6:9-13) The commentary on Isa 10:28-32 may have begun immediately in line 25 after the citation or at the beginning of line 26. In either case, there is no blank line following the lemma. The biblical text of Isa 10:28-32 continues the description of the fall of Assyria. The verses are here interpreted eschatologically; there is mention of the end of days (line 26) and a battle (line 27), probably the eschatological battle with the Kittim that was to take place before the end, see also 7-10 iii 6-13.

2-6 ii 26 (Allegro's 5-6:10) *The interpretation of the matter with regard to the end of days* (⌊*pšr h*⌋*ptgm lʾḥryt hymym*). Following the suggestion of Strugnell, I restore the formula *pšr hptgm lʾḥryt hymym*. There is no certain attestation of this formula elsewhere in the pesharim, but, as Strugnell points out, this formula could be restored in 4QpPs^b 2:1, where the word *pšr* is clearly followed by *hp* and a stroke that could be the right vertical stroke of a *t*. The formula might also be restored in 4QpHos^b 19:1, where the word *pšr* is followed by *h* and an unidentifiable trace of a letter.

In biblical Hebrew the noun *ptgm*, which is a Persian loanword, means "decision," "judgment," or "decree," and occurs only in Qoh 8:11; Esth 1:20; and Sir 3:11; 8:9. In Mishnaic Hebrew, the word takes on additional meanings such as "word," "affair," "event," and is analogous to the biblical Hebrew word *dbr.* In biblical Aramaic the word means "matter," "word," e.g., Dan 3:16, or "decree," e.g., Dan 4:14. The word is thus far unattested in Hebrew elsewhere in QL, but it occurs in Aramaic texts, e.g., 4QprNab 1-3:2; 11QtgJob 9:2; 29:4; 30:1; 34:3. In 1QapGen 22:27 the pl. occurs in the phrase *btr ptgmʾ,* "after these things," or "after these words" (see J. A. Fitzmyer, *The Genesis Apocryphon of Qumran Cave 1: A Commentary* [2nd rev. ed.; BibOr 18A; Rome: Biblical Institute Press, 1971], 180). If the formula restored here in 4QpIsa^a is correct, it is probably synonymous with the formula *pšr hdbr lʾḥryt hymym* (see 4QpIsa^b 2:1; 4QpIsa^c 6-7 ii [14]; 23 ii 10; 4QpIsa^e 5:[2]). The word *ptgm,* then, is used not as it is in biblical Hebrew, but as it is in biblical and Qumran Aramaic and in Mishnaic Hebrew; cf. Allegro's translation, "a decree."

2-6 ii 27 (Allegro's 5-6:11) The first visible letter of the line could be *d* or *r.* In the preliminary publication, Allegro read *r,* which seems to me to be the better reading.

when he goes up from the valley of Acco (*bʿlwtw mbqʿt ʿkw*). Geographically the Valley of Acco probably refers to the port of Ptolemais on the Mediterranean. Allegro thinks that the phrase in 4QpIsa^a refers to the location of the Messiah's point of departure on his triumphal march to Jerusalem ("Further Messianic References," 181; "Addendum," 183). The prophetic text, however, speaks of the Assyrian threat to Jerusalem, and it may be inferred that the pesher also would describe an enemy advancing toward Jerusalem. M. Burrows ("The Ascent," 105) suggests that the Qumran interpretation describes the march of the eschatological foe of the Qumran community rather than the Messiah. J. D. Amoussine ("L'interprétation de 4 Q 161," 387-90) treats the text as a historical allusion to the campaign of Ptolemy IX (Soter II) Lathyrus against Judea during the rule of Alexander Jannaeus (103-76 B.C.), and he identifies the Kittim mentioned in col. iii with the forces of Lathyrus. Elsewhere in the pesharim, however, the Kittim are almost certainly to be identified with the Romans. If the phrase is to be interpreted as a historical allusion rather than as a figurative description, it could refer to the Romans approaching from the West (see A. S. van der Woude, *Bijbelcommentaren,* 75-76, n. 7).

to fight (*llḥm*). This form could be the qal inf. cs. of *lḥm,* but it is more likely the niph. inf. cs. with the *h* elided. See the note above on 1QpHab 9:12-15.

against Philistia (*bpl*[*št*]). This is restored by Strugnell; at the end of the line Allegro reads *by* .[, but there is no space between the second and third letters.

2-6 ii 28 (Allegro's 5-6:12) *like it* (*kmwh*). There is a dot on the manuscript after the *h,* which Allegro reads as a doubtful *w,* giving the masc. form *kmwhw,* "like him." Strugnell, however, regards the dot as an accidental trace and reads *kmwh* as the fem. *kāmôhā.* Though another *h* might be expected as a vowel letter for the fem. sf. (*kmwhh*), the fem. is still the better reading.

At the end of the line the letter following the *h* could be either *m* or *š.*

Fragments 7-10, Column iii

See the introductory comments on the present arrangement of frgs. 8-10 and the restoration of the col., cf. Carmignac's reconstruction ("Notes," 512-15).

Frg. 7 probably refers to Isa 10:33, with *y*]*šplw*[restored in line 2. It could be part of the commentary or part of a second citation within the commentary. It is unlikely that it is part of the lemma, since the whole verse is too long for one line, and the letters in 7:1 do not correspond to any words of the biblical text. It might possibly be placed either in lines 5-6 (Allegro's 8-10:1-2) or in lines 9-10 (Allegro's 8-10:5-6). Since the frg. almost certainly belongs to col. iii, its number is included in the frgs. that make up the col. (7-10), but since the placement of it is uncertain, it is treated separately at the beginning of the col.

7-10 iii 2-3 The citation of Isa 10:34 is restored with the following variants from the MT in the light of the apparent repetitions of 10:34a below in lines 6 and 10:

(1) *wynqpw* (MT and 1QIsa^a: *wnqp*). In the repetition of the citation in line 10, the *y* of this form is written above the line and appears to be placed between the *n* and the *q,* so that Allegro reads *wnyqpw,* a spelling of the piel perf. of *nqp* that is attested in Mishnaic Hebrew. Strugnell notes that the form could also be read as *wnwqpw,* the pual perf.; he further suggests the possibility that the supralinear letter was badly placed by the scribe and that the form might be *wynqpw,* which could be the qal, piel, or pual impf. The form in the MT is the piel perf.; the pual is unattested in biblical and Mishnaic Hebrew, but a passive meaning is required by the context. Although it is not entirely satisfactory, the best choice in the context is the pual impf. (with the simple *w*), "and the thickets of the forest will be cut down."

(2) *swbky* (MT and 1QIsa^a: *sbky*). The form in 4QpIsa^a would be from the postulated substantive **sĕbōk,* while the form in the MT and 1QIsa^a is from *sĕbak.*

(3) *wlbnwn* (MT and 1QIsa^a: *whlbnwn*).

7-10 iii 5-14 (Allegro's 8-10:1-10) This long commentary on Isa 10:33-34 is structured around repetitions of short phrases of the biblical text followed by metaphorical identifications of key words. The interpretation follows the same theme as the preceding sections, speaking of the battle against the Kittim (line 11 = Allegro's 8-10:7).

7-10 iii 5 (Allegro's 8-10:1) Here Allegro restores a phrase of Isa 10:33: *wrmy hqw*]*mh* [*gdwʿy*]*m,* "those who are lofty in stature will be brought low," but none of the letters can be read with certainty.

7-10 iii 6-7 (Allegro's 8-10:2-3) The second citation of Isa 10:34 is partially restored. The following variants from the MT appear (see the note above on 7-10 iii 2-3):

(1) [*wynqpw*] (MT and 1QIsa[a]: *wnqp*).

(2) [*s*]*wbky* (MT and 1QIsa[a]: *sbky*). In the preliminary publication, Allegro read the letters that are preserved here as]*bkwl*[, a reading accepted by Carmignac ("Notes," 513). In the *editio princeps,* however, he reads]*sbky*[(so also Strugnell), but [*s*]*wbky* is better in the light of the repetition of this portion of the biblical text below in line 10.

(3) *wlbnwn* (MT and 1QIsa[a]: *whlbnwn*).

7-10 iii 7-13 (Allegro's 8-10:3-9) In these lines the interpretation about the battle between the Kittim and Israel continues, cf. 1QM 6:6; 11:8-13; 14:5-7.

7-10 iii 7 (Allegro's 8-10:3) *the Kittim* ([*h*]*ktyʾym*). It is uncertain whether or not the article should be restored with *ktyʾym.* In lines 9 and 11 below, the word occurs without the article. See the note above on 1QpHab 2:12.

who will fall by the hand of Israel (*ʾš*[*r*] *yp*[*lw*] *byd yśrʾl*). In the second half of this line Allegro restores *ʾš*[*r*] *ykt* [*w*] *byt yśrʾl,* "who will crush the house of Israel." This fits the visible traces of letters reasonably well, but it brings up the following problems: (1) The definite object sign *ʾt* would be expected to precede *byt yśrʾl* as the object of the verb *ktt.* (2) Would the Qumran author have said that the Kittim would "crush" the house of Israel? According to the Qumran salvation-historical scheme, at the end of the days the elect of God were going to triumph over the eschatological enemy, the Kittim (see e.g., 1QM 18:1-5). Moreover, the biblical text of Isa 10:33-34, which is here interpreted, describes how Assyria will fall. If it is assumed that Assyria, as the enemy of Israel, is here identified with the Kittim, then a description of the fall of the Kittim should follow. I therefore suggest *ʾšr yplw byd yśrʾl,* "who will fall by the hand of Israel," using the verb *npl* from the lemma. Compare 1QM 11:8-9 *lhpyl gdwdy blyʿl šbʿt gwy hbl byd ʾbywny pdwtkh,* "by causing the hordes of *blyʿl,* the seven nations of vanity, to fall by the hand of the poor whom you have redeemed."

Carmignac suggests *bp*]*tʾ*[*y y*]*śrʾl wʿnwy* [*yhwdh*], "against the simple ones of Israel and the poor ones of Judah," but this does not fit the visible traces of letters.

7-10 iii 7-8 (Allegro's 8-10:3-4) *and the poor ones of Judah will judge all the nations* (*wʿnwy* [*yhwdh yšpṭw ʾt*] *kwl hgwʾym*). I restore *yhwdh* at the beginning of line 8 as suggested by Carmignac ("Notes," 513). With "the poor ones of Judah" as the subject, a verb should be restored that would have as its object "all the nations." The text of 1QM 11:8-13 speaks of Yahweh's subjecting "all the nations" by the hand of the "poor" (the word for "poor" in 1QM 11:19, 13 is *ʾbywn,* while in 4QpIsa^{a} it is *ʿnw*). On the basis of 1QM 11:13, something like *yšpylw,* "will humble" might be restored. I tentatively suggest *yšpṭw* "will judge" (cf. 1QpHab 5:4; 1QM 14:5-7), but this may be a little short for the space.

7-10 iii 9 (Allegro's 8-10:5) Strugnell suggests restoring the formula *wʾšr ʾmr* to introduce the repetition of Isa 10:34a. However, when this formula is used to introduce a second citation, it is usually followed by an interpretation introduced by the word *pšrw* (see Part II, p. 243). The structure of this commentary section is similar to that of 1QpHab 12:9 and 4QpPs^{a} 1-10 iii 10-13, where the repeated biblical phrase is not introduced by any formula, and the interpretation that follows begins with the pronoun. Moreover, in line 11 below, the repetition of 10:34b is preceded only by a space.

7-10 iii 10 (Allegro's 8-10:6) To be restored at the beginning of the line is a predicate for "the warriors of the Kittim."

The first visible letter in the line could be either *d* or *r.* Allegro reads a *r* as part of the formula *wʾšr ʾmr,* but see the note above on line 9.

The text of Isa 10:34a is repeated again in this line, and the following variants from the MT appear (see the notes above on lines 2-3 and 6): (1) *wynqpw* (MT and 1QIsa^{a}: *wnqp*); (2) *swbky* (MT and 1QIsa^{a}: *sbky*).

7-10 iii 12 (Allegro's 8-10:8) At the beginning of the line Allegro restores *pšrw ʿl hktyʾym,* but compare the interpretation of 10:33bα above in line 9, which begins simply with the pronoun *hmh.* See the note above on line 9, and see further Part II, p. 242.

the Kittim ([*h*]*ktyʾym*). As in line 7 above, it is uncertain whether or not the article should be restored with *ktyʾym.*

his great ones (*gdwlw*). The form could also be read as *gdwly,* "the great ones of" (so Carmignac). As it is read here, the form could be the sing., "his great one," but it is more likely the defectively written pl. noun with the 3rd pers. sing. masc. sf., cf. *ʿlw* for *ʿlyw* of the MT below in line 15.

7-10 iii 13 (Allegro's 8-10:9) In the preliminary publication, Allegro read *yrw*]*šlym* by joining a small frg. to the edge of frg. 8. He described this juncture as very tenuous and omitted it from the *editio princeps.*

In this line Allegro joins the left upper part and the lower piece of frg. 8 in such a way as to read *bbrḥw mlpny l.*[ ]*m*[ ]. Strugnell, however, from his examination of the frgs. concludes that these two pieces should be farther apart and suggests that the traces of letters be read as *mlp*[*ny yś*]*rʾl.*

7-10 iii 15-20 (Allegro's 8-10:11-16) In these lines, which are made up of the lower portions of frgs. 8 and 9, and the first line of frg. 10, the text of Isa 11:1-5 is restored. Strugnell suggests that the beginning of the citation in line 15 should be indented as were the citations above in 2-6 ii 10, 21 (Allegro's 2-4:6; 5-6:5). Though this would be consistent with the structure of the document, there does not seem to be enough space for an indentation in line 15.

At the beginning of lines 15 and 16, Strugnell was able to match a previously unidentified frg., which gives the additional letters [*mgz*]ᶜ in line 15, and]*ḥwkmh* in line 16 (see "Notes," pl. I, frg., c).

7-10 iii 17 (Allegro's 8-10:13) In the citation of Isa 11:3, *lwʾ* is restored rather than *wlʾ* as in the MT and 1QIsaª in view of the repetition of 11:3b in line 26. This is not certain, since it is not unusual for a conjunction to be dropped in a second citation (cf. the omission of *kyʾ* in 2-6 ii 6), but the variant is supported by the LXX.

7-10 iii 19 (Allegro's 8-10:15) 4QpIsaª is restored in agreement with the MT of Isa 11:4, with the anarthrous *ʾrṣ* twice, but 1QIsaª has *hʾrṣ* (twice).

7-10 iii 20 (Allegro's 8-10:16) The citation of Isa 11:5 presents the following variant from the MT: *wʾmwnh* (MT: *whʾmwnh,* cf. 1QIsaª, which has *wʾmwnh* in agreement with 4QpIsaª).

7-10 iii 21 In the transcription in *Qumrân Cave 4,* Allegro does not indicate the blank line between the end of the citation in line 20 and the beginning of the interpretation in line 22.

7-10 iii 22-23 (Allegro's 8-10:17-18) At the beginning of line 22 I follow Allegro's restoration, *pšrw ᶜl ṣmḥ dwyd,* except that I prefer the formula *pšr hptgm ᶜl* (see above 2-6 ii 26), which fills the space better. The term "scion of David," a messianic designation in QL, is also found in 4QPBless 2, 4; and 4QFlor 1-2 i 11.

to save Israel and to exterminate his enemies ([*lhwšyᶜ ʾt yśrʾl wlklwt ʾt ʾw*]*ybw*). This is suggested in the light of 4QFlor 1-2 i 7-13; 1QpHab 13:3; 1QM 11:11; 13:16. The first letters preserved in line 23, which are read here as]*ybw,* could also be]*wbw.*

with a mighty spirit (*b*[*rwḥ g*]*bwrh*). This was suggested by P. Skehan; see R. E. Murphy, "GBR and GBWRH in the Qumran Writings," *Lex tua veritas: Festschrift für Hubert Junker zur Vollendung des siebzigsten Lebensjahres am 8. August 1961* (ed. H. Gross and F. Mussner; Trier: Paulinus-Verlag, 1961) 139, n. 8. Allegro reads *b*[. . . *h*]*twrh,* which is also possible.

7-10 iii 24 (Allegro's 8-10:19) *and God will give him* ([*wʾl ytn lw*]). The restoration is tentative.

garments of variegated stuff (*wbgdy ryqm*[*wt*]). Allegro and Strugnell read *rwqmw*[*t*], while Carmignac prefers *rwqmh.* I read *ryqmwt,* the biblical Hebrew form (see 1QM 5:6, 9, 14; 7:11; 4Q*179* 1 ii 12), which exhibits the orthographic phenomenon of a *y* representing the short *i*-vowel; see the note above on 1QpHab 7:13.

7-10 iii 25 (Allegro's 8-10:20) *and God will place a scepter in his hand* ([*wʾl yśym šbṭ*] *bydw*). The restoration is tentative. Allegro reads a trace of a final *n* at the right edge of the frg., but this is very doubtful.

Magog (*mgwg*). In Ezekiel 38-39, Magog is mentioned as the home of Gog, an enemy prince to the north of Israel. Gog is also mentioned in 1QM 11:16 as someone chastised by Yahweh in the last days. See also Rev 20:8, where Magog is treated as a nation, perhaps as here.

7-10 iii 26 (Allegro's 8-10:21) The repetition of Isa 11:3b presents the following variant from the MT: *lwʾ* (MT and 1QIsa[a]: *wlʾ*).

7-10 iii 29 (Allegro's 8-10:24) *one of the priests of repute* (*ʾḥd mkwhny hšm*), cf. *ʾnšy hšm,* "the men of repute," in 1QM 2:6; 3:4; 1QSa 2:11.

4QpIsa[b] (4Q*162*)

Editio princeps: "Commentary on Isaiah (B)" (J. M. Allegro), *Qumrân Cave 4,* Vol. I, pp. 15-17 and pl. VI.

Preliminary publication: J. M. Allegro, "More Isaiah Commentaries from Qumran's Fourth Cave," *JBL* 77 (1958) 215-21, esp. 215-18 and pl. I.

Secondary transcriptions and translations: J. Carmigmac, *Les Textes,* 2. 66-68; A. Dupont-Sommer, *Essene Writings,* 275; A. M. Habermann, *Megilloth,* 171-72; J. Maier, *Die Texte,* 1. 188, 2. 166-67; F. Michelini Tocci, *I manoscritti,* 285-88; L. Moraldi, *I manoscritti,* 525-27; G. Vermes, *Dead Sea Scrolls in English,* 227-28.

Secondary literature: W. R. Lane, "Pešer style as a reconstruction tool in 4Q Pešer Isaiah *b,*" *RevQ* 2 (1959-60) 281-83; J. Strugnell, "Notes," 186-88; Y. Yadin, "Some Notes on the Newly Published *Pesharim* of Isaiah," *IEJ* 9 (1959) 39-42.

In *Qumrân Cave 4,* the title 4Q*162* designates one large frg. of a commentary on Isaiah. Though this frg. preserves ten full lines of one col. and several words of two other cols., there are only a few words of the interpretation remaining. The frg. consists mainly of the following biblical verses: Isa 5:5b (?), 6a (?), 11-14, 24c-25, and 29b-30 (?). The number of lines in the cols. of this document cannot be determined, nor can a satisfactory estimate be made, since the biblical text of Isaiah does not seem to have been followed continuously. In the second col., for example, the citation of Isa 5:11-14 (lines 2-6) is followed by a brief interpretation (lines 6-7) and then by the citation of Isa 5:24c-25.

This irregularity of structure is not the only noteworthy feature of the text. According to J. Strugnell ("Notes," 188), the script of this MS differs from the rustic, semi-formal Herodian hand seen in several of the pesharim from Cave 4. He characterizes the hand of 4QpIsa^b as "semi-formel 'vulgaire'" and suggests that it could perhaps be dated before the Herodian period. In addition, the text exhibits a frequent use of defective spelling, e.g., *pqdt* (2:2); *lʾ* (twice), *ydw, wkbdw* (2:4); *whmnh, wšʾnh* (2:6); *bkl, lʾ* (2:9).

In this text are found the familiar introductory formulas *pšr hdbr ʾšr* (1:2), *wʾšr ʾmr* (1:3), *pšr hdbr lʾḥryt hymym* (2:1), and there are two short interpretations introduced simply by *ʾlh hm,* "they are the ones" (2:6) and *hyʾ,* "this is" (2:10). From what remains of the text, it appears that the interpretations were very short, only one line or a fraction of a line in length (1:2-3, 4, 5-6; 2:1-2, 6-7).

At the beginning of col. 2, the focus of the interpretation is eschatological as is evidenced by the introductory formula itself and by the eschatological images of "the sword," "the famine," and "the visitation of the land." The text of Isa 5:11-14 is a warning, probably directed against the "inhabitants of Jerusalem and the men of Judah" (5:3), those who seek pleasure and forget Yahweh. The Qumran author identifies the pleasure-seekers with *ʾnšy hlṣwn,* "the Scoffers," who are in Jerusalem (2:6). Later in 2:10, the "congregation of the Scoffers, who are in Jerusalem" is identified with those in Isa 5:24c-25 who rejected the Law of Yahweh. It is possible that the term "Scoffers" refers to the followers of the Wicked Priest (see the note on 2:6).

4QpIsa^b: Translation

Column 1

1. [(I SHALL) REMOVE ITS HEDGE THAT IT MAY BE FOR GRAZING; (I SHALL) BREAK D]OWN ITS WALL THAT IT MAY BECOME A TRAMPLED PASTURE, which — Isa 5:5b-6a
2. [I SHALL MAKE A VOID (?). IT WILL NOT BE PRUNED, NOR WILL IT BE WEEDED, AND THERE WILL GROW UP THORNS AND THIST]LES. The interpretation of the passage is that he abandoned them
3. [ ]*d* and when it says, THERE WILL GROW UP THORNS — 5:6aγ
4. [AND THISTLES, the interpretation of it]ʿ*t* and when {{and when}}

5. [it says, IT WILL NOT BE PRUNED, NOR WILL IT BE WEEDED, the interpretation of it].*nt* the way of 5:6aα·β
6. [ ]their eyes

Column 2

1. The interpretation of the passage with regard to the end of days concerns the condemnation of the land before the sword and the famine. And it will happen
2. in the time of the visitation of the land. WOE TO THOSE WHO, WHEN THEY RISE EARLY IN THE MORNING, RUN AFTER STRONG DRINK, WHO ARE INFLAMED BY WINE WHEN THEY STAY LATE IN THE EVENING. 5:11-14
3. AND THERE ARE ZITHER AND STRINGED INSTRUMENT, TAMBOURINE AND FLUTE, THE WINE OF THEIR FEASTS; BUT THE WORK OF YAHWEH
4. THEY DID NOT HEED, AND THE WORKS OF HIS HANDS THEY DID NOT REGARD. THEREFORE MY PEOPLE HAVE GONE INTO EXILE FOR LACK OF KNOWLEDGE. ITS HONORED ONES ARE DYING OF HUNGER,
5. AND ITS MULTITUDE IS PARCHED WITH THIRST. SO SHEOL OPENED ITS THROAT AND WIDENED ITS MOUTH WITHOUT LIMIT.
6. AND ITS SPLENDOR WILL GO DOWN, AND ITS THRONGS, AND ITS TUMULTUOUS CROWD EXULTING IN IT. These are the Scoffers,
7. who are in Jerusalem. They are the ones who REJECTED THE LAW OF YAHWEH, AND THE WORD OF THE HOLY ONE 5:24c-25
8. OF ISRAEL THEY TREATED WITHOUT RESPECT. SO THE ANGER OF YAHWEH FLARED AGAINST HIS PEOPLE, AND HE STRETCHED OUT HIS HAND AGAINST IT AND SMOTE IT. THE MOUNTAINS QUAKED
9. AND THEIR CORPSE(S) BECAME LIKE OFFAL IN THE MIDST OF THE STREETS. FOR ALL THIS [HIS ANGER] DID NOT TURN BACK,
10. [AND HIS HAND IS STILL STRETCHED OUT.] This is the congregation of Scoffers, who are in Jerusalem
11. [ ]*l*[ ]*l*[ ]

Column 3

1. AND THERE WILL BE NO DE[LIVERER; AND HE WILL GROAN OVER IT ON THAT DAY] 5:29b
2. LIKE THE ROA[R OF THE SEA. ONE LOOKS AT THE LAND, AND BEHOLD, (THERE IS) DISTRESSING DARKNESS, AND THE LIGHT BECOMES DARKNESS] 5:30 ?
3. WITH [ITS] CLOU[DS]
4. This is [ ]

5. These [ ]
6. tho[se] who come [and when]
7. it says .[ ]
8. LOOK IN[DEED, BUT DO NOT PERCEIVE] 6:9 ?
9. YOU UNDERSTA[ND]

4QpIsa^b: Notes

Column 1

1:1-2 In these lines the text of Isa 5:5b-6a is restored; it was probably preceded either by the citation of Isa 5:5a or by the closing words of a commentary begun in the preceding col. The following points are worthy of note in the citation as it is partially preserved and restored here.

(1) The inf. abs. *hsr* is restored according to the MT, but 1QIsa^a reads *ʾsyr,* "I shall remove." Both in the MT and in 1QIsa^a, this form is continued by the inf. abs. *prṣ,* but only the final *ṣ* of this word is preserved in 4QpIsa^b.

(2) The form *wyhy* is restored rather than *whyh* as in the MT in the light of *wyhy lmrms* later in the same line (where the MT also has *whyh*). In both cases 1QIsa^a has *wyhyh.*

(3) The inf. cs. *lbʿr* is restored in agreement with the MT; 1QIsa^a has *bʿr.* The root *bʿr* here is frequently translated "for burning," but see Isa 3:14; 6:13; Exod 22:4, where the meaning of the root is "to graze," which fits the context here and gives a good parallel to the following phrase *wyhy lmrms,* "that it may become a pasture." See H. Wildberger, *Jesaja. I. Teilband: Jesaja 1-12* BKAT X/1; Neukirchen-Vluyn: Neukirchener Verlag, 1972) 133, 163, 233.

(4) The last word in line 1, following the end of Isa 5:5 (*lmrms*) appears to be *ʾšr,* which is not part of the biblical text as it is in the MT and in 1QIsa^a. It has been suggested by W. R. Lane ("Pešer style," 281-83) that the reading is actually *ʾšy,* the erroneous beginning of the first word of Isa 5:6 (*wʾšythw*). The reading *ʾšr* is almost certain, though it may indeed have arisen through a scribal error as Lane suggests, by confusion with the following word (so also Carmignac, *Les Textes,* 2. 67, n. 3). Since the beginning of line 2 is lost, the function of the relative sign *ʾšr* cannot be determined. It is unlikely that *ʾšr* is used here to introduce an interpretation of the biblical text, as Allegro suggests, since the interpretation clearly begins in the end of line 2 with the formula *pšr hdbr ʾšr.* If it is not a scribal error, *ʾšr* is best understood as a connective between Isa 5:5 and 5:6; thus, I restore the first word of 5:6 (*ʾšythw*) at the beginning of line 2 without the conjunction of the MT and 1QIsa^a (*wʾšythw*).

(5) The form *bth* is restored according to the MT and 1QIsa^a, but the

meaning of the word is uncertain. The form occurs only here in biblical Hebrew, and it is usually translated "a ruin" or something similar according to the context. G. R. Driver has suggested that the form *bātâ* is an abstract noun from the root *bth,* which in Akkadian means "to reduce to ruins" or "to raze utterly" ("Linguistic and Textual Problems: Isaiah I-XXXIX," *JTS* 38 [1937] 38; see also H. Wildberger, *Jesaja,* 164). It is also possible that the form is the defective spelling of *bĕtōhû,* i.e., the noun *tōhû,* "void," with the preposition *bĕ* expressing equivalence. The phrase would be literally translated "which I shall make (it) as a void."

(6) The phrase *lʾ yzmr,* "it will not be pruned," is restored according to the MT of Isa 5:6, but 1QIsa^a has *wlwʾ yzmr.*

1:3 *and there will grow up* (*wʿlh*). In the transcription in *Qumrân Cave 4,* Allegro reads *yʿlh* in what is apparently the second citation of Isa 5:6aγ, but this is an unattested variant from the MT (*wʿlh*). A better reading is *wʿlh.*

This second citation of Isa 5:6aγ is introduced by the formula *wʾšr ʾmr,* and it was probably followed by a brief interpretation in line 4.

1:4-5 At the end of line 4 *wʾšr* is written twice; the second time it was marked for deletion with a dot below each letter. This is probably the first word of the introductory formula *wʾšr ʾmr,* in which case *ʾmr* is to be restored in line 5 followed by a second citation of some portion of the biblical text. It might be expected that the phrases of the biblical text would be repeated in order (cf. 1QpHab 6:2-8), but Isa 5:6aγ has already been cited for the second time (lines 3-4). With hesitation I restore Isa 5:6α-β, which would then be followed by a brief interpretation.

Column 2

2:1-2 For the formula *pšr hdbr lʾḥryt hymym l-,* see Part II, p. 240.

There is a problem with the syntax of this brief commentary. It is uncertain whether *whrʿb,* "and the famine," goes with *hḥrb,* "the sword," as the compound object of the preposition *mpny* (so Allegro, Carmignac, Dupont-Sommer, Maier, Vermes), or whether it begins a new sentence, in which case the following word would have to be read *yhyh,* "and the famine will be in the time of the visitation of the land." It seems to me more likely that the two substantives *hḥrb* and *hrʿb* form the compound object of *mpny,* since they occur together as an eschatological image in 4QpPs^a 1-10 ii 1, cf. Isa 51:19; Jer 5:12; 14:15; 32:24; Ezek 14:21. The result, however, is an ambiguous sentence that is really anacoluthon, "and it will happen in the time of the visitation of the land" (so Allegro, Dupont-Sommer, Maier). Carmignac supplies a subject, "(Ce) sera au temps de la visite de la terre" (apparently reading the verb as *yhyh*), and Vermes makes the following citation the predicate nominative, "At the time of the Visitation of the land there shall be 'Woe to those . . .''' (also apparently reading *yhyh*). Strugnell suggests the possibility of reading *mpnw* as the last word of the first phrase, and then *hḥrb whrᶜb yhyh*. However, this raises further problems on which he does not comment: (1) the antecedent of the 3rd pers. sing. masc. sf. of *mpnw;* (2) the compound subject with the sing. verb.

2:1 *the condemnation of the land* (*ḥwbt hʾrṣ*). The word *ḥwbh* does not occur in biblical Hebrew or elsewhere in QL. In biblical Hebrew the root *ḥwb* means "to do wrong," "to make guilty," and this verb is attested in QL in CD 3:10. There is also a biblical Hebrew noun *ḥwb,* "guilt." In Mishnaic Hebrew, the noun *ḥwbh* does occur, meaning "debt," "sin," or "condemnation." In the preliminary publication, Allegro translated *lḥwbt* with a question mark as "desolation" and commented that the form is probably a scribal error for *ḥrwbt,* a form of *ḥoreb,* "dryness," "drought." In the *editio princeps* he translated it as "at the doom of the earth." Dupont-Sommer, too, corrects *ḥwbt* to *ḥrwbt* and translates it "dévastation." But if they are suggesting that this is the construct form of the biblical Hebrew noun *ḥoreb,* how is the form to be explained? I agree with Y. Yadin ("Some Notes," 39) that the suggestion of a scribal error is unnecessary in view of the occurrence of the noun *ḥwbh* in Mishnaic Hebrew.

the sword (*hḥrb*). Strugnell questions whether *ḥrb* might be translated "scarcity" here; he feels that this meaning is favored by the context. There is no attestation of a substantive form with this meaning, though the root *ḥrb* means "to be without water," "to be desolate," "to be dried up." In view of the fact that the noun *ḥrb,* "sword," is coupled elsewhere with *rᶜb,* "famine" (see the comments above on the syntax of 2:1-2), the meaning "scarcity" is unlikely.

the famine (*hrᶜb*), see 4QpHos^a 2:12; 4QpPs^a 1-10 ii 1; 1-10 iii 3, 4.

2:2 *the time of the visitation of the land* (*bᶜt pqdt hʾrṣ*). The idea of the "visitation" is to be connected with the final judgment, which the Essenes believed would take place before their generation had passed (see e.g., 4QpHos^a 1:10; CD 7:21—8:3; see also A. Dupont-Sommer, *Essene Writings,* 277, n. 5).

2:2-6 The citation of Isa 5:11-14 presents the following variants from the MT:

(1) *ydlqm* (MT and 1QIsa^a: *ydlyqm*). This may be simply an orthographic variant (it was pointed out in the introductory remarks that this text exhibits defective spelling), or it could be that the form in 4QpIsa^b is the qal, where the MT and 1QIsa^a have the hiph. In biblical Hebrew, the verb *dlq* is used here and in Ezek 24:10 in the hiph., but elsewhere it is qal. In Mishnaic Hebrew the verb is used in the qal, niph., and hiph. conjugations.

(2) *wtwp* (MT: *tp;* at this point the text of 1QIsa[a] is not preserved).

(3) *yyn* (MT: *wyyn;* at this point the text of 1QIsa[a] is not preserved).

(4) *hbyṭw* (so also 1QIsa[a], but MT: *ybyṭw*).

(5) *wmʿśy* (MT and 1QIsa[a]: *wmʿśh*).

(6) *ṣḥy* (MT: *ṣḥh;* the text of 1QIsa[a] is not preserved). This is probably an orthographic variant, with *y* representing *ē* in place of the *ēh* in the MT.

(7) *ʿlyz bʾ* (MT and 1QIsa[a] [partially restored]: *wʿlz bh*). The form *bʾ* is probably an orthographic variant from the MT; see E. Y. Kutscher, *Isaiah Scroll,* 163-64.

2:2 Where the MT and 4QpIsa[b] have *mʾḥry,* 1QIsa[a] reads *mʾḥzy.*

2:2-3 *but the work of Yahweh* (*wʾt pʿl yhwh*). 1QIsa[a] reads *wʾt pʿlt yhwh.* The tetragrammaton is written here in the same script as the rest of the document; see the note above on 1QpHab 1:1.

2:4-5 *its honored ones . . . its multitude* (*wkbdw . . . whmnw*), i.e., the honored ones and the multitude of the people, with the 3rd pers. sing. masc. sf. referring to *ʿmy.*

2:6 *its splendor . . . its multitude . . . its tumultuous crowd* (*hdrh whmnh wšʾnh*), literally, "her splendor . . . her multitude . . . her tumultuous crowd." There is no fem. antecedent expressed preceding these words, but the fem. suffixes might have been understood as referring to the city of Jerusalem, which is mentioned in the interpretation in line 7.

The phrase *ʾlh hm ʾnšy hlṣwn ʾšr byrwšlym,* "these are the Scoffers, who are in Jerusalem," which follows the citation of Isa 5:11-14 does not begin with any of the usual introductory formulas for interpretations. For this reason, W. R. Lane regards this not as an interpretation of the biblical text, but as a device used to bridge the gap caused by the omission of Isa 5:15-24a. However, the interpretative phrase in line 10, which follows the citation of Isa 5:24c-25, also begins without an introductory formula. These phrases are clearly a sort of commentary, even though they do not follow the prevailing pesher form; see Part II, p. 242.

the Scoffers (*ʾnšy hlṣwn*), literally, "the men of arrogant boasting," see also below line 10. In CD 1:14, the Scoffer (*ʾyš hlṣwn*) appears as the enemy of the Teacher of Righteousness, who "shed over Israel the water of lies." This might be the same person identified as the One who Spouts the Lie (*mṭyp hkzb*) in 1QpHab 10:9. This figure, if not the Wicked Priest himself, was probably one of his followers. The Scoffers in Jerusalem, then, may be the allies and followers of the Wicked Priest.

2:7 In this line there is another exception to the usual pesher structure. The citation of Isa 5:24c-25 begins as a continuation of the pesher, with the phrase *hm ʾšr,* "they are the ones who," leading into the quotation.

2:7-10 The citation of Isa 5:24c-25 presents the following variants from the MT:

(1) In the MT, 5:24c begins with *ky,* which does not appear in 4QpIsa[b].

(2) *yhwh* (MT and 1QIsa[a]: *yhwh ṣbʾwt*).

(3) *ksḥh* (MT and 1QIsa[a]: *kswḥh*). It is likely that this is simply an orthographic variant, since defective spelling is frequent in this text. Strugnell, however, questions whether this form might be a morphological variant, since the omission of *w* when it represents *û* is very rare in QL. He does not suggest what type of noun the form of 4QpIsa[b] would be.

(4) *hḥwṣwt* (MT and 1QIsa[a]: *ḥwṣwt*).

2:8 *his hand* (*ydw*). This could be the sing. noun with the 3rd pers. sing. masc. sf. (as in the MT) or the defectively written pl. noun with the 3rd pers. sing. masc. sf. (as in 1QIsa[a], which has *ydyw*).

2:9 *their corpse(s)* (*nbltm*). This form is sing. as is the verb *wthy* (1QIsa[a]: *wthyh*), but the sf. is pl.

2:10 *his hand* (*ydw*). This is restored in agreement with the MT; 1QIsa[a] has *ydyw*. See the note above on 2:8.

Here as in line 6 above the interpretation begins without any of the usual pesher formulas.

2:11 On the photograph traces of two letters are visible, which are probably the tops of two *l*'s, but they were not transcribed by Allegro.

Column 3

This col. cannot be satisfactorily restored according to the width of cols. 1 and 2. In lines 1-3 there seem to be phrases of Isa 5:29b-30, and in lines 8 and 9, phrases of Isa 6:9. The structure is probably similar to that of the first col. with brief repetitions of biblical phrases followed by short interpretations or identifications. The word *hwʾ* in line 4 might introduce an interpretation, and *ʾmr* in line 7 might be part of the formula *wʾšr ʾmr* introducing a repetition of some portion of the biblical text.

3:1 *he will groan* ([*wynhm*]). This is restored according to the MT; 1QIsa[a] has *ynhm*.

3:7 In the transcription in *Qumrân Cave 4,* Allegro reads *ʾmr*[, but a space and a trace of a letter are visible after this, thus *ʾmr* . [.

3:8 In this line Allegro tentatively restores a phrase of Isa 6:9b, *rʾw r*[*ʾw wʿl tdʿw,* "look indeed, but do not perceive," (so 1QIsa[a], but MT: *wrʾw rʾw*). The phrase could be part of the citation or part of the commentary. Carmignac (*Les Textes,* 2. 69, n. 18) rejects Allegro's reading of a *r* just before the break; he suggests possible readings *b, k, m.* I agree with Strugnell, however, that Allegro's reading is better.

3:9 Here I follow Allegro's reading in the preliminary publication, *tbyn*[*w,* possibly part of Isa 6:9. In the *editio princeps,* he transcribes *tby* . [. Carmignac suggests either *tbwʾ,* "elle viendra," or *tbyʾ,* "elle fera venir."

4QpIsa^c (4Q*163*)

Editio princeps: "Commentary on Isaiah (C)" (J. M. Allegro), *Qumrân Cave 4,* Vol. I, pp. 17-27 and pls. VII-VIII.

Preliminary publication: J. M. Allegro, "More Isaiah Commentaries from Qumran's Fourth Cave," *JBL* 77 (1958) 215-21, esp. 218-20, with a photograph of frg. 23.

Secondary transcriptions and translations: J. Carmignac, *Les Textes,* 2. 72-74; A. Dupont-Sommer, *Essene Writings,* 275-76; A. M. Habermann, *Megilloth,* 172-73; J. Maier, *Die Texte,* 1. 188-89, 2. 166-67; L. Moraldi, *I manoscritti,* 531-35; G. Vermes, *Dead Sea Scrolls in English,* 228.

Secondary literature: J. Strugnell, "Notes," 188-95 and pl. III e, f, g, h.

Among the Qumran commentaries on Isaiah that are presented in *Qumrân Cave 4,* 4Q*163* designates a group of fifty-seven frgs., of which only a handful can be identified, matched, or restored with any degree of probability. In the preliminary publication, only frg. 23 was presented. To the frgs. given in the *editio princeps* J. Strugnell adds four more (see *RevQ* 7 [1969-71] 188-89 and pl. III e, f, g, h).

Strugnell finds two different scripts among the frgs. The first, a "semi-formal" Hasmonean hand, is found on most of the frgs. A second, more "cursive" script is represented, according to Strugnell, by frgs. 2, 37, 45-49, and possibly frg. 44. In the frgs. written in the "cursive" style the spelling tends to be defective, e.g., *htrh* "the Law" (?) in 2:5 (Allegro's 2-3:4), cf. *btwrh* in 23 ii 12 and *htwrh* in 23 ii 14a; *wlʾ* in 2:7 (Allegro's 2-3:6), cf. *wlwʾ* in 4, 6-7 i 19 (Allegro's 4-7:16) and 21:15, but *lwʾ* in 37:3, which Strugnell assigns to the "cursive" hand; *kl* twice in 2:3 (Allegro's 2-3:2) and *bkl* in 44:4, cf. *kwl* in 23 ii 9 and 41:2; *khn* "priest" (?) in 45:2; and *mrh* "teacher" (?) in 46:3; cf. *mwrh* in 21:6.

In contrast to the other pesharim studied here, which are written on skin, this document is written on papyrus. Consequently, the text on almost all of the frgs. is very badly preserved, and I have had to rely largely on Allegro's transcription and Strugnell's corrections and additions. There are a number of places, however, where I differ with them on placement of frgs., numbering of lines in some frgs., indications of spaces before and after lacunas, and indications of traces of letters that seem to be visible on the photographs in the *editio princeps.* The listing of these differences constitutes most of my commentary after the translation.

Owing to the fragmentary state of the text, it is impossible to determine with certainty the structure of the commentary. The document seems to follow the usual structure of a running commentary on the prophetic text. The familiar formulas occur: *kyʾ hwʾh ʾšr ʾmr* (1:[2]); *pšr hdbr ʿl* (6-7 ii 4); *wʾšr ʾmr* (6-7 ii 7, [15-16]; 8-10:4; 22:[4]; 24:2 ?); *pšr hdbr lʾḥryt hymym*

(6-7 ii [14]; 13:[4]; 23 ii 10); *pšrw* (29:3). In addition, the formula *k*ʾ*šr ktwb,* "as it is written," seems to be used in 1:[4]; 2:[6] (Allegro's 2-3:5); 4, 6-7 i [4] (Allegro's 4-7 i 1); 6-7 ii 18; 8-10:[8]; 47:[2]. Elsewhere in the biblical commentaries the only formula similar to this in the use of the verb *ktb* rather than ʾ*mr* is *w*ʾ*šr ktwb* in 4QpIsa[e] 1-2:2; see further Part II. p. 243.

An unusual feature of this document is the apparent use of implicit and explicit citations of other prophetic works in the commentary sections. In 1:4 the reading seems to be "[as it is w]ritten concerning him in Jere[miah]" (cf. 11QMelch 9-10, 24, and J. A. Fitzmyer, "The Use of Explicit Old Testament Quotations in Qumran Literature and in the New Testament," *Essays on the Semitic Background of the New Testament* [SBS 5; Missoula: Society of Biblical Literature and Scholars Press, 1974] 9). Following this phrase the text is lost, but a citation from Jeremiah would be expected. Similarly in 8-10:8, in the commentary on Isa 14:26-27, the restored reading is "[as it is writ]ten in the book of Zechariah from the mou[th of God]," cf. 4QFlor 1-2 i 2, 15; 1-3 ii 3. Following this, again, a citation from Zechariah would be expected. In 21:7-8, in what is presumably part of an interpretation of the last verses of Isaiah 29 (in lines 9-15 Isa 30:1-5 is quoted), there seems to be an allusion to Zech 11:11. Unfortunately, there is too little of the text preserved to determine the function of this allusion. Similarly in 23 ii 14, in the commentary on Isa 30:15-18, there may be an allusion to or a citation of Hos 6:9a. Such references to other biblical texts do not occur elsewhere in the "continuous" pesharim, but a similar structure is found in the "thematic" pesharim such as 11QMelchizedek and 4QFlorilegium (see above, pp. 2-3).

Another unusual aspect of the structure of the document concerns the use of biblical material. Several times it seems that verses are skipped, e.g., in 4, 6-7 i 6-8 (Allegro's 4-7 i 3-5) Isa 9:12 seems to have been omitted; between the end of col. i of frgs. 4, 6-7 and the beginning of col. ii, probably all of Isa 10:1-11 was skipped; in 8-10:1-4, Isa 14:9-25 seems to have been omitted. The omission of biblical verses, however, is not unknown from the other pesharim; see, e.g., 4QpIsa[b] col. 2.

Where the biblical text can be confidently restored, the full writing of some words has been supplied in accordance with the usual Qumran orthography, except in the frgs. of the "cursive" hand. Since so little of the text is preserved, the Qumran author's interpretation of Isaiah is almost entirely lost. However, the few phrases that can be read indicate that the commentary probably dealt with the history of the Qumran sect in a manner similar to that of the other pesher texts.

4QpIsa^{c}: Translation

Fragment 1

1. [ ]..[ ]
2. [fo]r this is wh[at it says:]
3. [ ] and he confused the way of .[ ]
4. [as it is w]ritten concerning him in Jere[miah]

Fragment 2

1. [ ].[ ].[ ].[ ].[ ]
2. [AND THEREFORE, BEHOLD, MY LORD IS BRING]ING UP AGAINST THE[M] {{THE WATERS OF}} THE RIVER, [MIGHTY AND MANY, THE KING OF ASSYRIA AND] Isa 8:7-8
3. [ALL HIS GLORY, AND IT WILL GO UP] OVER ALL ITS STREAMBEDS. IT WILL GO OVER ALL [ITS] BANKS [AND WILL SWEEP ON INTO JUDAH; IT WILL OVERFLOW AND WILL PASS BY;]
4. [IT WILL REACH TO THE NECK, AND] ITS OUTSTRETCHED WINGS WILL [BE] WHAT FILLS THE BREADTH OF [YO]UR LAND, [O IMMANUEL]
5. [ ]^{c}[ ]*m* the Law is. *ṣ.w* ..[ ]
6. [as it is wr]itten in[ ].[ ]
7. [ ]*h* and not [ ]

Fragment 3

]*w*^{c}*b*[

Fragments 4, 6-7, Column i

1. [ ]
2. [ ]
3. [ ]
4. [as it is] written
5. [ ].[upon] them.
6. [ARAM FROM THE EAST AND THE PHILISTINES FROM THE WEST, AND THEY DEVOURED I]SRAEL WITH OPEN 9:11a-e
7. [MOUTH. FOR ALL THIS HIS ANGER IS NOT TURNED AWAY].*wr* and it (?)
8. [AND YAHWEH CUT OFF FROM ISRAEL HEAD AND TAIL, REED AND RUS]H IN ONE DAY. THE OLD 9:13-16
9. [AND DISTINGUISHED ONE, HE IS THE HEAD; AND THE PROPHET, THE TEACHER OF LIES,] HE IS THE TAIL.
10. [THOSE WHO LEAD THIS PEOPLE LEAD (THEM) ASTRAY,

AND THOSE WHO ARE LED BY HIM ARE SW]ALLOWED UP. THEREFORE
11. [THE LORD DOES NOT REJOICE OVER HIS YOUNG MEN, AND FOR HIS FATHERLESS ONES AND HIS WI]DOWS HE HAS NO COMPASSION.
12. [FOR EACH OF THEM IS ALIENATED FROM GOD, AN EVILDOER, AND EVERY MOUTH SPEAKS NONSENSE. FOR ALL THI]S
13. [HIS ANGER IS NOT TURNED AWAY, AND HIS HAND IS STILL STRETCHED OUT].
14. [ ].*šh*
15. [ ] (*vacat?*)
16. [FOR WICKEDNESS BURNS LIKE FIRE; IT DE]VOURS [THORNS AND WEEDS] AND ENKINDLES 9:17-20
17. [THE THICKETS OF THE FOREST, AND THEY ASCEND IN A COLUMN OF SMOKE. ON ACCOUNT OF THE ANGER OF YAHWEH OF] HOSTS, [THE LAND IS BLA]CKENED (?),
18. [AND THE PEOPLE ARE LIKE FOOD FOR THE FIRE.] NO ONE SPARES [HIS] BROTHER.
19. [THEY GORGE THEMSELVES ON THE RIGHT, BUT ARE (STILL) HUNGRY, AND THEY DEVOUR ON] THE LEFT, BUT THEY ARE NOT ..[ ]*bt*
20. [EVERY MAN DEVOURS THE FLESH OF HIS ARM: MANASSEH,] EPHRAIM, AND EPHRAI[M,]
21. [MANASS]EH. [THEY] ARE TOGETHER [AGAINST JUDAH. FOR ALL THIS] HIS ANGER [IS NOT] TURNED AWAY.

Fragment 5

1.]. soul[
2.]*h* he will kill[
3.]. *ʿš*.[

Fragments 6-7, Column ii

1. [AND IT WILL HAPPEN,] WHEN [THE LORD] FINISHES [ALL HIS WORK ON MOUNT ZION AND IN JERUSALEM, THAT I WILL AVENGE THE FRUIT OF] 10:12-13b
2. [THE PRI]DE OF THE KING OF AS[SYRIA, AND HIS HAUGHTY ARROGANCE, FOR HE SAID, "BY THE POWER OF MY HAND HAVE I ACTED."]
2a-h. [ ] 10:13c-19a
3. [(THE NUMBER) WILL BE SUCH] THAT [A CHIL]D COULD WRITE [IT] DOWN [ ]
4. The interpretation of the passage concerns the region of Babylon[ ]
5. the precepts of the peoples *h* . . . [ ]

6. to deal treacherously with many. He[ ]
7. Israel. And when it says, [AND AS FOR THE REST OF THE TREES IN HIS WOOD, THE NUMBER WILL BE SUCH THAT A CHILD COULD WRITE IT DOWN,] 10:19
8. the interpretation of it concerns "the few" (?) of humanity[ ]
9. (*vacat*) [ ]
10. AND IT WILL HAPPEN ON THAT DAY [THAT THE REMNANT OF ISRAEL AND THOSE] OF THE HOUSE OF JACOB [WHO ESCAPED WILL NO LONGER] 10:20-22bα
11. LEA[N ON THE ONE WHO SMOTE THEM, BUT WILL LEAN ON YAHWEH, THE HOLY ONE OF]
12. [IS]RAEL IN TRUTH. A R[EM]NANT [WILL RETURN, THE REMNANT OF JACOB, TO THE MIGHTY GOD.]
13. IF YOUR PEOPLE, O I[SRAEL,] WERE [AS THE SANDS OF THE SEA, ONLY A REMNANT WOULD RETURN]
14. The interpretation of the passage with regard to the end of [days]
15. they will walk among the re[turnees of Israe]l[and when]
16. it says, [IF YOUR PEOPLE, O ISRAEL, WERE AS THE SANDS OF THE SEA, ONLY A REMNANT WOULD RETURN,] 10:22a-bα
17. the interpretation of it concerns "the few" (?) [of humanity]
18. as it is written, [ANNIHILATION IS DECIDED, OVERFLOWING WITH RIGHTEOUSNESS, FOR — IT IS DETERMINED —] 10:22bβ-23
19. [THE LORD YAHWEH OF H[OSTS WILL WORK COMPLETE DESTRUCTION IN THE MIDST OF ALL THE LAND.]
20. (*vacat*) [ ]
21. [THEREFORE, THUS SAYS THE LORD Y[AHWEH OF HOSTS, "DO NOT BE AFRAID, O MY PEOPLE, WHO DWELL] 10:24

Fragments 8-10

1. [ ]. against the king of Babylon .[INDEED, THE CYPRESSES] 14:8
2. [REJOICE AT] YOU, THE CEDARS OF LEBANON, (SAYING), "SINCE [YOU LAY DOWN, THERE HAS NOT COME UP]
3. [A HEWER] AGAINST THEM." The cypresses and the cedar[s of Lebanon are]
4. [ ] . . . and when it says, THI[S IS THE PLAN PROPOSED] 14:26-27
5. [CONCERNING ALL] THE EARTH, AND THIS IS THE HAND [THAT IS STRETCHED OUT OVER ALL THE NATIONS.]
6. [FOR YAHWE]H OF HOSTS HAS DECI[DED, AND WHO WILL INVALIDATE (IT)? HIS HAND IS STRETCHED OUT,]
7. [AND WHO WILL T]URN IT BACK? This is . .[ ]
8. [as it is writ]ten in the book of Zechariah from the mouth of [God]
9. [ ].[ ]

10. ʿl[ ].[ ]
11. [IN THE YEAR OF THE DEA]TH OF KING AHA[Z CAME THIS ORACLE: DO NOT RE]JOICE, 14:28-30
12. [O PHILISTIA, A]NY OF YOU, THAT THE ROD [THAT SMOTE YOU] IS BROKEN, [FOR FROM THE SCION OF THE] SERPENT WILL CO[ME]
13. [A VIPER, AND ITS OFF]SPR[ING WILL BE A] FLYING S[ERPENT.] AND [THE FIRST-BORN OF THE POOR WILL FEED,] AND THE NEEDY
14. [WILL LIE DOWN SAFELY, BUT I SHALL KILL YOUR SCION WITH STARVATION, AND THE REST OF] YOU HE (or IT) WILL SLAY.

Fragment 11, Column i

1. [ ]*b* . . .
2. [ ]*h* the workers of
3. [ ]. they
4. [ ] . . . *ṣy* . .*m*
5. [ ]this

Fragment 11, Column ii

1. AND THE WEAVERS [GREW PALE. ITS WEAVERS WILL BE CRUSHED: ALL] HIRED [WORKERS] 19:9b-12
2. WILL BE GRIEVED [OF SOUL. INDEED, THE PRINCES OF ZOAN ARE UTTER FOOLS. THE WISE ONES OF THE COUNSELORS OF]
3. PHARAOH (GIVE) [STUPID] AD[VICE. HOW CAN YOU SAY TO PHARAOH, "WE ARE SONS OF THE WISE;]
4. WE ARE SONS OF [ANCIENT] KIN[GS"? WHERE, THEN, ARE YOUR WISE MEN? PLEASE LET THEM TELL]
5. YOU [AND MAKE KNOWN]

Fragment 12

1.]*r* his coming (?) [
2.]. at the head[
3.].*dy* . . . [
4.]. and a remnant will remain .[
5.] the stone tha[t
6. p]riests and ʾ . .[
7.]. as a measuring instrument and . . .[
8. whi]ch he commanded . . .[
9.] *bʿy* . *w*.[
10.] .*h*. [ ]*h*ʾ[ ] . . .
11.]. it (?) [

Fragment 13

1.].[
2.]. . . .[ ].[
3.] . . those who are far away (?) .[
4. The interpretation of the passage with regard to the en]d of days concerns [
5. on] t[ha]t day [they] will see[k
7.].*ṣy*.[

Fragment 14

1.]integrity (?) [
2.].*yt wbmw*[
3.]it *ʾb* . . . [
4.]*mh* not *ty*[
5.].*mh* a lion[
6.]*bh ʾ.ry*.[
7.]his soul [
8.] (*vacat?*) [
9.] . . . . .[
10.]*tw* .[
11.]. *l*[

Fragments 15-16

1. [UPON Y]OU YAHWEH [(HAS POURED OUT) A SPIRIT OF D]EEP SLEEP, AND HE HAS CLOSED [YOUR EYES, THE PROPHETS] 29:10-11
2. [AND] YOUR [H]EADS, THE SE[ERS,] HE HAS COVERED, AND THE V[ISION OF THE WHOLE THING] WAS FOR YOU [LIKE THE WORDS OF]
3. [THE BOOK THAT IS S]EALED—WHEN [THEY GIVE I]T TO ONE WHO KNOWS HOW TO READ SA[YING: "PLEASE READ THIS."]
4. [AND HE SAYS, "I CANNOT, F]OR [IT IS] S[EALED."] AND HE GIVES THE BOO[K TO ONE WHO DOES NOT KNOW HOW TO READ]

Fragment 17

1. [WHO] SEES US AND WHO [KNOWS US. YOUR PERVERSITY IS AS IF THINGS WERE UPSIDE DOWN. SHALL THE POTTER BE CONSIDERED AS THE CLAY, THAT] 29:15-16
2. THE WORK [WOULD SAY] ABOUT [ITS MAKER, "HE DID NOT MAKE ME."]

Fragments 18-19

(AND ON THAT DAY THE DEAF WILL HEAR) 29:18-23

1. [THE WORDS OF A BOOK,] AND OUT OF GLOOM AND

D[ARKNESS THE EYES OF THE BLIND WILL SEE. THE POOR WILL AGAIN FIND IN YAHWEH]

2. [JOY, AND THE NEE]DY ONES OF HUMANITY IN THE HO[LY ONE OF ISRAEL WILL REJOICE, FOR THE RUTHLESS ONE WILL COME TO AN END, THE SCORNER WILL DESIST,]
3. [AND AL]L WHO WATCH FOR (AN OPPORTUNITY TO DO) EVIL [WILL BE CUT OFF,] THOSE WHO [BY A WORD CONDEMN A PERSON, WHO LAY A SNARE FOR THE ONE REPROVING AT THE GATE.]
4. [WHO TURN ASIDE A RIGHTEOUS ONE WITH GROUNDLESS ARGUMENTS.] THEREFORE, THUS S[AYS YAHWEH TO THE HOUSE OF JACOB, WHO REDEEMED]
5. [ABRAHAM, "NEVER AGAIN WILL] JACOB [BE ASH]AMED [AND NEVER AGAIN WILL HIS FACE GROW PALE, FOR WHEN HE SEES HIS CHILDREN,]
6. [THE WORK OF MY HAND, IN HIS MIDST THEY] WILL SANCTIFY MY [N]AME, AND [THEY] WILL RE[VERE THE HOLY ONE OF JACOB]

Fragment 20

1.].[
2.]. . . .*yw* .[
3.].*htb*. ʾ.[
4.]it *by*[

Fragment 21

1. [ ]*t*. [ ]
2. [Lebanon is reckoned .[ ]
3. [ ]*l* to Carmel, and they returned .[ ]
4. [ ]. by the sword, as[ ]
5. [ ]*ṣ.m* . .[ ].[ ]
6. [ ] . . . *yn*[ ]the Teacher[ ]
7. [AND IT WAS BROKEN ON THAT DAY, AND] THEY [KNEW] THEREFORE, THE POOR OF THE FLOCKS WHO [WATCH] Zech 11:11
8. [ME, THAT] IT WAS [THE WORD OF YAHWEH.]
9. [WOE TO REBELLIOUS CHILDREN!—ORACLE OF] YAHWEH—IN MAKING A PL[AN THAT IS NOT] Isa 30:1-5
10. [MINE, AND ENTERING AN ALLIANCE,] BUT NOT (OF) MY SPIRIT, SO THAT THEY A[DD SIN]
11. [UPON SIN, IN SETTING OUT TO GO] DOWN TO EGYPT, AND N[OT ASKING] MY OPINION,

12. [IN TAKING REFUGE IN THE PROTECTION OF PHARAOH AND SEEKING SAFE]TY IN THE SHADOW OF EGY[PT, BUT FOR THEM]
13. [THE REFUGE OF PHARAOH WILL BE A SHAME, AND SEEKING REFU]GE IN THE SHADOW OF EGYP[T WILL BE AN INSULT, FOR]
14. [HIS OFFICERS ARE AT ZOAN; AND HIS MESSENGERS] REACH HANES. EVERY[THING TURNS TO SHAME]
15. [ON ACCOUNT OF A PEOPLE WHO DO NOT BENEFIT THEM, NEITHER] FOR H[EL] P NOR FOR [PROFIT]

Fragment 22

1.]The interpretation of the passage[
2.]*m* who walked[
3.] the sons of Zadok [
4. and whe]n it says, GRAIN, THE PRO[DUCE OF THE SOIL, AND IT WILL BE FAT 30:23
5.].*ʾm* it (?) [
6.]. .*l*[

Fragment 23, Column i

16. [ ].
17. [ ]*bʿṣ*
18. [ ] . .

Fragment 23, Column ii

1. [ ].*yw* . . . . [ ]. all .[ ]. *h*.[ ]
2. [ ]*hb*. .*l*.[ ]. .[ ].[ ]
3. [FO]R TH[U]S SAYS YAHWEH, THE HOLY ONE OF ISRAEL: "WITH RETURN AND R[ES]T [YOU WILL BE SAVED,] 30:15-18
4. [IN QU]IET AND IN TRUST WILL BE YOUR STRENGTH." BUT THIS YOU WOULD NOT HAVE; YOU [SAID:]
5. "NO! FOR ON HORSEBACK WE WILL FLEE." THEREFORE, YOU SHALL FLEE INDEED! "ON SWIFT STEEDS WE WILL RIDE." AND SWIFT SHALL
6. YOUR PURSUERS BE! A THOUSAND BEFORE THE THREAT OF ONE, BEFORE THE THREAT OF
7. FIVE YOU SHALL FLEE, UNTIL YOU ARE LEFT LIKE A FLAGSTAFF ON A MOUNTAINTOP,
8. AND A STANDARD ON A HILL. YET THE LORD WAITS TO BE GRACIOUS TO YOU AND RISES UP TO

9. BE MERCIFUL TO YOU, FOR YAHWEH IS THE GOD OF JUSTICE. BLESSED ARE ALL WHO WAIT FOR HIM!
10. The interpretation of the passage with regard to the end of days concerns the congregation of the S[eekers-After-]Smooth Things
11. who are in Jerusalem ... *h*.[ ]
12. in the Law, but (they did) not *yh*[ ] . . [ ]
13. heart, for to trample .[ ]
14. AS THE RAI[DERS] LIE IN WAIT FOR ONE, [A BAND OF PRIESTS *wʾt*] Hos 6:9a (?)
14a. they have rejected the Law
15. F[O]R, O PEOPLE IN ZION, [WHO DWELL IN JERUSALEM, YOU SHALL SURELY WEEP NO MORE. HE WILL INDEED BE GRACIOUS TO YOU AT THE SOUND OF] Isa 30:19-21
16. YOUR CRY. WHEN HE HEAR[S, HE WILL ANSWER YOU. THOUGH THE LORD GIVE YOU THE BREAD OF TROUBLE AND THE WATER OF OPPRESSION,]
17. [YOUR TEACHER] WILL NO LON[GER] HIDE HIMSELF. [YOUR EYES WILL SEE YOUR TEACHER,]
18. AND YOUR EARS WILL H[EAR A WORD BEHIND YOU, SAYING, "THIS IS THE WAY; WALK IN IT]
19. WHEN YOU WOULD TURN [TO THE RIGHT OR TURN TO THE LEFT."]
20. concerning the transgression of .[ ]

Fragment 23, Column iii

7. ʿ[ ]
8. *l*[ ]
9. *y*.[ ]

Fragment 24

1.] on the mountain of Ya[hweh
2.] who said [

Fragment 25

1. [ ]. the king of Babylon .[ ]
2. [ ].[ ] on the tambourine and on the ly[re]
3. [rain and] thunder, the instruments of battle. They are[ ]
4. [ ] (*vacat*) [ ]
5. [WOE TO THOSE WHO GO DOWN] TO EGYPT. [THEY RELY] ON HORSES [AND THEY TRUST IN CHARIOTS—] 31:1
6. [F]OR THEY ARE MANY—AND IN HORSEMEN—FOR

THEY ARE [VERY] STRONG, [BUT THEY DO NOT LOOK TOWARD]
7. [THE HO]LY ONE OF ISRAEL, NOR DO THEY [SEEK] YAHWE[H]
8. [ ] . . . . who tr[ust].[ ]

Fragment 26

1.]*yqr*[
2.]foolishness[
3.].*lh* [

Fragment 27

1.]the times *h*. [
2.]*k* the people and ʾ[
3.] ʿ*h* your cattle[

Fragment 28

1.]Egypt [
2.]*kw* who (?) *y*[
3.]. . [

Fragment 29

1.].*w* he wept (?) [
2.]*lh* sh[e (?)
3.]*mh* The interpretation of it[

Fragment 30

1.]. ʾ*t*
2.]*h bk*ʾ*l*
3.]the Wicked [Pr]iest (?)
4.]it
5.]*b*. the ki[n]gs of

Fragment 31

1.] it will be [
2.] humanity [
3.]*ym* ʿ*š*.[
4.]*w* taking possession[
5. 1]and [

Fragment 32

1.]. [
2.] precious things [
3.].*d* . . [
4.]. .[

Fragment 33

1.] *t*.[
2.]*rm* [
3.].[

Fragment 34

1.] .*m* [
2.] *l*.[
3.] *w*.[

Fragment 35

]*b* thi[s

Fragment 36

1.]*m* [
2.]*t*ʿ*w* [
3.]water [
4.]coming .[
5.]. ʾ*lyh*[

Fragment 37

1.].*r* [
2.].*m*.[
3.] not[
4.] *š*.[

Fragment 38

1.]ʾ*m* .[
2.] . .*d*.[

Fragment 39

1.]*kmtm*[
2.]*šlt*.[

Fragment 40

1.]Assyria[
2.]*r lhzʿ*.[

Fragment 41

1.]*t h*.[
2.] all [

Fragment 42

1.].*h*.[
2.]*dh* [
3.] . .[

Fragment 43

1.].*y*.[
2.]*mh*[
3.]*bb*.[

Fragment 44

1.] . . . [
2.].ʾʾ.[
3.].. *tš*[
4.] in all (?) .[

Fragment 45

1.]. *m*[
2.]priest (?) [
3.] *š*.[

Fragment 46

1.] . [
2.] .*zrm*[
3.] Teacher (?) [
4.] *hhm*[
5.] *b*ʾ. [
6.]*šbt*[

Fragment 47

1.]he broke .[
2. a]s it is writt[en

Fragment 48

1.].[
2.].*g*.[
3.] ʿ*t* [

Fragment 49

1.] . . . .[
2.]days in[
3.]*l*[

Fragment 50

1.] . . .[
2.] *l*ʾ . . . [

Fragment 51

1.] .[
2.] . .[
3.] *sn*.[

Fragment 52

1.] . . .*ḥ*[
2.] . .*qy*[

Fragment 53

]*khw*[

Fragment 54

] *šl*[

Fragment 55

] *kns*.[

Fragment 56

].ʿ*b* they snorted (?) [

Fragment 57

] Hor the mountain . . . *hkl*

Fragment 58 (Strugnell's IIIe)

]therefore, thus [

Fragment 59 (Strugnell's IIIf)

1.]. *wzptw*[
2.]*mh b*.[
3.] . . [

Fragment 60 (Strugnell's IIIg)

1.] . . [
2.]*b w*.[
3. [holy[
4.]the hand . . [
5.] . . [

Fragment 61 (Strugnell's IIIh)

1.] . . [
2.].*m*. [
3.]*h*.[

4QpIsa^c: Notes

Fragment 1

1:2 The letter preceding *hwʾh,* which Allegro does not identify, is almost certainly ʾ, and a trace of the first letter of the word following *hwʾh* is visible, possibly also ʾ. This, then, may be the introductory formula *kyʾ hwʾh ʾšr ʾmr,* which is used in 1QpHab (3:2; 3:13-14; 5:6) to introduce the second citation of a biblical text; see further Part II, p. 243.

1:3 A trace of the first letter of the word following *drk* is visible.

Allegro notes a possible connection between the two words preserved in this line (*wblʿ drk,* "and he confused the way of") with Isa 3:12 (*wdrk ʾrḥtyk blʿw,* "and they confuse the course of your paths").

1:4 Though the reading is not at all certain, I follow Allegro in restoring the formula *kʾšr ktwb,* "as it is written." This formula does not occur elsewhere in the pesharim (cf. *wʾšr ktwb* in 4QpIsa^e 1-2:2), but it is attested in 1QS 5:17; 8:14, 4QFlor 1-2 i 2, 12; CD 7:19; cf. *ʾšr ktwb* in 4QFlor 1-2 i 15, 16. If Allegro's suggested restoration is correct, the formula continues "concerning him in Jere[miah]," which might indicate that there was a secondary citation from Jeremiah; see the comments above on this feature of 4QpIsa^c.

in Jeremiah (*byr*[*myh*]). This might be an elliptical expression for "in (the book of) Jeremiah," cf. 8-10:8 *bspr zkryh,* "in the book of Zechariah," or it could be translated "by Jeremiah," cf. Jn 6:45, ἔστιν γεγραμμένον ἐν τοῖς προφήταις.

Fragment 2

Allegro places frgs. 2 and 3 together; however, too little is preserved of frg. 3 for positive identification. Strugnell suggests that frg. 3 perhaps belongs to the semi-formal hand of the majority of the frgs., while frg. 2 is clearly from the cursive group. These frgs. are transcribed separately here.

2:1 There seem to be few traces of letters visible on frg. 2 above the first line transcribed by Allegro. They are thus designated as line 1, and the rest of the lines have been renumbered accordingly.

2:2-4 In lines 2-4, the restoration of the text has been adjusted, giving a better line length and a more accurate vertical alignment than the transcription in the *editio princeps.*

2:3 Strugnell reads *wᶜl*]*h,* with the *h* doubtful, as the first partially preserved word of the line, but in the photograph in the *editio princeps* I can see no trace of a *h.*

2:4 The apparent citation of Isa 8:8 may offer the following variant from the MT: *wh*]*yw* (MT and 1QIsa^a: *whyh*).

2:5 In this line Allegro reads *htrh hyʾ rṣyn rᶜ*[*w.* He translates the first three words as "the Torah is Rezin," and he suggests that *rᶜw* "be evil" may be the beginning of the citation of Isa 8:9. He regards the phrase "the Torah is Rezin" as a pesher on Isa 8:6, but this reading is impossible. Moreover, it is hard to imagine a context in which an Essene commentator would identify the Torah with Rezin, who, as king of Damascus in 735 B.C., allied himself with Pekah of Israel and attacked Judah (2 Kgs 15:37; 16:5-9).

I agree with Strugnell that *rᶜ*[*w* at the end of the line is impossible; he suggests possibly *wbn* [*rmlyhw,* "the son of Remeliah," referring to Isa 8:6.

2:6 There seems to be a trace of a letter visible under the *w* of *ṣ.w* in line 5, but it was not transcribed by Allegro.

2:7 Before *wlʾ,* Allegro reads a final *m,* but I agree with Strugnell that *h* is more plausible.

Fragments 4, 6-7, Column i

Allegro takes frgs. 4-7 as one group, but his placement of frg. 5 is based on questionable readings (see further below, frg. 5). Frgs. 4, 6-7 form two cols., and the lines in col. i have been numbered here to correspond to those in col. ii, rather than independently as Allegro numbered them. The two fragmentary cols. seem to contain the text of parts of Isaiah 9—10, but satisfactory restoration of the biblical text with accurate vertical alignment is impossible. There are unusual signs in the margin between the cols., but their significance is unknown (see Allegro's description and comments in *Qumrân Cave 4,* p. 19).

4, 6-7 i 4 *as it is written* ([*k*ʾ*šr*] *ktwb*), see also 1:[4]; 2:[6]; 6-7 ii 18; 8-10:[8]; 47:[2]; and see the note above on 1:2. A space should be indicated in the transcription before *ktwb*.

4, 6-7 i 5 There might be a trace of a letter of line 5 visible on a little part of frg. 6 that extends up on the right, and there is a trace of a letter after the *l*, which might be the top of the *l* in line 6.

upon them ([ʿ]*lyhmh*). If this reading is correct, it is an example of the preposition ʿ*l* with the long suffix *hmh*. Similar suffixal forms occur in 4QFlor 1-2 i 9, 16 (ʿ*lyhmh*) and 11QMelch 6 (*lhmh*).

4, 6-7 i 6-7 For line 6 I follow Allegro's reading, *y*]*śr*ʾ*l bkwl*, and restore the text of Isa 9:11. The trace of a letter, possibly the *t* of ʾ*t*, seems to be visible on the right edge of the frg. Strugnell suggests reading ʾ*l* instead of *bkwl*, but he admits that it is impossible to read the line with certainty. It is more likely that Allegro is on the right track, since Isa 9:13-16b seems to be correctly restored in lines 8-13 (Allegro's 4-7:5-10), but there are problems with lines 6 and 7. There is not enough room for all of vv 11-12 to be restored, and part of the biblical text must have been abbreviated or omitted. Moreover, there seems to be very little room for an interpretation of the biblical text. It is unclear how *whw*ʾ*h* at the end of line 7 fits syntactically, but it probably belongs somehow with the commentary. It appears to be hanging by itself, since the citation of Isa 9:13 probably starts at the beginning of the next line. Could *whw*ʾ*h* be a sort of abbreviated introductory formula for a quotation? There is no similar instance elsewhere among the pesharim.

In the group of letters preceding *whw*ʾ*h*, Allegro reads]*bw*ʿ, but the first letter is very doubtful, and the third might be better read as *r*.

4, 6-7 i 8 At the end of this line Allegro has]*m wbywm* ʾ*ḥd zqn*. It is impossible to read any of the letters in the first two words with certainty, but the present restoration of Isa 9:13 fits the visible traces. Strugnell restores the line similarly and is able to read *w*ʾ*g*]*mwn*.

If this restoration is correct, the citation of Isa 9:13 presents the following variant from the MT: *bywm* (MT: *ywm*, but cf. 1QIsa^{a}, which also has *bywm*).

4, 6-7 i 12-15 Though Allegro treated lines 12-13 (his numbers 9-10) as blank lines, they probably contained the text of Isa 9:16c-d. In fact, part of a letter seems to be visible at the end of line 12, and there may be a trace of a letter at the end of line 13. The citation could have been followed by a short commentary section that continued through line 15.

At the end of line 14 Allegro reads]*bštm*. Strugnell regards this as impossible but proposes no alternative.

4, 6-7 i 15-17 This is where Allegro places frg. 5 (his lines 12-14), but the present restoration of Isa 9:17-20 excludes this positioning of frg. 5, which is thus transcribed separately.

4, 6-7 i 16-21 It is almost certain that the citation of Isa 9:17-21 constituted the text of these lines; however, restoration according to the MT leaves a puzzling variation in the length of the lines.

4, 6-7 i 16 *and enkindles* (*wtṣyt*). Although the reading is not certain, it appears that the form of 4QpIsa[c] is the hiph., while the MT and 1QIsa[a] have the qal (*wattiṣṣat*). The meaning is the same.

4, 6-7 i 17 A trace of the *ṣ* of *ṣbʾwt* seems to be visible.

is blackened (?) ([*nt*]*ʿm*). This is also the reading of 1QIsa[a], but the MT has *neʿtam.* KB lists the form under the root *ʿtm* but suggests that *ntʿh* be read in Isa 9:18, which would have to be the niph. part. fem. sing. of *tʿh,* "to be led astray." W. L. Holladay accepts the reading *nʿtm* and derives it from *nwʿ,* "to quiver" (qal perf. 3rd pers. sing. fem. with an enclitic *m*). (See *A Concise Hebrew and Aramaic Lexicon of the Old Testament Based upon the Lexical Work of Ludwig Koehler and Walter Baumgartner* [Grand Rapids: Eerdmans, 1971] 287, under the root *ʿtm;* he follows W. L. Moran ["The Putative Root *ʿTM* in Is. 9:18," *CBQ* 12 (1950) 153-54].) Neither Allegro nor Strugnell comments on the form in 4QpIsa[c], which is here taken to be the nithpael perf. 3rd pers. sing. masc. of *ʿmm,* "to be black" (the nithpael is a reflexive-intensive formation that occurs in later Hebrew; see GKC §55k 9; Beer-Meyer, Vol. II, §70 3h; Bauer and Leander §38s). Though this meaning fits the context well, if *ʾrṣ* is to be restored as the subject, the verb would be expected to be fem. in form.

4, 6-7 i 18 In the transcription in *Qumrân Cave 4, ʾyš* should have been preceded by a bracket ([).

4, 6-7 i 19 The last word of the line is completely unclear on the photograph. In the MT of Isa 9:19 the phrase is *wĕlōʾ śābēʿû,* "but they are not satisfied." Allegro reads *yšbt,* which he translates "will cease (?)" (the question mark is his), and he comments that the reading may originally have agreed with the MT but that a heavy *t* was written over the last two letters of *śbʿw.* Strugnell, however, sees the last letter not as a *t* but as a *b,* and he reads *yśb*[*ʿ*. Though the last letter is illegible, the visible traces seem to exclude reading *b.* Moreover, the top of a *b* is visible before the last letter.

4, 6-7 i 20 A trace of a letter is visible before *ʾprym.*

4, 6-7 i 21 Allegro's placement of frg. 4 at the beginning of this line is possible, since the word *yḥdyw* is clear on the frg. and fits the citation of Isa 9:20. But this is the only word preserved on the frg., so the identification cannot be verified.

In the transcription no space should be indicated before *šb.*

4, 6-7 i 22 ff. The col. probably continued on with the text of Isa 9:20 and may have gone into Isaiah 10. What is preserved of col. ii gives Isa

10:12 as the first lemma, and this citation is probably the first line of the col. It seems very unlikely that all of Isa 10:1-11 would have appeared in col. i. This would have required at least fourteen lines for the biblical text alone, making a col. of at least thirty-five lines; see the note on 6-7 ii 1-3, and see the comments above on the structure of this document.

Fragment 5

Allegro positions this frg. as part of lines 15-16 (his numbers 12-14) of col. i of frgs. 4, 6-7. This identification is based on his reading]*h šmyr*[(=Isa 9:17) in line 2 and]*wt* ᶜ*šn*[(=Isa 9:17) in line 3. His reading of line 2, however, is impossible. The *h* can be clearly read, but the *š* is incorrect as is also probably the final *r*. Strugnell, too, regards Allegro's reading of *šmyr*—and consequently the identification of the frg.—as very doubtful.

5:2 *he will kill* (*ymyt*), or possibly *ymwt,* "he will die."

Fragments 6-7, Column ii

6-7 ii 1-3 Lines 1-2 belong to frg. 7 and are almost certainly part of the citation of Isa 10:12-13. Allegro places this frg. directly over the second col. of frg. 6 and reads the first line of frg. 6 (my line 3) as the continuation of this citation, *wbḥkmt*]*y ky*ᵓ[(Isa 10:13). Strugnell, however, regarding *ky*ᵓ as an impossible reading, suggests that line 3 (i.e., the first line of frg. 6) is part of the citation of Isa 10:19, *wn*ᶜ]*r ykt*[*bm*. His suggestion may be correct in view of the fact that the next citation (line 10) is that of Isa 10:20. Thus, if Allegro's arrangement were adopted, Isa 10:14-19 would have to be omitted. Strugnell would move frg. 7 up in order to make room for these verses and a commentary. It was seen above in col. i that if the biblical text of Isa 9:20bβ—10:11 were to be included at the end of the col. at least fourteen lines would have to be added to the bottom, and therefore also to the bottom of col. ii, making cols. of at least thirty-five lines so far. Now, if frg. 7 is moved up to allow enough space for the text of Isa 10:14-19, at least eight more lines are required for the biblical material alone, giving cols. of at least forty-three lines. This seems too long, and I suspect that some of the biblical text was omitted. The text of Isa 10:1-11, 13-19 is an oracle against Assyria, interrupted by 10:12, which is an editorial comment. This makes 10:1-11 look like a unit by itself, and the Qumran commentator may have taken 10:12 as the beginning of a new section. It seems to me more likely, therefore, that 10:1-11 would have been omitted rather than 10:14-19, since the continuity of the text would not have been seriously disrupted. If the text of Isa 10:1-11 was omitted, col. i would have ended with Isa 9:20, perhaps followed by a brief commentary. This would reduce the length of the cols. to an acceptable thirty lines.

If this reconstruction of col. ii is correct, one further difficulty should be noted. There is here, as elsewhere in the document, a puzzling variation in the length of the lines. Lines 1 and 2 as restored are considerably longer than the rest of the lines in the col.

6-7 ii 1 In the transcription no space should be indicated after *ybṣʿ*.

I will avenge ([*ʾpqwd*]). The 1st pers. form of the verb is restored in agreement with the MT and 1QIsaª, but cf. the emendation suggested in *BHS,* the 3rd pers. form *ypqwd,* "he will avenge," and the Greek ęριavei.

6-7 ii 2a-h If the text of Isa 10:13c-19a is to be included as was suggested above, there must have been at least eight lines between what is preserved on frg. 7 and the first line of frg. 6.

6-7 ii 3 I follow Strugnell and restore Isa 10:19b.

6-7 ii 4 *region* (*ḥbl*). This is Allegro's reading, and it is better than Strugnell's suggestion *hm*[*w*]*n*. For the meaning "region," see Deut 3:4, 13; 1 Kgs 4:13.

6-7 ii 5 After *ʿmym* Allegro transcribes *h*[.]*t*.[, but it is misleading to use brackets after the *h*—especially with a trace of a letter indicated within the brackets—since there are traces of two or three letters visible before the break.

6-7 ii 6 *to deal treacherously* (*lbgwd*). The first letter of the first word is unclear; Strugnell suggests the impf. *ybgwd,* "he will deal treacherously," with the *y* doubtful.

6-7 ii 7 In the transcription there should not be an indication of a space after *ʾmr.*

6-7 ii 8 *the interpretation of it concerns "the few"* (?) *of humanity* (*pšrw lmʿwṭ hʾdm*), cf. *pšrw lmwʿṭ* [*hʾdm* below in line 17. Since the immediate context of both these phrases is lost, the translation and meaning are uncertain. In biblical Hebrew there is a verb *mʿṭ,* "to be few," and a noun *mĕʿaṭ,* "a little," "a few." The noun is treated as a qatl type by Bauer and Leander, but it is noted that this is an Aramaizing form and that the root form is unknown (§61j′). Elsewhere in QL the only noun form that occurs is *mwʿṭ,* apparently a qutl type, in *byn rwb lmwʿṭ,* "whether great or small" (1QS 4:16; similarly 1QSa 1:18); and *lmwʿṭ,* "at least" (CD 13:1) In later Hebrew, the noun forms *mĕʿaṭ* and *mûʿaṭ* occur. Both of the forms that appear in 4QpIsaᶜ, *lmʿwṭ* and *lmwʿṭ,* could represent the same segolate noun, and the difference in spelling could be either a scribal error or, more likely, an example of the fluctuation of segolate forms in Qumran Hebrew. A parallel fluctuation can be seen with the biblical Hebrew noun *lahab,* "flame," or "blade," which appears as *lhwb* in 1QH 2:26; 3:30; 4QpNah 3-4 ii 3, but as *lwhb* in 1QM 5:7, 10; 6:2 (see further M. H. Goshen-Gottstein, "Linguistic Structure," 127, §§51-52).

If this explanation of the forms is accepted, there remains the problem of translating the phrase. Both of the biblical texts that are apparently interpreted by the phrase (Isa 10:19; 10:22) contain the word *šĕʾār,* "remainder." In 10:19 it is the "rest of the trees" in the forest of Assyria, and in 10:22 it is the "remainder" or the "remnant" of Israel. The word *mʿwṭ* is probably a pesher on *šʾr,* and so I translate it "the few." The preposition *l* is taken here as the signal of the topic of the interpretation, i.e., "the interpretation of it concerns 'the few' of humanity," cf. the possible parallels *pšr hdbr lʾḥryt hymym l-* in 4QpIsa[b] 2:1 and *pšr hptgm lʾḥryt hymym l-* in 4QpIsa[a] 2-6 ii 26. In this case the function of the *l* is the same as that of *ʿl* in other pesher formulas; see further Part II, p. 240. Or the preposition could indicate the group at which the interpretation is directed, i.e., "the interpretation of it with regard to 'the few' of humanity [concerns," with the *l* functioning as it does in the formula *pšr hdbr lʾḥryt hymym,* "the interpretation of the passage with regard to the end of days."

6-7 ii 10 In the transcription there should be no indication of a space after *hhwʾh.*

6-7 ii 12 A trace of the *r* of *yśrʾl* seems to be visible on the right edge of the frg., and a trace of the *r* of *šʾr* on the left edge.

6-7 ii 14 *the interpretation of the passage with regard to the end of days* (*pšr hdbr lʾḥryt hymym*), see also below 23 ii 10; 4QpIsa[b] 2:1 and Part II, p. 240. For the translation "end of days," see the note above on 1QpHab 2:5-6.

6-7 ii 15-17 Following Strugnell's suggestion, I restore a second citation of Isa 10:22a-b here.

6-7 ii 15 *the returnees of Israel* (*š[by yśrʾ]l*). This phrase occurs also in 4QpHos[a] 1:[16-17] and 4QpPs[a] 1-10 iv [24], cf. *šby hmdbr* in 4QpPs[a] 1-10 iii 1, and see the note below on 4QpHos[a] 1:16-17.

The top of the *l* of *yśrʾl* seems to be visible beneath the *r* of *lʾḥryt* in line 14.

6-7 ii 17 See the comments above on line 8; Allegro reads *myʿṭ* here.

6-7 ii 18 The citation of Isa 10:22b is introduced by the formula *kʾšr ktwb;* see the introductory comments above.

In the transcription there should be an indication of a space after *ktwb.*

6-7 ii 19 A trace of the *ṣ* of *ṣbʾwt* is visible on the left edge of the frg.

Fragments 8-10

According to Allegro, frgs. 8-10 preserve the biblical text of Isa 14:8 (lines 1-3), 26-27 (lines 4-7), 28-30 (lines 11-14) and commentary; apparently Isa 14:9-25 is omitted. Strugnell notes the possibility that line 1 is a pesher on Isa 14:22-25 with a second citation of 14:8.

8-10:1 Since there is so little space following *bbl* before the apparent citation of Isa 14:8, this line is probably the end of a commentary, rather than the beginning as Allegro suggests (he restores [*pšr hdb*]*r* ᶜ*l*).

the king of Babylon (*mlk bbl*). Here I follow Strugnell; Allegro reads *klh bbl,* "the destruction of Babylon." The biblical text that is being interpreted—whether it is 14:8 as Allegro suggests, or possibly 14:22-25 as noted by Strugnell—is part of the oracle against Babylon (Isa 13:1—14:32). That Babylon may have been significant in the history of the Essenes should be considered in the light of J. Murphy-O'Connor's thesis regarding the origins of the sect ("The Essenes and Their History," *RB* 81 [1974] 215-44); see above, p. 7, n. 16. Unfortunately, the Qumran author's interpretation is entirely lost.

8-10:2 In the transcription there should be an indication of a space after *m*ʾ*z*.

8-10:3 The apparent citation of Isa 14:8 presents the following variant from the MT: ᶜ*lymw* (MT and 1QIsaᵃ: ᶜ*lynw*).

Following the citation of Isa 14:8 an interpretation begins. It is not introduced by a formula using the word *pēšer,* but it seems to be a figurative identification of the terms *hbrwšym w*ʾ*rzy lbnwn,* "the cypresses and the cedars of Lebanon," similar in structure to 1QpHab 1:[13]; 12:3-5, 7; 4QpIsaᵃ 7-10 iii 9, [10], [12] (Allegro's 8-10:5, 6, 8); 4QpNah 1-2 ii 3, 7; 3-4 i 10-12; 3-4 ii 1; 3-4 iii 9; 4QpPsᵃ 1-10 iii 12, cf. 4QpIsaᵇ 2:6, 10 (?); 4QFlor 1-2 i 2, 3, 11, 12, 16, 17. See further Part II, p. 242.

8-10:4 At the beginning of the line, Allegro is able to read]*lbnwn,* but the traces on the photograph in the *editio princeps* are illegible. After *w*ʾ*šr* ʾ*mr,* only the tops of letters are visible. Allegro reads *zw*ʾ[*t,* while Strugnell prefers *zwt*[. In the light of *wzw*ʾ*t* in line 5, Allegro's reading is probably better.

In the pesharim the formula *w*ʾ*šr* ʾ*mr* is generally used to introduce second citations of a biblical text; see Part II, p. 243. It would seem then, that 14:26 must have been quoted previously, apparently before 14:8. Otherwise the formula is being used here simply to introduce a biblical text for the first time, as *k*ʾ*šr ktwb* is used elsewhere in this document.

8-10:4-5 I restore ᶜ*l* at the beginning of line 5 rather than at the end of line 4 as Allegro suggests.

8-10:7 After *hw*ʾ*h* (or *hy*ʾ*h*) Allegro reads *m.*[, but nothing is clear from the photograph in the *editio princeps.*

In this line another interpretation seems to begin without any introductory formula using the word *pēšer,* cf. above line 3.

8-10:8-10 Line 8 apparently begins with the formula *k*ʾ*šr kt*]*wb bspr zkryh mp*[*y* ʾ*l,* "as it is written in the book of Zechariah from the mouth of God." A citation from Zechariah would be expected to follow, but Allegro treats lines 9-10 as though they were blank. It is more likely that these lines contained some text that cannot be read because of the poor state of preservation of these papyrus frgs. In fact, there seem to be some traces of letters visible on the first two lines of frg. 10, which gives the last half of lines 9-10, and on the left side of line 10 of frg. 8. For similar intrusions of secondary citations from or allusions to other biblical books, see above 1:[4]; 21:[7-8]; 23 ii [14]. See further the introductory comments to this text.

from the mouth of God (*mpy* [*ʾl*]). This is restored in the light of 1QpHab 2:2-3.

A trace of a letter is visible after the *p* in line 8 at the left edge of frg. 8.

8-10:11 At the end of the line Allegro reads *tš*]*mḥy,* but a trace of the *š* is visible.

8-10:12 I suggest the following revisions in the transcription: (1) *kw*]*lk* for Allegro's *k*]*wlk;* (2) no indication of a space after *šbṭ*; (3)]*nḥš yṣ*[ʾ for Allegro's *n*] *ḥš y*[*ṣ*ʾ.

8-10:13 The tops of at least two letters are visible before *mʿwpp* along the lower edge of frg. 9. Allegro reads the trace of a letter after *mʿwpp* as a *b* and restores *b*[*kwry* from the biblical text, commenting that *wrʿw* must have been omitted. That letter, however, is not at all clear, and it could just as well be a *w,* in which case the citation would correspond to the MT. If a *b* is read, however, perhaps the words of the MT were transposed, a possibility noted by Strugnell, and *bdwry dlym yrʿw* could be restored. If *wrʿw* is omitted entirely, the line is not filled.

8-10:14 Allegro reads the visible traces at the end of the line as *wš*]ʾ*ryt* [*k,* but this makes the vertical alignment unsatisfactory.

he (or *it*) *will slay* (*yhrwg*). This word cannot be read with any certainty. This 3rd pers. form is also that of the MT, but 1QIsaᵃ has the 1st pers. ʾ*hrwg,* "I shall slay," which makes better sense and might possibly be read here.

Fragment 11, Column i

This col. apparently preserves part of a commentary section, since there seem to be no biblical verses that fit the visible traces of letters.

11 i 1 Allegro reads]*b*[. . .].*m*.

11 i 2 Perhaps this part of the commentary is related to Isa 19:9 (*wbšw ʿbdy pštym,* "those who work in flax will be in despair").

11 i 3 There is a trace of a letter visible on the right edge of the frg.

11 i 4 Allegro reads].*ṣyh* . . . . Strugnell's suggestion of *hṣyḥym* could fit the visible traces, but he neither explains nor translates the form. I translate "the dried up (things)," see Isa 5:13.

11 i 5 Compare the full writing of *wzw*ʾ*t* above in 8-10:5.

Fragment 11, Column ii

11 ii 1 *grew pale* ([*ḥwrw*]). Allegro reads *ḥwry* in agreement with the MT *ḥôrā*(*y*), but this form is a problem. The form restored here, i.e., *ḥāwērû,* is the conjectured qal perf. of *ḥwr*; it is also apparently the reading of 1QIsa[a].

its weavers ([*štwtyh*]). The form is restored as in the MT (*šātōte*[*y*]*hā*) —another form that is a problem in the MT—but cf. *šwtthy* in 1QIsa[a].

11 ii 2 *the wise men of* ([*ḥkmy*]). The form is restored according to the MT, which has *ḥakĕmê,* but cf. *ḥkmyh* in 1QIsa[a].

11 ii 3 Allegro reads ᶜ[*ṣh,* but Strugnell rightly notes a trace of the *ṣ* before the break.

sons of the wise ([*bny ḥkmym*]). The pl. cs. form *bny* is restored rather than the sing. *bn* as in the MT and 1QIsa[a] in the light of the parallel variant *bny ml*[*ky qdm*] in line 4, cf. the Greek υἱοὶ συνετῶν ἡμεῖς, υἱοὶ βασιλέων τῶν ἐξ ἀρχῆς.

11 ii 4 *we are sons of ancient kings* (*ʾnw bny ml*[*ky qdm*]). The pl. cs. form *bny* is read here by both Allegro and Strugnell rather than the sing. *bn* of the MT and 1QIsa[a]. If the pl. is the correct reading, there is a difficulty with Allegro's reading of the preceding word as the sing. personal pronoun *ʾny* in agreement with both the MT and 1QIsa[a]. I therefore follow Strugnell in reading the pl. *ʾnw,* though this is not certain. The biblical Hebrew form for the 1st pers. pl. personal pronoun is *ʾănaḥnû; ʾănû* occurs once as the *kĕtîb* in Jer 42:6. In QL both forms, *ʾănaḥnû* (e.g., CD 20:29) and *ʾănû* (e.g., 1QM 13:7, 12), occur. In Mishnaic Hebrew *ʾănû* is the regular form.

I read *ml*[*ky* for Allegro's *m*[*lky.*

11 ii 5 I read *lkh*[*wy*]*d*ᶜ[*w* for Allegro's *l*[*kh wyd*ᶜ*w.*

Fragment 12

This frg. is extremely difficult to read. Except for the following revisions Allegro's transcription is reproduced here. In lines 5-7 Allegro notes a possible connection with Isa 28:16 (*ʾbn*) and 28:17 (*lmšqlt*). He might be correct in relating this to Isaiah 28; further support might be *.dy* in line 3, cf. *mdy* in Isa 28:19, and [*k*]*whnym* in line 6, cf. *khn* in Isa 28:7.

12:4 Allegro reads]*wytr,* but a trace of a letter is visible before this word.

12:5 There should be an indication of a space before *hʾbn.*

12:6-8 Allegro indicates that the frg. breaks off after *wʾ* in line 6, *w* in line 7, and *ṣwh* in line 8, but the frg. extends on, and there are traces of letters visible in all three lines, though most of the text has been obliterated.

12:7 There is a trace of a letter visible on the right edge of the frg. before *lmšqlt.*

12:8 Allegro restores *k*ʾ]*šr.*

12:9 Allegro reads] *rʿwt h*[, but the first letter is better read as a *b* or a *k*.

Fragment 13

In this frg. line 4 is the only line that is clear on the photograph in the *editio princeps.* There is room at the top of the frg. for another line, which was not indicated by Allegro; it could be a blank line or the top margin, but there seem to be traces of letters visible. This is designated here as line 1, and the rest of the lines have been renumbered accordingly. According to papyrologist Dr. John Barnes (see *Qumrân Cave 4,* p. 21), frg. 13 belongs in a vertical plane with frg. 15.

13:3 (Allegro's 13:2) Allegro reads]*ky* at the beginning of the line, but this does not seem to fit the visible traces of letters.

For the next word Allegro reads *hrḥqwt,* which is by no means a certain reading; he translates it "distant," but he does not comment on the form. Is it *hārōḥăqôt,* a fem. pl. part. of *rḥq,* "those who are far away," or possibly an abstract formation *hāraḥăqût* (?), "distance"?

13:4 (Allegro's 13:3) A space should be indicated in the transcription after *ʿl.*

Fragment 14

Regarding frg. 14, Allegro refers again to Dr. John Barnes, who suggests that the frg. belongs in a vertical plane with frg. 16.

14:2 I agree with Strugnell that Allegro's reading of *hymym* for the second word is impossible. Strugnell suggests *wbpny*[or *wbmw*[; the latter fits the visible traces of letters better.

14:3 Allegro's reading]*hwʾ ʾbdn* .[is not entirely satisfactory, but the traces on the photograph are too faint to read. If the personal pronoun is intended, the form *hwʾh* would be expected as in 1:2.

14:5 Strugnell's suggestion, *kpyr,* is better than Allegro's reading, *kprm.*

14:6 Allegro reads *ʾtrw.,* but the *t* is not certain. Perhaps either *ʾḥrwn* or *ʾḥryt* could be read.

14:7-8 The space after *npšw* in line 7 could indicate that this is the end of a commentary section, which may be supported by the fact that line 8 appears to be blank.

Fragments 15-16

These frgs. apparently contain the text of Isa 29:10-11, but the interpretation is entirely lost. Allegro's restoration of the biblical text has been revised in order to even out the lines.

15-16:2 In the transcription there should be no indication of a space before *ksh.*

15-16:3 The apparent citation of Isa 29:11 presents the following variant from the MT: *spr* (MT: *hspr,* cf. 1QIsa[a], which has *spr* with *h* added above the line).

15-16:4 Allegro does not transcribe the traces of letters that are visible on the lower edge of frg. 15; Strugnell reads them as *l*[*w*ʾ] ʾ[*wkl,* but according to the present restoration of the line they might be *k*]*y*ʾ *ḥ*[*twm.* For the last line of frg. 16, Allegro reads] *ḥtwm hw*ʾ[, but Strugnell thinks that it is better to read *hs*[*pr* than *hw*ʾ. I agree with Strugnell in reading the second word, but a trace of the *p* is also visible on the photograph.

Fragment 17

17:1 Allegro reads]*r*ʾ*nw,* but there is room for]*rw*ʾ*nw,* though the visible traces of letters are inconclusive. Compare 1QIsa[a], which has *r*ʾ*nw* with a *w* or a *y* added above the line. Strugnell accepts Allegro's reading, noting that this would be the perf. form rather than the sing. masc. part. as in the MT. In the light of this he restores the parallel verb form *yd*ʿ*nw* in the next phrase rather than the part. *yôd*ʿ*ēnû* as in the MT; see also *yd*ʿ*nw* also in 1QIsa[a].

17:2 Allegro reads]*m*ʿ*śh*[, but there should be an indication of a space after the *h,* and it seems that there is a trace of the *l* visible on the left edge of the frg.

Fragments 18-19

These two frgs. give the last lines of a col.; the bottom margin is visible on both frgs. The text of Isa 29:18-23 can be restored with fair certainty, but the present arrangement of the lines differs from Allegro's. The commentary is entirely lost.

18-19:1 In the transcription Allegro indicates with dots that only traces of letters appear, but I agree with Strugnell that the text of Isa 29:18 is not incompatible with these traces.

18-19:3 Allegro reads *kwl*] *šwqdy,* but there is a trace of the *l* of *kwl* visible on the right edge of the frg. (so also Strugnell).

18-19:5 In the transcription there should be no indication of a space after *y*ʿ*qwb.*

18-19:6 In the transcription there should be no indication of a space before *yqdyš*[*w.*

Fragment 20

Regarding frg. 20, Allegro comments (*Qumrân Cave 4,* p. 22), "This fragment is placed by Dr. Barnes 'almost certainly' on a line with f. 16 which would put it into the following column and thus part of a *pēšer* on Isa 30:1-5 (f. 21): note *ml*ʾ*kyw* in l. 2 and in Isa 30.4." I agree with Strugnell, however, that the reading *ml*ʾ*kyw* is impossible. Thus, the placement of the frg. must be abandoned.

20:2 Allegro reads *pšrw*] ʿ*l ml*[ʾ]*kyw w*[. Strugnell rejects Allegro's reading of the line, but does not offer an alternative suggestion. The only clear letters on the photograph are *yw*.

20:3 For the first word, Allegro reads]. *hmh,* and Strugnell suggests]*whmh*. The first *h* is certain, and there are one or two letters before it, but the next two letters do not look like *mh;* perhaps *tb* can be read.

20:4 I agree with Allegro's reading, *by,* though Strugnell regards the *y* as impossible.

Fragment 21

21:1 Allegro reads a trace of only one letter in this line, but there seem to be two letters partially visible and the first may be a *t*.

21:2-3 These lines may be related to Isa 29:17 (*wšb lbnwn lkrml whkrml ly*ʿ*r yḥšb,* "and Lebanon will be turned to an orchard, and the orchard will be regarded as a forest").

21:2 Although there is a hole in the frg., a trace of the *b* of *hlbnwn* is visible.

21:3 At the end of the line Allegro reads *h* [, but the vertical strokes that are visible could also be *w, z, ḥ, y,* or *t*.

21:4 I read *k*ʾ*šr* for Allegro's *w*ʾ*šr*.

21:5 A trace of a letter is visible beneath the *š* of *k*ʾ*šr* in line 4.

21:6 Though Allegro indicates only a couple of letters at the beginning of the line, there are traces of several letters visible.

21:7-8 Here, as above in 1:4 and 8-10:8 and below in 23 ii 14, there is apparently a secondary citation or allusion. These lines seem to contain the text of Zech 11:11, but it is unlikely that the verse appeared exactly as in the MT, since it does not fill the lines satisfactorily.

21:7 A trace of the final *w* of *wyd*ʿ*w* is visible before *kn;* this is noted also by Strugnell.

21:9-15 The apparent allusion to Zech 11:11 must have been considered as part of the interpretation rather than as a separate lemma, since it is followed immediately by the citation of Isa 30:1-5. When the text of Isa 30:1-5 is restored according to the MT, the length of the lines and the vertical alignment are not entirely satisfactory.

21:11 There are traces of letters visible after *mṣrym*.

21:12 A stroke of the *w* is visible before the *t* of *wlḥswt*.

21:14-15 Strugnell lines up the biblical verses differently, making *bṣ*ʿ*n* the first word in line 14, and *yw*ʿ*ylw* the first word in 15.

21:14 In the transcription there should be no indication of a space before *ḥns*.

21:15 I read the visible traces of letters as]*l*[*ᶜz*]*r wlw*ʾ *l*[rather than as Allegro reads them,] *wlw*ʾ [; Strugnell suggests *lw*ʾ]*l*[*ᶜzr*].

Fragment 22

Allegro notes that in the opinion of Dr. Barnes frg. 22 probably lies on a horizontal plane with frg. 23 (see *Qumrân Cave 4,* p. 23).

22:2 *who walked* (*ʾšr drk*). Allegro reads *ʾšr drš,* "who sought," but the last letter is probably a final *k*. The lower part of it is visible next to the *q* in line 3.

22:3 *sons of Zadok* (*bny ṣdwq*); see 1QS 5:2, 9; 9:14 (*hṣdwq*); 1QSa 1:2, 24; 2:3; 1QSb 3:22; 4QFlor 1-2 i 17; CD 3:21—4:1; 4:3. In the transcription spaces should be indicated before *bny* and after *ṣdwq*.

22:4 Following Strugnell, I restore Isa 30:23 with the introductory formula *wʾšr ʾmr;* it cannot be determined, however, whether this is a first or a second citation.

The apparent citation of Isa 30:23 presents the following variant from the MT: *lḥm* (MT and 1QIsa[a]: *wlḥm*). Allegro reads *lhm,* "to them."

22:6 Allegro reads *bl*[.

Fragment 23, Column i

23 i 17 The ᶜ is written above the line.

Fragment 23, Column ii

23 ii 1-2 These lines apparently end a commentary section.

23 ii 1 Strugnell regards Allegro's reading,]*m whmy* .[, at the beginning of the line as doubtful. The photograph is illegible, but it looks as if some of the letters of the word may have been deliberately crossed out.

23 ii 2 Allegro's reading, *yś*]*rʾl,* does not fit the traces of letters that are preserved.

23 ii 3-4 Allegro's transcription of line 3 indicates that the *y* and the first *h* of *yhwh* and the *y* of *yśrʾl* are not visible, but traces of all three letters are preserved, and probably also the *t* of *wnḥt*.

For the first word of line 4 Allegro reads *bhš*]*qt,* but I follow Strugnell, who is able to see a trace of the *š*.

The citation of Isa 30:15 presents the following variants from the MT: (1) *yhwh* (MT: *ʾdny yhwh,* cf. 1QIsa[a], which reads *yhwh* with *ʾdwny* written above the line); (2) *wbṭḥ* (MT and 1QIsa[a]: *wbbṭḥh*).

23 ii 6 Though there is a small hole in the frg., the *m* and *p* of the first *mpny* are partially visible, but Allegro reads [*mp*]*ny,* and Strugnell has [*m*]*pny*.

23 ii 7-8 The citation of Isa 30:17-18 presents the following variants from the MT: (1) *tnwswn* (MT: *tnsw,* cf. 1QIsa[a], which has *tnwsw*); (2) *hr*

(MT: *hhr,* but 1QIsa[a] also has *hr*); (3) *gbʿh* (MT and 1QIsa[a]: *hgbʿh*); (4) *ʾdwny* (MT and 1QIsa[a]: *yhwh*); (5) as the fourth word of line 8 Allegro reads *wlkn* in agreement with the MT and 1QIsa[a], but the correct reading is probably *lkn*.

23 ii 10 *the interpretation of the passage with regard to the end of days* (*pšr hdbr lʾḥryt hymym*). See the note above on 6-7 ii 14.

the Seekers-After-Smooth-Things (*d*[*wršy*] *hḥlqwt*). See the note on 4QpNah 3-4 i 2.

23 ii 11 *who are in Jerusalem* (*ʾšr byrwšlym*), cf. 4QpIsa[b] 2:6-7, 10.

Traces of letters are visible where Allegro indicates a lacuna after *byrwšlym*.

23 ii 13 *to trample* (*ldwš*). I follow Strugnell here; Allegro reads *ldrš,* "to seek," which is not impossible. In the preliminary publication he read *kyʾ lrwš*.

A trace of the first letter of the word after *ldwš* seems to be visible on the left edge of the frg.

23 ii 14-14a In line 14 Allegro restores the biblical text of Hos 6:9a, giving apparently a secondary citation or allusion similar to those in 1:4; 8-10:8; 21:7-8. Line 14 and the following line, designated as 14a by Allegro, are unusually close together, and it is likely that one of them is an interlinear addition. There is a problem, however, in determining which line is actually the addition. Judging from the average space between the lines in this col., line 14 looks like the addition. This would make sense also in terms of content; the phrase from Hos 6:9a could have been added as a gloss on the commentary, perhaps inspired by the verb *ḥkh,* "to wait for," in both Isa 30:18 and Hos 6:9a. However, the first word of line 14a, *htwrh,* seems to be indented, which could indicate that this line is the addition. Strugnell suggests that 14a is the addition, but that it was added to line 15, the citation of Isa 30:19. He suggests that the phrase was omitted through haplography: *kyʾ htwrh mʾsw kyʾ ʿm bṣywn.* But the phrase *kyʾ htwrh mʾsw* is part of an interpretation and not part of the biblical text. It seems to me unlikely that the commentary would end at the beginning of a line and be followed immediately by the next biblical citation; compare above where the citation of 30:15 begins line 3. I think it is better to take line 14 as the addition, an interlinear gloss on the commentary, but I cannot explain why line 14a is apparently indented.

23 ii 14 In the MT of Hos 6:9a the first word, *ûkĕḥakê,* is a problem. The allusion in 4QpIsa[c] has the form *kyḥkh,* apparently the piel impf. 3rd pers. sing. masc. This presents a difficulty if the line is restored according to the MT of Hos 6:9a, since the subject of this sing. verb would be pl.

23 ii 14a *they rejected the Law* ([*ʾt*] *htwrh mʾsw*), cf. 1QpHab 1:11; 5:11-12 (where it is said of the House of Absalom); 4QpIsa[b] 2:7-10 (where

it is said of the "Scoffers," *ʾnšy hlṣwn*). Here this might be the offense of the Seekers-After-Smooth-Things, who are the subject of the interpretation (see line 10).

23 ii 15 Carmignac thinks that the traces of letters could also be read as *ʿm ṣ[ywn] ywš[b]*.

In the citation of Isa 30:19 *byrwšlym* (so also 1QIsa[a]) is restored rather than *byrwšlm* as in the MT, cf. *byrwšlym* above in line 11. For the spelling of the name Jerusalem, see the note on 1QpHab 9:4.

23 ii 16 The citation of Isa 30:19 presents the following variant from the MT: *zwʿqkh* (MT and 1QIsa[a]: *zʿqk*). In biblical Hebrew the noun *zaʿaq* is a segolate, and the form in 4QpIsa[c] is probably an example of the preference in Qumran Hebrew for the qutl noun type in segolates. See the note above on 6-7 ii 8.

23 ii 19 The citation of Isa 30:21 presents the following variant from the MT: *tym[ynw* (MT: *tʾmynw,* cf. 1QIsa[a], which has *tyʾmynw*).

23 ii 20 Allegro reads the trace at the left edge of the frg. as ʿ.

Fragment 24

On the basis of a possible relation of Isa 30:29 (*bhr yhwh*), Allegro suggests that frg. 24 may belong immediately before frg. 25.

24:1 In the transcription there should be an indication of a space before *bhr.*

24:2 In the transcription there should be an indication of a space before *ʾšr.*

Fragment 25

25:2 I follow Strugnell's transcription of the second word rather than Allegro's (*wbknw*[), but the photograph is illegible.

25:2-3 These lines could be a commentary on Isa 30:50 (*npṣ wzrm*) and 30:32 (*btpym wbknrwt*). Strugnell points out that there is a trace of a letter from the beginning of line 2 visible above the *z* of *zrm* (line 3).

25:5 The citation of Isa 31:1 presents the following variant from the MT: *mṣrym* (MT and 1QIsa[a]: *mṣrym lʿzrh*).

In the transcription there should be no indication of a space before *mṣrym.*

25:7 Allegro indicates that the *d* of *qdwš* is partially preserved, but this is very doubtful.

25:8 For this line Allegro transcribes *pšrw*] *ʿl hʿm ʾšr yb*[*ṭḥw,* "the interpretation of it concerns the people who trusted." This is too long for the beginning of the line, and Strugnell regards *ʿl* as an impossible reading. At the end of the line Strugnell reads *ybṭ* [*ḥw.*

Fragment 26

Allegro restores the biblical text of Isa 32:5-6 in this frg., but his reading of line 3, *yhwh tw*] *ʿh,* is probably incorrect. Though the frg. may preserve part of a commentary on these verses, satisfactory restoration of the biblical text is impossible.

Fragment 27

In line 3 Allegro reads] . . *ḥsnkh*[and suggests a possible connection of this frg. with Isa 33:6. However, the letter that he reads as *s* is clearly *q*. I follow Strugnell in reading]*ʿh mqnkh*[; he suggests a relation to Isa 30:23, where the words *yrʿh mqnyk,* "your cattle will graze," occur. Perhaps this frg. belongs with frg. 22, though no direct join is evident.

Fragment 28

28:1 In the transcription there should be an indication of a space after *mṣrym.*

28:2 Allegro restores *pš*]*rw ʾšr y*[, but his reading of the first visible letter as *r* is doubtful.

Fragment 29

29:2 In this line I follow Allegro, but Strugnell suggests that the letter that is read as an ʾ could also be a *ḥ,* e.g., *hyḥ* [*d*].

29:3 Again I follow Allegro; Strugnell suggests that the letter that is read as a *p* is more likely a *n.*

Fragment 30

This frg. is almost completely illegible; Allegro's transcription is reproduced here. It appears that the left margin of a col. is visible.

Fragment 31

31:1 Allegro reads the second letter as *ḥ,* but a *h* is more likely; Strugnell suggests *yhwh.*

Fragment 32

There are traces indicating a line above the first line transcribed by Allegro. This is designated as line 1, and the rest of the lines have been renumbered accordingly.

32:3 (Allegro's 32:2) Allegro transcribes].*dt hʾ*[, but only the *d* is clear, and there seems to be no space between the letters that he reads as *t* and *h.*

32:4 (Allegro's 32:3) Allegro reads] ʾ[.

Fragment 33

33:1 In the transcription there should be an indication of a space before the *t* and a trace of a letter after it.
33:3 There seems to be a trace of a letter of a third line, but it is impossible to tell from the photograph in the *editio princeps.*

Fragment 34

34:1 In the transcription there should be an indication of a space after the *m*.
34:3 Allegro reads]*wp*[, but the first letter could be either *w* or *y*.

Fragment 36

36:2 In the transcription there should be an indication of a space after *tʿw*.
36:5 There is a trace of a letter visible at the right edge of the frg.
Allegro's reading, *ʾlyh*[, is followed here, but Strugnell thinks that the *h* is not certain.

Fragment 37

According to Strugnell, this frg. belongs with the other frgs. of the more "cursive" hand, i.e., frgs. 2, 45-49, and possibly frg. 44.
37:2 The letter that is read here as *m* could also be *ṭ*.

Fragment 38

38:2 Strugnell suggests reading]. *ṣdq*[.
There may be traces of another line at the bottom of the frg.

Fragment 39

39:1 I follow Strugnell's reading; Allegro has].*mhm*[.
39:2 Allegro reads]*šlšt*[.

Fragment 40

40:1 I follow Allegro's reading, but the *š* is not certain, and a space should be indicated after the *r*.

Fragment 41

41:1 There is a trace of a letter visible after the *h*.
41:2 With Strugnell I read]*kwl*[.

Fragment 42

42:2 There is no trace of a letter visible before the *d* on the photograph in the *editio princeps*.
42:3 There seem to be traces of a third line at the bottom of the frg.

Fragment 43

43:2 Allegro reads]*sh* [, but the line is better read as]*mh*[.

Fragments 44-49

According to Strugnell, frg. 44 may belong to the group of frgs. of the "cursive" script; frgs. 45-49 are surely from this group.

44:2 There may be a trace of a letter visible after the second ʾ, but it might be simply a dark spot on the edge of the frg.

44:4 There is a trace of a letter visible on the left edge of the frg. after the *l*.

45:2 The line is transcribed here as Strugnell suggests; Allegro reads]*nḥ*. [.

46:1 There seem to be traces of letters visible above the first line transcribed by Allegro. This is designated here as line 1, and the rest of the lines have been renumbered accordingly.

46:2 (Allegro's 46:1) Allegro reads]*ḥr m*[; Strugnell suggests]*zrm*[, noting that this may be part of a citation of Isa 4:6 with the following lines as part of the commentary.

48:2 The letter that Allegro reads as *g* could also be *t*.

49:2 Allegro's reading seems to be better than Strugnell's suggestion of]*wymwt*[.

49:3 There is a dot on the frg., which may be the top of a *l* in line 3.

Fragment 50

50:2 Allegro's reading,]ʾ *lʾwmy*[*m*, does not fit the visible traces of letters.

Fragment 52

52:1 Allegro reads].*ṣḥ* [, but Strugnell regards the *ṣ* as impossible.

Fragment 56

Allegro reads]*rʿb*, but as Strugnell points out, the *r* is not at all certain according to the photograph in the *editio princeps*.

Fragment 57

Allegro reads]*hwr hhr* . . *ʾwkl*[, but Strugnell suggests either]*hwr hhr thy hkl*[or]*hwr hhr wzh hkl*[.

Fragments 58-61

These frgs. were added to 4Q*163* by Strugnell; see *RevQ* 7 (1969-71) 259, pl. IIIe-h.

4QpIsa[d] (4Q*164*)

Editio princeps: "Commentary on Isaiah (D)" (J. M. Allegro), *Qumrân Cave 4,* Vol. I, pp. 27-28 and pl. IX.

Preliminary publication: J. M. Allegro, "More Isaiah Commentaries from Qumran's Fourth Cave," *JBL* 77 (1958) 215-21, esp. 220-21 and pl. III.

Secondary transcriptions and translations: J. Carmignac, *Les Textes,* 2. 74-76; A. Dupont-Sommer, *Essene Writings,* 276; A. M. Habermann, *Megilloth,* 173; J. Maier, *Die Texte,* 1. 189, 2. 166-67; F. Michelini Tocci, *I manoscritti,* 290; L. Moraldi, *I manoscritti,* 535-36; G. Vermes, *Dead Sea Scrolls in English,* 228-29.

Secondary literature: J. M. Baumgarten, "The Duodecimal Courts of Qumran, Revelation, and the Sanhedrin," *JBL* 95 (1976) 59-78; D. Flusser, "*Pšr yšᶜyhw wrᶜywn šnym ᶜśr hšlyḥym brʾšyt hnṣrwt* [The *Pesher* of Isaiah and the Twelve Apostles]," *E. L. Sukenik Memorial Volume* (*1889-1953*) (ed. N. Avigad *et al.;* Eretz-Israel 8; Jerusalem: Israel Exploration Society, 1967) 52-62; "Qumran und die Zwölf," *Initiation* (ed. C. J. Bleeker; Studies in the History of Religions [Supplements to *Numen*] 10; Leiden: Brill, 1965) 134-46; B. Gärtner, *The Temple,* 42-44; J. Strugnell, "Notes," 195-96; Y. Yadin, "Some Notes on the Newly Published *Pesharim* of Isaiah," *IEJ* 9 (1959) 39-42.

The text entitled 4QpIsa[d] (4Q*164*) in *Qumrân Cave 4* consists of three frgs.: two small pieces and one larger piece that preserves parts of eight lines and shows the top and right margins of a col. J. Strugnell places the script in the semi-cursive Hasmonean line with elements of the semi-formal vulgar Herodian style; he would date this text in the early Herodian period.

In what remains of this document the structure conforms to that of the other pesharim, with the biblical text of Isa 54:11-12 and its interpretation partially preserved. This portion of Isaiah describes the rebuilding of Jerusalem after the Babylonian captivity, and parts of the city are pictured as various precious stones. In the commentary, the author identifies the parts of the city with different groups in the structure of the Qumran community, e.g., the council of the community (*ᶜṣt hyḥd,* line 2), priests (*kwhnym,* line 2), the people (*hᶜ*[*m*], line 2), the congregation of his chosen ones (*ᶜdt bḥyrw,* line 3), the twelve (*šnym ᶜśr,* line 4), cf. 1QS 8:1-12.

Except in one partially restored instance in line 7, (*rʾšy šbṭy yśrʾl lʾ*[*ḥryt hymym*], "the heads of the tribes of Israel at the e[nd of days]"), there is no eschatological terminology preserved in this text. It is likely, however, that the interpretation refers to the New Jerusalem at the end of days. Reference to a group of twelve in this context has prompted studies on the relation of the eschatological community envisioned in 4QpIsa[d] to that described in Revelation 21 and the relation of a group of twelve in the structure of the Qumran community to the twelve apostles of Jesus (see the articles of D. Flusser and J. M. Baumgarten listed above).

The image of building, or of the community as the temple or house of God, occurs elsewhere in QL (e.g., 1QS 5:5-6; 8:5-6). It is also used in the NT (e.g., Matt 16:17-18; Eph 2:19-20; Rev 3:12); see further B. Gärtner, *The Temple,* 16-122; and G. W. MacRae, "Building the House of the Lord," *AER* 140 (1959) 361-76.

4QpIsa^{d}: Translation

Fragment 1

1. [ ]*k* all Israel like mascara around the eye. AND I SHALL ESTABLISH YOU AS LAPIS [LAZULI. The interpretation of the passage is] Isa 54:11c
2. [tha]t the council of the community was established [among the priests and the p[eople in the midst of]
3. the congregation of his chosen ones, like a stone of lapis lazuli in the midst of the stones [AND I SHALL MAKE (OF) RUBY (?)] 54:12a
4. ALL YOUR PINNACLES. The interpretation of it concerns the twelve [men of the council of the community, who]
5. give light by the decision of the Urim and Thummim[ ]
6. the ones that are absent from them, like the sun {{*l*}} with all its light. AND A[LL YOUR GATES AS STONES OF BERYL (?)] 54:12b
7. The interpretation of it concerns the heads of the tribes of Israel at the e[nd of days]
8. his lot, the offices of .[ ]

Fragment 2

1.]. and as for all of them, are they not [
2.]ᶜ.[ ]*wd* for to all[
3.]*l*[

Fragment 3

1.]*lm*[
2.]ᶜ.[

4QpIsa^{d}: Notes

Fragment 1

1:1 This line preserves part of the commentary on Isa 54:11b and part of the citation of 54:11 c.

like mascara around the eye (*kpwk bʿyn*). In the preliminary publication, Allegro read *kpwk bʿwk* (followed by Carmignac and Habermann) and translated the phrase with a question mark "all Israel like antimony they have sought thee." He identified *bʿwk* as a 3rd pers. pl. perf. of *bʿh* with a 2nd pers. sing. masc. sf., but he notes that the use of direct address would be unusual in a pesher document. In the *editio princeps* he has revised the reading to *kpyk bʿwk,* "all Israel sought thee according to thy word." Y. Yadin's reading of the two words as *kpwk bʿyn* (he refers to 2 Kgs 9:30 and Jer 4:30) is better and is regarded as certain by J. Strugnell.

Yadin restores the beginning of the interpretation as *pšrw ky yrby*]*ṣ kwl yśrʾl kpwk bʿyn,* "Its interpretation is that He will lay all Israel like antimony in the eye." I agree with Strugnell, however, that the first visible letter in the line should not be read as a final *ṣ,* because of the horizontal stroke that goes off to the left. Moreover, while Yadin's translation of *kpwk* as "antimony" fits the use of the word in Isa 54:11, it does not make sense here. What is the meaning of "antimony in the eye"? The biblical Hebrew word *pwk* is defined as either a black paint for the eye or a type of hard mortar. The Septuagint of Isa 54:11 uses the word ὁ ἄνθραξ, which refers either to charcoal or to a precious stone of red color such as ruby or garnet. The latter meaning is better suited to the context of Isa 54:11, where other precious stones are mentioned, but it does not fit the context of the interpretation.

Carmignac thinks that the word *pwk* in Isa 54:11 refers to a mortar composed of colored matter, but that in the Qumran commentary it refers to a rare stone more or less like marble. He translates the phrase "tout Israël T'a recherché [*bʿwk*] comme une pierre rare," but the reading *bʿwk* is incorrect. Without more of the context preserved the meaning cannot be determined with certainty, but the best definition of *kpwk* in the phrase *kpwk bʿyn* is probably "black paint for the eye" or "mascara." The Qumran author, therefore, is making a deliberate play on the two meanings of *pwk,* cf. the similar play on the two meanings of *šmš* below in line 6. Baumgarten follows Yadin's reading of the phrase (*kpwk bʿyn*) and suggests restoring either [*ysr*]*k* or [*yʿr*]*k* at the beginning of the line, "[he will ar]ray all Israel like antimony around the eye" ("Duodecimal Courts," 60-61, 63).

and I shall establish you as lapis lazuli (*wysdtyk bspy*[*rym*]). Following this apparent citation of Isa 54:11c, a formula such as *pšrw ʿl* or *pšr hdbr* should be restored to begin the interpretation. If the restoration of line 6 can be taken as an indication of the length of the lines in this col., the longer formula is needed to fill the space. Baumgarten suggests *pšrw ʿl* and a short substantive designating the founders of the community ("Duodecimal Courts," 61), but see the note on 1:2.

The text is not perfectly clear, but if the reading *wysdtyk* is correct, it agrees with the consonants of the MT; 1QIsa[a] has *wyswdw* with *tyk* added above the line.

1:2 *the council of the community was established among the priests and the people* (*ysdw ʾt ʿṣt hyḥd* [*b*]*kwhnym whʿ*[*m*]), literally, "they established the council of the community among the priests and the people." I follow Yadin in restoring [*b*]*kwhnym,* making the phrase parallel to *wysdtyk bspyrym* of the biblical text; Allegro, followed by Baumgarten, restores [*h*]*kwhnym*. There is not enough room for Habermann's restoration *ʿṣt hyḥd* [*hm h*]*kwhnym*.

While it is grammatically possible that the subject of the verb *ysdw* was named at the end of line 1, as Baumgarten suggests, it would be difficult in terms of content; the subject is the agent who establishes the council of the community. If the verb were sing., then God or the Teacher of Righteousness could be the subject, cf. 4QpPs[a] 1-10 iii 15-16 and CD 1:11, where the Teacher of Righteousness is the one established by God to build a congregation. It is hard to imagine what group might be named as those who founded the council of the community. It is impossible to tell whether *ysdw* is the qal, "they established," the conjugation of the MT of Isa 54:11, or the piel, "they appointed."

For the designation "the council of the community," see the note above on 1QpHab 12:4.

In 1QS 8:1 the council of the community is said to be composed of twelve men and three priests, which could support Allegro's reading *whʿ*[*m*], "and the people" following [*b*]*kwhnym* in this line (so also Baumgarten). Yadin restores *whʿ*[*ṣh hyʾ*], "and the Council, it is (the congregation of his chosen ones)," but this is too short for the space. Moreover, it is clear from 1QS 8:1 that the council was a group of at least twelve (see E. F. Sutcliffe, "The General Council of the Qumran Community," *Bib* 40 [1959] 971-83), while the congregation was a larger group of all those who observe the Law, probably the Qumran sect itself, cf. 4QpPs[a] 1-10 ii 1-5; 1-10 iii 3-6 [16]. Based on the length of line 6 as restored, there is room for about seventeen units at the end of line 2, in which one might restore a phrase describing the relationship of the council of the community to the *ʿdt bḥyrw,* "the congregation of his chosen ones." The phrase might be parallel to *kʾbn hspyr btwk hʾbnym* in line 3.

1:3 *the congregation of his chosen ones* (*ʿdt bḥyrw*). The form *bḥyrw* is here taken to be the defectively written pl. noun with the 3rd pers. sing. masc. sf. (*pace* Baumgarten, "Duodecimal Courts," 61); see the note above on 1QpHab 5:4.

1:3-4 At the end of line 3 the first words of Isa 54:12a are restored, though this does not completely fill the space. Baumgarten restores the formula *wʾšr ʾmr* to introduce the citation ("Duodecimal Courts," 60), but in the pesharim this formula regularly introduces a second citation or repetition of a portion of the biblical text. Although it is not impossible that this is a second citation, it seems to me very unlikely. In the citation I restore *kdkwd* with the full writing as it appears in 1QIsa^a rather than *kdkd* as in the MT. The first word in line 4, *kwl,* appears neither in the MT nor in 1QIsa^a.

It is uncertain what should follow the number "twelve" in line 4. The commentary section in lines 4-7 is a complex of images based on the description of the city of Jerusalem in Isa 54:11 and connected by elements involving the number twelve. In Isa 54:11 the city of Jerusalem, though not named, is implied and is described in terms of precious stones. In Ezek 48:30-34 the New Jerusalem is said to have twelve gates inscribed with the names of the twelve tribes of Israel. In Exod 28:15-30 the breastplate of the High Priest is described: on it are twelve precious stones inscribed with the names of the twelve tribes of Israel (see line 7 below), and within it are the Urim and Thummim (see line 5 below). In Rev 21:18-21 the New Jerusalem has for its foundation stones twelve precious stones as in Isa 54:11, and the city is said to have twelve gates inscribed with the names of the twelve tribes of Israel.

The interpretation that begins in line 4 probably does not refer directly either to the twelve foundation stones or to the stones of the breastplate, since the word *ʾbn,* "stone," is treated as fem. in Hebrew and would require *štym ʿśrh* as the form of the number twelve. Habermann restores *šnym ʿśr [šbṭy yśrʾl ʾšr hm]*, "the twelve tribes of Israel, who" (cf. line 7). Carmignac mentions as a possible restoration "douze chefs des prêtres," referring to 1QM 2:1 *rʾšym šnym ʿśr*. Baumgarten restores the line similarly, *šnym ʿśr [rʾšy hkwhnym ʾšr]*, "the twelve [chief priests who]" ("Duodecimal Courts," 61, 63). Yadin suggests *šnym ʿśr [hkwhnym ʾšr* (?)], "the twelve priests who," implying that this group is the same as that constituted in line 2. I agree that the group referred to here may be the same as that in line 2, but I restore *šnym ʿśr [ʾyš bʿṣt hyḥd ʾšr]*, "the twelve men in the council of the community, who" because membership in the council was not restricted to priests (see 1QS 8:1).

1:5 *give light* (*mʾyrym*). In the preliminary publication Allegro read *mʾwrym,* which he translated "luminaries," the pl. of *māʾôr*. Carmignac and Yadin objected to this reading, because they expected the pl. form to be fem. (*mʾwrwt*), but in biblical Hebrew the pl. is attested in both masc. and fem. forms.

by the decision of (*bmšpṭ*). This is read also by Yadin, Strugnell, Carmignac, and Baumgarten. Allegro reads *kmšpṭ,* but one need only compare the form of the *b* and the *k* in *bkwl* in line 6 to verify the present reading.

the Urim and Thummim (*hʾwrym whtwmym*). This phrase does not occur elsewhere in QL, but in 4QTestim 14 there is a quotation of Deut 33:8, "And of Levi he said, 'Give to Levi your Thummim, and your Urim to your pious one,'" cf. Lev 8:8; Num 27:21. Mention of these ancient divining instruments here is probably occasioned by the image of giving light (*mʾyrym* in line 5, *kšmš* in line 6) and the mention of precious stones.

1:6 *the ones that are absent from them* (*hnʿdrwt mhmh*). The form *hnʿdrwt* is here taken as the niph. part. pl. fem. of *ʿdr,* but *mhmh* is the pl. masc. form. Thus, whatever or whoever are absent are fem., while the group from which they are absent is masc. Yadin thinks that the use of the part. here is based on Zeph 3:5 and might refer to the stones of the Urim and Thummim. He suggests that *wʾyn hʾbnym* might be restored at the end of line 5. Baumgarten rightly criticizes this restoration as being too short, but his translation of Yadin's restoration (which he contends "yields no meaning") is incorrect. He translates "and the stones which are missing from them are *not* (?) like the sun in all its light," but Yadin's text should be translated "and there are no stones missing from them, like the sun. . . ." Baumgarten's solution is to look for another meaning for *hnʿdrwt.* The possibility that he suggests is that the root *ʾdr* was intended and that the form in 4QpIsa^{d} is an example of "the confusion of gutturals common in Qumran orthography" ("Duodecimal Courts," 62). He translates the form with a question mark "which shine forth." But the interchange of laryngals in Qumran Hebrew is not as common as Baumgarten seems to think (see M. H. Goshen-Gottstein, "Linguistic Structure," 107-108; and E. Y. Kutscher, *Isaiah Scroll,* 507), and there is no reason to assume that the form as it stands is in need of emendation.

like the sun (*kšmš*). After this word a *l* has been partially erased. As Carmignac points out (*Les Textes,* 2. 47), the appearance of the word *šmš* here meaning "sun" shows either that the Qumran commentator understood *šmšwtyk* of Isa 54:12 as "sun" rather than as "pinnacle," or that he was making a deliberate play on the double meaning of the word, cf. a similar play on the meaning of *pwk* in line 1 above.

At the end of the line Yadin restores Isa 54:12c (so also Carmignac), *wkwl gbwlk lʾbny ḥpṣ,* "and all your boundaries as precious stones," thinking that the letters *wk*[just before the break could not be part of Isa 54:12b, *wšʿryk lʾbny ʾqdḥ,* "and your gates as stones of beryl (?)." If 54:12c is preferred, then either 54:12b was omitted, or the clauses of verse 12 were not known to the Qumran author in the order of the MT. At the suggestion of J. Strugnell (followed also by Baumgarten), I restore 54:12b with the addition of *wkwl,* similar to the variant in the citation of 54:12a (line 4). The commentary in line 7 mentions the heads of the tribes of Israel, and it was pointed out above that in Ezek 48:30 the twelve gates of the New Jerusalem are inscribed with the names of the twelve tribes, cf. Rev 21:12. This supports the restoration of Isa 54:12b.

1:8 *his lot* (*gwrlw*). This word does not occur elsewhere in the pesharim, but it is frequent in 1QS, 1QM, and 1QH, where it refers to a member's position in the community (e.g., 1QS 2:23) or among the followers of Belial (e.g., 1QS 2:5, cf. 3:24), to one's predetermined position in the divine plan (e.g., 1QS 1:10; 2:17; 4:24), or to a judgment by the leaders of the community (e.g., 1QS 6:16, 18, 22; 9:7). Baumgarten reads the pl. cs. *gwrly,* which he translates as "their allotted stations," but the pl. of the word *gwrl* both in biblical Hebrew and in the Qumran documents (e.g., 1QS 4:26; 1QM 1:13) is fem., *gwrlwt*.

In the *editio princeps* Allegro transcribes the second word in the line as *mᶜmdy*[, but on the photograph a trace of the first letter of the next word is visible.

Fragment 2

2:1 The *h* of *hlwʾ* is written above the line.

2:2 For the first word, which Allegro reads as]. *ᶜmwd,* "stand," Strugnell suggests *ᶜwd,* "yet," with a trace of a letter before it. He comments that the two parts of the frg. were originally touching directly.

4QpIsa^e (4Q*165*)

Editio princeps: "Commentary on Isaiah (E)" (J. M. Allegro), *Qumrân Cave 4,* Vol. I, pp. 28-30 and pl. IX.

Secondary literature: J. Strugnell, "Notes," 197-99 and pl. II g.

The ten frgs. that J. M. Allegro identifies as 4QpIsa^e were not published in any preliminary form. To these frgs. J. Strugnell adds one previously unidentified frg. (frg. 11) that preserves parts of 5 lines. He describes the script of this document as "formal," belonging to the early Herodian period.

The frgs. of this commentary preserve portions of the biblical text of Isaiah 11, 14, 15, 21, 32, and 40. Only isolated words and letters of the interpretation remain, so that even the basic thrust of the commentary is lost.

4QpIsa^e: Translation

Fragments 1-2

1. *hn*[ ].*ʾw*.[ ]*šy*[ ]

2. and Jerusalem[ ]*d* and as for what is written, [HE WILL FEED HIS FLOCK LIKE A SHEPHERD,] Isa 40:11
3. the interpretation of the passage [concerns the Teacher of Righteousness, who] revealed the Torah of right[eousness. WHO HAS MEASURED THE WATERS IN THE HOLLOW OF HIS HAND,] 40:12
4. OR [MARKED OFF] THE HEAVENS WITH [A SPAN, OR HELD THE DUST OF] THE EARTH [IN A MEASURE,] WEIGHED [THE MOUNTAINS ON A SCALE OR THE HILLS IN A BALANCE?]

Fragment 3

1. THOSE WHO GO DOWN TO THE STONES OF] THE PIT LIKE A CORPSE [TRODDEN DOWN 14:19
2.]*ll*[

Fragment 4

1. [(THE ARMED MEN OF MOAB)] RAISE A CRY OF BITTERNESS AND [HIS SOUL TREMBLES AT IT. MY HEART CRIES OUT FOR MOAB. HER FUGITIVES (FLEE) TO ZOAR, EGLATH SHELISHIYAH, FOR BY THE ASCENT OF LUHITH] 15:4-5
2. THEY GO UP [IN] TEARS, [FOR ON THE ROAD TO HORONAIM THEY KEEP RAISING A CRY OF DESTRUCTION. The interpretation of the passage]
3. [ ]*b.l*[ ]

Fragment 5

1. [ ].ʾ.[O MY TRAMPLED AND THRESHED ONE, WHAT I HAVE HEARD FROM THE LORD OF HOSTS, THE GOD OF ISRAEL,] 21:10
2. [I RECOUNT TO YO]U. The interpretation of the passage with regard to [the end of days]
3. [AN ORACLE ABOUT DUMAH: SOMEONE CALL]S [TO ME] FROM SEIR, "WATCHMAN, WHAT OF THE [NIGHT, WATCHMAN, WHAT OF THE NIGHT?" THE WATCHMAN SAID, "MORNING COMES AND SO DOES NIGHT. IF YOU WILL INQUIRE, INQUIRE;] 21:11-15
4. [COME BACK AGAIN." AN ORACLE CONCERNING ARABIA:] YOU WILL SPEND THE NIGHT IN THE WOODLAND OF ARABIA, O C[ARAVANS OF DEDANITES. WHEN YOU ENCOUNTER THE THIRSTY, BRING WATER, O INHABITANTS OF THE LAND OF TEMA. WITH BREAD FOR HIM]
5. [MEET THE FUGITIVE, FOR]

5a. HE HAS FLED [FR]OM THE SWORDS,

5. [FROM] THE DRAWN SWORD,
5a. FROM [THE BENT BOW,]
5. FRO[M THE FURY OF BATTLE]
6. [ ]the peoples, and the bread [ ]
7. [ ]the despoiler ʿ[ ]

Fragment 6

1. [the ch]osen ones of Israel .[ ]
2. [ ]ever, and as for what is w[ritten, THE FOOL WILL NO LONGER BE CALLED NOBLE] 32:5
3. NOR WILL [THE KNAVE (?)] BE SAID (TO BE) MAGNANIMOUS, FOR A F[OOL SPEAKS FOLLY; HIS HEART PREPARES WICKEDNESS SO AS TO PRACTICE UNGODLINESS] 32:6-7
4. [AND TO SPEAK] ERROR [A]GAINST ‹YAHWEH› AND TO SL[AY THE HUNGRY, AND TO DEPRIVE THE THIRSTY OF DRINK]
5. [AND THE INSTRUMENTS OF HIS CUNNING (?) ARE EVIL.] HE ADVISED LEWD CONDUCT [TO RUIN THE POOR WITH DECEITFUL WORDS EVEN WHEN THE SPEECH OF]
6. [THE NEEDY WAS PR]OPER. The interpretation of it concerns[ ]
7. [ ]. the Torah[ ]*šr* .[ ]

Fragment 7

1.]*t* he will sa[y
2.] poor one[s
3.] and the instruments of[

Fragment 8

1. the ki]ng of Babylon, who *y*[
2. and as for wh]at is w[ritten

Fragment 9

1.]*mwty* the beginning of[
2.]who ruled in .[
3.]the men of the commun[ity
4.].*y*ʾ.[
5.]. .[

Fragment 10

1. .[
2. *nwy*.[
3. *tb*[
4. *šm*[

Fragment 11

1. [ ].[ ]
2. [ ]you become known (?) [ ]
3. [AND IT WILL HAPPEN ON THAT DAY THAT THE LORD WILL AGAIN] LIFT [HIS HAND TO REDEEM THE REM- 11:11-12a

NANT OF HIS PEOPLE WHO]
4. [ARE LEFT FROM ASSYRIA, AND FROM EGYPT, FROM PATHROS,] AND FROM ETHIOPIA [AND FROM ELAM AND FROM SHINAR AND FROM HAMATH]
5. [AND FROM THE ISLANDS OF THE SEA. AND HE WILL RAISE A STANDARD FOR THE NATIONS; HE WILL GATH-E]R [THOSE OF ISRAEL WHO ARE SCATTERED]

4QpIsa[e]: Notes

Fragments 1-2

1-2:1-2 Frg. 1 almost certainly shows the top and right margins of the col. In the first line Allegro restores *hn*[*b*]*wʾwt,* "the prophecies," which he presumes to be the title of the work. At the end of the line he restores [*ʾšr ḥzh ʿl yhwdh*], "which he saw concerning Judah," as a possible citation of Isa 1:1. I agree with Strugnell that this restoration is questionable. In frgs. 1-2, the first one and one-half lines must be part of a commentary. The only citation that is partially preserved is that of Isa 40:12 in lines 3-4.

Jerusalem (*yrwšlm*). See the note above on 1QpHab 9:4.

In the middle of line 2 the formula *wʾšr ktwb,* "and as for what is written," is preserved. Among the pesharim this formula is attested without doubt only here; it is restored below in 6:2 and possibly 8:2. The similar formula *kʾšr ktwb,* "and as it is written," occurs in 4QpIsa[c] 6-7 ii 18; 1QS 5:17; 8:14; 4QFlor 1-2 i 2, 12; CD 7:19, cf. *ʾšr ktwb* in 4QFlor 1-2 i 15 and *whmh ʾšr ktwb* in 4QFlor 1-2 i 16. See further Part II, p. 243. If this formula is used analogously to *wʾšr ʾmr,* i.e., to introduce a second citation of the biblical text, then a phrase from Isa 40:11 might be restored in line 2.

1-2:3 To be restored at the end of line 2 are the first words of Isa 40:12. Preceding the lemma, Allegro restores the introductory formula *wʾšr ktwb,* which is not impossible. The citation of Isa 40:12 is restored according to the MT, except for differences that would be expected in Qumran spelling, but the following variant is preserved: *šql* (MT and 1QIsa[a]: *wšql*). 1QIsa[a] contains several other variants from the MT (*myʾ, my ym, bzrtw, bšlyš, bmwznym*), but there is no way of knowing if they appeared in this text as well.

Fragment 3

3:2 The tops of two *l*'s are visible but were not transcribed by Allegro. Strugnell suggests restoring]*l*[ʿ]*l*[*m,* "forever," i.e., the defective spelling of *lʿwlm* (Isa 14:20). This would mean that the citation of Isa 14:19, part of which is preserved in line 1, might have continued through 14:20. This is possible, but *ʿwlm* is not spelled defectively elsewhere in the Qumran writings.

Fragment 4

If the restoration of line 1 is correct, this frg. is part of an unusually wide col., as is frg. 5.

4:1 The apparent citation of Isa 15:4-5 presents the following variant from the MT: *wnpšw* (MT and 1QIsa[a]: *npšw*).

4:2-3 Strugnell accepts Allegro's reconstruction, which continues the citation through Isa 15:6, restoring in line 3: *klh dšʾ*] *yrq lw*[ʾ *hyh,* "new grass dies and green plants are no more" (Strugnell prefers the spelling *lʾ*, cf. 6:3). The problem is that there is no space before the *l,* and so it cannot be the first letter of a word. Therefore, line 3 must be the continuation of a commentary begun in line 2.

Fragment 5

5:1 There are three letters partially preserved in this line. Allegro reads]. ʾ*r*[, but Strugnell suggests]*lʾr*[*ṣ,* the last word of Isa 21:9, and he proposes restoring Isa 21:9-10 in lines 1-2. This would fit the space, but I should expect the lower part of the final *ṣ* of *lʾrṣ* to be visible, and I should not expect the lower point of the *l* to extend down as far as the ʾ, cf. the *l*'s in 1:2; 8:1; 9:2. It seems to me more likely that the traces of letters in line 1 are part of a commentary section.

my threshed one (*bn grny*), literally, "my child of the threshing floor." This is restored according to the MT of Isa 21:10; 1QIsa[a] has *wbn gdry,* "child of my stone wall" (?).

5:2 In the transcription of this line, Allegro should have placed the formula *pšr hdbr* about five spaces to the left, giving the lines a better vertical alignment and reflecting the fact that there is space between the word partially preserved at the beginning of the line and the formula. He reads the formula as *pšr hdbr* ʿ[*l.* However, the letter just before the break is better read as *l,* and thus the formula is probably *pšr hdbr lʾḥryt hymym,* cf. 4QpIsa[b] 2:1; 4QpIsa[c] 6-7 ii 14; 23 ii 10.

The *h* that is visible at the beginning of the line must be the end of a citation, since it is followed by the beginning of an interpretation. I accept Strugnell's suggestion that it is the last word of Isa 21:10, *lkm*]*h* for *lkm* of the MT and 1QIsa[a].

5:3-5 These lines appear to contain the biblical text of Isa 21:11-15. When the entire text of these verses is restored according to the MT the lines are extraordinarily long, cf. 4:1 above, but they are of uniform length.

The citation is restored according to the MT; 1QIsa[a] differs in the following words: (1) *bʿyw* (1QIsa[a]: *bʿw*); (2) *ddnym* (1QIsa[a]: *dwdnym* or *dydnym*); (3) *htyw* (1QIsa[a]: *hʾtyw*); (4) *blḥmw* (1QIsa[a]: *blḥm*). The following variants from the MT are preserved in the text of 4QpIsa[e]: (1) *ndd* (MT: *nddw,* cf. 1QIsa[a], which has *ndd*); (2) *mpny qšt* (MT and 1QIsa[a]:

wmpny qšt); (3) *mpny kwbd* (MT: *wmpny kbd,* cf. 1QIsa[a], which has *wmpny kbwd*).

5:5a-5 Between lines 4 and 5 is an interlinear addition designated as line 5a. It is easy to account for a scribal error of omission, since Isa 21:15 has four short clauses, each containing the word *mpny.* Allegro comments that the scribe's eye jumped from *ndd* of 21:14d to the *ndd* of 21:15a (MT: *nddw*), and he later inserted verse 15a above the line. As Strugnell points out, however, this explanation is not entirely satisfactory. While it explains the interlinear addition of verse 15a, it does not take into account the fact that line 5a continues with another "*mpny*-clause" indicating that another of the clauses of the biblical text was omitted in the first writing. I reproduce Strugnell's transcription, using arrows as he did to indicate that there are two distinct scribal errors, each involving the haplography of *mpny.* Thus, there are two distinct interlinear additions. Strugnell thinks that the corrections are not the work of the first scribe but seem to have been made by a corrector in the scribal tradition of 4QpIsa[b].

5:6 Allegro restores *mdbr*] *hᶜmym,* "the wilderness of the peoples," cf. 4QpIsa[a] 2-6 ii [18] (Allegro's 5-6:2).

5:7 *the despoiler* (*šwdd*). Allegro restores *whšwdd*] *šwdd* ᶜ[*ly* ᶜ*ylm,* "the despoiler despoils. Go up O Elam," from Isa 21:2.

Fragment 6

6:1 Allegro reads the letter partially preserved just before the break as ᵓ.

6:1-2 These lines preserve part of a commentary section, probably followed by a citation introduced by the formula *wᵓšr ktwb;* see above 1-2:2. If the width of the col. can be judged from the restoration of lines 3-5, restoring Isa 32:5a in line 2 neither fills the line nor does it leave enough space for a commentary before the citation of 32:5b-7 in lines 3-5.

6:2-6 The citation of Isa 32:5-7 is restored according to the MT. In the following places the text of 1QIsa[a] is different: (1) *lᵓ yqrᵓ* ᶜ*wd* (1QIsa[a]: *lᵓ yqrᵓw* ᶜ*wd*); (2) *yᵓmr* (1QIsa[a]: *ywᵓmr*); (3) *wlbw y*ᶜ*śh* ᵓ*wn* (1QIsa[a]: *wlbw ḥwšb* ᵓ*wn*); (4) ᵓ*bywn* (1QIsa[a]: ᵓ*bywnym*).

6:4 A space was left for the tetragrammaton; it was probably to be added at a later time in paleo-Hebrew script. See the note above on 1QpHab 1:1.

and to slay (*wlhk*[*wt*] *n*[*pš*]), literally, "to smite the life of." Only *wlh* is clearly visible on the frg. before the lacuna. There is part of a letter after the *h,* which can only be *k, m,* or *p,* and thus, the reading of the MT and 1QIsa[a] *lhryq,* "to cause to lack," is excluded. Allegro reads the partially preserved letter as *m* and restores *wlhm*[*yt*], "and to kill." Strugnell reads a *k* and suggests either *wlhkryt,* "and to cut off," or *wlhkwt,* "and to smite." The verb *nkh* is used with *npš* in Lev 24:18 and Deut 19:6, meaning "to slay," and seems to me to be the better choice. Other possibilities include *wlhpyṣ,* "and to disperse," or *wlhpryd,* "and to separate," cf. the LXX, which has τοῦ διασπεῖραι, "to scatter."

6:5 On earlier photographs of this frg. Strugnell was able to see traces of letters before *hwʾh,* which he reads as *r*]*šʿ*[*ym,* "wicked," rather than *rʿym,* "evil" of the MT and 1QIsa[a]. He further notes that one might read *w*]*hwʾh* as in 1QIsa[a] rather than *hwʾh* as in the MT.

6:6 The commentary begins with the phrase *pšrw ʿl,* after which there is a break in the skin. After the lacuna a mark or part of a sign is visible, but I cannot identify it with any letter.

6:7 The *r* of]*šr*[is written above the line.

Fragment 7

Allegro suggests that this frg. might belong to the commentary begun in 6:6.

7:1 I follow Strugnell's suggestion of reading *ydb*[*r,* "he will say," which might connect the frg. with Isa 32:6.

7:2 Strugnell is able to read *ʿnwym,* with the *m* doubtful, but there is no trace of a *m* on the photograph in the *editio princeps.* This might be related to *ʾbywn* in Isa 32:7 (above line 6:[6]).

7:3 The visible letters could be]*bylw*[as read by Allegro, but according to Strugnell the second letter is certainly a *k.* He reads]*wkyly*[, "and the instruments of," suggesting that this might be an allusion to *wkly* in Isa 32:7 (above line 6:[5]). The same spelling is found in 1QIsa[a].

Fragments 8-10

These frgs. may possibly refer to some portion of Isaiah 14 or 39, where the king of Babylon is mentioned (14:4; 39:1, 7).

8:2 In this line it is possible to restore the introductory formula *wʾšr ktwb;* see above 1-2:1; 6:[2].

9:1 For the first word Allegro reads].*wty.* The letters are here read as *mwty,* which could be the pl. cs. of *mwt,* "the deaths of." Also possible is]*myty,* which might be part of the hiph. part. pl. masc. cs. of *mwt,* i.e., *mmyty,* "the killers of."

9:2 Cf. *ml*]*k bbl* in line 8:1.

9:3 *the men of the community* (*ʾnšy hyḥd*). This phrase does not occur elsewhere in the pesharim, but it is frequent in 1QS, e.g., 5:2-3, 15-16; 6:21; 7:20.

9:5 Traces of two letters are visible, the second of which Allegro reads as *k.*

10:1 There is a trace of a word visible in the line above the first line transcribed by Allegro. This is here designated as line 1, and the rest of the lines are renumbered.

Fragment 11

Strugnell has placed this previously unidentified frg. pertaining to Isa 11:11-12 with the group of frgs. that make up this document (see "Notes," 199 and pl. I g).

11:3 The citation of Isa 11:11 presents the following variant from the MT: *śʾt,* "to lift" (MT and 1QIsa[a]: *šnyt,* "second time"). This variant is reflected in the LXX, which has τοῦ δεῖξαι.

11:4 Strugnell reads *mptrw]s mkwš*[, with both words lacking the conjunction of the MT and 1QIsa[a]. It might be better to read]*wmkwš*[and to restore *wmptrws* preceding it.

4QpHos[a] (4Q*166*)

Editio princeps: "Commentary on Hosea (A)" (J. M. Allegro), *Qumrân Cave 4,* Vol. I, pp. 31-32 and pl. X.

Preliminary publication: J. M. Allegro, "A Recently Discovered Fragment of a Commentary on Hosea from Qumran's Fourth Cave," *JBL* 78 (1959) 142-47 [with a photograph of col. 2].

Secondary transcriptions and translations: J. Carmignac, *Les Textes,* 2. 77-80 (entitled 4Qp Os[b]); A. Dupont-Sommer, *Essene Writings,* 277-78; "Résumé des cours de 1969-70: Hébreu et Araméen," *Annuaire du Collège de France* 70 (1970-71) 399-414, esp. 411-13; J. Maier, *Die Texte,* 1. 189-90, 2. 167 (both entitled 4QpHos[b]); F. Michelini Tocci, *I manoscritti,* 259-62 (entitled 4Q p Os[b]); L. Moraldi, *I manoscritti,* 537-40; G. Vermes, *Dead Sea Scrolls in English,* 230.

Secondary literature: J. D. Amoussine, "Observatiunculae qumraneae," *RevQ* 7 (1969-71) 533-52, esp. 545-52; J. Strugnell, "Notes," 199-201.

In *Qumrân Cave 4,* the number 4Q*166* refers to a large frg. that preserves parts of two cols. of a commentary on Hos 2:8-14 (English 2:6-11). The text is designated 4QpHos[a], and 4Q*167,* the next text in *Qumrân Cave 4,* is designated 4QpHos[b]. In the preliminary publications of these two texts, the titles were reversed, i.e., 4Q*167* was designated 4QpHos[a] and 4Q*166* was entitled 4QpHos[b]. The resulting confusion is evident in the secondary works cited above. Those that appeared prior to the publication of the *editio princeps* refer to the two texts according to the designations of the preliminary publications, and most of the later works use the titles of the *editio princeps.*

In the preliminary publication, Allegro observes that the script of 4QpHos[a] is identical to that of 4QpPs[a]. Strugnell describes the writing as belonging to the "rustic semi-formal" school of the Herodian era. Subsequent to the preliminary publication, Allegro was able to join to the large frg. a small piece giving additional letters at the beginning of lines 11 and 12 in col. 1.

Like the other pesharim, this text quotes one or two biblical verses and then presents a brief commentary. The top, bottom, and right side margins of the second col. are clearly preserved, and restoration of the biblical text in 2:14-15 establishes the left side margin with certainty. There are about 35-40 units in a line, and nineteen lines in a col. Following two of the commentary sections are blank lines (1:14 and 2:7), but it is impossible to tell if these lines indicate any deliberate division in the text.

In what is preserved of the interpretation of the prophetic text, there are both eschatological and historical allusions. Though most of col. 1 is lost, the few phrases that are left seem to have an eschatological thrust, namely *qṣ mwᶜlm,* "the time of their infidelity" (1:9), *dwr hpqwdh,* "the generation of the visitation" (1:10), *qṣy ḥrwn,* "the times of wrath" (1:12). In the second col. there may be several clues to the historical background of the document: *mtᶜyhm,* "those who led them astray" (2:5), *rᶜb,* "famine" (2:12), *hgwʾym,* "the nations" (2:13, 16), *mwᶜdy hgwʾym,* "the appointed times of the nations" (2:16).

The text of Hos 2:8-14 is part of a section of sayings about the relation of Yahweh to Israel, picturing Yahweh as the husband and Israel as the unfaithful wife. In 4QpHosa the unfaithful ones are those who are led astray. In 1QpHab 10:9 the subject of the verb *tᶜh* is the One who Spouts the Lie (*mṭyp hkzb*), and similarly in 4QpPsa 1-10 i 26-27 (Allegro's 1-2 i 18-19) the Man of the Lie (*ʾyš hkzb*) is said to lead many astray. Those referred to in 4QpHosa 2:5, therefore, may be the followers of the Man of the Lie or the One who Spouts the Lie, though Dupont-Sommer ("Résumé 1969-1970," 413) and Amoussine ("Observatiunculae," 547) think that they are the Pharisees. In this text the famine is the affliction and destruction of those blind and confused ones who are led astray and lean on "the nations" for support, casting behind them the commandments of God, cf. 4QpIsab 2:1; 4QpPsa 1-10 ii 1; 1-10 iii 3, 4. In 4QpPsa 1-10 i 26-27, those who are led astray by the Man of the Lie will perish by the sword, by famine, and by plague, cf. 1QpHab 2:1-15. The famine mentioned in 4QpHosa could be a metaphorical famine as in Amos 8:11, but Dupont-Sommer ("Résumé 1969-1970," 413) thinks it is a reference to the great drought that preceded the arrival of Pompey in 63 B.C. According to Amoussine this is the drought referred to by Josephus in *Ant.* 14.2.1 §19-23, which was brought to an end by the prayers of Onias the Just.

While the authors who comment on this text agree that the general historical background is the end of the Maccabean period, the time of civil strife preceding the Roman takeover in 63 B.C., there is disagreement about the identification of "the nations." Dupont-Sommer (*Essene Writings,* p.

278, n. 1) argues that "the nations" refers to the Romans in their exchange of support with the High Priest Hyrcanus II. Carmignac and Amoussine, however, reject this identification on the grounds that the Romans would more likely have been referred to as the Kittim. Carmignac thinks that the "nations" are the Seleucids, on whom the unfaithful Jews leaned for support, and Amoussine identifies them as the troops of the Nabatean king Aretas, who came to the aid of Hyrcanus II; he refers to *Ant.* 14.2.2 §28 ("Observatiunculae," 550-52).

The reference to the appointed times of the nations alludes in some way to the calendaric differences between the Qumran sect and the Jews in Jerusalem. See the note above on 1QpHab 11:7.

The subjects of these historical allusions cannot be identified with certainty here, but future studies should include a detailed comparison of this text with 1QpHab 2:1-15; 4QpIsa^{b}, and 4QpPs^{a}, all of which contain similar phrases juxtaposed in the same way as they are in this text. The parallels in 4QpPs^{a} could be especially important in view of the fact that the manuscripts may have been written by the same scribe.

4QpHos^{a}: Translation

Column 1

1. [ ]
2. [ ]
3. [ ].*ṣwr*
4. [ ] and they were pleased with
5. [ ] but they went astray
6. [ ] (*vacat*)
7. [THEREFORE BEHOLD, I SHALL HEDGE] HER [WAY] WITH THORNS, SO THAT Hos 2:8a, c
8. [SHE CANNOT FIND] HER PATHS.[The interpretation of it is that with madness] and with blindness and bewilderment
9. [of mind]*r* and the time of their infidelity [ ]not
10. [for] they are the generation of the visitation
11. [ ] from *m*[ ].*y* [the e]nd
12. [of days to] be gathered in the times of wrath, for
13. [ ] (*vacat*)
14.]] (*vacat*)
15. [THEN SHE WILL SAY, "I SHALL GO AND RETURN TO MY FI]RST [HUSBAND,] FOR Hos 2:9b, c
16. [IT WAS BETTER FOR ME THEN THAN NOW." The interpretation of it is that] when the returnees [of Israel] return
17. [ ]*ṭ* . . *p* . .

18. [ ]
19. [ ]

Column 2

1. [SHE DID NOT KNOW THAT] I MYSELF HAD GIVEN HER Hos 2:10
THE GRAIN [AND THE WINE]
2. [AND THE OIL, AND] (THAT) I HAD SUPPLIED [SILVER] AND GOLD {{ . . . }} (WHICH) THEY MADE [INTO BAAL. The interpretation of it is]
3. that [they] ate [and] were satisfied, and they forgot God who [had fed them, and all]
4. his commandments they cast behind them, which he had sent to them [by]
5. his servants the prophets. But to those who led them astray they listened, and they honored them [ ]
6. and as if they were gods, they fear them in their blindness.
7. (*vacat*)
8. THEREFORE, I SHALL TAKE BACK MY GRAIN AGAIN IN 2:11-12
ITS TIME AND MY WINE [IN ITS SEASON,]
9. AND I SHALL WITHDRAW MY WOOL AND MY FLAX FROM COVERING [HER NAKEDNESS.]
10. I SHALL NOW UNCOVER HER PRIVATE PARTS IN THE SIGHT OF [HER] LO[VERS AND]
11. NO [ONE] WILL WITHDRAW HER FROM MY HAND.
12. The interpretation of it is that he smote them with famine and with nakedness so that they became a disgra[ce]
13. and a reproach in the sight of the nations on whom they had leaned for support, but they
14. will not save them from their afflictions. AND I SHALL PUT AN 2:13
END TO ALL HER JOY,
15. [HER] PIL[GRIMAGE,] HER [NEW] MOON, AND HER SABBATH, AND ALL HER FEASTS. The interpretation of it is that
16. they make [the fe]asts go according to the appointed times of the nations. And [all]
17. [joy] has been turned for them into mourning. AND I SHALL 2:14
MAKE DESOLATE [HER VINE]
18. [AND HER FIG TREE,] OF WHICH SHE SAID, "THEY ARE THE HIRE [THAT MY LOVERS HAVE GIVEN] ME."
19. AND I SHALL MAKE THEM A FOREST, AND THE W[ILD BEAST OF THE FIELD] WILL DEVOUR THEM.

4QpHos^a: Notes

Column 1

1:3 There is a trace of a letter visible before the *ṣ*. In the preliminary publication, Allegro had transcribed it] *ṣyr.* If the reading].*ṣwr* is correct, it could be a verbal form from *ṣwr* (I), "to confine," *ṣwr* (II), "to be hostile to," or *ṣwr* (III), "to shape." It could also be the substantive *ṣwr*, "rock."

1:4 *and they were pleased with* (*wyrṣw*). This form is translated as a form of *rṣh* (I). It could also be from *rṣh* (II), "to pay," or from *rwṣ*, "to run." It could be the impf. with a simple *w* or *w* conversive, which is operative elsewhere in this text, e.g., *wyškḥw* (2:3), *wykbdwm* (2:5), and possibly *wylwzw* (1:5). Since it is preceded by a space that is larger than the normal space between words, it may be the first word of a sentence.

1:5 *but they went astray* (*wylwzw*). The form is translated as the niph. impf. (with *w* conversive) of *lwz,* though it could also be qal (so apparently Dupont-Sommer, who translates it "et ils ont cédé" ["Résumé 1969-1970," 412]). Like the verb in line 4, the form could be the impf. with simple *w* or *w* conversive. This word, too, is preceded by an unusually large space and may be the first word of a sentence.

1:6 The commentary probably ended at the beginning of this line, and the second half of the line is blank.

1:7-8 In these lines Hos 2:8a is restored followed by 2:8c. Verse 2:8b must have been omitted. The width of col. 1 cannot be determined with certainty, but if it is the same as that of col. 2, then the text of Hos 2:8a does not fill the space at the beginning of line 7. Assuming that the line is, in fact, part of a citation and not part of a commentary, it must be concluded either that the beginning of the citation was indented, as for example in 4QpIsa^a 2-6 ii 10 (Allegro's 2-4:6), or that the text differs from the MT. Strugnell suggests restoring as in the MT *drk*]*k bsyrym,* "your paths with thorns," with the final *k* doubtful. I prefer *drkh bsyrym,* "her paths with thorns," an emendation suggested in *BHS,* cf. the LXX τὴν ὁδὸν αὐτῆς.

1:8-14 A commentary section begins in line 8 and continues presumably through part of line 13, the last part of which is blank. Line 14 seems to have been completely blank preceding the next citation, cf. below 2:7.

1:8 *with madness* ([*bšgʿwn*]). I follow Dupont-Sommer, Carmignac, and Strugnell, restoring this in the light of the parallel phrase in Deut 28:28. On the basis of the same text, I restore *lbb* at the beginning of line 9. See also Zech 12:4, where the three words *šgʿwn, ʿwrwn,* and *tmhwn* occur in the same verse. Dupont-Sommer restores the beginning of the interpretation in line 8 as follows, but he does not give the Hebrew text: ["L'explication de ceci, c'est qu'ils se sont égarés dans la folie] . . . " ("Résumé 1969-1970," 412).

1:9 The first letter that is partially preserved in line 9 could be *r* as read by Allegro, or possibly *d* or *h*.

and the time of their infidelity (*wqṣ mwʿlm*). The form *mwʿl,* "infidelity," which also occurs in CD 1:3, is a morphological variant of the biblical Hebrew form *maʿal,* which is well-attested elsewhere in QL; see e.g., *bqṣ mʿl yśrʾl,* "in the time of Israel's infidelity," in CD 20:23.

1:10 *they are* (*hm*), but cf. *whmh* below in 2:13.

the generation of the visitation (*dwr hpqwdh*), cf. 1QpHab 1:[2-3], *bʿt pqdt hʾrṣ* (4QpIsa^b 2:2), *ʿd mwʿd pqwdtw* (1QS 3:18, similarly 1QS 4:18-19), and *bqṣ hpqwdh* (CD 7:21, similarly CD 19:10). See the note above on 4QpIsa^b 2:2.

1:11 The reading of this line is uncertain because there are two holes in the skin; the only clear letters are *mn m . . . ryt.* In the preliminary publication, before he identified the small frg. on the right side of the col., Allegro read *[d]wr ʾḥryt,* "the last generation" (similarly Dupont-Sommer [*Essene Writings*], Carmignac, Maier). In the *editio princeps* Allegro transcribes the visible traces as *mn m*[ ]*.r* [ ]*ryt,* but the letter after the first break, which he reads as a *r,* could also be a *y* or a *h.* In a later publication, Dupont-Sommer translates "depuis .[. . . .] . . .[la f]in (?) [des jours(?)]," restoring *hymym* at the beginning of line 12 ("Résumé 1969-1970," 412). Strugnell suggests *mn m*[*ḥzy*]*qy h*[*b*]*ryt,* "from those who hold fast to the covenant." If the reading *bryt* were correct, however, I should expect the lower horizontal stroke of the *b* to be visible extending over toward the *r,* perhaps even forming a ligature with it; compare the *b*'s in *wntybwtyh* (1:7), *wbtmhwn* (1:8), *bšwb šby* (1:16), and *ʿbdyw* (2:5). Moreover, when the hiph. of *ḥzq* means "to hold fast to" it is usually used with the preposition *b.* Otherwise I should expect the definite object sign *ʾt,* "those who support the covenant."

1:12 Following Dupont-Sommer, I restore *hymym* at the beginning of the line.

to be gathered ([*l*] *ʾsp*). Allegro translates *ʾsp* as "gather," apparently a qal form from *ʾsp,* but he does not explain the form further. Since *ʾsp* is not followed here by a direct object, it is probably better taken as a niph. form (so also Strugnell). It is true that the object could precede the verb (see below 2:[16]), but it would be awkward here. I restore the niph. inf. cs., which could appear either with the *h,* as *lhplh* in 1QpHab 7:8, or with the *h* elided as in *lnṣl* in 1QpHab 9:13. See the note above on 1QpHab 9:13.

in the times of wrath (*bqṣy ḥrwn*), cf. CD 1:5; 1QH 3:28; 1QH frg. 1:5.

1:15-19 Following Allegro, I restore Hos 2:9bβ-c in lines 15-16. Apparently 2:9a-bα was omitted, perhaps as Strugnell suggests through homoioteleuton; *tmṣʾ* is the final word of Hos 2:8 and also of 2:9bα. The citation was followed by a commentary that continued through the rest of col. 1.

1:16-17 *when the returnees of Israel return* (*bšwb šby* [*yśrʾl*]). The form *šby* is here taken as *šābê,* the qal part. pl. masc. cs. of *šwb,* rather than as the noun *šĕbî,* "captivity" (so Allegro, Dupont-Sommer [*Essene Writings*]). This part. could be translated literally "those who return," as it is here, or it could be translated figuratively "those who repent" (so apparently Dupont-Sommer ["Résumé 1969-1970," 412], who translates "les pénitents"). Carmignac also takes the form as the part. and translates the phrase "lors du retour des convertis de [la faute]," making reference to the use of *šwb* meaning "to repent" in Isa 59:20; 1QS 10:20; 1QH 2:9; 6:6; 14:24; CD 2:5; 20:17. H. Stegemann ("Der Pešer Psalm 37 aus Höhle 4 von Qumran [4QpPs37]," *RevQ* 4 [1963-64] 261, n. 150) translates *šby hmdbr* in 4QpPs^a 1-10 iii 1 "diejenigen . . . die zur Wüste umkehren." He interprets that phrase and *šby yśrʾl* here in 4QpHos^a as designations for the Qumran community insofar as they have turned from sin and returned to the Teacher of Righteousness.

Without rejecting the possibility that the figurative meaning "repent"—or even a double meaning—may have been intended by the Qumran interpreter, I have adopted the literal translation of S. Iwry (see "Was There a Migration to Damascus? The Problem of *šby yśrʾl,*" *W. F. Albright Volume* [ed. A. Malamat; Eretz-Israel 9; Jerusalem: Israel Exploration Society, 1969] 80-88, esp. 86-88). He argues that the phrase *šby yśrʾl,* which occurs also in CD 4:2; 6:5; 8:16; 19:29 and is generally translated "penitents of Israel," refers rather to an actual historical return of people from the Jewish settlement in Syria (*wygwrw bdmśq,* "who had sojourned during their exile in Damascus" CD 6:5), who returned to Israel when the political and economic climate seemed favorable under the Maccabees. This position is elaborated by J. Murphy-O'Connor ("The Essenes and their History," *RB* 81 [1974] 215-44), who believes that the Essenes originated among the Jews in exile in Babylon and that they returned to Palestine after the victories of Judas Maccabaeus, which began in 165 B.C.

See also *šby hmdbr* in 4QpPs^a 1-10 iii 1, cf. 1 Macc 2:29; *bšwbm mmdbr hʿ[my]m* in 4QpIsa^a 2-6 ii 18.

The visible traces of letters at the end of line 17 cannot be read with certainty. Allegro reads *ṭw*[ ].*pr* .[, and Carmignac suggests perhaps *ṭw*[*b*]*ym,* "bo[n]s." Strugnell rejects Carmignac's reading and offers *ṭḥ*[*w*]*rym* with the *ḥ* and *r* doubtful. However, he does not translate the word, so it is impossible to tell if he intends the noun "hemorrhoids."

Column 2

2:1 I agree with Carmignac and Strugnell that the lacuna at the beginning of the line is too short for the first four words of Hos 2:10. Either the first word, *whyʾ*, stood at the end of col. 1, or this text varies from the MT, perhaps by the omission of *whyʾ*, which is not syntactically necessary in this clause.

2:2 The citation of Hos 2:10 presents the following variant from the MT: *hrbyty* (MT: *hrbyty lh*).

After *wzhb* a word of two or three letters has been erased. The diagonal stroke visible just to the left of the *b* of *zhb* can only be part of a *l*, an ʿ, or a *š*, and the last letter may have been a *h*. Strugnell tentatively suggests that the scribe began to write *wzhb* a second time, but this does not fit the traces of the first letter.

2:2-6 At the end of line 2 a commentary probably began, continuing through line 6. Line 7 is blank.

2:3 *they ate and were satisfied* (*ʾkl*[*w wy*]*śbʿw*). Following Strugnell's suggestion, I transcribe *ʾkl*[*w* as the second word of the line, though none of the letters is clear. The three words *ʾkl, śbʿ*, and *škḥ* occur together e.g., in Deut 6:11-12; 8:10-11, 12-14; 26:12-13; 31:20-21.

At the end of the line I restore [*wʾt kwl*] as suggested by Strugnell. Preceding this I suggest *ʾl hmʾ*[*klm*]. "God who had fed them," cf. *hammaʾăkilĕkā* in Deut 8:16. This use of an objective suffix on a participle with the definite article occurs infrequently in biblical Hebrew; see G. Bergsträsser, *Hebräische Grammatik* (Leipzig: J. C. Hinrichs'sche Buchhandlung, 1929) II. Teil, §13a, p. 68, and C. Brockelmann, *Hebräische Syntax* (Neukirchen: Verlag der Buchhandlung des Erziehungsvereins, 1956), 68. Carmignac suggests either *ʾl hm*[*wšʿwt wʾt*], "le Dieu des dé[livrances]" from Ps 106:21 and 68:21, or *ʾl hm*[*špṭ wʾt*], "le Dieu du jugement," cf. Isa 30:18 or Mal 2:17. Dupont-Sommer interprets the phrase differently. Rather than restoring a word to modify *ʾl*, "God," he supplies a modifier for "they," the group that is the subject of the three preceding verbs. He translates "et qu'ils ont oublié Dieu, eux qui ont mé[prisé la Loi]" ("Résumé 1969-1970," 412).

2:4 *his commandments* (*mṣwwtyw*). The form is not printed clearly in the transcription in *Qumrân Cave 4*, where it appears to be *mṣyytyw*.

At the end of the line, either *byd* (so Vermes) or *bpy* (so Allegro) should probably be restored. I prefer *byd*, which is much more frequently used in the OT to indicate the instrumentality of the prophets, e.g., 1 Sam 28:15, 2 Kgs 17:13, 23; 21:10; 24:2; Hos 12:11; Dan 9:10; see also 1QpHab 2:9 (*bydm spr ʾl*); 1QS 1:3 (*kʾšr ṣwh byd mwšh wbyd kwl ʿbdyw hnbyʾym*). Strugnell's suggestion, *bpy kwl*, may be too long for the line.

2:5 *his servants the prophets* (*ʿbdyw hnbyʾym*), cf. 1QpHab 2:9; 7:5.

those who led astray (*mtʿyhm*). The verb *tʿh* describes the activity of the *mṭyp hkzb*, "the One who Spouts the Lie," in 1QpHab 10:9, and of the *ʾyš hkzb*, "the Man of the Lie," in 4QpPs[a] 1-10 i 26-27, cf. CD 3:14; 4:1; 5:20.

In the transcription of line 5 Allegro did not indicate that there is a break at the end of the line; *wykbdwm* is probably not the last word in the line.

2:6 *and as if they were gods* (*wkʾlym*). The pl. form *ʾēlîm* is infrequent in biblical Hebrew, occurring only in the phrase *bny ʾlym,* "sons of gods," i.e., heavenly beings, in Ps 29:1; 89:7, and in Exod 15:11, but the form is well-attested in QL, e.g., 1QM 1:10, 11; 14:16; 15:14; 17:7; 1QH 7:28. This word is indented slightly, so it appears to go with what follows, thus emphasizing the phrase "as if they were gods" by placing it before the verb. It is not impossible, however, that the word could go with the preceding text, which is lost.

2:9 The citation of Hos 2:11 presents the following variants from the MT:

(1) *wpyšty* (MT: *wpšty*). Strugnell prefers to read *wpwšty,* noting the form *pštym* in 1QIsaª 19:9, which may have been corrected by a supralinear addition to *wpwštym,* but the corrected form in 1QIsaª could just as well be *wpyštym.* In 4QpHosª I read *wpyšty,* following Allegro. Thus, this is an orthographic variant with the *y* representing a short *i*-vowel. See W. F. Albright, "The Gezer Calendar," *BASOR* 92 (1943) 22, n. 34. See also the note above on 1QpHab 7:13.

(2) *mlkswt* (MT: *lkswt*). The form in the MT, the preposition *l* + the inf. cs. is translated "which were to cover," but the form in 4QpHosª has the compound preposition *mn* + *l* + the inf. cs., which must be translated "from covering" (see GKC §119c), cf. the LXX τοῦ μὴ καλύπτειν.

2:12 *with famine* (*brʿb*), cf. 4QpIsaᵇ 2:1; 4QpPsª 1-10 ii 1; 1-10 iii 3-4.

2:13 *the nations* (*hgwʾym*). The word is spelled here with a medial ʾ as in 1QpHab 3:5; 4QpIsaª 7-10 iii 8; 4QpHosᵇ 10:[3]. The usual spelling in biblical Hebrew is *gwym* as in 1QpHab 5:3, 4; 6:9; 8:5, 15; 9:3; 12:13; 13:1; 4QpNah 3-4 i 1; 3-4 ii 5, 7; 3-4 iii 1. See the note above on 1QpHab 3:5.

2:15 The citation of Hos 2:13 presents the following variant from the MT: *mwʿdyh* (MT: *mwʿdh*).

2:15-16 The reading, restoration, and translation of the beginning of this interpretation are uncertain, but it is clear that the lines refer in some way to the calendaric differences between the Qumran community and the Jews in Jerusalem (see the note above on 1QpHab 11:7). In the preliminary publication Allegro read the first visible letters in line 16 as]*ʿdwt* and stated that this might be *ʿdwt,* "congregations," or part of the form *mw*]-*ʿdwt,* the fem. pl. form of *mwʿd,* "festivals," as in CD 6:18; 12:4. In the *editio princeps* he transcribes]*ʿdwt* at the beginning of the line but translates only what is preserved, "they will bring into the Gentile festivals." Dupont-Sommer translates "[toutes les f]êtes, ils les font venir aux dates des païens," apparently restoring [*kwl hmw*]*ʿdwt* at the beginning of line

16 ("Résumé 1969-1970," 413). Vermes supplies a different idea, "[they have rejected the ruling of the law, and have] followed the festivals of the nations." Since the verb *ywlykw* is causative, "to cause to go," a direct object is needed, presumably at the beginning of line 16. This word order is a little awkward, but cf. line 6 above. The object is probably *mwᶜdwt,* as has been suggested by others, in the light of *mwᶜdyh* in the lemma. If the definite object sign *ʾt* is restored, there is not enough room for *kwl.* I thus restore [*ʾt hmw*] *ᶜdwt* at the beginning of line 16.

2:16-17 *and all joy* (*w*[*kwl śmḥh*]). This is restored following Strugnell's suggestion, cf. the contrast of joy and mourning e.g., in Qoh 7:4.

2:18 The citation of Hos 2:14 presents the following variants from the MT:

(1) *ʾtnm* (MT: *ʾtnh*). The usual biblical Hebrew word for the harlot's reward is *ʾtnn;* only in Hos 2:14 does *ʾtnh* occur (see James A. Montgomery, "Hebraica," *JAOS* 58 [1938] 135). It is difficult to explain the form that occurs in 4QpHos[a] with a final *m.* Strugnell offers two possible explanations: (a) the final *m* arose through a paleographic corruption of a ligature *ny* in *ʾtnny;* or (b) the final *m* reflects a phonetic evolution of final *n* to final *m.* The second suggestion raises a problem. The phenomenon of final *m* turning into *n* is known. E. Y. Kutscher, for example, in discussing proper names, suggests that it is this phenomenon that gave rise to the form Μαρια, i.e., *mrym* became *mryn,* and then the *n* "was understood as an appended [n], so *mryh,* Μαρια arose through backformation" ("The Language of the 'Genesis Apocryphon': A Preliminary Study," *Aspects of the Dead Sea Scrolls* [ed. C. Rabin and Y. Yadin; Scripta Hierosolymitana 4; Jerusalem: Hebrew University, Magnes Press, 1958] 23-24, n. 118; see also H. L. Ginsberg, "Zu den Dialekten des Talmudisch-Hebräischen," *MGWJ* 77 [1933] 421-22; H. Yalon, "Zur palästinischen Aussprache des Schluss-*m* wie *n,*" *MGWJ* 77 [1933] 429-30). In the same article Kutscher points out that in Mishnaic Hebrew, Galilaean Aramaic, and Christian Aramaic there was a tendency to affix a *n* to a non-declined word that ended with an open syllable and that this *n* was often represented graphically by a *m* (p. 23). This could possibly explain the appearance of the form *ʾtnm* in 4QpHos[a], but J. A. Fitzmyer responds to Kutscher's explanation that it is more likely that "the difference between final *m* and *n* is due to the analogy of such endings as *-îm* and *-în*" (*The Genesis Apocryphon of Qumran Cave 1: A Commentary* [2nd rev. ed.; BibOr 18A; Rome: Biblical Institute, 1971] 162). Thus, the alleged change from final *n* to final *m* is not a phenomenon of phonetic evolution. Strugnell's first suggestion is possible, although this presupposes at some point the textual variant *ʾtnny.* In the light of Kutscher's explanation of the form Μαρια, it

could be that both the form of the MT and 4QpHos[a] are backformations of the biblical Hebrew word *ʾtnn.*

(2) *hm* (MT: *hmh*).

4QpHos[b] (4Q*167*)

Editio princeps: "Commentary on Hosea (B)" (J. M. Allegro), *Qumrân Cave 4,* Vol. I, pp. 32-36 and pls. X-XI.

Preliminary publication: J. M. Allegro, "Further Light on the History of the Qumran Sect," *JBL* 75 (1956) 89-95, esp. p. 93 and pl. 2 (photograph of frg. 2).

Secondary transcriptions and translations: J. Carmignac, *Les Textes,* 2. 80-81 (entitled 4Qp Os[a]); A. Dupont-Sommer, *Essene Writings,* 276-77; J. Maier, *Die Texte,* 1. 189, 2. 167 (both entitled 4QpHos[a]); F. Michelini Tocci, *I manoscritti,* 262 (entitled 4Q p Os[a]); L. Moraldi, *I manoscritti,* 540.

Secondary literature: J. Strugnell, "Notes," 201-203 and pl. III b, c, d; E. Vogt, "Prima nomina historica in Qumrân (4QpNah)," *Bib* 37 (1956) 530-32, esp. 532.

The number 4Q*167* (4QpHos[b]) in *Qumrân Cave 4* designates a group of thirty-eight frgs. It was noted in the introductory remarks to the preceding text (4Q*166* or 4QpHos[a]) that the titles of these two documents were reversed in the preliminary publications, i.e., 4Q*167* was designated 4QpHos[a] and 4Q*166* was entitled 4QpHos[b]. In the preliminary publication of this text, only frg. 2, which is actually two frgs. put together, was presented. Of the thirty-eight frgs. that appear in the *editio princeps,* only about seventeen can be identified with any probability as preserving parts of the biblical text of Hosea or a commentary on the text.

J. Strugnell describes the script of the document as "rustic semi-formal," but he finds some characteristic differences from the hand of the preceding text. Subsequent to Allegro's publication of the *editio princeps,* Strugnell was able to add two other frgs. and to join several of the frgs. that appear in *Qumrân Cave 4.* He joined frgs. 4, 18, and 24 to a previously unidentified frg. that he designated 10[a]. Similarly, he joined frgs. 10 and 26, and frgs. 15, 33, 16, and 4Q*168* frg. 2. Moreover, he questions whether frgs. 27, 28, 30, and 31 belong to this document, and he suggests that frgs. 9 and 36 are part of the next text, 4Q*168.*

Allegro's transcription presents many problems. Depending on how the frgs. are matched, there are approximately 105 lines partially preserved. I differ with Allegro's reading of almost one-third of the lines. In some cases it seems to be that Allegro made the transcription from different photographs, e.g., frg. 30, where the transcription clearly does not reflect the photograph that appears in *Qumrân Cave 4.*

I have not succeeded in matching or restoring any further frgs. Though there is little of the document preserved, it is apparent that the structure of the commentary is the same as that of the other pesharim. A short section of the biblical text is cited, followed by a brief commentary introduced by a formula using the word *pšr* (2:[1]; 7-8:[1]; 10, 26:[2]; 11-13:[4]; 11-13:[9]; 16:[1]). In 19:1, the word *pšr* is clear, and it is followed by *h* and traces of one or two letters. The familiar formula *pšr hdbr* does not fit the visible traces of letters, but they are not incompatible with *pšr hptgm;* see 4QpIsa[a] 2-6 ii [26] (Allegro's 5-6:10) and 4QpPs[b] 2:[1]. This formula is probably synonymous with *pšr hdbr.* One other noteworthy feature of the structure is the possible use of *wʾšr* by itself as an introduction to a biblical quotation (10, 26:1). This may be an abbreviation of the formula *wʾšr ʾmr,* which is used elsewhere in the pesharim to introduce the second citation from a biblical passage already quoted; see further Part II, p. 243.

Only isolated phrases of the Qumran author's interpretation of the prophetic text are preserved, but it clearly deals with the history of the community. There is mention of the Lion of Wrath (2:2), who also appears in 4QpNah 3-4 i 5-6 as an enemy of the Qumran sect "who hangs men alive" (see the note below on 4QpNah 3-4 i 5). In the same fragment of 4QpHos[b] there are references to the last priest and to Ephraim (2:3). It is impossible to tell from this text whether these terms refer to friends or foes of the Essene community. Elsewhere, however (4QpNah 3-4 i 12; 3-4 ii 2, 8; 3-4 iii 5; 4QpPs[a] 1-10 i [24]; 1-10 ii 18), Ephraim designates enemies of the Qumran sect. Thus, the last priest mentioned here is probably on the side of the Qumran community. In 5-6:2, the word *mwryhm,* "their teacher," may be a reference to the Teacher of Righteousness.

4QpHos[b]: Translation

Fragment 1

1.]the plain of[
2.]in front of .[

Fragment 2

1. [NOR CAN HE HEAL (?) YOU]R SORE. The in[terpre- tation of it] Hos 5:13-14a
2. [ ]. the Lion of Wrath. FOR I AM LIKE A YOUNG LIO[N TO E]PH[RAI]M [AND LIKE A LION]
3. [TO THE HOUSE OF JUDAH. The interpretation of it con]cerns the last priest, who will stretch out his hand to smite Ephraim

4. [ ]*dw*
5. [I SHALL GO, I SHALL RETURN T]O [MY PLACE UN]TIL THEY [ARE] CONVICTED AND THEY SEEK MY PRESENCE. IN [THEIR] TROUBLE 5:15
6. [THEY WILL SEEK ME. The interpretation of it]God [will hi]de his face fro[m the l]a[nd]
7. [ ]*hw* but they did not listen[ ]

Fragment 3

1.]*nh* ᶜ[
2.]night to look fo[r
3.]a covering (?) on [his] prey[
4.]to the threshing floor[s

Fragment 4

See below, frgs. 10a, 4, 18, 24.

Fragments 5-6

1. [ ]the men of[ ]
2. [ ]. their teacher[ ]upon[ ]
3. [WHAT SHALL I] DO WITH YOU, [EPHRAIM?] WHAT [SHALL I DO WITH YOU, JUDAH?] 6:4a

Fragments 7-8

1. [AND THEY LIKE ADAM] HAVE TRANSGRESSED THE COVENANT. The interpretation[of it] 6:7a
2. [ ]they abandoned God; they walk[ed] according to the precepts of [ ]*lym* [th]em in all [ ]

Fragment 9

] ʾ*t* Is[rae]l[

Fragments 10, 26

1. and that [THEY ACT] LEWDLY; [IN THE HOUSE OF ISRAEL I HAVE SEEN A HORRIBLE THING. THE FORNICATION OF EPHRAIM IS THERE;] ISRAEL [IS DEFILED.] 6:9bβ-10
2. The inter[pretation of it]
3. [the wi]cked ones of the nation[s]
4. all *mk*.[ ]
5. [ ]*l*[ ]

Fragments 10a, 4, 18, 24

1. [AND HE HAS SET A H]ARVEST FOR YOU [TOO, JUDAH] 6:11a
2. [ ]on the day
3. [ ]*m* to us

4. [ ]
5. [ ]*tw* and that
6. [ ]who will bring back [ ]
7. [ ]*yhm wht.*[ ]*l*[ ]

Fragments 11-13

1. [ ]*ḥt ls*[ ]
2. [ ] son . .[ ]
3. [FOR IT IS FROM ISRAEL; THA]T THING AN ARTISAN MADE; [THAT THING IS NOT GOD. FOR THE CALF OF SAMARIA HAS BEEN CHOPPED TO SPLINTERS (?)] 8:6
4. [The in]terpretation of it [is th]at they were among the peoples [ ]
5. [and when it says,] FOR THE C[ALF OF SAMARIA] HAS BEEN CHOPPED [TO SPLIN]TERS, [the interpretation of it] 8:6b
6. [ ]God[FOR (IT IS)] THE WIND THEY SOW; [BUT THEY WILL REAP] STORMWINDS. [THE STANDING GRAIN HAS NO SPROUT; IT WILL NOT MAKE] 8:7-8
7. [FLOUR. AND IF PERCHANCE IT SHOU]LD, STRANGERS WOULD DEVOUR I[T. ISRAEL IS SWALLOWED UP. NOW THEY ARE AMONG THE NATIONS LIKE A VESSEL]
8. [WITH NO USE TO IT] (*vacat*) [ ]
9. The interpretation[of it]*hs*[ ]
10. *hb*[ ]

Fragment 14

1.] . . .[
2.]*ḥšb*[

Fragments 15, 33, 4Q*168* frg. 2, Column i

1. [ ].*yry*
2. [ ]*l*

Fragments 15, 33, 4Q*168* frg. 2, Column ii

(TO EGYPT) 8:13-14
1. THEY [WILL RE]TURN. AND [ISRAEL] HAS FORGOT[TEN THE ONE WHO MADE IT AND HAS BUILT PALACES, AND JUDAH]
2. HAS MULTIPLIED CITIE[S]
3. [ ]
4. to beco[me]
5. befor[e]

Fragment 16

1. the in]terpretation of it is that[

2. and] each one will lay hold of [
3.] God was n[ot] pleased [

Fragment 17

1. the interpretation] of it concerns Egypt [
2.]. . .[ ]*l*[

Fragment 18

1.]*tw w'm*[
2.]*'šr yšy.*[
3.]*l*[

Fragment 19

1.]the interpretation of *h.*[
2.].*ḥ 't* .[
3. o]ld people *yš*[
4.]. *'šr* .[
5.]*sr* .[
6.].*dh h.*[
7.]*hws.*[
8.]*l* .[

Fragment 20

1.]. .[ ].[
2.]*m* in the holy place of Is[rael
3.]*bnm wbʿ*[

Fragment 21

1. [ ]*hnh*
2. [ ]and all

Fragment 22, Column i

1. [ ].
2. [ ].*w*
3. [ ]*lm*

Fragment 22, Column ii

1. God[ ]
2. .[ ]

Fragment 23

]commandments[

Fragment 24

See above, frgs., 10a, 4, 18, 24.

Fragment 25

1. J]uda[h
2.]*l* the day[of

Fragment 26

See above, frgs. 10, 26.

Fragment 27

1.]*m*
2.].

Fragment 28

]not . .[

Fragment 29

1. *t*[
2. .[

Fragment 30

1.].*m*[
2.]. [

Fragment 31

1.].*m*
2.]*h*

Fragment 32

1.]*ʾt*[
2.].[

Fragment 33

See above, frgs. 15, 33, 4Q*168* frg. 2.

Fragment 34

] . *yrʾ* .[

Fragment 35

]*mʿš*[

Fragment 36

]*yš*[

Fragment 37

]ʾ.[

Fragment 38

1. ʾ.[ ]
2. [ ]
3. ʿ[ ]
4. *y*.[ ]
5. *m*.[ ]
6. *g*.[ ]
7. *hmy*.[ ]
8. *ṭrp*[ ]
9. *mš*.[ ]
10. ʾ.[ ]

4QpHos^{b}: Notes

Fragment 1

Either this frg. preserves the bottom margin of a col., or these lines are followed by two blank lines. If the frg. is correctly identified as part of a commentary on Hosea, it might refer to Hos 1:5 (*ʿmq yzrʿʾl*) or 2:17 (*ʿmq ʿkwr*).

1:1 In the transcription a space should be indicated after *ʿmq*.

1:2 Following *ngd* a space and a trace of the first letter of the next word are visible but were not transcribed by Allegro.

Fragment 2

2:2 *the Lion of Wrath (kpyr hḥrwn)*; see also 4QpNah 3-4 i 5-6. In

4QpNah, the Lion of Wrath appears as one who "hangs men alive." See the note on 4QpNah 3-4 i 5.

I follow Allegro and Strugnell in reading the words following *kpyr hḥrwn* as the beginning of the citation of Hos 5:14a. In the preliminary publication, Allegro suggested *hm*] *ᶜykw,* and Carmignac restores similarly [*khm*] *ᶜykw* and translates the phrase "le Lionceau Furieux [dans] son [ét]reinte comme (celle du) fau[ve." Dupont-Sommer translates "the furious Young Lion to [gr]ind him down (?) like the li[on" (the question mark is his).

In the transcription in *Qumrân Cave 4,* Allegro indicates that he is able to read a trace of the *l* of *kšḥl,* but this letter is not visible on the photograph.

2:3 *the last priest . . . Ephraim* (*kwhn hʾḥrwn . . . ʾprym*). From the context it cannot be determined whether these terms refer to friends or enemies of the Qumran sect. It was noted in the introductory remarks that from other documents it is clear that Ephraim is the foe, and consequently the last priest must be the ally. Elsewhere Ephraim is identified both with the Seekers-After-Smooth-Things (4QpNah 3-4 ii 2) and with those whom they lead astray by their false teaching (4QpNah 3-4 ii 8). There is a section in 4QpPs^{a} (1-10 ii 18, cf. 1-10 i 24) that seems to be just the opposite of this passage in 4QpHos^{b}. It describes how the "wicked ones of Ephraim" seek to lay their hands on the priest; in 4QpHos^{b} it is the last priest who will smite Ephraim. The use of the term Ephraim to designate those who are led astray may be traced to Isa 7:17, which is quoted twice in the Damascus Document (CD 7:12; 14:1): "He will bring upon you, and upon your people, and upon your father's house, days such as have not come since the day that Ephraim departed from Judah." See further the notes on 4QpPs^{a} 1-10 ii 18-20.

2:5 The commentary probably ended in line 4, since the last part of the line is blank. There is not enough room at the beginning of line 5 to restore Hos 5:14b, which must have been omitted. Strugnell is apparently correct in suggesting that the first word of 5:15 was indented. It is also possible, however, that the scribe began to write 5:14b and then skipped mistakenly to 5:15 because of the repetition of the word *ʾlk.* In that case the restored text would be *ʾny ʾny ʾṭrwp wʾlk ʾšwbh,* "I, even I, shall rend and go away; I shall return."

The upper tip of a *l* is visible to the lower left of *dw* in line 4 but was not transcribed by Allegro.

2:6 *from the land* (*m*[*n hʾ*]*r*[*ṣ*]). This is restored in the light of CD 2:8, *wystr ʾt pnym mn hʾrṣ*

In *Qumrân Cave 4* Allegro indicates a *n* following the *m* after *pnyw,* but this is not visible on the photograph.

Fragment 3

It is impossible to identify this frg. with certainty, but Allegro suggests that it might be related to Hos 5:15 (*yshṛnny*), 5:14 (*ʾṭrp*), or 6:1 (*ṭrp*), but see Mic 4:12 (*grnh*).

3:1 Allegro reads the first visible letter as a *b,* but the horizontal base stroke is shorter than that of other *b*'s in this text; see e.g., *wbqšw* and *bṣr* in 2:5 or *yblʿwh*[*w* in 11-13:7. The letter is more likely to be read as *n, ṣ,* or *t.*

3:2 *to look for* (*lšḥ*[*r*]), or possibly "to dawn," cf. Hos 6:3 (*kšḥr*).

3:3 *on his prey* (*bṭrp*[w]), or possibly, "when he tears." Allegro transcribes *bṭrpw,* but in the photograph in *Qumrân Cave 4* the frg. is broken off in the middle of the *p,* and the *w* is not visible at all.

Fragment 4

See below, frgs. 10a, 4, 18, 24.

Fragment 5-6

These frgs. may preserve part of a citation of Hos 6:4a (line 3), and *mwryhm* in line 2 may be part of a pesher on *ywrh* of Hos 6:3.

5-6:1 A space after *ʾnšy* should be indicated in the transcription.

5-6:3 The citation of Hos 6:4a presents the following variant from the MT: *lkh* (MT: *lk*). This variant is preserved once and restored once.

Contrary to Allegro's transcription, there is no space visible before or after *mh.*

Fragments 7-8

Allegro took frgs. 7-9 as one group, placing frg. 9 on a level with frg. 8 as the continuation of line 2 of frg. 7. Strugnell, however, thinks that frg. 9 belongs to 4QpMic (see further 4Q*168* in the Appendix, pp. 261-63). It cannot be determined from the photographs in the *editio princeps* whether or not this is correct, but frg. 9 is transcribed separately here.

The lower margin is visible on both frgs. 7 and 8, and they may preserve part of the citation of Hos 6:7a and a pesher.

7-8:1 It seems that a trace of a letter is visible before *brw* at the beginning of the line.

like Adam (*kʾdm*), or possibly "like humanity." This is restored in agreement with the MT, but it is suggested in *BHS* that the text be emended to *bʾdm,* "at Adam," cf. Jos 3:16. There are only a few words of the interpretation preserved, and they give no indication of how the Qumran author understood the biblical text.

Fragment 9

See the comments above on frgs. 7-8. There is no space visible before *ʾt*. I follow Strugnell's suggestion of restoring the frg., though he transcribes] *ʾt yśr*[*ʾ*]*l*.

Fragments 10, 26

To frg. 10 Strugnell joins frg. 26 (see "Notes," 167-68 and pl. III c). These frgs. match at the *l* of line 4, the top of which is visible on frg. 10 but was not transcribed by Allegro.

10, 26:1 Following Allegro, I restore the citation of Hos 6:9bβ-10, but this may be too long.

The apparent citation of Hos 6:9bβ-10 presents the following variant from the MT: *wʾšr* (MT: *ky*). This may be a textual variant, or it could be an abbreviated introductory formula for the citation. See Part II, p. 243.

The form *šʿrwryh,* "a horrible thing," which is the *qĕrê* of the MT, is restored here rather than *šʿryryh,* the *kĕtîb* of the MT; see also 4QTestim 27 and cf. *šʿrwrywt* in 1QpHab 9:1.

Fragments 10a, 4, 18, 24

Strugnell joins frgs. 4, 18, and 24 to a previously unidentified frg. that he designates 10a (see "Notes," 202 and pl. III b). This group of frgs. preserves the left margin of a col. In line 1 Strugnell restores Hos 6:11a with *lkh* for *lāk* of the MT.

10a, 4, 18, 24:5 In 18:1 Allegro reads]*tw wʾmr*[, but if it is joined to frg. 4, *wʾšr* can be read.

10a, 4, 18, 24:6 In 18:2 Allegro reads *yšwb,* but Strugnell prefers *yšyb.* Either is possible on the basis of the script.

10a, 4, 18, 24:7 On the basis of other photographs, Strugnell is able to read]*yhm* on the right side of frg. 24, but this cannot be verified from the photograph in *Qumrân Cave 4.*

Fragments 11-13

This group of frgs. preserves parts of the biblical text of Hos 8:6-8 with commentary, though Allegro remarks that the positions of frgs. 11 and 12 are uncertain. The vertical alignment presented by Allegro is impossible; specifically, *ky* cannot be the first word in line 5.

11-13:1 Allegro's transcription indicates that he can read a trace of a letter after *ls,* but this is not visible on the photograph in the *editio princeps.*

11-13:3 There seems to be a trace of a letter visible at the right edge of frg. 13 (13:3)

The text of Hos 8:6b is restored with the following variants from the

MT in the light of line 5, the second citation of 8:6b:

(1) *šwbbym* (MT: *šĕbābîm*). The form *šwbbym* is restored also by Strugnell rather than *šybbym* as suggested by Allegro. The form could be explained as the qal part. pl. masc. from *šbb,* but this verb is unattested in biblical Hebrew. If it is a substantive, the form in 4QpHos[b] may have arisen by analogy with the qutl noun types frequent in Qumran Hebrew.

(2) *hyh* (MT: *yhyh*).

If the length of the lines in this col. can be judged from the restoration of lines 6-7, there must have been more in line 3 than Hos 8:6a as restored by Allegro, since the commentary does not begin until line 4.

11-13:4 From an earlier photograph, Strugnell is able to read *p*]*šrw* (12:1), but on the photograph in *Qumrân Cave 4* only the *š* and the *r* are partially preserved.

11-13:6 Contrary to Allegro's transcription, there is no space visible before *rwḥ* or after *swpwt*.

The apparent citation of Hos 8:7 presents the following variant from the MT: *swpwt* (MT: *wswpth*).

Fragment 14

From the condition of the skin, Strugnell suggests that this frg. might be related to Hos 6:1 rather than to 8:12, as Allegro proposes.

Fragments 15, 33, 4Q*168* frg. 2

Treated separately by Allegro, these frgs. were joined by Strugnell on the basis of their distinctive appearance. They form parts of two cols. relating to Hos 8:13-14 (see "Notes," 203 and pl. III d). He also adds frg. 16, which he places as the lefthand part of the last three lines of col. ii. While I agree that frg. 16 is probably to be related to Hos 8:13, the placement of it is uncertain. It might precede frgs. 15, 33, 4Q*168* frg. 2, but it might also follow. I transcribe it separately.

15, 33 4Q*168* frg. 2 ii 2 (= 15:2). Allegro's transcription is *hrbḥ,* but the photograph shows *hrbh* clearly.

Fragments 17-38

These frgs. preserve only a few words and partially preserved letters. Strugnell questions whether frgs. 27, 28, 30, and 31 belong with this document, and he suggests that frgs. 9 and 36 belong with 4QpMic (4Q*168*). I suggest the following revisions of Allegro's transcription of these frgs.

19:2].*ḥ* *ʾt* .[(Allegro has]*wḥ* *ʾt y*[).

19:4]. *ʾšr* .[(Allegro has]. *ʾšr*[).

19:7]*hws*.[(Allegro has]*yws*.[).

20:1 There are traces of letters visible on the photograph, but the line was not indicated by Allegro.

Fragment 28:]*lw*ʾ . .[(Allegro has]*lw*ʾ*m.*[).

Fragment 29

The brackets should be reversed; it is the right margin that is preserved, not the left as shown in the transcription.

Fragment 30

Allegro's transcription indicates that there are several letters partially visible in line 1 before the *m,* and a few traces visible in line 2. On the photograph in *Qumrân Cave 4,* however, only one or at the most two letters are partially visible before the *m,* and in line 2 there is only one small dot on the right edge of the frg.

31:1].*m* (Allegro has]*ym*).

Fragment 34:]. *yr*ʾ.[(Allegro has]*m wr*ʾ.[).

38:2 There should be some indication of a line even though no letters are preserved.

38:4 *y.*[(Allegro has *yh*[).

4QpNah (4Q*169*)

Editio princeps: "Commentary on Nahum" (J. M. Allegro), *Qumrân Cave 4,* Vol. I, pp. 37-42 and pls. XII-XIV.

Preliminary publications: J. M. Allegro, "Further Light on the History of the Qumran Sect," *JBL* 75 (1956) 89-95, especially pp. 90-93 and pl. I (photograph of frgs. 3-4, col. i); "More Unpublished Pieces of a Qumran Commentary on Nahum (4QpNah)," *JSS* 7 (1962) 304-308 and pls. I-III (photographs of frgs. 3-4, cols. ii, iii, and iv). J. Licht, "*Dpym nwspym lpšr nḥwm* [Additional Leaves of the Pesher Nahum]," *Molad* 19 (1961) 454-58.

Secondary transcriptions and translations:* J. Carmignac, *Les Textes,* 2.

*The list of works under this and the following heading is not exhaustive. Only those secondary works that are especially important for the study at hand are included. Additional titles are incorporated into the general bibliography.

Several authors limit their presentations to frgs. 3-4, col. i, with brief comments on the historical importance of the text, e.g., H. Bardtke, *Die Handschriftenfunde,* 297-98; "Neue Funde und Forschungen am Toten Meer," *Die Zeichnen der Zeit* 10 (1956) 448-55, esp. pp. 453-55; P. Boccaccio and G. Berardi, *Interpretatio Habacuc,* Appendix I: "Interpretatio Nahum," 36-37; M. Burrows, *More Light,* 404; A. Dupont-Sommer, *Essene Writings,* 268-70; A. M. Habermann, *Megilloth,* 153; J. Maier, *Die Texte,* 1. 180, 2. 162; E. F. Sutcliffe, *The Monks* 180-81; E. Vogt, "Prima nomina historica in Qumrân (4QpNah)," *Bib* 37 (1956) 530-32; A. S. van der Woude, *Bijbelcommentaren,* 55-58; Y. Yadin, *Hmgylwt hgnwzwt mmdbr yhwdh* [*The Hidden Scrolls from the Judaean Desert*] 119-20; *The Message of the Scrolls,* 102-104.

85-92 (not including frgs. 1-2); A. Dupont-Sommer, "Le Commentaire de Nahum découvert près de la Mer Morte (4Q p Nah): Traduction et notes," *Sem* 13 (1963) 55-88 (not including frgs. 1-2); T. H. Gaster, *Dead Sea Scriptures,* 240-43 (not including frgs. 1-2); E. Lohse, *Die Texte,* 261-69; F. Michelini Tocci, *I manoscritti,* 267-72 (not including frgs. 1-2); L. Moraldi, *I manoscritti,* 545-52; G. Vermes, *Dead Sea Scrolls in English,* 231-35 (not including frgs. 1-2).

Secondary literature: J. M. Allegro, "*Thrakidan,* the 'Lion of Wrath' and Alexander Jannaeus," *PEQ* 91 (1959) 47-51; J. D. Amoussine, "Éphraïm et Manassé dans le Péshèr de Nahum (4 Q p Nahum)," *RevQ* 4 (1963-64) 389-96; J. M. Baumgarten, "Does *TLH* in the Temple Scroll Refer to Crucifixion?" *JBL* 91 (1972) 472-81; A. Dupont-Sommer, "Lumières nouvelles sur l'arrière-plan historique des écrits de Qoumran," *E. L. Sukenik Memorial Volume (1889-1953)* (ed. N. Avigad *et al.;* Eretz-Israel 8; Jerusalem: Israel Exploration Society, 1967) 25-36; "Observations nouvelles sur l'expression 'suspendu vivant sur le bois' dans le Commentaire de Nahum (4Q pNah II 8) à la lumière du Rouleau du Temple (11Q Temple Scroll LXIV 6-13," *CRAIBL* (Novembre-Décembre, 1972) 709-20; "Observations sur le Commentaire de Nahum découvert près de la Mer Morte," *CRAIBL* (Juillet-Décembre, 1963) 242-43; "Observations sur le Commentaire de Nahum découvert près de la Mer Morte," *Journal des Savants* (Octobre-Décembre, 1963) 201-27; "Résumé des cours de 1969-70; Hébreu et Araméen," *Annuaire du Collège de France* 70 (1970-71) 399-414; J. A. Fitzmyer, "Crucifixion in Ancient Palestine, Qumran Literature, and the New Testament," *CBQ* 40 (1978) 493-513; J. Maier, "Weitere Stücke zum Nahumkommentar aus der Höhle 4 von Qumran," *Judaica* 18 (1962) 215-50; H. H. Rowley, "4QpNahum and the Teacher of Righteousness," *JBL* 75 (1956) 188-93; P. W. Skehan, "A New Translation of Qumrân Texts," *CBQ* 25 (1963) 119-23, esp. pp. 120-21; J. Strugnell, "Notes," 204-10; R. Weiss, "A Comparison Between the Massoretic and the Qumran Texts of Nahum III, 1-11," *RevQ 4* (1963-64) 433-39; "*Hʿrwt ldpym hnwspym mpšr nḥwm* [Notes on the Additional Columns of the Pešer of Nahum]," *Beth Mikra* 2 (1962-63) 57-63; "*kʾwrh* (*pšr nḥwm b', w'*) [*kʾwrh* (Pesher Nahum 2.6)]," *Beth Mikra* 3 (1963-64) 156; Y. Yadin, "Pesher Nahum (4QpNahum) Reconsidered," *IEJ* 21 (1971) 1-12 and pl. I (photograph of 11QTemple 64:6-13).

The number 4Q*169* in *Qumrân Cave 4* designates the Qumran commentary on Nahum, one of the most important and best-preserved of the pesharim. In the *editio princeps* there are photographs of five frgs. giving portions of seven cols. of the document, though only five cols. are substantially preserved. In 1956, J. M. Allegro presented col. i of frgs. 3-4 in a preliminary publication, and in 1962 he published the other three cols. of frgs. 3-4. Between these two preliminary publications, according to A. Dupont-Sommer ("Le Commentaire," p. 56, n. 2), photographs of 4QpNah appeared in a catalogue for visitors to the Palestine Archaeological Museum. On the basis of these photographs, J. Licht published a transcription of cols. ii, iii, and iv of frgs. 3-4 in 1961 (see the article by Licht listed above; see also H. Stegemann, "Weitere Stücke von 4 Q p Psalm 37, von 4 Q Patriarchal Blessings und Hinweis auf eine unedierte Handschrift aus Höhle 4 Q mit Exzerpten aus dem Deuteronomium," *RevQ 6* [1967-69] 195-96).

J. Strugnell describes the script of 4QpNah as the "formal" type, and he dates it to the end of the Hasmonean era or the beginning of the Herodian period. The document is structured like the other Qumran biblical commentaries, with short citations of the biblical text followed by brief interpretations introduced by the familiar formulas *pšrw* ʿ*l* or *pšrw*. On the basis of what is preserved, it is possible to give a rough estimate of the length of the document, if one may assume that none of the biblical text was omitted. Col. i of frgs. 1-2 was probably the first col. of the work (see the note below on frgs. 1-2), followed by col. ii of frgs. 1-2. Between the latter and col. i of frgs. 3-4, there would have to be room for twenty and one-half verses of the biblical text with commentary. The cols. that are preserved are twelve lines long and contain from two and one-half to six and one-half verses and commentary each (1-2 i: apparently two and one-half verses; 1-2 ii: apparently three and one-half verses; 3-4 i: two and one-half verses; 3-4 ii: five verses; 3-4 iii: six and one-half verses), so that there were probably from four to eight cols. lost. On frg. 5 the top margin of a col. is visible, and in line 3 some of the text of Nah 3:14b is preserved. This frg., therefore, must be part of the col. that immediately followed col. iv of frgs. 3-4. Frg. 5 probably contained at least one or two more biblical verses, leaving three more verses of Nahum, probably one more col. The whole document, then, was probably between twelve and sixteen cols. long.

A noteworthy feature of the structure of this commentary is the spacing. In the text that is preserved a space is always left after the biblical citation before the pesher. (Sometimes, however, either the citation or the pesher ends a line, but the beginning of the next line is not indented; compare the structure of 4QpIsa[a].) Similarly, there is a space after the pesher and before the citation except at 3-4 iii 1, 5. There is no space following the pesher in 3-4 i 8, but this is a special case; see the note on this line below. This pattern is consistent enough that it proves useful in restoring the text, as will be seen below.

The commentary sections contain both historical and eschatological interpretations of the biblical text. In col. ii of frgs. 1-2 much of the Qumran commentary is lost, but what remains deals with the eschatological fate of the Kittim (1-2 ii [3]). In the pesher sections of col. i of frgs. 3-4, there is an interpretative account of the incidents connected with Demetrius III's attempt to conquer Alexander Jannaeus, and Jannaeus's reprisals against the Pharisees (see below). At the end of this col. and in cols. ii, iii, and iv of frgs. 3-4, the tense in the interpretations changes to the impf., and the commentaries are a mixture of *vaticinia ex eventu* about the power struggles in Jerusalem and eschatological description of the fate of all the principals at the end of days.

Much has been written about the historical events underlying the Qumran commentary on Nahum, but this brief study can give a detailed account neither of the historical events themselves nor of the many scholarly discussions (see the secondary works listed above and in the general bibliography). Since there is almost complete agreement among the modern authors, a brief summary of the main historical events, noting specific references to 4QpNah, will suffice to make the setting of the commentary clear. The several historical and metaphorical identifications in the commentary can be summarized as follows: the Kittim = the Romans; Demetrius = Demetrius III Eukerus (95-88 B.C.); the Seekers-After-Smooth-Things = the Pharisees; the Lion of Wrath = Alexander Jannaeus; Ephraim = the Pharisees; Judah = the Qumran Community; Manasseh = the Sadducees (it is uncertain to what group the phrase "House of Peleg" refers).

The events alluded to in 4QpNah occurred during the reigns of Alexander Jannaeus (103-76 B.C.), Salome Alexandra (76-67 B.C.), Hyrcanus II and Aristobulus II (67-63 B.C.). See the accounts of Josephus in *Ant.* 13.12.1—14.4.5 (13, §320-432; 14, §1-79), especially 13.13.5—13.16.3 §372-416; *J.W.* 1.4.1—1.6.4 §85-131.

As ruler of Israel, Alexander Jannaeus proved to be an aggressive warrior; he employed foreign mercenaries (*rsʿy gwym* [?] 4QpNah 3-4 i 1; *gdwdy ḥylw* 3-4 i 10) for his military campaigns. Within the nation his policies favored the Sadducees (*gdwlyw wʾnšy ʿṣtw* 3-4 i 5 and similarly restored in 3-4 i 11). These policies and his abuse of the office of high priest made him unpopular with the Pharisees. Civil strife was rampant during his rule, and the Pharisees finally turned outside for help. They called on the Seleucid ruler of Damascus, Demetrius III to aid in their revolt (3-4 i 2-4). Demetrius did not succeed in taking Jerusalem (3-4 i 3), because he had to leave the country, even though he had put Jannaeus and his mercenaries to flight at Shechem (3-4 i 5-6). The prospect of living under Seleucid rule, however, apparently drove the Jewish rebels back to the camp of Alexander Jannaeus. But when he regained his authority in Jerusalem he ordered 800 Pharisees to be crucified (3-4 i 7-8). After the death of Alexander Jannaeus, the Pharisees became the ruling power in Jerusalem during the reign of Salome Alexandra (3-4 i 11-12; 3-4 ii 4-6; 3-4 iv 5-6). However, after Salome Alexandra's death, civil war raged again in the struggle between Hyrcanus II and Aristobulus II (3-4 ii 4-6; 3-4 iii 9, 11), with the final outcome being the fall of the nation to Pompey and the Roman army in 63 B.C.

4QpNah: Translation

Fragments 1-2, Column i

3. [ ] . .
4. [ ] . .
5. [ ] .

Fragments 1-2, Column ii

a. [ ]
1. [HIS WAY IS IN THE WHIRLWIND AND IN THE Nah 1:3b
STORM, AND] CLOUDS ARE THE D[UST OF HIS FEET.
The interpretation of it: "the whirlwind and the storm"
2. *h*[ ]*t r*[ ]*ʿy* his heaven and his earth, which he cre[ated,
and "the clouds" are]
3. HE REBU[KED] THE SEA AND DRIED [IT UP. The in]ter- 1:4aα
pretation of it: "the sea"—that is all the K[ittim, whom God
will rebuke,]
4. so as to ren[der] a judgment against them and to wipe them out
from the face of [the earth. AND HE DRIED UP ALL THE 1:4aβ
RIVERS.]
4a. [The interpretation of it: "the rivers" are the Kittim,]
5a. with [all] their [ru]lers, whose dominion will be ended [ ]
5. [BASHAN IS WITHERED] AND CARMEL, AND THE BLOS- 1:4b
SOM OF LEBANON IS WITHERED. The in[terpretation
of it: "Bashan and Carmel" are]
6. [and] they [will make] many deso[la]te (at) the height of wickedness, for *hb*[ ]
7. [Car]mel and regarding its rulers, Lebanon. And the "blossom of
Le[ba]non" is [the congregation of the Seekers-After-Smooth-
Things]
8. [and] their [partis]ans, but they will perish before [the congregation of] the elect [of God]
9. [and al]l the inhabitants of the world. MOUN[TAINS 1:5-6
QUAKED BEFORE HIM, AND THE HILLS MELTED
AWAY.]
10. THE EARTH [IS LAID WASTE] BEFORE HIM, AND BEFORE
[HIM THE WORLD AND AL]L [WHO INHABIT IT. BE-
FORE HIS INDIGNATION WHO CAN STAND, AND WHO]
11. [CAN ENDURE] HIS ANGER. [HIS] WR[ATH IS POURED
OUT LIKE FIRE, AND THE ROCKS ARE PULLED DOWN
BY HIM]

Fragments 3-4, Column i

1. [The interpretation of it concerns Jerusalem, which has become] a dwelling for the wicked ones of the nations. WHERE THE LION WENT TO ENTER, THE LION'S CUB 2:12b
2. [AND NO ONE TO DISTURB. The interpretation of it concerns Deme]trius, King of Greece, who sought to enter Jerusalem on the advice of the Seekers-After-Smooth-Things,
3. [but God did not give Jerusalem] into the power of the kings of Greece from Antiochus until the rise of the rulers of the Kittim; but afterwards [the city] will be trampled
4. [and will be given into the hand of the rulers of the Kittim] THE LION TEARS ENOUGH FOR HIS CUBS AND STRANGLES PREY FOR HIS LIONESSES. 2:13a
5. [The interpretation of it concerns Demetrius, who made war] against the Lion of Wrath, who would strike with his great ones and his partisans,
6. [but they fled before him (i.e., Demetrius). AND IT FILLS UP] ITS CAVE (?) [WITH PREY,] AND ITS DEN WITH TORN FLESH. The interpretation of it concerns the Lion of Wrath, 2:13b
7. [ ]*mwt* in the Seekers-After-Smooth-Things; he would hang men up alive
8. [upon the tree,] in Israel before, for regarding one hanged alive upon the tree [it] reads: BEHOLD I AM AGAINST YO[U] 2:14
9. SAY[S YAHWEH OF HOSTS. I SHALL BURN UP YO]UR [ABUNDANCE IN SMOKE,] AND THE SWORD WILL DEVOUR YOUR LIONS. AND [I] SHALL CUT OFF ITS [PR]EY [FROM THE EARTH,]
10. AND [THE VOICE OF YOUR MESSENGERS] WILL NO [LONGER BE HEARD. The inter]pretation of it: "your abundance"—they are the detachments of his army th[at are in Jerusale]m; and "his lions"—they are
11. his great ones [and his partisans, who perished by the sword;] and "his prey"—that is the wealth that the [prie]sts of Jerusalem have amas[sed,] which
12. they [will] give ʿ[E]phraim Israel will be given[ ]

Fragments 3-4, Column ii

1. and "his messengers" are his envoys, whose voice will no longer be heeded by the nations. WOE, CITY OF BLOODSHED! ALL OF IT [DECEIT!] FILLED WITH [RAPI]NE! 3:1a-bα
2. The interpretation of it: this is the city of Ephraim—the Seekers-After-Smooth-Things at the end of days—who in deceit and false[hood c]onduct themselves.
3. PREY DOES NOT CEASE. AND THE CRACK OF THE WHIP, 3:1bβ-3

THE RUMBLING SOUND OF THE WHEEL, THE DASHING HORSE AND THE BOUNDING CHARIOT, THE HORSEMAN CHARGING, THE FLASH (OF A SWORD)

4. AND THE GLITTER OF A SPEAR, A MULTITUDE OF SLAIN AND A WEIGHT OF CORPSES. THERE IS NO END TO DEAD BODIES, AND THEY STUMBLE OVER THEIR CARCASSES. The interpretation of it concerns the dominion of the Seekers-After-Smooth-Things;
5. the sword of the nations will not depart from the midst of their congregation. Captives, plunder, and heated strife (are) among them, and exile for fear of the enemy. A multitude of
6. guilty corpses will fall in their days, and there will be no end to the sum-total of their slain. In fact, they will stumble over their decaying flesh because of their guilty counsel.
7. (IT IS) BECAUSE OF THE MANY HARLOTRIES OF THE CHARMING HARLOT, THE WITCH OF SORCERIES, WHO TRADES (?) NATIONS FOR HER HARLOTRY AND CLANS FOR HER [SORCER]IES. 3:4
8. The interpretation [of it con]cerns those who lead Ephraim astray—with their false teaching, their lying tongue, and deceitful lip they lead many astray—
9. [th]eir kings, princes, priests, and people, joined with the resident alien. Cities and clans will perish by their counsel; ho[no]red ones and ru[lers]
10. will fall [on account of] their [inso]lent speech. BEHOLD, I AM AGAINST YOU, SAYS YAHWEH OF H[OST]S. YOU WILL LIFT UP 3:5
11. [YOUR] SKIRTS OVER YOUR FACE(S), AND YOU WILL SHOW NATIONS [YOUR] NAKEDNESS AND KINGDOMS YOUR SHAME. The interpretation of it .[ ] . .
12. [ ]cities of the East, for the skirts[ ]

Fragments 3-4, Column iii

1. the nations because of their impurity [and because of] the [fi]lth of their abominations. I SHALL CAST UPON YOU FILTH, [AND] I [SHALL] TREAT YOU WITH CONTEMPT. I SHALL MAKE YOU 3:6-7a
2. REPULSIVE (?), AND ALL WHO SEE YOU WILL FLEE FROM YOU.
3. The interpretation of it concerns the Seekers-After-Smooth-Things, whose wicked deeds will be revealed to all Israel at the end of time,
4. and many will discern their sin, will hate them, and consider them repulsive (?) on account of their guilty insolence. But when the glory of Judah is [re]vealed,

5. the simple ones of Ephraim will flee from the midst of their assembly. They will abandon those who led them astray and will join .[I]srael. AND THEY WILL SAY 3:7b-c
6. "NINEVEH IS DEVASTATED. WHO WILL MOURN FOR HER? WHENCE, INDEED, SHALL I SEEK COMFORTERS FOR YOU?" The interpretation of it [concerns] the Seekers-After-
7. Smooth-Things, whose council will perish, and whose congregation will be dispersed. They will not again lead [the] assembly astray, and the sim[ple ones]
8. will no longer support their policy. WILL YOU DO BETTER THAN AM[ON, SITUATED BY] THE RIVERS? 3:8a
9. The interpretation of it: "Amon"—they are Manasseh, and "the rivers"—they are the gr[ea]t ones of Manasseh, the honored ones of the [city, who suppo]rt M[anasseh.]
10. WATER SURROUNDING HER, WHOSE POWER IS (THE) SEA, AND (THE) WATER, HER WALLS. 3:8b
11. [The in]terpretation of it: they are the men of her [ar]my, her warrior[s.] ETHIOPIA IS HER STRENGTH, [AND EGYPT (TOO) WITHOUT LIMIT.] 3:9a
12. [ ] . . . [ ] . .[ ]. . . . . [ ].*m*[P]UT AND THE [LIBYANS ARE YOUR HELP.] 3:9b

Fragments 3-4, Column iv

1. The interpretation of it: they are the wicked one[s of Manasse]h, the House of Peleg, who are joined to Manasseh. YET SHE TOO W[ENT] INTO EXILE, [INTO CAPTIVITY. EVEN] 3:10
2. HER CHILDREN, TOO, ARE DASHED TO PIECES ON EVERY STREET CORNER, AND FOR HER HONORED ONES THEY WILL CAST LOTS, AND ALL [HER] G[REA]T [ONES WERE BOUND]
3. IN FETTERS. The interpretation of it concerns Manasseh at the last time, whose reign over Is[rael] will be brought down [ ]
4. his wives, his children, and his infants will go into captivity. His warriors and his honored ones [will perish] by the sword. [YOU TOO WILL BE DRUNK] 3:11a
5. AND YOU WILL BE HIDDEN. The interpretation of it concerns the wicked ones of E[phraim]
6. whose cup will come after Manasseh[ ]*l*[YOU TOO WILL SEEK] 3:11b
7. A HAVEN IN THE CITY FROM (THE) ENEMY. The inter[pretation of it con]cerns[ ]
8. their enemies in the city[ALL YOUR FORTRESSES] 3:12a
9. ARE (LIKE) FIG TREES W[ITH FIRST-FRUITS]
10. .[ ]

11. [ ]
12. [ ]

Fragment 5

1. [ ].*ym* .[ ]
2. [ ].*l* the boundary of Israe[l] . .*m*[ ]
3. [STRENGTHEN] YOUR [FORTIFI]CATIONS, GO INTO THE CLAY[ ] 3:14 (?)

4QpNah: Notes

Fragments 1-2

The first two frgs. preserve parts of two cols. Several traces of letters of the upper lines of col. i are visible on frg. 1. Though none of the letters can be read with certainty, the lines of col. i should be indicated in the transcription, and the lines read by Allegro should be designated col. ii of frgs. 1-2. Allegro suggested that the lost first col. of the work would have contained all of Nah 1:2-6, and that the biblical phrases in the col. he transcribed are repetitions of relevant phrases. Elsewhere in the document, however, there are no second citations of the biblical text presented in this way. It is more likely, therefore, that the commentary moves along in order verse by verse, with col. i containing Nah 1:1-3a quoted in short sections, each followed by an interpretation.

In attempting to restore col. ii of frgs. 1-2, there are problems both with the width of the col. and with the number of lines in the col. There is no line that can be restored with certainty in order to determine the width of the col. Nor can the length of the lines be judged by the other cols. that are preserved; col. ii of frgs. 3-4 is 155-160 mm. wide, but col. iii is only about 135 mm. wide. Thus, the length of the lines in col. ii of frgs. 1-2 remains uncertain, and the restorations suggested here are tentative.

Allegro reads portions of eleven lines and one interlinear addition between lines 4 and 5, which he designates 5a. Strugnell also reads portions of eleven lines, but with two interlinear additions. Besides Allegro's line 5a, Strugnell restores part of a line between lines 3 and 4, which he designates 4a (see further below). In cols. i and ii of frgs. 3-4 both the upper and lower margins are preserved, and each col. has twelve lines. Prescinding from the question of the interlinear additions, I agree with Dupont-Sommer ("Résumé 1969-1970," 407) that a col. of twelve lines should be restored. (In lines 1-2, however, Dupont-Sommer restores Nah 1:1-2a, 3b, taking this col. as the beginning of the pesher, but it was pointed out above that this is probably the second col. of the commentary.) In order to avoid unnecessary confusion by renumbering all the lines of the col. here, I simply restore line "a" as the first line of the col., thus making a col. of twelve lines. The first line would have contained either the text of Nah 1:3a or a commentary, or both.

1-2 ii 1-2 These lines are restored according to the pesher structure found below in 1-2 ii 3; 3-4 i 10; 3-4 iii 9; and 3-4 iv 1 (cf. 1QpHab 1:[13]; 12:3-4, 7-10; 4QpIsa[a] 7-10 iii 9-13 [Allegro's 8-10:5-9]; 4QpPs[a] 1-10 iii 12; 1-10 iv [1]), where key elements of the biblical text are explained metaphorically by phrases that begin with a form of the personal pronoun. The exact restoration of the end of line 1 is uncertain, but it is likely that one or more substantives from the biblical text were presented for explanation. If this is correct, then the first word in line 2, of which the first letter (*h*) is preserved, is probably a form of the personal pronoun. The fem. pl. *hnh,* agreeing with *hswph* and *hśʿrh* might be expected, but elsewhere in this document in similar identifications the form of the personal pronoun agrees with what follows, rather than with what precedes it. Allegro's restoration of the beginning of line 2, *h*[*swpwt whśʿrw*]*t,* "the whirlwinds and the storms," is too short for the lacuna, and the change from the sing. in the biblical text to the pl. in the apparent interpretation is unexplained.

Before *šmyw,* "his heavens," Allegro restores the word *r*[*qy*]*ʿy,* which he translates "the firmaments of." But there is no pl. form of *rāqîaʿ* attested in biblical or Qumran Hebrew. Only the final *y* of the form can be read with certainty; the letter preceding it is probably an ʿ, but the first letter of the word could be a *w* as well as a *r.*

which he created (*ʾšr br*[*ʾm*]). At the end of line 2 Strugnell would restore a phrase identifying *ʾrṣw ʾšr brʾ* (he regards the suffix *m* of *brʾm* as uncertain) with *ʿnn* of the biblical text. According to the pesher structure, however, the phrase *ʾrṣw ʾšr brʾ*(*m*) should go with the preceding phrase as part of the identification of the "whirlwind" and the "storm." Moreover, it is unlikely that the pair "heaven and earth" would be separated as Strugnell suggests. At the end of line 2 I restore the beginning of an identification of *ʿnn,* "clouds." Again, the form of the personal pronoun that would introduce the explanation is uncertain, but it would probably agree with what follows.

1-2 ii 3-5 These lines probably contain the text of Nah 1:4 divided into three sections, each with a commentary. The text of 1:4aα is almost certainly restored at the beginning of line 3, and a short commentary is partially preserved following the citation. The text of 1:4aβ is not included by Allegro, but I follow Strugnell in filling out line 4 with this half-colon, since otherwise it would be omitted.

Between lines 4 and 5 (which almost certainly contains the text of 1:4b) a line has been added that is clearly part of an interpretation. Allegro designates this line as 5a but does not attempt to restore the beginning of the interpretation. Strugnell proposes that line 5a is a continuation of a line that was added between lines 3 and 4. He designates this as line 4a and restores the beginning of a commentary on 1:4aβ with the formula *pšrw ʿl hktyym,* "the interpretation of it concerns the Kittim." In view of the pesher structure indicated in line 3, which seems to have been used throughout the col., it is probably better to restore the beginning of the interpretation something like *pšrw hnhrwt hm hktyym,* "the interpretation of it: 'the rivers' are the Kittim." A similar suggestion is offered by Dupont-Sommer ("Résumé 1969-1970," 407), but he restores the beginning of the interpretation at the end of line 4, which would make the line too long. I therefore follow Strugnell in placing it between lines 3 and 4, to be continued by the line between lines 4 and 5.

1-2 ii 3 *he rebuked the sea and dried it up* (*gwʿ*[*r*] *bym wywb*[*yšhw*]). The form *gôʿēr* is here taken to be the poel perf. 3rd pers. sing. masc., and *wywb*[*yšhw* is restored as the hiph. impf. 3rd pers. sing. masc. In the MT *wayyabšēhû* is vocalized as a piel impf., but the meaning of the conjugations is the same. If the form in 4QpNah were the piel, I should expect two *y*'s to be represented. Even though *w* and *y* are not always clearly distinguishable in this document, the reading *wyyb*[*šhw*] as the piel in agreement with the MT is unlikely.

1-2 ii 4a *"the rivers" are the Kittim* ([*hnhrwt hm hktyym*]). The restoration seems to fit, but compare 3-4 iii 9, where "the rivers" (*hyʾrym*) are identified with Manasseh. The spelling *ktyym* is restored as it appears below in 3-4 i 3; see the note above on 1QpHab 2:12.

1-2 ii 5a *their rulers* ([*mw*]*šlyhm*), see 1QpHab 4:[12] (referring to the rulers of the Kittim); the phrase *mwšly hktyym* appears below in 3-4 i 3, see also 1QpHab 4:5, 10.

1-2 ii 5 The first word of Nah 1:4b (*ʾmll*) is restored in agreement with the MT, but it is suggested in *BHS* that the form be emended to *dāldlû,* "(Bashan and Carmel) are weak," in order to preserve the alphabetic structure of this section of the prophetic text.

The citation of Nah 1:4b presents the following variant from the MT: *lbnn* (MT: *lbnwn*), but cf. *lbnwn* below in line 7.

In the transcription in *Qumrân Cave 4,* Allegro did not indicate that the *w* of *wkrml* is partially legible and that a trace of the *p* of *pšrw* is visible on the left edge of the frg.

1-2 ii 5-9 Following the citation of Nah 1:4b in the first half of line 5, a commentary begins that continues through the beginning of line 9. In line 7 the words *wprḥ l*[*b*]*nwn hyʾ,* "and 'the blossom of Lebanon' is," can be read, which is surely the beginning of a figurative identification of *prḥ lbnwn* in the manner observed elsewhere in the col. It is therefore likely that the interpretation began in line 5 with a similar identification of *bšn* and *krml.* These two were probably treated together, since there does not seem to be enough room for separate explanations. They may have been connected in some way with the Kittim, who are almost certainly the subject of the preceding interpretations. This is supported by *wlmwšlyw* in line 7, cf. *mwšlyhm* in line 5a, which also probably refers to the Kittim.

At the beginning of line 6 Allegro has [*yʾb*]*dw bw rbym,* which he translates "[and] (*sic*) many [shall per]ish by it." Except for the spelling of *yʾbdw* (the verb *ʾbd* appears in the impf. as *ywbdw* below in 3-4 ii 9 and as *twbd* in 3-4 iii 7, but cf. *wʾbdw* below in line 8), this restoration has been generally accepted. It is true that the phrase "many will perish," or "to destroy many" is paralleled elsewhere in the pesharim in similar contexts, e.g., 1QpHab 2:13; 6:10; 4QpIsa^{a} 2-6 ii 8 (Allegro's 2-4:4); 4QpPs^{a} 1-10 i 27—1-10 ii 1; 1-10 iii 3, 8; 1-10 iv 18. To restore such a phrase here, however, creates a very awkward syntax with the verb preceding the subject but separated from it by a prepositional phrase. Furthermore, if *bw* is read as the preposition with the suffix, it would presumably refer back to the individual or instrument—necessarily masc. sing.—named at the end of line 5, by whom or by which many will perish. The identification could, of course, have been the name of a historical figure, or possibly *hkwhn hršʿ,* "the Wicked Priest" (cf. *rwm ršʿh* in line 6), or *ʾyš hkzb,* "the Man of the Lie" (see 4QpPs^{a} 1-10 i 27—1-10 ii 1), but the most likely identification in the context of these lines—the Kittim—would be excluded by the sing. form.

In view of these problems I reject Allegro's reading and suggest instead [*wh*]*ḥr*[*y*]*bw rbym,* "and they make many desolate," cf. *hḥryb* in Nah 1:4aβ and *lḥrym ʾrṣwt rbwt,* "to lay waste many lands," in 1QpHab 6:8 (the subject is the Kittim). This reading fits the visible traces of letters, gives a more acceptable syntax, and allows restoration of some identification of the Kittim at the end of line 5.

(*at*) *the height of wickedness* (*rwm ršʿh*). The exact function of this phrase in line 6 is unclear, but I interpret it adverbially, as does Allegro. The phrase *rwm ršʿh* also occurs in 1QH frg. 5, line 7, but the context is lost. Dupont-Sommer ("Résumé 1969-1970," 407) apparently understands the phrase in 4QpNah as being in apposition with someone or something named at the end of line 5; he translates it "les impies orgueilleux." Strugnell questions whether the phrase would not be the object of the verb with *rbym* as the subject. Both of these explanations, however, assume that the verb is *yʾbdw* and that *bw* is a preposition with the 3rd pers. sing. masc. sf.

Just before the break in line 6 Allegro reads *hb*[, and there is probably room for about twenty-eight letters following this. Strugnell restores *hb*[*šn* (so also Dupont-Sommer, "Résumé 1969-1970," 407), but he does not explain why the proper name would have the article here.

At the beginning of line 7 Allegro restores [*kr*]*ml,* which is probably correct, but the syntax of the line is difficult. The word *krml* must be joined to the following prepositional phrase *wlmwšlyw* and seemingly also to the next word, *lbnwn,* since the phrase *wprḥ lbnwn hyʾ* begins a new section of the interpretation. Strugnell proposes a restoration such as *ky hb*[*šn hyʾ hktyym wlmlkm qrʾ*]/*krml wlmwšlyw lbnwn,* "for Bashan is the Kittim, and its kings are called Carmel, and its rulers, Lebanon." While there are problems with the specific Hebrew words he supplies, Strugnell offers a possible syntactical solution to this awkward passage.

The only other mention of Carmel in the pesharim is in 4QpIsa^c 21:3 in what may have been a commentary on the last verses of Isaiah 29. It follows the mention of *hlbnwn* in 21:2, but the context is entirely lost.

Lebanon and the blossom of Lebanon (*lbnwn wprḥ l*[*b*]*nwn*). In line 7 Allegro transcribes *lbnwn* (the second time), but I see no trace of the *b* in the photograph in *Qumrân Cave 4.*

At the end of line 7, following *prḥ lbnwn,* the personal pronoun is preserved. Although *w* and *y* are not always clearly distinguished in this text, the fem. form *hyʾ* is almost certainly to be read here. What follows, therefore, should agree with this form. I suggest restoring *ʿdt dwršy hḥlqwt,* "the congregation of the Seekers-After-Smooth-Things" (see 4QpIsa^c 23 ii [10]), though this may be a little short for the space. Also possible are *ʿṣt dwršy hḥlqwt,* see 3-4 i 2; or *mmšlt dwršy hḥlqwt,* see 3-4 ii 4. See the note below on 3-4 i 2. Identification of Lebanon with the Kittim as presumably in 4QpIsa^a 7-10 iii 6-7, 11-12 (Allegro's 8-10:2-3, 7-8) is excluded by the fem. form of the personal pronoun. In 1QpHab 12:3-4, Lebanon is identified as the "council of the community" (*ʿṣt hyḥd*), but this would not fit the context of these lines, where Lebanon is apparently an enemy of the Qumran sect, who "will perish before the congregation of the elect of God" (line 8). See the note on 1QpHab 12:3.

1-2 ii 8-9 *and their partisans* ([*wʾnšy ʿṣ*]*tm*). This is restored by Allegro, without the conjunction. Strugnell suggests *bny ʾšm*]*tm,* "their guilty followers." On the translation of the phrase, see the note above on 1QpHab 5:10.

the congregation of the elect of God ([*ʿdt*] *bḥyr*[*y ʾl*]), cf. *ʿdt bḥyrw* in 4QpIsa^d 1:3; 4QpPs^a 1-10 ii 5; 1-10 iii 5; and *bḥyry ʾl* in 4QpPs^a 1-10 iv [14]. See the note above on 1QpHab 5:4.

At the end of line 8 and the beginning of line 9 Strugnell proposes restoring something like [*kʾšr ʾmr mmnw*/*ygwrw k*]*wl ywšby tbl,* "as it says, 'all the inhabitants of the world stand in awe before him,'" a secondary citation of Ps 33:8. While this suggestion cannot be rejected out of hand, no similar secondary citations or allusions are found elsewhere in this text.

1-2 ii 9-11 Although these lines seem to have contained the text of Nah

1:5-6a, restoration of the biblical passage is difficult. In the second half of line 9 Allegro restores 1:5aα followed by a commentary, and in the second half of line 10 he restores 1:6a continuing into line 11. He thus omits 1:5aβ-b. This may be owing to his opinion that the preceding col. contained all of Nah 1:2-6 and that this col. repeats and interprets only selected phrases of the biblical text. Strugnell restores the full text of Nah 1:5-6a, beginning in the second half of line 9, with the following variants from the MT: *mmnw wlmpnyw* (MT: *mpnyw*) and *tbl* (MT: *wtbl*). In addition, he thinks that it is possible to restore [*h*]*hr*[*ym*] as the first word of Nah 1:5, an emendation suggested in *BHS* on the basis of a text from Murabbaᶜat (Mur 88 [XII], col. 16, line 12; see *Les grottes de Murabbaᶜât* [ed. P. Benoit *et al.*; DJD 2; Oxford: Clarendon, 1961], p. 197 and pl. LXVI), but this seems to me to be unlikely on the basis of the photograph in *Qumrân Cave 4*.

I follow Strugnell in restoring Nah 1:5-6a, but I continue the citation through the end of verse 6. In line 11, both Allegro and Strugnell read the letter that is partially preserved on the left edge of the frg. as *p*, restoring *p*[*šrw* as the beginning of the interpretation. But an analysis of the structure of this document indicates that there would almost certainly have been a space between the end of the citation and the beginning of the interpretation. This letter is better read as *ḥ* thus continuing the citation of Nah 1:6.

The three words at the beginning of line 9 ([*wkw*]*l ywšby tbl*) in what is apparently the end of the commentary on Nah 1:4b seem to be an allusion to the text of Nah 1:5b which follows. See Part II, p. 245.

Fragments 3-4, Column i

The restorations offered tentatively here for the beginnings of some of the lines in this col. are probably too short, but they are included in order to present the accord of recent scholarly debate. Lines 7 and 8, however, the most difficult lines of this controversial col., have not been filled in, since the meaning of the lines is not certain and all of the evidence is not yet in. Moreover, all the restorations that have been proposed are too short for the space that is left at the beginning of these lines (see the discussion of these lines below). The length of the lines cannot be determined with certainty, but if the restoration of the biblical text of Nah 2:14 in lines 8-10 is accepted, then line 9 contains about 68 units and is about 8 units shorter than the other lines. Thus, the length of the lines in the col. is probably about 76 units, which is about the same as the length of the lines in col. ii of frgs. 3-4. Then by observing the vertical alignment with the preceding lines, the approximate number of missing units can be determined for lines 1-8: line 1, 28 units; line 2, 27 units; line 3, 28 units; line 4, 37 units; line 5, 38 units; line 6, 36 units; line 7, 36 units; line 8, 33 units.

3-4 i 1 Beginning either at the end of the preceding col. or in the first line of this col. is an interpretation presumably of Nah 2:12a, "where is the lion's den, the cave of the young lions?" (probably with *mĕʿārâ,* "cave," for *mirʿeh,* "pasture," of the MT).

From what is preserved in this line, the structure of the pesher cannot be determined, but it is likely that Nah 2:12a, which originally referred to Nineveh, is here applied to Jerusalem (Dupont-Sommer, "Le Commentaire," 57). The commentary may have been structured as a figurative identification of the sort found above in col. ii of frgs. 1-2 and below in lines 10 and 11. However, I restore the commentary with the formula *pšrw ʿl* (as below in line 6), since it places the beginning of the formula at the beginning of the line and the col., though this restoration is about four or five units too short. Dupont-Sommer ["Le Commentaire," 58] does not restore the Hebrew text but translates "L'explication de ceci concerne Jérusalem. . . , qui est devenue."

the wicked ones of the nations (*ršʿy gwym*). The usual biblical Hebrew spelling *gwym* is used throughout this document; see the notes above on 1QpHab 3:5 and 4QpHos^{a} 2:13.

The citation of Nah 2:12b, which begins in the middle of the line, presents the following variants from the MT:

(1) *ʾry* (MT: *ʾryh*). Both nouns are used in biblical and Qumran Hebrew meaning "lion."

(2) *lbwʾ,* "to enter" (MT: *lābîʾ,* "lion"). Since *w* and *y* are not clearly distinguishable at times in this document, the reading is not certain. I prefer to read *lbwʾ* (so also Bardtke [*Die Handscriftenfunde*], Vermes, Dupont-Sommer); this emendation is suggested in *BHS* and is supported by the Greek τοῦ εἰσελθεῖν and by the pesher on this verse (line 2) where *lbwʾ* is certain. Many commentators, however, read *lbyʾ,* "lion" in agreement with the MT (e.g., Allegro, Carmignac, Habermann, Lohse, Maier, Vogt, Yadin). Boccaccio and van der Woude, too, read *lbyʾ,* but they interpret it as the hiph. inf. cs. of *bwʾ,* "to bring." Syntactically this requires a direct object. Boccaccio freely supplies one, "ut afferret (praedam)," while van der Woude apparently takes *gwr ʾry* as the object, "om daar te brengen het leeuwenwelp."

At the end of the line on the photograph in *Qumrân Cave 4,* there is a mark that appears to be a vertical stroke of a pen, though it could be simply a darkening of the skin along a fold. It has not been indicated in any of the transcriptions of this line, and it is very unlikely that it should be read as one of the letters of the next word of the biblical text (*wʾyn*).

3-4 i 2 At the beginning of the line the last two words of Nah 2:12b are restored. Following this the formula *pšrw ʿl* is restored at the beginning of the interpretation (as below in line 6), leaving a space of about seven units between the citation and the commentary (as below in line 6 and apparently also in line 10; see the introductory comments on the structure of the commentary).

Demetrius (*[dmy]ṭrws*). The spelling of the name could also be *dmy]-ṭrys* (as read by Habermann and Yadin ["Pesher Nahum," 1]). Dupont-Sommer ("Le Commentaire," 57) transcribes *dmy]ṭrys,* but in his note on that line (p. 62) he apparently follows the reading *dmyṭrws.* In the preliminary publication Allegro noted that either reading is possible; he referred to S. Krauss, *Griechische und lateinische Lehnwörter im Talmud, Midrasch und Targum* (Berlin: S. Calvary & Co., 1898-1899) 2. 520b, for alternations in spelling such as *qwryys* and *qyrys* for κύριος. As was pointed out above, most scholars believe that this is a reference to the Seleucid ruler Demetrius III Eukerus (95-88 B.C.).

the king of Greece (*mlk ywn*). The term *yāwān* is used variously in biblical Hebrew to indicate all or part of the Greek-speaking Hellenistic realm. In Dan 8:21 the phrase *mlk ywn* designates Alexander the Great, cf. *śar yāwān,* "the prince of Greece" in 10:20, referring to the "guardian angel" of Greece, and *malkût yāwān,* "the kingdom of Greece" in 11:2, referring to the realm of Alexander the Great.

on the advice of the Seekers-After-Smooth-Things (*bʿṣt dwršy hḥlqwt*), or "at the instigation of the Seekers-After-Smooth-Things." This group also appears below in line 7; 3-4 ii 2, 4; 3-4 iii 3, 6-7. The only other mention of them in the pesharim is *ʿdt dwršy hḥlqwt byrwšlym,* "the congregation of the Seekers-After-Smooth-Things in Jerusalem," in 4QpIsa^c 23 ii [10], cf. 1QH 2:[15], 32. As was noted in the introductory remarks to this text, this group is almost certainly to be identified with the Pharisees; see further J. Maier, "Weitere Stücke," 233-49.

3-4 i 3 The letters that are partially preserved at the beginning of this line were read by Allegro in the preliminary publication as *]ryd* and so he restored *mḥ]ryd* from Nah 2:12b. An alternative reading that fits the visible traces of letters better is *]byd* "into the power of," literally, "into the hand of." Other suggestions for restoring the beginning of the line with this reading are similar to that proposed here, e.g., [*wlwʾ bʾ ky lwʾ ntnh ʾl*] *byd,* "mais celuici n'y entra pas, car Dieu ne l'a pas livrée] dans la main" (Dupont-Sommer, "Le Commentaire," 57-59); or similarly "[But God did not permit the city to be delivered] into the hands (*sic*) of" (Vermes).

The Qumran interpretation preserves the phrase *mʾntykws,* "from Antiochus." Since this is followed by the temporal phrase *ʿd ʿmwd mwšly ktyym,* "until the rise of the rulers of the Kittim," it seems necessary to interpret the preposition *mn* temporally, i.e., "from (the time of) Antiochus," though no such usage is attested in Hebrew. The commentary refers in some way to the independence of Judea and seems to be saying that

Jerusalem (or Judea) was independent from the time of Antiochus until the coming of the Kittim (i.e., the Romans). It is unclear which Antiochus is meant, since it was not from Antiochus that Judea gained political independence. It was from Demetrius II that Simon, the son of Mattathias, was able to negotiate independence in 142 B.C. From that time until the Roman conquest (63 B.C.) Judea enjoyed relative freedom. The Qumran commentator could be referring to religious liberty, which was denied by Antiochus IV Epiphanes but was regained after his death. It is likely, therefore, that Antiochus IV Epiphanes is meant.

until the rise of (*ʿd ʿmwd*). For similar uses of this phrase, see Ezra 2:63; Neh 7:65; CD 5:5; 12:23; 20:1.

the Kittim (*ktyym*). See the note above on 1QpHab 2:12.

3-4 i 3-4 [*the city*] *will be trampled* (*trms* [*hʿyr*]), i.e., Jerusalem, which is presumably the subject of the preceding interpretations. The verb form *trms* is here taken to be the niph. impf. sing. fem. *tērāmēs,* though the niph. of *rms* is attested in biblical Hebrew only in Isa 28:3. As it stands the form could be read as the qal impf., but it would be awkward. The subject of the verb must be fem., and in the context of this col. it seems that it can be none other than Jerusalem. Moreover, with the qal, a direct object would be needed, but what would Jerusalem trample? For the idea of a city being trampled, see Isa 26:6, cf. Ezek 26:11, where "all your streets" are trampled, and Isa 1:12, where "courts" are trampled.

3-4 i 4 Following the commentary on Nah 2:12b, which ends at the beginning of the line, there is a space before the citation of 2:13a, though the exact length of the space cannot be determined. See the introductory remarks on the structure of this pesher.

The citation of Nah 2:13a in the second half of line 4 presents the following variants from the MT:

(1) *ʾry* (MT: *ʾryh*); see the note above on 3-4 i 1.

(2) *gwryw,* i.e., *gûrā*(*y*)*w* (MT: *grwtyw,* i.e., *gōrôtā*(*y*)*w*). Two different noun forms are used, though the meaning is the same. The MT has *gôr* in the pl. fem. with the 3rd pers. sing. masc. sf., while 4QpNah uses *gûr* in a pl. masc. suffixal form.

(3) For the fifth word of the citation, it is not certain whether 4QpNah has *wmḥnq* (as read by Allegro in the preliminary publication) in agreement with the MT, or *mḥnq* (as read by Allegro in the *editio princeps*). Strugnell regards *wmḥnq* as certain, questioning whether the transcription of this word in *Qumrân Cave 4* might be an error in printing, but Yadin ("Pesher Nahum," 1, 11) reads *mḥnq.* The *w,* if present, is almost totally obscured by a crack in the manuscript.

(4) *llbywtyw* (MT: *llbʾtyw*). Here again different nouns with the same meaning are found. The form in the MT is a pl. suffixal form of

lĕbāʾâ, while the form in 4QpNah is a pl. suffixal form of *lĕbîyāʾ* spelled without the ʾ.

(5) The last word in the line, *ṭrp,* "prey," is not in the MT.

enough for his cubs (*bdy gwryw*). The form *bdy* is here to taken to be *bĕdê,* "enough" as in the MT (so e.g., Allegro, Maier, and Yadin). Others interpret the form as *baddê,* "the limbs of," i.e., "the lion tears the limbs of his own cubs" (so e.g., Gaster, van der Woude, Dupont-Sommer, Strugnell). Gaster refers to Job 18:13 to support this interpretation, but the context there is entirely different.

3-4 i 5-6 Allegro leaves the beginning of line 5 blank and restores *pšrw* at the end of the lacuna, giving the formula *pšrw*] *ʿl kpyr hḥrwn,* "the interpretation of it] concerns the Lion of Wrath." But this leaves a large indentation at the beginning of the line before the pesher, which is not consistent with the structure of this document. There is room for the text of Nah 2:13b, but this appears in line 6. The absence of repeated citations elsewhere in the document argues against restoring 2:13b at the beginning of line 5. Carmignac (*Les Textes,* 2. 86) places the introductory formula at the beginning of the line and translates what is preserved after the break as "contre le Lionceau Furieux," but he does not make any further restoration of the interpretation. Following this lead I tentatively restore the line in the light of the historical setting described in the introductory remarks, but the present reconstruction is about nine units too short. In lines 1-2 the noun *ʾry* is connected with Demetrius, so a similar commentary is restored here, *ʾry* in Nah 2:13a being identified with Demetrius. If the Lion of Wrath is identified with Alexander Jannaeus, the smiting of the Lion of Wrath could refer to Alexander Jannaeus's defeat at Shechem, suggesting something like "but they fled before him" for the beginning of line 6.

For the phrase *ʿśh mlḥmh,* see, e.g., Gen 14:2; Deut 20:12.

The impf. verb form *ykh* should be noted. In the context as restored, it could have the nuance of repeated past action, referring to Jannaeus's many military campaigns.

his great ones (*gdwlyw*) or "his nobles." Dupont-Sommer ("Le Commentaire," 65) is probably correct in taking this as a reference to the Sadducees, the aristocratic partisans of Alexander Jannaeus.

his partisans (*ʾnšy ʿṣtw*). See the note above on 1QpHab 5:10.

Following the end of the interpretation of Nah 2:13a at the beginning of line 6, there was probably a space before the citation of Nah 2:13b.

3-4 i 6 The citation of Nah 2:13b presents the following variants from the MT;

(1) *ḥwrh* or possibly *ḥyrh* (MT: *ḥryw*). The form in the MT, *ḥōrā(y)w,* "his holes," or "his dens," is the pl. of *ḥōr* with the 3rd pers. sing. masc. sf. The form in 4QpNah cannot be read with certainty; the first letter—or

what is presumably the first letter—is mutilated, as is the last letter. Some read *ḥyrh* (e.g., Allegro, Habermann, Lohse, Strugnell), a noun with a suffix (?), but *ḥyr* is an unattested noun. Others read *ḥwrh* (e.g., Dupont-Sommer, Yadin). In both cases, however, the final *h* is explained as the old 3rd pers. sing. masc. sf. Though this suffix is attested in biblical Hebrew in pre-exilic times (GKC §91e), no clear example of it can be found in Qumran Hebrew (*pace* Dupont-Sommer, "Le Commentaire," 65; see the note above on 1QpHab 10:11). If the suffix is taken as the 3rd pers. sing. fem., then it is not parallel to the other noun of the compound object (*wmᶜwntw,* "its den[s]"), which has the 3rd pers. sing. masc. sf. It seems then that either some other word is to be read, or possibly a scribal error is involved. Such an error could have arisen through misreading of the suffix *yw,* if the letters were similar in form and written closely together. Compare the *h* in [*y*]*thlkw* in 3-4 ii 2, which could easily be mistaken for *yw* or *wy*. This would not necessarily presuppose that the manuscript is a copy rather than an autograph, since the error could have arisen at some point in a biblical manuscript used by the scribe.

(2) *wmᶜwntw* (MT: *wmᶜntyw*). The form in 4QpNah could be the sing. noun with the sing. sf. (so Dupont-Sommer, "Le Commentaire," 66), a variant in number from the MT. More likely it is the defectively written pl. fem. with the defectively written 3rd pers. sing. masc. sf., cf. *ṣyrw* below in 3-4 ii 1, *mḥšbtm* in 1QpHab 3:5, and *wbbhmtm* in 1QpHab 3:10.

3-4 i 6-8 This interpretation of Nah 2:13b has been the subject of much discussion. In these lines are references to the Lion of Wrath (*kpyr hḥrwn,* line 6), the Seekers-After-Smooth-Things (*dwršy hḥlqwt,* line 7), and hanging men alive (*ytlh ʾnšym ḥyym,* line 7). Though there is virtually unanimous agreement among modern scholars that these lines refer to Alexander Jannaeus's crucifixion of the Pharisees who had turned their allegiance to Demetrius III (see the sketch of the events in the introduction to this text), opinions differ as to how the beginning of lines 7 and 8 should be restored and as to how the last words of the pesher should be treated.

In the preliminary publication, Allegro read the first letters that are preserved in line 7 as]*mwt,* which he translated (with a question mark) "death" (so also Carmignac). More recently, Y. Yadin, too, has read]*mwt,* and in the light of his analysis of the Temple Scroll he has restored *mšpṭ*] *mwt,* "sentence of death," suggesting an allusion to Deut 21:22 ("Pesher Nahum," 10-11; see further below). Other commentators restored *nq*]*mwt,* "vengeance" (e.g., Dupont-Sommer, Vermes).

The first attempts at restoring the beginning of line 8 were based on the view that the sect would have been horrified at the crucifixion of the Seekers-After-Smooth-Things by the Lion of Wrath. In the preliminary publication Allegro supplied *ʾšr lʾ yᶜśh,* "which was not done (in Israel before)." In the *editio princeps,* however, he did not restore the beginning of line 8. Many commentators have followed Allegro's original suggestion with minor variations, e.g., Dupont-Sommer, who proposes [*ʿl hʿṣ ʾšr lwʾ ʿśh ʾyš*] *byśrʾl mlpnym,* "(lui qui suspendait des hommes vivants) [sur le bois. . . , ce que nul n'avait fait] en Israël antérieurement" ("Le Commentaire," 57, 59).

Recently, the presuppositions on which such restorations are based, i.e., that the sect would have been critical of Alexander Jannaeus in this instance and would have been horrified by crucifixion, have been challenged by Y. Yadin ("Pesher Nahum," 3-12). He argues, first, that the sect would not have used the designation "Lion of Wrath" to refer to someone whom they were criticizing. In the light of 4QpHos^b 2:2-3 and his analysis of the use of the word *ḥrwn* in biblical Hebrew (referring to the wrath of Yahweh), Yadin concludes that the sect looked upon the Lion of Wrath as God's instrument. Next Yadin presents a passage from the Temple Scroll (11QTemple 64:6-13) that he thinks prescribes crucifixion as punishment for certain political crimes. He concludes that something like the following should be restored in lines 7-8: *ʾšr ytlh ʾnšym ḥyym* [*ʿl hʿṣ ky zʾt* (or *kn htwrh*) *mšpṭ*] *byśrʾl mlpnym,* "who hangs men alive [upon the tree as this is the law] in Israel as of old."

Yadin's conclusions have been questioned by J. M. Baumgarten ("*TLH* in the Temple Scroll," 472-81). To Yadin's first assertion he replies that 4QpHos^b is too fragmentary to give a clear characterization of the Lion of Wrath, and in answer to Yadin's statement that *ḥrwn* in the Bible is generally associated with God's wrath, he cites 1QpHab 3:12, where *ḥrn ʾp* refers to the Kittim. With regard to Yadin's interpretation of 11QTemple, Baumgarten argues that *tlh* there refers to hanging and not to crucifixion. He concludes (p. 481) that it is plausible that the sect held the Seekers-After-Smooth-Things to be deserving of death for treason, but that the assertion that the sect believed crucifixion to be in accord with the Law of Moses is unsubstantiated.

That many questions surrounding the practice of crucifixion in Palestine in the first century B.C. and the first century A.D. cannot be treated here. Involved is not only the whole interpretative tradition of Deut 21:23 ("for a hanged man is accursed of God"; see Yadin ["Pesher Nahum," 4-11], Baumgarten ["*TLH* in the Temple Scroll," 473-79], L. Díez Merino ["La crucifixión en la antigua literatura judía (Período intertestamental)," *Estudios Eclesiásticos* 51 (1976) 5-27; "El suplicio de la Cruz en la literatura judía intertestamental," *SBFLA* 26 (1976) 31-120]), but also the juxtaposition of this tradition with the Roman practice of crucifixion (see, e.g., M. Wilcox, "'Upon the Tree'—Deut 21:22-23 in the New Testament," *JBL* 96 [1977] 85-99; M. Hengel, *Crucifixion* [Philadelphia: Fortress,

1977]). The evidence from Jewish tradition that Baumgarten and Yadin present is conflicting, and the Hebrew terminology is subject to varying interpretations. Full publication of 11QTemple and more detailed study of it will be needed to determine more exactly what sort of punishment is being prescribed there.

Archeological evidence bearing on this point that has recently come to light has been presented by J. A. Fitzmyer, who has examined the positions of Yadin and Baumgarten in the light of this evidence ("Crucifixion in Ancient Palestine," 498-507). He concludes that Yadin is probably correct in his interpretation of 11QTemple and its implications for 4QpNah, and he suggests, following Yadin's lead, restoring at the beginning of line 7 [*ʾšr mṣʾ ḥṭʾ mšpṭ*] *mwt,* "[who has found a crime punishable by] death," and at the beginning of line 8 [*ʿl hʿṣ ky kn nʿśh*] *byśrʾl mlpnym,* "(whom he hangs as live men) [on the tree, as it was thus done] in Israel from of old." But these restorations are about 15-20 units too short for the space (see the remarks above about the length of the lines in this col.). The content of these restorations may be the best presentation of the evidence at present, but no satisfactory suggestion of the exact Hebrew words to be supplied in lines 7 and 8 has thus far been offered.

It should be noted that the verb at the end of line 7 in the phrase *ʾšr ytlh ʾnšym ḥyym,* "who hung men alive," is impf., but the nuance of this impf. form in the historical context that is assumed is unclear.

Another problem of this interpretation section is the meaning of the last phrase *ky ltlwy ḥy ʿl hʿṣ* [*y*]*qrʾ*. The phrase seems to be anacoluthon, and it has been translated in various ways. The proposal made by Allegro in the preliminary publication was suggested to him by F. M. Cross and D. N. Freedman, who considered the phrase to be an elliptical allusion to Deut 21:23. They suggested that *qllt* (or *qllt ʾlhym* as in Deut 21:23) was to be understood and had to be supplied in order to fill out the phrase; thus, "for one hanged alive upon a tree is called (cursed)." They explained that the word *qllt* had been deliberately omitted for pietistic reasons (cf. Gal 3:13), but that the Qumran community knew what was meant. Similar translations have been offered by Gaster, Habermann, and van der Woude.

Other attempts to translate the phrase include "mais celui qui a été suspendu vivant sur [le] bois [on (l') in]voque[ra]" (Dupont-Sommer, "Le Commentaire," 67); "since the hanged one is called alive on the tree" (Yadin, "Pesher Nahum," 10-11, who further explains "since the hanged one is called [hanged] alive on the tree"); "for he (the Young Lion of Wrath) took 'hanged' (Deut 21:23) to mean 'alive on a tree'" (Baumgarten, *"TLH,"* 481).

What all these translations have in common is the attempt to avoid anacoluthon. In my opinion, the best suggestion is that of H. Bardtke, who interprets the phrase as a sort of introduction to the citation of Nah 2:14, "denn über den lebendig [das] Holz Gehängten [hei]sst es:" (similarly Allegro in *Qumrân Cave 4,* Lohse, Maier, Vermes, Skehan, and Fitzmyer). Such a translation has been rejected by others because it was thought to violate the normal pesher structure (see Dupont-Sommer, "Le Commentaire," 67, who regards this irregularity of structure as just as arbitrary as the ellipse suggested by Cross and Freedman). This structure, however, is not entirely unsupported among the pesharim; see 4QpIsa[b] 2:7, where the citation seems to be a continuation of the preceding commentary in one syntactical unit.

If this is accepted it remains to determine the best translation of the verb *yqrᵓ*. There are three possible meanings for the verb *qrᵓ,* and the form in 4QpNah could be the qal of niph. impf.: (1) With the meaning "to call," the form in 4QpNah could be translated either "for he/it (scripture ?) calls one hanged alive upon the tree" (qal), or "for one hanged alive upon the tree is called" (niph.). But neither of these translations gives a smooth introduction to the citation. (2) With the meaning "to proclaim," the form could be translated either "for with reference to living men hanged on a tree He—i.e., God—declares:" (P. W. Skehan, "A New Translation," 120-21, taking the form as the qal), or "for with reference . . . it is declared" (niph.). (3) With the meaning "to read," the form could be translated either "for with regard to . . . one (or 'it') reads" (qal), or "for with regard to . . . it is read" (niph.). I prefer the qal meaning "to read," either with an indefinite subject "one" or with "scripture" understood as the subject. This makes the smoothest transition to the citation. Moreover, if "scripture" is understood as the subject, this may be associated with formulas such as *wᵓšr ᵓmr,* "and as for what it (i.e., scripture) says." See further Part II, p. 243.

3-4 i 8 *against you* (*ᵓly*[*kh*]). This form is restored with the 2nd pers. sing. masc. sf., as suggested by Allegro, in the light of the masc. sf. of *wkpyrykh* in line 9. The form of the MT has the 2nd pers. sing. fem. sf. referring to the city of Nineveh.

3-4 i 9-12 For the *editio princeps* Allegro has added frg. 3 to the col., giving the first letters of lines 9-12.

3-4 i 9-10 The citation of Nah 2:14 presents the following variants from the MT:

(1) *rwbkh,* "your (masc.) abundance" (MT: *rkbh,* "her chariot"). This is restored in the light of the commentary in line 10. The reading of 4QpNah is supported by the LXX, which has πλῆθός σου.

(2) *wkpyrykh* (MT: *wkpyryk*). The form of the MT has the 2nd pers. sing. fem. sf., and 4QpNah has the 2nd pers. sing. masc. In the commentary in line 10, the form *wkpryw* has the 3rd pers. sing. masc. sf., cf. the

alternation in the suffixes on *ṭrp* below. A better translation of *kpyr* in the context of the MT would be "your villages," cf. Neh 6:2, in the light of the Aramaic word *kpryh,* "village," which is attested in Sefîre III 23,26. The word is also preserved as *kpyr* in Hadad 10 and Panammu 10 (see J. A. Fitzmyer, *The Aramaic Inscriptions of Sefîre* [BibOr 19; Rome: Pontifical Biblical Institute, 1967] 119). I have retained the translation "your lions" in the citation in 4QpNah, because it seems from the commentary that is partially preserved in line 11 that this is how the Qumran author understood the phrase.

(3) [*ṭ*]*rph* (MT: *ṭrpk*). The form in the MT has the 2nd pers. sing. fem. sf., while the form in 4QpNah ends in *h,* apparently the 3rd pers. sing. fem. sf. Because the form *ṭrpw* with the 3rd pers. sing. masc. sf. occurs in the commentary in line 11, it has been suggested that the *h* of the form *ṭrph* is a 3rd pers. sing. masc. sf. (so Allegro, Dupont-Sommer), but see the note above on 3-4 i 6.

(4) The form *mlʾkykh* is restored rather than *mlʾkkh* as in the MT in the light of the form *wkpyrykh* above in line 9. It is suggested in *BHS* that the form of the MT be emended to *mlʾkyk,* parallel to *wkpyryk.* See GKC §91*l,* where the *h* is explained as dittography with the following word; see also K. Cathcart, *Nahum in the Light of Northwest Semitic* (BibOr 26; Rome: Biblical Institute, 1973) 110-11.

According to Strugnell, there are masc. suffixes on *rwbkh* and *wkpyrykh* because the verse is being applied to a man—the Lion of Wrath—while the fem. suffixes in the MT refer to the city of Nineveh. He sees in the 3rd pers. sing. fem. sf. of *ṭrph* a reference to *ḥrb.* The problem with his explanation of the masc. suffixes is the assumption that the Qumran author would have altered the gender of words in the biblical text to suit the interpretation. The change from fem. to masc. in *wkpyryk* might not have been a deliberate alteration; the masc. could have arisen through misreading of a consonantal text. Similarly, *ṭrph* could have arisen through a scribal error, with *k* at some point being lost through haplography of the similar-looking letters *k* and *p.*

3-4 i 10-11 In the preliminary publication Allegro read]*ṭ* after the first lacuna in line 10 on the right edge of frg. 4 (so also Dupont-Sommer, "Le Commentaire," 10), but the restoration in the *editio princeps* of the word *pš*]*rw* is certainly correct.

the detachments of his army (*gdwdy ḥylw*). The 3rd pers. sing. masc. sf. certainly refers back to the Lion of Wrath, the subject of the preceding pesher (line 10).

and his lions (*wkpryw*). The change from the 2nd pers. sing. masc. sf. in the biblical text to the 3rd pers. sing. masc. is understandable in the context of the pesher, probably influenced by the preceding *ḥylw.* Although the reading is not certain, it looks as if the spelling here is defective (*wkpryw*), cf. *wkpyryw* above in line 9. The same change in suffix occurs in words *ṭrpw* (line 11) and *mlʾkyw* (3-4 ii 1) in the continuation of the commentary on this verse.

It was noted above in the comment on *wkpyrykh* in line 9 that it would be possible to translate the word *kpyr* as "village," but the translation "and his lions," is preferred here because of the lion imagery of this whole col. The commentary in line 11 identifies the "lions" as "his great ones," a group also named in line 5, where the citation and interpretation include the words *ʾry, gwr, lbyʾ, kpyr hḥrwn,* all words referring to lions.

3-4 i 11 The beginning of line 11 is restored in the light of the phrase *bgdwlyw wʾnšy ʿṣtw* above in line 5, and the mention of *ḥrb,* "sword," in Nah 2:14 suggests the verb *ʾbd,* "to perish," see 1QpHab 2:[13]; 6:10; 4QpPs[a] 1-10 ii 1; also 1-10 iii 3-4.

the wealth (*hhwn*). This is read by Allegro, but only the first *h* and the final *wn* can be read with probability. Carmignac (*Les Textes,* 2. 88, n. 21) thinks that there is room for another letter in addition to the second *h*. On the basis of the photograph in *Qumrân Cave 4,* I have to agree with Carmignac. It is possible, however, that a fissure in or a stretching of the skin has caused the letters to appear farther apart in the photograph than they actually are. I can think of no other word that would fit the context here.

that the priests of Jerusalem have amassed (*ʾšr qb*[*ṣw kwh*]*ny yrwšlym*), see 1QpHab 9:4-5. Allegro's restoration fits the visible traces of letters and the space. I side with Strugnell in rejecting the *l* that Carmignac and Dupont-Sommer ("Le Commentaire," 70) prefer to read just after the break.

The subject of the pesher since line 6 has been the Lion of Wrath, presumably Alexander Jannaeus, and there is no reason to think that the 3rd pers. sing. masc. sfs. of *gdwlyw* and *wṭrpw* in line 11 do not also refer to the Lion of Wrath. The wealth of the priests of Jerusalem could be said to be "his prey" inasmuch as Jannaeus himself was the high priest.

3-4 i 12 *Ephraim* ([*ʾ*]*prym*), see below 3-4 ii 2, 8; 3-4 iii 5. For the identification of Ephraim with the Seekers-After-Smooth-Things, see 3-4 ii 2. This, then, is almost certainly a reference to the Pharisees.

In the preliminary publication Allegro joined a small frg. by which he read at the end of this line *l*[ ]*ṭ y*[ ], but in the *editio princeps* the frg. has been removed. See below 3-4 iii 12.

Israel will be given (*yntn yśrʾl*). On the photograph in *Qumrân Cave 4* it looks as if "Israel" is the last word in the line, followed by a *vacat*. However, there must have been a whole phrase, now obliterated, because it does not make sense for the commentary to break off after "Israel will be given" (unless it is to be translated "Israel will be given up," cf. Hos 11:8). Moreover, the first line of the next col. is a continuation of the same pesher, and it is unlikely that the interpretation would have been interrupted by such a large space.

Fragments 3-4, Column ii

3-4 ii 1 The first half of the line gives the fourth part of the interpretation of Nah 2:14, which began above in 3-4 i 10. Following this is a short space and then the text of Nah 3:1a-bα.

his messengers (*wmlʾkyw*); see the note above on 3-4 i 9-10.

his envoys (*ṣyrw*). For the defectively written pl. noun with a suffix, cf. *wmʿwntw* above in 3-4 i 6; elsewhere in this document such forms usually appear with the full writing.

The citation of Nah 3:1a-bα presents the following variant from the MT: *hdmym* (MT: *dmym*).

3-4 ii 2 *at the end of days* (*lʾḥryt hymym*). This phrase is a signal that the interpretation is shifting from a historical thrust to an eschatological focus. These words are sometimes incorporated into the introductory formula itself, e.g., *pšr hdbr lʾḥryt hymym* (4QpIsa[b] 2:1; 4QpIsa[c] 6-7 ii [14]; 23 ii 10). See the note above on 1QpHab 2:5-6.

3-4 ii 3-4 The citation of Nah 3:1bβ-3 presents the following variants from the MT:

(1) *ymwš* (MT: *ymyš*). The form of the MT is from *myš,* while the form in 4QpNah is from *mwš.*

(2) *wqwl* [first] (MT: *qwl*).

(3) *lhwb* (MT: *wlhb ḥrb*). The omission of *ḥrb,* "sword," in 4QpNah is almost certainly a scribal error, perhaps owing to homoioteleuton. Instead of the segolate form *lahab* that appears in the MT, 4QpNah has *lhwb,* probably to be vocalized as a *qĕtōl* form. This variation in form might have arisen under the influence of Aramaic, or it could reflect an accentual variation that developed within Hebrew. Elsewhere in QL the usual biblical Hebrew segolate form *lahab* is attested in 1QM 5:10; CD 2:5; 1QH frg. 58, line 4; *lhwb* appears in 1QH 2:26; 3:30; and *lwhb,* a qutl type (?), appears in 1QM 5:7, 10; 6:2. See the note above on 4QpIsa[c] 6-7 ii 8. See also M. H. Goshen-Gottstein, "Linguistic Structure," 126-27; J. Maier, "Weitere Stücke," 215-25; G. S. Glanzman, "Sectarian Psalms from the Dead Sea," *TS* 13 (1952) 506-507, n. 18.

(4) *wkbwd* (MT: *wkbd*). Here the noun *kōbed* of Nah 3:3, a qutl type, is replaced in 4QpNah by *kbwd,* which could be vocalized *kābôd,* a qatāl type, or *kĕbôd,* a qĕtōl form, cf. *lhwb* above. Both forms are attested in biblical Hebrew, but in QL *kbwd* is used exclusively.

(5) *qṣ* (MT: *qṣh*). Both of these nouns mean "end." The noun *qāṣeh* occurs only once in QL in 1QH 6:31, but the noun *qēṣ* is used frequently. Though it usually connotes the "endtime," it bears no such eschatological nuance here or below in line 6; see the note above on 1QpHab 5:7-8.

(6) *wkšlw* (MT: *ykšlw*). The *kĕtîb* of the MT is vocalized *yikšĕlû,* the qal impf. 3rd pers. pl., but the *qĕrê* is *wkšlw* (*wĕkāšĕlû*), which agrees with the form in 4QpNah, the converted qal perf.

(7) *wgwytm* (MT: *bgwytm*). This is certainly a scribal error; the pesher on this verse has *bgwyt* (line 6).

3-4 ii 4-6 *heated strife* (*ḥrḥwr*). This noun occurs only once in biblical Hebrew (Deut 28:22) meaning "feverish heat." The meaning "strife" is found in later Hebrew.

guilty corpses (*pgry ʾšmh*), cf. *pgry hʾšmh* in 1QM 14:3.

they will fall . . . they will stumble (*ypwlw . . . ykšwlw*), cf. *wkšlw* in line 4 (MT: *ykšlw*). A different system of accentuation may be reflected in the impf. forms *yippôlû* and *yikšôlû,* where the usual biblical Hebrew forms would be *yippĕlû* and *yikšĕlû.* Similar impf. forms are found in 1QpHab 4:6 (*yśḥwqw*); 4:11 (*yʿbwrw*); and 9:5 (*yqbwṣw*); see the note above on 1QpHab 4:6.

to the sum-total of (*lkll*). The noun *kĕlāl* does not occur in biblical Hebrew, but in Mishnaic Hebrew it is attested meaning "principle," "community," or "total."

over their decaying flesh (*bgwyt bśrm*), literally, "over the corpse(s) of their flesh."

3-4 ii 7 *the witch* (*bʿlt*). Strugnell suggests restoring the conjunction [w]*bʿlt* in order to fill what appears to be an abnormally large space between words and to make the text correspond to the reading of other versions, but compare on the photograph the space below between *ʾprym* and *ʾšr* (line 8).

The citation of Nah 3:4 presents the following variants from the MT:

(1) *hmmkrt* (MT: *hmkrt*). For the form *hammōkeret* (qal part. fem. sing. of *mkr,* "sell"), the *apparatus criticus* of *BHS* suggests reading *hakkōmeret* (qal part. fem. sing. of *kmr,* "ensnare"). The form in 4QpNah looks like a piel part. fem. sing. of *mkr* (*mĕmakkeret*), but *mkr* is unattested in the piel in biblical Hebrew, Mishnaic Hebrew, and Qumran Hebrew. It is possible that one of the *m*'s is a dittography, in which case the corrected form would correspond to that of the MT. I can find no evidence to support Dupont-Sommer's conjecture ("Le Commentaire," 75) that the *m*'s may be a graphic indication of the doubling of a consonant after the article. Carmignac apparently understands the form as the hiph., though this conjugation of *mkr,* too, is unattested. He translates "elle qui faisait vendre les nations par ses prostitutions." Maier ("Weitere Stücke," 226,

228) emends the form in 4QpNah to *hmkmrt,* the piel part. of *kmr.* He suggests that the form in the MT arose through metathesis of *k* and the second *m,* with the subsequent loss of one *m* through haplography. The form in 4QpNah, then, would represent the middle stage in this transformation. See further, M. Dahood ("Causal *Beth* and the Root NKR in Nahum 3,4," *Bib* 52 [1971] 395-96), who takes the form as *mammukkeret,* the hophal part. of *nkr.* This suggestion is followed by K. Cathcart (*Nahum,* 129-30), who translates "who is known by the nations," but this explanation sheds no light on the form in 4QpNah. Nor does the pesher on this verse give any indication of how the Qumran author understood the form.

(2) *bznwth* (MT: *bznwnyh*). The form in 4QpNah is the noun *zĕnût,* while the MT uses the noun *zĕnûnîm;* both mean "fornication." Strugnell calls attention to the fact that the *t* of this word in 4QpNah is mutilated, and he suggests that it may have been deliberately altered to a *n,* giving a form *bznwnh,* which would be closer to that of the MT.

3-4 ii 8 *those who lead Ephraim astray* (*mtʿy ʾprym*), cf. below 3-4 iii 5. Ephraim here probably refers to the followers of the Pharisees (cf. *ptʾy ʾprym* in 3-4 iii 5), who are led astray by the leaders. After *ʾprym* there is an unusually large space before the next word.

by their false teaching (*btlmwd šqrm*). The noun *talmûd* does not occur in biblical Hebrew; in Mishnaic Hebrew it means "teaching," "study." It does not occur elsewhere in QL, though it was read, at first, by mistake in 1QH 2:17. In biblical Hebrew there are other noun formations from the root *lmd: talmîd,* "scholar," "disciple" (only in 1 Chr 25:8) and *malmād,* "ox-goad" (an instrument for teaching ?). There is no need to recount here the controversy initiated by S. Zeitlin, who saw in this word support for his thesis that the scrolls were of medieval origin, a thesis incompatible with the archeological and paleographical evidence. (See S. Zeitlin, "The Dead Sea Scrolls: A Travesty on Scholarship," *JQR* 47 [1956-57] 1-36; "The Expression BeTalmud in the Scrolls Militates Against the Views of the Protagonists of their Antiquity," *JQR* 54 [1963-64] 89-98; "Asher Betalmud," *JQR* 54 [1963-64] 340-41; "The Word BeTalmud and the Method of Congruity of Words," *JQR* 58 [1967-68] 78-80; N. Drazin, "What can 'Betalmud' prove?" *JQR* 54 [1963-64] 333; S. B. Hoenig, "What is the Explanation for the Term 'BᵉTalmud' in the Scrolls?" *JQR* 53 [1962-63] 274-76; "BeTalmud and Talmud," *JQR* 54 [1963-64] 334-39; "Dorshé Ḥalaḳot in the Pesher Nahum Scrolls," *JBL* 83 [1964] 119-38; "The Pesher Nahum 'Talmud,'" *JBL* 86 [1967] 441-45; B. Z. Wacholder, "A Qumran Attack on the Oral Exegesis? The Phrase *ʾšr btlmwd šqrm* in 4 Q Pesher Nahum," *RevQ* 5 [1964-66] 575-78.) The form in 4QpNah seems to be the earliest attestation of the noun *talmûd,* "teaching."

3-4 ii 9 In this line I prefer Strugnell's reading *mlkyh*[*m*] to Allegro's *mlkym*. The stroke just before the break looks more like a *h* than a *m*.

joined with the resident alien (*ʿm gr nlwh*), literally "with the joined resident alien." Strugnell suggests reading *nlwm*, the niph. part. sing. masc. of *lwh* with the 3rd pers. pl. masc. sf., but such a form would probably have appeared as *nlwhm*.

will perish (*ywbdw*). The impf. form is spelled without the ʾ as is *twbd* below in 3-4 iii 7, but cf. e.g., *yʾbdw* in 1QpHab 6:10.

3-4 ii 10 *they will fall* (*ypwlw*). See the note above on lines 4-6.

on account of their insolent speech ([*mz*]*ʿm lšwnm*), literally, "on account of the insolence of their tongue." This was suggested by Dupont-Sommer ("Le Commentaire," 58, 77) in the light of *mzʿm lšwnm* in Hos 7:16. Allegro reads [*m*]*ʿm lšwnm*, "because of what they say."

3-4 ii 10-11 The citation of Nah 3:5 presents two parallel variants from the MT: *wglyt . . . whrʾ* [*y*]*t*, "you will lift up . . . and you will show" (MT: *wglyty . . . whrʾyty*, "I shall lift up . . . and I shall show"). The form *wglyt* in 4QpNah is the qal perf. 2nd pers. sing. fem., while the form in the MT is the piel perf. 1st pers. sing. The reading *whrʾ*[*y*]*t* is not certain; Allegro reads *whrʾt*, the defectively written hiph.

In the middle of line 11 after *wmmlkwt* a word has been erased. Though the traces visible on the photograph in *Qumrân Cave 4* are to me illegible, except for the upper point of a *l*, Strugnell is able to make out *g*, *l*, and *t*. He suggests that the word may have been *gdwlwt*, possibly written by mistake under the influence of Jer 28:8, *wʿl mmlkwt gdlwt*.

3-4 ii 11-12 Only a few phrases of the pesher on Nah 3:5 are preserved. Near the end of line 11 Allegro reads a doubtful *h*, but this is not certain.

Fragments 3-4, Column iii

The column opens with the conclusion of the pesher on Nah 3:5. The "nations" must be either the subject or the object of a verb lost at the end of col. ii.

3-4 iii 1 *because of their impurity* (*bndtm*). This reading is suggested by Dupont-Sommer ("Le Commentaire," 58) rather than *bnwtm*, "between them," as read by Allegro.

and because of the filth of their abominations ([*wbš*]*qwṣy twʿbwtyhm*). Allegro restores simply [*š*]*qwṣy*, but this does not fill the space. I suggest [*wbš*]*qwṣy*, parallel to *bndtm*. If this restoration is accepted, then the pesher anticipates the word *šqwṣym* in the following citation of Nah 3:6-7a; see above 1-2 ii 9, and see further Part II, p. 245.

3-4 iii 1-2 The citation of Nah 3:6-7a presents the following variants from the MT:

(1) *kʾwrh*, "repulsive" (?) (MT: *krʾy*, "like a spectacle"). The form

in 4QpNah is difficult to explain. Since the same consonants appear in both 4QpNah and the MT, it is possible that there is a scribal error involved; namely, metathesis of ʾ and *r* in a defectively written text. As it stands, however, the form in 4QpNah could be either one word or the preposition *k* and a form *ʾwrh.* The latter form could be a noun *ʾôrâ,* "light," or a qal part. *ʾôreh* from *ʾrh,* "to pluck" (?), but neither of these meanings makes sense here. In the pesher on this text the form *wkʾrwm* is clearly a 3rd pers. pl. verb form. It seems, then, that the Qumran author did not intend the preposition *k* to be read, but rather had in mind a root *kʾr,* but no such root is attested in biblical Hebrew. In Mishnaic Hebrew, however, *kʾr* occurs as a by-form of *kʿr,* "to be dark, ugly, repulsive." The identification of the form in 4QpNah as a pass. part. of this root has been generally accepted, and the meaning fits the context (see further R. Weiss, "A Comparison," 437; *"Kʾwrh,"* 156).

(2) *ydwdw* (MT: *ydwd*). The pl. form in 4QpNah may have arisen under the influence of the pl. force of the subject *kwl rwʾyk,* cf. *wʾmrw* below in line 5. It should be noted that *kwl* appears in this instance with the full writing, as below in line 3 and 3-4 iv 2, but cf. *kl* in 1-2 ii 3 and 3-4 iv 2.

3-4 iii 3 *at the end of time* (*bʾḥryt hqṣ*). This phrase is probably synonymous with the phrase *ʾḥryt hymym,* cf. *lʾḥryt hqṣ* in 4QpPs[b] 1:[5], and see the note above on 1QpHab 2:5-6.

3-4 iii 4 *consider them repulsive* (*wkʾrwm*). See the note above on *kʾwrh* in line 2. In Mishnaic Hebrew the verb *kʾr* (with the by-form *kʿr*) is intransitive in the qal, but in the piel it can mean "to declare repulsive." Thus, the form in 4QpNah is probably best understood as the piel *wĕkēʾărûm.*

when the glory of Judah is revealed (*wbh*[*g*]*lwt kbwd yhwdh*). In the preliminary publication Allegro read *wbhlwt,* "and the ruin of Judah's glory" (similarly Carmignac). In the *editio princeps,* however, at the suggestion of K. G. Kuhn, he restores *wbh*[*g*]*lwt,* which fits the context much better (see *Qumrân Cave 4,* 41).

the simple ones of Ephraim (*ptʾy ʾprym*). This phrase probably refers to those who were intellectually vulnerable and easily "led astray" by the Seekers-After-Smooth-Things; see the note above on 1QpHab 12:4. See further Dupont-Sommer, "Le Commentaire," 79.

3-4 iii 5-6 *and will join* .[*I*]*srael* (*wnlww ʿl* .[*y*]*śrʾl*). After *ʿl* there is a short lacuna with a trace of a letter visible just before it. The space seems too long for *yśrʾl* alone. Strugnell suggests *k*[*wl y*]*śrʾl, b*[*yt y*]*śrʾl,* or *b*[*ny y*]*śrʾl,* but—judging from the photograph in *Qumrân Cave 4*—these restorations are too long. Moreover, the letter that is partially preserved before the break does not look to me like either a *b* or a *k*.

The citation of Nah 3:7b-c presents the following variants from the MT:

(1) *wʾmrw* (MT: *wʾmr*). This variant is parallel to *ydwdw* (MT: *ydwd*) in line 2.

(2) *šwddh* (MT: *šddh*). The form in the biblical text is the pual perf., and the consonants in the MT could be vocalized either as *šuddĕdâ* or as *šoddĕdâ* (see KB under the root *šdd;* Bauer and Leander, §58 p′). The form in 4QpNah could be simply an orthographic variant, with the *w* representing a short *u,* or more likely, a short *o*-vowel. The *w,* however, could also represent a long vowel, in which case the form in 4QpNah would be the polal perf.

(3) *ʾbqšh* (MT: *ʾbqš*). Though the form in the MT is the simple impf., the form in 4QpNah is the cohortative. See M. H. Goshen-Gottstein, "Linguistic Structure," 124-25.

for you (*lk*). Strugnell observes correctly, I think, that the *k* of *lk,* the last word of Nah 3:7, was written over an original *h.* The first reading was *lh,* "for her," probably under the influence of the preceding clause, cf. the LXX, which has αὐτῇ.

3-4 iii 7 *whose council will perish* (*ʾšr twbd ʿṣtm*). In this context the noun *ʿṣh* is probably the designation of a group of leaders, the "council," parallel to *knst,* "congregation." The word *ʿṣh,* however, is frequently ambiguous, and the meaning "counsel" or "policy" (as below in line 8) cannot be excluded. See the note above on 1QpHab 12:4.

whose congregation (*ʾšr . . . knstm*). The noun *kĕneset,* unattested in biblical Hebrew, also appears in 4QpBless 6. While the root *kns* means simply "to gather," in Mishnaic Hebrew the noun *knst* takes on the technical meaning "synagogue." That is the way Gaster translates the word here, but that rendering may be anachronistic.

lead astray (*ltʿwt*). The form is here taken to be the hiph. inf. with the *h* elided; see the note above on 1QpHab 3:1.

the assembly ([*h*]*qhl*). I follow Allegro in restoring this word, but I add the definite object sign *ʾt.* The small frg. that contains the end of this line could be moved a little to the left to make room for *ʾt,* but this might make the lacuna in line 8 a little too long for the biblical text restored there.

3-4 iii 8 The citation of Nah 3:8a presents the following variants from the MT:

(1) *htyṭyby* (MT: *htyṭby*). The consonants of the form in the MT could represent the defectively written hiph. *hătêṭībî,* "will you do better," or the qal *hătîṭĕbî,* "are you better?". The mixed vocalization of the MT (*hătîṭĕbî*) indicates a choice of reading. The form in 4QpNah is clearly the hiph. impf. with the full writing. The second *y* is mutilated and may have

been deliberately erased. The corrected form would then correspond to the consonants of the MT.

(2) *mny ᵓmwn,* "than Amon" (MT: *mnᵓ ᵓmwn,* "than No-Amon"). The form in the MT, *minnōᵓ,* is the preposition *min* with the place name No-Amon, i.e., Thebes. Several commentators read the form in 4QpNah as *mnw,* an orthographic variant from the MT (so Dupont-Sommer ["Le Commentaire," 58], Lohse, Weiss ["A Comparison," 438]). I prefer Allegro's reading *mny,* which is a poetic form of the preposition *min.* This is supported by the commentary in line 9, where the place name is simply "Amon." Carmignac, too, reads *mny,* but he interprets it as Ni-Amon, a variant of the place name No-Amon.

3-4 iii 9 *they are Manasseh* (*hm mnšh*). It was noted in the introductory comments that Manasseh is probably to be identified with the Sadducees. The word is apparently understood here as a collective, since it is preceded by the pl. form of the personal pronoun.

the honored ones of the city who support Manasseh (*nkbdy h*[*ᶜyr hmḥzq*]*ym ᵓt m*[*nšh*]). Dupont-Sommer suggests restoring at the end of the lacuna [*hswb*]*bym ᵓt m*[*nšh*], "[qui soutienn]ent Ma[nassé]," but this is too short for the space. Moreover, I should expect the object of *sbb* to be introduced by the preposition *l* rather than by the definite object sign *ᵓt,* cf. *sbyb lh* in line 10. I suggest restoring *hᶜyr* in the light of the fem. suffixes in the interpretation below in line 11, which indicate that a fem. antecedent should probably be restored here. Another possibility might be *ᶜdh,* "congregation." The restoration of the piel part. of *ḥzq* is based on the verb *yḥzqw* in the preceding interpretation (line 8).

3-4 iii 10 The citation of Nah 3:8b presents the following variants from the MT:

(1) *ḥylh* (MT: *ḥyl*). The form in the MT is vocalized *ḥêl,* "rampart," but it could also be *ḥayil,* "power." In the *apparatus criticus* of *BHS* it is suggested that *ḥylh* be read, which is the form of 4QpNah, cf. the LXX, which has ἡ ἀρχή (with αὐτῆς, e.g., in codex Alexandrinus and added by a corrector in the Freer codex).

(2) *wmym* (MT: *mym*). In the MT the form is vocalized *mîyyam,* "from the sea," but it is suggested in *BHS* that *mayim,* "water," be read. I, therefore, read the form in 4QpNah as *ûmayim.*

(3) *ḥ*{{*w*}}*mwtyh* (MT: *ḥwmth*). In the MT the noun is sing. while in 4QpNah it is pl. In 4QpNah the first *w* has been obliterated, perhaps deliberately erased.

3-4 iii 11 *the men of her army, her warriors* (*ᵓnšy* [*ḥ*]*ylh gbwr*[*y m*]*lḥmth*). The pesher on Nah 3:8b is very brief, and the antecedent of the fem. sing. suffix is unclear. The biblical text refers specifically to Thebes. The Qumran interpretation might be applying the verse to a city, possibly

Jerusalem, cf. the fem. verb in 3-4 i 3 and the present restoration at the end of the preceding line.

After *mlḥmth* something has been erased, but an ᶜ is still visible.

The citation of Nah 3:9a presents the following variant from the MT: *ᶜwṣmh* (MT: *ᶜṣmh*). In the 3rd ed. of *Biblia Hebraica* (ed. R. Kittel; Stuttgart: Württembergische Bibelanstalt, 1966) the form is vocalized as *ᶜāṣĕmâ,* the qal perf. 3rd pers. sing. fem. of *ᶜṣm,* and the phrase would be translated "Ethiopia is mighty." In *BHS* the form is vocalized as *ᶜoṣmâ,* a substantive meaning "might," but the *apparatus criticus* suggests *ᶜoṣmāh,* i.e., the noun *ᶜoṣem* with the 3rd pers. sing. fem. sf., cf. the LXX, which has ἡ ἰσχὺς αὐτῆς. In the latter case, the form in 4QpNah would be simply an orthographic variant.

I restore *qṣ* rather than *qṣh* as in the MT in the light of 3-4 ii 4, where 4QpNah reads *qṣ* for *qṣh* in Nah 3:3.

3-4 iii 12 The interpretation of Nah 3:9a is lost except for a few traces of letters, but it was probably a brief identification like that in line 11.

At the end of the col. I follow Carmignac's suggestion that a frg. first placed by Allegro at the end of col. i of frgs. 3-4 be placed here (see the preliminary publication and the note above on 3-4 i 12). Thus, a few of the letters of Nah 3:9b can probably be read: *p*]*wṭ wh*[*lwbym* (MT: *pwṭ wlwbym*).

your help (*bᶜzrtk*). This is restored in agreement with the MT. In *BHS,* however, it is suggested that *bᶜzrth,* "her help," be read, cf. the LXX, which has βοηϑοὶ αὐτῆς. There is no way of knowing if this was also the reading of 4QpNah.

Fragments 3-4, Column iv

3-4 iv 1 *the wicked ones of Manasseh* (*ršᶜy mnšh*). This is restored in the light of the parallel *ršᶜy* ʾ[*prym*] below in line 5, cf. 4QpPsᵃ 1-10 ii 18. Allegro restores *ršᶜ*[*y ḥyl*]*h,* "the wicked ones of its army." Dupont-Sommer ("Le Commentaire," 58) reads the word before the break as *ršy,* "les chefs," and suggests either *ršy* [*mnš*]*h,* "les chefs de Manassé," or *ršy* [*yhwd*]*h,* "les chefs de Judah." But the letter just before the lacuna cannot be a *y.*

the House of Peleg (*byt plg*), or possibly "house of division." This phrase also occurs in CD 20:22, where it is applied to those "who went out from the Holy City and leaned on God at the time of Israel's unfaithfulness; they defiled the Temple but returned. . . ." Neither text gives a clear indication of the identity of the group to which this phrase refers. Carmignac thinks it is a group from within the Qumran community who joined the adversaries, while Dupont-Sommer regards the phrase as a term of derision for the Hasmonean dynasty as it was divided under Hyrcanus II and Aristobulus II ("Le Commentaire," 83-84). J. Murphy-O'Connor ("The Essenes and their History," 239-44) follows H. Stegemann in identifying the House of Peleg with Ephraim. But this equation is based on the restoration of *ršʿ[y yhwd]h,* "the wicked of Judah," in the lacuna in line 1, and this appears to me to be too long for the space. The present tentative restoration describes the House of Peleg as a group joined to Manasseh, presumably then a group of Sadducee-sympathizers.

3-4 iv 1-2 The citation of Nah 3:10 presents the following variants from the MT:

(1) *bgwlh* (MT: *lglh).*

(2) *ʿylwlyh* (MT: *ʿllyh*). Because of the difficulty of distinguishing *w* and *y* in the script of this document, the reading is not certain. The form in 4QpNah could also be *ʿwlwlyh* (so Lohse, Strugnell), or *ʿwlylyh,* but *ʿylwlyh* is preferred here in the light of the commentary in line 4, where *ʿylwlyw* seems certain. In biblical Hebrew both *ʿôlāl* (the noun used here in the MT) and *ʿôlēl* are attested meaning "child." There is no form *ʿylwl,* nor does such a form occur in Mishnaic Hebrew. Elsewhere in QL the forms *ʿwlwl* (1QH 7:21) and *wʿwlwlyhmh* (1QIsa^{a} XI:23 for *wĕʿōlĕlêhem* of Isa 13:16) are possible readings, but such *"qwṭwl"* forms are regarded as "palaeographically questionable" by M. H. Goshen-Gottstein (see "Linguistic Structure," 127).

(3) *ywrw,* hiph impf. 3rd pers. pl. of *yrh* (MT: *ydw,* qal perf. 3rd pers. pl. of *ydd*). The verb *ydd* occurs twice in biblical Hebrew in a phrase "to cast a lot upon" (Joel 4:3; Obad 11); it does not occur in QL. The verb *yrh* occurs only once in biblical Hebrew with the meaning "to cast lots" (Josh 18:6); it does not occur elsewhere in QL with this meaning. See further R. Weiss, "A Comparison," 439.

3-4 iv 3 *the interpretation of it* (*pšrw*). The suffix *w* is written above the line.

at the last time (*lqṣ hʾḥrwn*). This phrase is probably synonymous with *bʾḥryt hqṣ;* see the note above on 3-4 iii 3.

3-4 iv 4 *his children* (*ʿylwlyw*). See the note above on line 2. The 3rd pers. sing. masc. sf. presumably refers to Manasseh.

will perish (*ywbdw*). This is restored in the light of such texts as 1QpHab 6:10; 4QpPs^{a} 1-10 ii 1. Strugnell proposes *ypwlw,* "will fall"; he refers to 1QM 11:11; 19:11 (so apparently Carmignac, who translates "tomberont").

3-4 iv 5 The citation of Nah 3:11a preserves the following variant from the MT: *wthy* (MT: *thy*).

the wicked ones of Ephraim (*ršʿy ʾ[prym]*), cf. *ršʿ[y mnš]h,* "the wicked ones of Manasseh," restored in line 1 of this col.

3-4 iv 7 The citation of Nah 3:11b preserves the following variant from the MT: *bʿyr,* "in the city," is not in the MT.

3-4 iv 10-12 The last lines of this col. are not preserved, but there were probably twelve lines in the col. as in the preceding three.

Fragment 5

Strugnell interprets line 1 of frg. 5 as part of a citation of Nah 3:13a, [*hnh ʿmk n*]*šym b*[*qrbk*], which would be followed by the rest of v 13. According to Strugnell, line 2, then, is part of a commentary. This is possible, but restoring all of v 13 in line 1 would make the line unusually long. Moreover, v 14a would have to begin at the end of line 2, and this would leave little room in the line for an interpretation of v 13.

5:2 Allegro reads the first word that is partially preserved in this line as]*kwl,* but on the photograph in the *editio princeps* only the *l* is clear. He reads the letters that are preserved at the end of the line as *lym.*

5:3 Allegro reads the word before *bṭyṭ* as *bwʾy,* but only the tops of the letters are preserved, and none can be read with certainty.

4QpZeph (4Q*170*)

Editio princeps: "Commentary on Zephaniah" (J. M. Allegro), *Qumrân Cave 4,* Vol. I, p. 42 and pl. XIV.

Secondary literature: J. Strugnell, "Notes," 210-11.

This document is comprised of two small frgs. J. Strugnell describes the script as "rustic semi-formal" but different from the usual hand of the pesharim. Frg. 1 preserves part of the citation of Zeph 1:12-13, and the top margin of a col. is visible. Frg. 2 contains only part of the word *lmšwsh* (line 1), which suggests the identification with Zeph 1:13a, and the introductory phrase *pšrw ʿl* (line 2). Too little is preserved for certain identification or restoration of this text. The arrangement of the frgs. is also open to question.

Allegro places the frgs. on the same level, giving parts of two lines. The problem with this arrangement is that the interpretation (*pšrw ʿl*) follows the phrase *lwʾ ywkl,* which is not part of the biblical text. Allegro comments that there is apparently a quotation but not from the biblical text of Zephaniah as it is in the MT. I follow J. Strugnell's rearrangement of the frgs., which places frg. 2 below frg. 1, giving parts of four lines. This eliminates the problem of the nonbiblical quotation by making *lwʾ ywkl* part of the commentary on the first citation of Zeph 1:12-13a, and it leaves room for a second citation of Zeph 1:13a (*lmšwsh* in line 3).

The thrust of the commentary sections cannot be determined, since only the introductory formula and the words *lwʾ ywkl* are preserved.

4QpZeph: Translation

Fragments 1-2

1. YAHWEH [WILL NOT DO GOO]D, NOR WILL HE DO EVIL. BUT [THEIR WEALTH] WILL BE [FOR PLUNDER AND THEIR HOUSES FOR DESOLATION. The interpretation of it] Zeph 1:12-13a
2. [ ] . . [ ] he will not devour [ ]
3. [And when it says, THEIR WEALTH WILL BE FOR PL]UNDER, [the interpretation of it] 1:13a α
4. [AND THEY WILL BUILD HOUSES, BUT THEY WILL NOT INHABIT (THEM).] The interpretation of it [con]cerns [ ] 1:13b

4QpZeph: Notes

1-2:1 Strugnell is probably correct in restoring *lmšwsh* (from the first line in frg. 2, where Allegro reads *lm*]*šysh*) rather than *limšissâ* as in the MT. The form *lmšwsh* is attested in 1QIsa^{a} XXXVI:5 (=MT 42:22), though it is transcribed in the *editio princeps* as *lmšysh* (*The Dead Sea Scrolls of St. Mark's Monastery,* Vol. I, pl. XXXVI).

The tetragrammaton, *yhwh,* is written in the same script as the rest of the text; see the note above on 1QpHab 1:1.

1-2:2 *he will not devour* (*lwʾ ywkl*). Here Strugnell thinks that *lwʾ ywklw,* "they will not devour," should be read, but no final *w* is visible on the photograph in *Qumrân Cave 4.*

1-2:3 For *lmšwsh* here rather than *lmšsh* as in the MT, see above, line 1. After *lm*]*šwsh,* there is a dot, which Allegro reads hesitatingly as *w,* and so he continues the citation of Zeph 1:13a. The dot, however, is better taken as the top of a *l,* giving the phrase *pšrw* [ᶜ]*l* in the next line.

4QpPs^{a} (4Q*171*)

Editio princeps: "Commentary on Psalms (A)" (J. M. Allegro), *Qumrân Cave 4,* Vol. I, pp. 42-50 and pls. XIV-XVII.

Preliminary publications: J. M. Allegro, "A Newly-Discovered Fragment of a Commentary on Psalm XXXVII from Qumrân," *PEQ* 86 (1954) 69-75, with a photograph of 1-10 ii 1-10 and 1-10 iii 1-19 (Allegro's 1-2 ii 1-9 and 1, 3-4 iii 1-19); "Further Light on the History of the Qumran Sect," *JBL* 75 (1956) 89-95, esp. 94-95 and pls. III (=1-10 iv 7-18) and IV (=1-10 ii 16-27); see also *The People of the Dead Sea Scrolls in Text and Pictures,* 86-87 and pls. 48, 50.

Secondary transcriptions and translations:* H. Bardtke, *Die Handschriftenfunde,* 295-97; P. Boccaccio and G. Berardi, *Interpretatio Habacuc,* Appendix II: "Interpretatio Ps 37," 38-40; M. Burrows, *More Light,* 401-403; J. Carmignac, *Les Textes,* 2. 119-26; A. Dupont-Sommer, *Essene Writings,* 270-73; T. H. Gaster, *Dead Sea Scriptures,* 253-55; A. M. Habermann, *Megilloth,* 154-56; J. Licht, *Mgylt hhwdywt mmgylwt mdbr yhwdh* [*The Thanksgiving Scroll from the Scrolls from the Wilderness of Judea*], 243; E. Lohse, *Die Texte,* 271-79; J. Maier, *Die Texte,* 1. 180-82; F. Michelini Tocci, *I manoscritti,* 253-58; L. Moraldi, *I manoscritti,* 517-24; D. Pardee, "A Restudy of the Commentary on Psalm 37 from Qumran Cave 4 (Discoveries in the Judaean Desert of Jordan, vol. V, n° 171)," *RevQ 8* (1973) 163-94; H. Stegemann, "Der Pešer Psalm 37 aus Höhle 4 von Qumran (4Q p Ps 37)," *RevQ 4* (1963-64) 235-70; "Weitere Stücke von 4 Q p Psalm 37, von 4 Q Patriarchal Blessings und Hinweis auf eine unedierte Handschrift aus Höhle 4 Q mit Exzerpten aus dem Deuteronomium," *RevQ* 6 (1967-69) 193-227; E. F. Sutcliffe, *The Monks,* 182-83; G. Vermes, *Dead Sea Scrolls in English,* 243-45; E. Vogt, "Fragmentum Ps 37 ex Qumran," *Bib* 36 (1955) 263-64; A. S. van der Woude, *Bijbelcommentaren,* 61-67; Y. Yadin, *Hmgylwt hgnwzwt mmdbr yhwdh* [*The Hidden Scrolls from the Judaean Desert*], 116-19; *The Message of the Scrolls,* 99-102.

Secondary literature: J. Carmignac, "À propos d'une restitution dans le commentaire du Psaume 37," *RevQ* 1 (1958-59) 431; "Notes," 521-26; R. B. Coote, "'MWᶜD HTᶜNYT' in 4 Q 171 (Pesher Psalm 37), fragments 1-2, col. II, line 9," *RevQ* 8 (1972) 81-86; S. B. Hoenig, "Qumran Pesher on 'Taanit,'" *JQR* 57 (1966-67) 71-73; J. Strugnell, "Notes," 211-18; E. Vogt, "Prima nomina historica in Qumrân (4QpNah)," *Bib* 37 (1956) 531.

When frgs. of this text first came to light the document was entitled 4QpPs 37. It became clear, however, with the identification and publication of additional frgs. in the *editio princeps* that this commentary was not restricted to one psalm. In col. iv after the interpretation of Psalm 37, a pesher on Psalm 45 begins. In *Qumrân Cave 4,* therefore, the text is given the title 4QpPsᵃ.

The fact that Allegro offered in three different places preliminary photographs and transcriptions of portions of cols. ii-iv led to some complications in the early presentations of the text and translation by other scholars. The state of the publications after the first flurry of secondary studies was organized and summarized by H. Stegemann ("Pešer Psalm 37," 235-70). Before the appearance of the *editio princeps* another photograph appeared

*Only the works of Lohse, Pardee, Michelini Tocci, and the combined articles of Stegemann contain the entire text of the document (excluding frgs. 11-13). The others present more or less of the text as it was given in Allegro's preliminary publications.

in 1961 in a catalogue of the Qumran collection of the Palestine Archaeological Museum. This photograph showed previously unpublished portions of col. i of the text and was the subject of another article by Stegemann ("Weitere Stücke," 193-96). (This was the same catalogue that included a photograph of frgs. 3-4 of 4QpNah.)

As the text appears in the *editio princeps,* portions of four or possibly five cols. are preserved, presenting the biblical text of Ps 37:7-40; 45:1-2; 60:8-9 (?) and commentary. The document is structured like the other pesharim with one or two verses of the biblical text followed by a commentary. Sometimes a space is left between a pesher section and a following citation (1-10 i 24 [Allegro's 1-2 i 16]; 1-10 ii 12, 20; 1-10 iii 6, 13; 1-10 iv 5), but the pesher always follows the lemma immediately. The usual introductory formulas occur, *pšrw ᶜl* (1-10 i [26] [Allegro's 1-2 i 18]; 1-10 ii 2, 9, 14, 18; 1-10 iii 7, 10, 15; 1-10 iv 8, [14], 18), *pšrw hmh* (1-10 ii 4-5; 1-10 iv [1], [23]), *pšrw ʾšr* (1-10 iii [3]), *pšr hdbr ᶜl* (1-10 iii [18-19]), and there is one instance of the repetition of a previously cited biblical phrase (1-10 iii 11-12).

In the *editio princeps* Allegro treated in three groups the frgs. that contain the four main cols. of this document; he numbered the cols. 1-2 i; 1-2 ii, 1, 3-4 iii; and 3-10 iv. However, since these are four continuous cols. formed by fragments 1-10, I have designated them 1-10 i, ii, iii, iv.

The content of Psalm 37 is especially well-suited to the Qumran community's world-view, since it is a psalm of personal tribulation offering reassurance for the righteous in the face of the prosperity of the wicked (see further D. Pardee, "Restudy," 170-71). In the interpretation of Psalm 37 "wickedness" and "the wicked" are associated with the Man of the Lie (1-10 i 26; 1-10 iv 14), the ruthless ones of the covenant (1-10 ii 14; 1-10 iii 12) and the ruthless ones of the Gentiles (1-10 ii 20), while "the righteous" are identified with the Teacher of Righteousness (1-10 iii [15], [19]), the Interpreter of Knowledge (1-10 i 27), the congregation of the elect (1-10 ii 5; 1-10 iii 5), the congregation of the poor ones (1-10 ii 10; 1-10 iii 10), the Priest and his partisans (1-10 ii 19). The Man of the Lie, the Interpreter of Knowledge, and the Wicked Priest appear in clauses that use the perf. tense, while the wicked ones of Ephraim and Manasseh, the time of testing, and the congregation of the poor ones occur with impf. verbs. The thrust of the interpretation of Psalm 37 is mainly eschatological, and there are no clear allusions to identifiable historical events. According to the Qumran commentator, the wicked will ultimately perish, and the righteous will take possession of the inheritance (1-10 iii 1, 10).

4QpPsª: Translation

Fragments 1-10, Column i

9. [ ].
10. [ ]
11. [ ]
12. [ ]
13. [FOR LIKE THE GREEN GR]ASS Ps 37:2 (?)
14. [THEY WILL QUICKLY FADE, AND LIKE THE NEW GREEN PLANTS THEY WILL WITHER. The interpretation of it]
15. [ ]*r*
16. [ ].*r*
17. [ ].
18. [ ].*t*
19. [COMMIT YOUR WAY TO YAHWEH, AND TRUST IN HI]M, 37:5-6 (?)
20. [AND HE WILL ACT. HE WILL BRING FORTH YOUR VINDICATION LIKE LIGHT, AND YOUR RIGHT LIKE THE N]OONDAY.
21. [The interpretation of it concerns the congregation of the poor ones, who chose to do God]'s bidding,
22. [ ]*t* foolish ones chose
23. [ ]those who [li]ke laxity and those who lead astray
24. [ ]wickedness at the hand of Eph[rai]m.
25. [MOA]N BEFORE [YAHWEH AND] WRITHE BEFORE HIM. DO NOT BE ANGRY WITH THE ONE WHO MAKES HIS WAY PROSPEROUS, WITH THE ONE 37:7
26. [WHO CARRIES] OUT EVIL PLANS. [The interpretation] of it concerns the Man of Lie, who led many astray with deceitful words,
27. for they chose empty words and did not lis[ten] to the Interpreter of Knowledge, so that

Fragments 1-10, Column ii

1. they will perish by the sword, by famine, and by plague. ABANDON ANGER AND FORSAKE RAGE. DO NOT 37:8-9a
2. BE ANGRY; IT RESULTS ONLY IN EVIL, FOR THOSE WHO DO EVIL WILL BE CUT OFF. The interpretation of it concerns all those who return
3. to the Law, who do not rebelliously refuse to turn back from their evil; for all those who refuse
4. to turn back from their sin will be cut off. AND THOSE WHO WAIT FOR YAHWEH, THEY WILL INHERIT THE LAND. The interpretation of it: 37:9b
5. they are the congregation of his chosen ones, those who do his bidding. AND AGAIN A LITTLE WHILE, AND THE WICKED ONE WILL BE NO MORE. 37:10

6. (*vacat*)
7. WHEN I LOOK CAREFULLY AT HIS TERRITORY, HE WILL NOT BE THERE. The interpretation of it concerns all the wicked at the end of
8. forty years: they will be consumed, and there will not be found on earth any [wi]cked man.
9. AND THE POOR WILL INHERIT THE LAND AND WILL DELIGHT IN PROSPEROUS ABUNDANCE. The interpretation of it concerns 37:11
10. the congregation of the poor ones, who will accept the appointed time of affliction (or "who will take upon themselves the appointed time of fasting"), and they will be delivered from all the traps of
11. Belial. But afterwards they will delight [in] all .[ ].*y* of the land and will grow fat in all *t*ʿ. . [ ]
12. of flesh.
13. THE WICKED PLOTS AGAINST THE RIGHTEOUS AND GNASHES [HIS TEETH] AT [HIM.] YAHWEH LAUGHS AT HIM, FOR HE SEES 37:12-13
14. THAT HIS DAY HAS COME. The interpretation of it concerns the ruthless ones of the covenant who are in the house of Judah:
15. they will plot to destroy completely those who observe the Law, who are in the council of the community. But God will not abandon them
16. into their power. THE WICKED DREW THE SWORD AND BENT THEIR BOW TO FELL THE POOR AND NEEDY, 37:14-15
17. TO SLAUGHTER THOSE WHO ARE UPRIGHT IN (THEIR) CONDUCT. THEIR SWORD WILL ENTER THEIR (OWN) HEART, AND THEIR BOWS WILL BE BROKEN.
18. The interpretation of it concerns the wicked ones of Ephraim and Manasseh, who will seek to lay their hands
19. on the priest and on his partisans in the time of testing that is coming upon them. But God will ransom them
20. from their hand, and afterwards they (i.e., the wicked ones of Ephraim and Manasseh) will be given into the hand of the ruthless ones of the Gentiles for judgment.
21. (*vacat*)
22. BETTER IS THE LITTLE THAT THE RIGHTEOUS HAS THAN ABUNDANCE OF MAN[Y] WICKED. [The interpretation of it concerns everyone who] 37:16
23. observes the Law, who (does) not *y*[ ].*h*
24. for evil. FOR THE ARM[S OF THE WICKED WILL BE BROKEN. BUT] YAH[WEH SUPPORTS THE RIGHTEOUS] 37:17
25. [The interpretation of it concerns to do]

26. [his] bidding. Y[AHWEH KNOWS THE DAYS OF THE BLAMELESS, AND THEIR INHERITANCE WILL BE FOREVER]. 37:18-19a
27. THEY [WILL] N[OT] BE PUT TO SHAME IN [THE TIME OF EVIL. The interpretation of it concerns]

Fragments 1-10, Column iii

1. those who return to the wilderness, who will live for a thousand generations in saf[ety]; to them will belong all the inheritance of
2. Adam and to their seed forever. AND IN THE DAYS OF FAMINE, THEY WILL BE SA[TISFIED,] FOR THE WICKED 37:19b-20a
3. WILL PERISH. The interpretation of it is th[at] he will keep them alive in famine, in the appointed time of af[flic]tion (or "fa[st]-ing"), but many
4. will perish on account of the famine and the plague, all who do not go out [from here] to be [wi]th
5. the congregation of his chosen ones.
5a. AND THOSE WHO LOVE YAHWEH ARE LIKE THE SPLENDOR OF PASTURES (?). The interpretation [of it concerns the congregation of his chosen ones,] 37:20b-c
5. who will be chiefs and princes o[ver all the people, like] shep[herds]
6. in the midst of their flocks.
7. THEY ARE CONSUMED LIKE SMOKE, ALL OF THEM. The interpretation «of it» concerns the wi[cke]d princes who oppress his holy people, 37:20d
8. who will perish like smoke that is los[t in the w]ind. THE WICKED ONE BORROWS BUT DOES NOT REPAY. 37:21-22
9. BUT THE RIGHTEOUS ONE IS GRACIOUS AND GENEROUS, FOR THOSE WHO ARE BLESSED [BY HIM WILL IN]HERIT THE LAND, BUT THOSE WHO ARE CURSED BY HIM [WILL BE C]UT OFF.
10. The interpretation of it concerns the congregation of the poor ones; [their]s is the inheritance of all the great [ones;]
11. they will take possession of the high mountain of Isra[el, and on] his holy [moun]tain they will delight, and [THOSE WHO ARE CURS]ED BY HIM 37:22
12. WILL BE CUT OFF—They are the ruthless ones of the co[venant, the wi]cked ones of Israel, who will be cut off and will be exterminated
13. forever.
14. For FROM YAHW[EH ARE THE STEPS OF A MAN. THEY] ARE MADE FIRM [AND] HE DELIGHTS IN HIS [W]AY, FOR [IF] HE SHOULD [CHAR]GE, HE WOULD [NOT] 37:23-24
15. BE HURLED DOWN, FOR Y[AHWEH SUPPORTS HIS HAND.] The interpretation of it concerns the Priest, the Teacher of [Righteousness, whom]

16. God [ch]ose as the pillar. F[or] he established him to build for him a congregation of [his chosen ones in truth;]
17. his [wa]y is straight to the truth. I [WAS YOUNG] BUT NOW I AM OLD, AND [I HAVE] NOT [SEEN THE RIGHTEOUS ONE] 37:25-26
18. ABANDONED, NOR HIS OFFSPRING SEEKING BREA[D. ALL DAY LONG] HE IS GRACIOUS AND GENEROUS, AND [HIS] OFFSPR[ING BECOMES A BLESSING. The interpretation]
19. of the passage concerns the Teache[r of Righteousness, whom] God *m*[ ]
20. *w*ʾ*t*[ ]
21-
26 [ ]
27. [FOR YAHWEH LOVES] 37:28

Fragments 1-10, Column iv

1. JUS[TICE, AND HE WILL NOT ABANDON THOSE WHO ARE LOYAL TO HIM.] THEY ARE PRESERVED [FOREV]ER, BUT THE CHILDREN OF THE WI[CKED ARE CUT OFF. The interpretation of it:] they are the ruthless ones of
2. [the covenant, who will be cut off, for they rejected] the Law. RIGHTEOUS [ONES WILL TAKE POSSESSION OF THE LAND AND WILL DWELL] UPON IT [FOR]EVER. 37:29
3. [The interpretation of it: they will take possession of the land] for a thousand [generations. THE MOUTH OF THE RIGHTEOUS ONE UTTERS W]ISDOM, AND HIS TONGUE SPEAKS 37:30-31
4. [JUSTICE. THE LAW OF HIS GOD IS IN HIS HEART; HIS FEET NEVER SLIP. The interpretation of it concerns of] the truth, who spoke
5. [justice]declared to them.
6. (*vacat*)
7. THE WICKED ONE LIES IN AMBUSH FOR THE RIGHTEOUS ONE AND SEEKS [TO MURDER HIM. YAH]WEH [WILL NOT ABANDON HIM INTO HIS HAND,] N[OR WILL HE] LET HIM BE CONDEMNED AS GUILTY WHEN HE COMES TO TRIAL. 37:32-33
8. The interpretation of it concerns [the] Wicked [Pr]iest, who l[ay in ambush for the Teache]r of Righteous[ness and sought to] murder him[ ]*n* and the Law
9. that he sent to him; but God will not ab[andon him into his hand,] nor [will he let him be condemned as guilty when] he comes to trial. But as for [him, God will] pay [him] his due, giving him
10. into the hand of the ruthless ones of the Gentiles to wreak [vengeance] on him[WAIT FOR YA]HWEH AND 37:34

GUARD HIS WAY, AND HE WILL RAISE YOU UP TO TAKE POSSESSION OF

11. THE LAND; AND WHEN THE WICKED ARE CUT OFF YOU WILL G[LOAT. The interpretation of it concerns the last generation,] which will gloat over the judgment of wickedness; and with [the congregation of]

12. his chosen ones they will rejoice in the inheritance of truth .[ ]

13. I [HAVE SEEN] A WICKED ONE, A TERRIBLE ONE, AND 37:35-36
HE DIS[PLAYS] HIMSELF [LIKE A NATIVE TREE OF LUXURIANT GROWTH (?). AND] I PASSED BY BEFORE HIS [PLA]CE, BUT L[O!] HE WAS [NOT] THERE. I [SOUGHT FOR HIM,] BUT HE WAS NOT

14. [FOUND. The interpretation of it] concerns the [M]an of the Lie, [who].*l*.[ ]against the chos[en] ones of God, and [he sou]ght to put an end to

15. [ ] . . *m* . [ ]to do [ ].ʿ*y* judgment[ ]acted in high-handed arrogance

16. [ ]*l*.*l*..[OBSERVE THE BLAMELESS ONE, AND 37:37
WATCH] THE UPRIGHT ONE, [FOR THERE IS POS]TER[ITY FOR THE ON]E OF INTEGRITY. The interpretation of it con[cerns]

17. [ ].*dm h*ʾ[ ].[ ]*t* integri[ty].
AND THE REBELS 37:38

18. WILL BE ALTOGETHER DESTROYED, AND THE POSTER[ITY OF THE] WI[CKED WILL BE CUT OFF. The interpretation of it concerns the ruthless ones of the covenant, who] will perish and will be cut off

19. from the midst of the congregation of the community. AND THE 37:39
S[ALVATION OF THE RIGHTEOUS IS FROM YAHWEH, THEIR HAVEN IN THE TIME OF DISTRESS. YAHWEH HELPS THEM,]

20. AND HE SAVES THEM; HE RESCUES THEM FROM THE WICKED, [AND HE DELIVERS THEM, FOR THEY SEEK REFUGE IN HIM. The interpretation of it]

21. God will save them, and [he will] deliver them from the hand of the wi[cked ones of]

22. (*vacat*)

23. TO THE CHOIRMASTER, ACCORDING TO [LILIE]S. [A Ps 45:1
MASKIL OF THE SONS OF KORAH, A LOVE SONG. The interpretation of it: th]ey are the seven divisions of

24. the returnees of Is[rael, who] MY H[EART IS 45:2a
AS]TIR WITH A GOOD THING;

25. [I] AD[DRESS MY SONG TO THE KING. The interpretation of it] . . holy, for

26. [ ]the books of[ ]
AND MY TONGUE IS THE PEN OF 45:2b

27. [A SKILLED SCRIBE. The interpretation of it] concerns the Teacher of [Righteousness, who be]fore God with purposeful speech

Fragment 11

1.]to return together to the Law in[
2.]the chosen [ones of] Israel [ ].ʾ.[

Fragment 12

1.]with the lip of ᶜ[
2.]*l*[

Fragment 13

1. [ ].[ ]
2. [ ] (*vacat*) [ ]
3. [GO]D SAID [IN HIS SANCTUARY: "I SHALL EXULT, I SHALL DIVIDE SHECHEM,] Ps 60:8-9
4. [AND THE VALLEY OF SUCC]OTH I SHALL MEASURE OUT. [GILEAD IS] MINE, [AND MANASSEH IS MINE, AND EPHRAIM IS MY HELMET."]
5. [The interpretation of it: Gilea]d and the half-tribe of [Manasseh are]
6. [ ] and they are gathered [ ]

4QpPsa: Notes

Fragments 1-10, Column i

Portions of lines 9-27 of this col. are preserved on frg. 1. In the transcription in *Qumrân Cave 4* Allegro began numbering the lines with the first one in which a letter is visible (line 9), but the lines should be renumbered to correspond to the lines in the following cols.

Most of the text of Ps 37:7 is preserved in lines 25-26 of col. i (Allegro's 1-2 i 17-19). The preceding twenty-four lines, therefore, must have contained Ps 37:1-6 and commentary. About five lines would be needed for the biblical text of those verses, leaving about nineteen lines for the interpretation, or about three and one-third lines for each biblical verse. In the following cols., however, the interpretation sections are generally only about one to two lines for each lemma, except at 1-10 i 21-24; 1-10 ii 14-16; and 1-10 iii 10-13. Thus, twenty-four lines appears to be too much for the beginning of this commentary. The question then arises about what, if anything, might have preceded the beginning of this pesher. The fact that col. iv preserves part of the beginning of a commentary on Psalm 45 suggests that an interpretation of another psalm might have preceded that of Psalm

37. This document was clearly not part of a commentary on the whole Psalter, but may have been part of an interpretation of a collection of psalms grouped around a central theme.

1-10 i 9 (Allegro's 1-2 i 1) There is a trace of a letter visible at the end of this line; Allegro reads a doubtful *h,* but it is not clear from the photograph. Stegemann ("Weitere Stücke," 199) indicates only a trace of a letter.

1-10 i 13 (Allegro's 1-2 i 5) The trace of the letter visible before the *r* at the end of this line could be one of several letters, e.g., *h, w, y, m.* If Allegro is correct in reading a *y,* then this line might contain Ps 37:2 as Strugnell suggests. I tentatively restore the biblical text accordingly.

1-10 i 15 (Allegro's 1-2 i 7) Strugnell regards Allegro's reading of a *b* at the end of this line as very doubtful. Stegemann ("Weitere Stücke," 199) indicates no trace at all. If it were a *b,* I should expect some trace of a horizontal bottom stroke to be visible. The only other possibilities that would fit the existing trace seem to be *d* and *r.* No trace of the preceding letter is visible on the photograph in *Qumrân Cave 4,* contrary to Allegro's transcription.

1-10 i 16 (Allegro's 1-2 i 8) At the end of the line there are traces of two letters, which Allegro reads as].*r*. Stegemann's restoration ("Weitere Stücke," 200) of Ps 37:5 followed by *pšrw ʿl . . . ʾ*]*šr* is too long for one line. Nor can his reconstruction be adjusted by beginning the citation of 37:5 in line 15, since there is no word in the biblical verse that ends in a letter that would fit the traces preserved at the end of line 15. Strugnell, too, proposes restoring a biblical verse here; he suggests reading *kʾ*]*wr* (from Ps 37:6) at the end of line 16 and restoring Ps 37:5-6. But see below, lines 19-20.

1-10 i 18 (Allegro's 1-2 i 10) Allegro reads]*yt* at the end of this line, with the *y* doubtful, but the letter partially visible before the *t* could also be a *h* or a *w*.

1-10 i 19-20 (Allegro's 1-2 i 11-12) The letter that is partially preserved at the end of line 19 is almost certainly a *w* or a *y;* Allegro indicates only that a trace is visible (so also Stegemann, "Weitere Stücke," 200). Strugnell suggests the possibility of reading *ʿly*]*w* (Ps 37:5b) at the end of line 19 and restoring Ps 37:5-6 in lines 19-20. But for him this would be a second citation, since he had proposed the restoration of Ps 37:5-6 in line 16 above. There is one instance of a second citation in this document (1-10 iii 11-12), but it is only a short phrase. I follow Strugnell's suggestion here, but I take it as the first citation of Ps 37:5-6.

The tetragrammaton restored in line 19 would probably have been written in paleo-Hebrew script, as it appears below in 1-10 ii 4, 25; 1-10 iii

14, 15; and 1-10 iv 10, but cf. 1-10 iii 5a (second hand). See the note above on 1QpHab 1:1.

Reading *ṣ]hrym* at the end of line 20 supports the restoration of Ps 37:5-6 in these lines (see *kṣhrym* in Ps 37:6b). Allegro, followed by Pardee ("Restudy," 164) reads *]ṣhrym.* Stegemann gives *kṣ(w)]hrym,* indicating that in the Qumran text the word might have appeared with the full writing, though elsewhere in this document there is only one possible occurrence of a similar representation of a short *o* vowel by a *w,* i.e., *ḥ]wkmh* in 1-10 iv 3. In the citation I restore *drkkh, ṣdqkh,* and *wmšpṭkh* (MT: *drkk, ṣdqk, wmšpṭk*) in the light of the similar orthography of the 2nd pers. sing. masc. sf. on the verb *wy]rwmmkh* in 1-10 iv 10.

1-10 i 21-24 (Allegro's 1-2 i 13-16) These lines almost certainly contained the Qumran interpretation of Ps 37:5-6, but only a few words are preserved.

At the end of line 21 Allegro transcribes]*.t* before *rṣwn,* but on the photograph in the *editio princeps* there does not appear to be any letter visible before the *t.*

Stegemann ("Weitere Stücke," 200, 202, and n. 34) is almost certainly correct in applying the verses to the Qumran community. In lines 21-22 he restores: *[pšrw ʿl ʿdt hʾbywnym ʾšr mtndbym lʿśwt ʾ]t rṣwn/* [*ʾl*], "Damit ist die Gemeinde der Armen gemeint, die (ständig) bereit sind, zu tun was Gott wohlgefällig ist." Although this suggestion fits the space, there is a problem with the syntax. A pl. part. serving as the predicate after *ʾšr* in the pesher formula is not normal. In this formula, *ʾšr* should be followed by a finite verb. I suggest *bḥrw,* "who chose," cf. the use of this verb with *rṣwn* in CD 3:2-3, 11. This might also be supported by the occurrence of the same verb in the next line (if *bḥrw* is read; see the note below).

the congregation of the poor ones ([*ʿdt hʾbywnym*]). See below 1-10 ii 10; 1-10 iii 10; see also the note on 1QpHab 12:3.

God's bidding (*rṣwn* [*ʾl*]), literally, "the pleasure of God." At the beginning of line 22 I follow Stegemann in restoring *ʾl,* see *rṣwn ʾl* in 1QS 9:13, 24; 1QM 2:5; and *rṣwnw* (with the 3rd pers. sing. masc. sf. referring to God) below in 1-10 ii 5.

Without a clear context it is difficult to translate the two words preserved at the end of line 22. The reading *hwllym* is certain, but the next word has been read as *bḥry* (so Allegro, who translates "in the burning of," followed by Pardee ["Restudy," 171], who translates "with burning") and as *bḥrw,* "they chose" (read by Stegemann ["Weitere Stücke," 200] and noted as a possible reading by Strugnell). Stegemann comments that *bḥrw* is clear on the original but is obscured on the photographs because of a wrinkle in the skin. He asserts further (pp. 202-203, n. 35) that the participle would probably have been fully written as *bwḥry,* cf. the participles in 1-10 ii 5, 13, 15, 23; 1-10 iii 5a; 1-10 iv 17. On this I agree with Stegemann, reading *bḥrw* here and also restoring it in the preceding line, which could be a parallel description.

The form *hwllym* could be the pl. of *hwll,* a noun attested in 1QH 2:36; 4:8, 20 meaning "folly." In biblical Hebrew no such noun is attested in the sing. but a pl. fem. form *hwllwt,* "madness," occurs several times in Qoheleth, e.g., 1:17; 2:12. More likely, the form *hwllym* is to be understood as the qal part. pl. masc. of *hll* (so Allegro), a root that can mean "to boast" or "to be mad." It is attested in 1QH in the qal (4:17) and in the hithpolel (3:33; 4:12; 10:33), and it occurs in biblical Hebrew infrequently in the qal, polel, and hithpolel. The qal part. pl. masc. is found in Ps 5:6; 73:3; 75:5. From the context of these passages, Stegemann concludes that the word is probably to be taken as a collective term with a negative connotation such as "the boastful," "the arrogant," "the foolish" (see further "Weitere Stücke," 202, n. 35). Pardee translates it similarly as "the boasters" ("Restudy," 166).

As Stegemann suggests, the *t* that is preserved before *hwllym* might be part of *ᶜdt, qhlt, knst,* or a similar collective, making a "community of foolish ones" stand in opposition to the Qumran congregation. Such opposition between the righteous and the wicked is very frequent in biblical literature and in the Qumran writings; see, e.g., Psalm 1 and 1QpHab 1:[13]; 5:8-12.

For the use of a pl. verb with a sing. collective subject, see below 1-10 ii 7-8.

1-10 i 23 (Allegro's 1-2 i 15) This line continues the condemnation of the wicked group.

those who like laxity ([ʾ]*whby prᶜ*), literally, "those who love hair hanging loose" (similarly Allegro and Pardee). The reading of the word *ʾwhby* is not certain; the only clear letters on the photogrpah are *h* and *b.* For the translation of *prᶜ* as "laxity," cf. 1QS 6:26; CD 8:8; 19:21, where the verb *prᶜ* is used in the general sense of "to let go," "to neglect." This meaning of the root *prᶜ* is attested in biblical Hebrew in verb forms, e.g., Exod 32:25; Prov 1:25; 4:15. Although no such meaning is known for a substantive form, it is reasonable to suppose that the root meaning could take a noun form, "laxity." See further Stegemann ("Weitere Stücke," 202, 203, and n. 35), who translates it similarly as "Ungebundenheit," understanding it specifically with reference to the attitude of the wicked ones toward the Law.

1-10 i 24 (Allegro's 1-2 i 16) This line ends the section of interpretation; the last part of the line is blank.

at the hand of Ephraim (*byd ʾp*[*ry*]*m*). "Ephraim" is suggested by

Strugnell, and it fits the visible traces of letters better than Allegro's reading *ʾl[why]m*, "God." For Ephraim, see the notes above on 4QpHos^b 2:3; 4QpNah 3-4 i 12.

1-10 i 25-26 (Allegro's 1-2 i 17-18) The citation of Ps 37:7 presents the following variants from the MT (see further Pardee, "Restudy," 190):

(1) *wʾl* (MT: *ʾl*).

(2) *tḥr,* qal impf. (MT: *ttḥr,* hithpael impf.).

moan before Yahweh and writhe before him (*[dw]m l[yhwh w]htḥwll lw*). The form *dwm* is here derived from *dmm,* "to mourn," "to moan" (see M. Dahood ["Textual Problems in Isaia," *CBQ* 22 (1960) 400-403], who prefers this derivation for the form *dommû* in Isa 23:2). The form *dwm* in this verse is usually derived from *dmm,* "to be silent," but in this case the sense of the text requires that the next verb form (*whtḥll*) be emended, as suggested in *BHS,* to *wĕhôḥēl* (hiph. impv. sing. masc. of *yḥl,* "to wait," cf. Ps 37:9b). The second verb form in 4QpPs^a, however, clearly agrees with the MT, *htḥwll,* and must be derived from the hollow stem *ḥyl/ḥwl,* "to writhe." In the light of this, the derivation of the form *dwm* from *dmm,* "to moan," is preferred here.

the Man of the Lie (*ʾyš hkzb*). See below 1-10 iv [14]; 1QpHab 2:1-2; 5:11; see also the note on 1QpHab 2:1-2.

1-10 i 27 (Allegro's 1-2 i 19) *the Interpreter of Knowledge* (*mlyṣ dʿt*). The same phrase occurs in 1QH 2:13, and *mlyṣy ḥydwt,* "interpreters of riddles," appears in 1QpHab 8:6; see the note above on 1QpHab 8:4-8.

Fragments 1-10, Column ii

1-10 ii 1 *they will perish* (*ywbdw*). The impf. form is spelled without the ʾ; the biblical Hebrew form is *yōʾbĕdû,* cf. *ywbdw* below in 1-10 iii 3, 4, and 4QpNah 3-4 ii 9; *twbd* in 4QpNah 3-4 iii 7; but cf. *yʾbdw* in 1QpHab 6:10.

by the sword, by famine, and by plague (*bḥrb wbrʿb wbdbr*). This is the only place in the pesharim where the three nouns *ḥrb, rʿb,* and *dbr* occur together. Elsewhere there is mention of *ḥrb whrʿb* (4QpIsa^b 2:1), *brʿb wbdbr* (below 1-10 iii 4), *brʿb* (4QpHos^a 2:12), *bḥrb* (1QpHab 6:10; 4QpNah 3-4 iv 4), cf. Jer 32:24; Ezek 14:21. See further Pardee, "Restudy," 172-173.

1-10 ii 1-2, 4 The citation of Ps 37:8-9 presents the following variants from the MT:

(1) *wʾl* (MT: *ʾl*).

(2) *tḥr* (MT: *ttḥr*); see above 1-10 i 25-26.

(3) *ykrtw* (MT: *ykrtwn*).

(4) *wqwʾy* (MT: *qwy*). This variant shows the intervocalic insertion of ʾ, as in *gwʾym* and *ktyʾym;* see the notes above on 1QpHab 2:11, 12.

(5) *yršw* (MT: *yyršw*). This should be considered an orthographic variant rather than the use of the perf. where the MT has the impf. (this is also the opinion of Stegemann, "Pešer Psalm 37," 247, n. 42), cf. below 1-10 ii 9; 1-10 iii 11. For the defective spelling of the impf. of this verb in biblical Hebrew, see Obad 20; Jer 32:23; Josh 12:1; 21:43; 2 Kgs 17:24.

1-10 ii 4-5 For the structure of this pesher, cf. 4QpNah 3-4 iv 1, and see further Part II, p. 242.

the congregation of his chosen ones (*ʿdt bḥyrw*). The noun *bḥyrw* is here taken to be the defectively written pl. with the sing. masc. sf.; see the note above on 1QpHab 5:4.

1-10 ii 6 This line is blank and was left unnumbered by Allegro. But since it does correspond to a line of text in col. iii, it should be designated as line 6, and the numbering of the following lines should be adjusted.

1-10 ii 7 (Allegro's 1-2 ii 6) The citation of Ps 37:10 presents the following variant from the MT: *wʾtbwnnh,* hithpolel impf. 1st pers. sing. with simple *w* (MT: *whtbwnnt,* hithpolel perf. 2nd pers. sing. masc. with *w* conversive).

1-10 ii 7-9 (Allegro's 1-2 ii 6-8) The syntax of this brief interpretation of Ps 37:10 is difficult. The syntactic features to be noted are (1) the sing. *ršʿh* with the pl. verb *ytmw;* (2) the ambiguity of the phrase *lswp ʾrbʿym hšnh;* and (3) the ambiguity of the relative sign *ʾšr.*

The fact that a pl. verb is used with the subject *ršʿh* suggests that the noun is to be interpreted as a collective. Moreover, the use of the article with the fem. abstract form *ršʿh* might indicate that a specific, concrete group—possibly the enemies of the Qumran community—constituted the "collection of all the wicked." I agree with Pardee ("Restudy," 174) that Strugnell's suggestion of reading *kwl* as a form of *klh* or *kll,* "to destroy," is unnecessary.

The translators have treated the phrase *lswp ʾrbʿym hšnh ʾšr ytmw* differently. Some take the whole pesher as one sentence with *lswp ʾrbʿym hšnh* subordinated to *hršʿh,* and the *ʾšr*-clause as an adverbial clause of time with "wicked" understood as the subject of *ytmw,* e.g., "all the wicked at the end of forty years, when they will be consumed" (Allegro; Yadin [*Message,* 101]; Pardee ["Restudy," 167]). Others who treat the whole pesher as one sentence subordinate the *ʾšr*-clause to *hršʿh* adjectivally, "all the wicked who will be consumed at the end of forty years" (e.g., van der Woude). Most authors, however, divide the pesher either after *lswp ʾrbʿym hšnh,* "all the wicked at the end of forty years; when they are finished, there will not be found . . ." (e.g., Burrows, who takes "forty years" as the subject of *ytmw* [but the verb is masc. and the form *ʾrbʿym hšnh* is fem.] and Carmignac, who takes "the wicked" as the subject) or after *hrš*ᶜ*h,* "all the wicked. At the end of forty years they (i.e., the wicked) will be consumed . . ." (e.g., Dupont-Sommer, Gaster, Vermes).

These translations all assume that the phrase *lswp* ʾ*rb*ᶜ*ym hšnh* must fit syntactically into the pesher, but the possibility that the phrase is a gloss or a parenthetical remark should not be overlooked. For similar syntactic interruptions, see 1QpHab 12:2-3; 4QpNah 3-4 ii 8-9. If the phrase is interpreted parenthetically, then the ʾ*šr*-clause fits smoothly, "all the wicked—at the end of forty years—who will be consumed . . . ." Or, the ʾ*šr* could be left untranslated, "all the wicked at the end of forty years: they will be consumed and there will not. . . ."

Regardless of how the pesher is analyzed syntactically, the sense is clear from the allusion. The "forty years" refers to the Holy War at the end of days (1QM 2:6-14) when all the wicked will be wiped out, see CD 20:15. See further Pardee, "Restudy," 174-75.

For this meaning of *tmm,* see e.g., Num 14:33; 17:28; Josh 8:24; 10:20.

1-10 ii 9 (Allegro's 1-2 ii 8) The citation of Ps 37:11 presents the following variant from the MT: *yršw* (MT: *yyršw*). See the note above on lines 1-2, 4.

1-10 ii 9-12 (Allegro's 1-2 ii 8-11) *the congregation of the poor ones* (ᶜ*dt h*ʾ*bywnym*). See above, 1-10 i 21.

who will accept the appointed time of affliction, or *who will take upon themselves the appointed time of fasting* (ʾ*šr yqblw* ʾ*t mw*ᶜ*d ht*ᶜ*nyt*). Strugnell objects to Allegro's translation of the verb *qbl* as "accept" in the sense of supporting passively. Although in biblical Hebrew this verb means "to receive," in later Hebrew two roots are attested, one meaning "to accept," "to take an obligation upon one's self," "to agree," and another meaning "to cry out." In addition, the first root is attested elsewhere in QL meaning "to accept (someone's testimony)," e.g., CD 9:22, 23. Since the verb is transitive in 4QpPs^a, the translation "to cry out" is impossible.

The reading of the word *ht*ᶜ*nyt* is not certain, since there is a break in the skin. In the preliminary publication Allegro read *mw*ᶜ*d ht*ᶜ*nyt,* which he translated "season of affliction" ("Newly-Discovered Fragment," 71, 73), but in the *editio princeps* he revises the reading to *mw*ᶜ*d ht*ᶜ*wt,* "season of error." His first reading is certainly the better one and is confirmed by the examination of Strugnell, who suggests either *ht*ᶜ*nwt* or *ht*ᶜ*nyt.* Since *t*ᶜ*nwt* is unattested, it is better to read *ht*ᶜ*nyt,* a noun attested in biblical and later Hebrew and also in Qumran Hebrew in CD 6:19 (*ywm ht*ᶜ*nyt*). But the phrase *mw*ᶜ*d ht*ᶜ*nyt* is difficult to translate.

In the preliminary publication Allegro rejected the translation "time of fasting" as reflecting a later technical rabbinic significance. He felt that such a meaning was excluded by the following phrase *wnṣlw mkwl pḥy blyᶜl*, "and they will be delivered from all the traps of Belial," which he took to imply real affliction from outside ("Newly-Discovered Fragment," 73). Following Allegro, some commentators translate "the appointed time of affliction" (Burrows, Dupont-Sommer, Pardee ["Restudy," 167], Stegemann ["Pešer Psalm 37," 258-59]). The case for the translation "affliction" is strengthened if one reads *bmwᶜd htᶜnyt* below in 1-10 iii 3, where it is connected with the eschatological *rᶜb*, "famine," and *dbr*, "plague"; see further below 1-10 iii 3-4.

However, there is also evidence to support the translation "time of fasting." The only attestation in biblical Hebrew of the noun *tᶜnyt* is in Ezra 9:5, where it refers to some kind of penitential exercise, possibly fasting. Fasting is also the predominant meaning of the word in later Hebrew. In QL the only clear occurrence is in CD 6:19 (*ywm htᶜnyt*), which is generally taken as a reference to the Day of Atonement, and therefore to fasting. S. Talmon regards as synonymous the phrases *ywm ṣwm*, "the Day of the Fast," in 1QpHab 11:8 and *mwᶜd htᶜnyt*, taking both as references to the Day of Atonement ("The Calendar Reckoning of the Sect from the Judaean Desert," *Aspects of the Dead Sea Scrolls* [ed. C. Rabin and Y. Yadin; Scripta Hierosolymitana 4; Jerusalem: Magnes Press, Hebrew University, 1958] 180-81).

Some commentators give an ambiguous translation for this phrase, e.g., "de tijd der kastijding" (van der Woude), "Zeit der Busse" (Bardtke, Maier), "season of penance" (Vermes), or "le temps de l'humiliation" (Carmignac). In the most recent study of the phrase, R. B. Coote ("'MWᶜD HTᶜNYT,'" 81-86) concludes that both "time of affliction" and "time of fasting" are correct interpretations and that, in fact, both meanings were intended by the Qumran author. He extends the double meaning further to the verb *qbl*, which with "affliction" would have the root meaning "to feel oppressed," or "to cry out," but see the comments above on this transitive verb. With "fasting," according to Coote, it would have the root meaning "to accept," "to take upon one's self." He places the pesher in the context of the sectarian calendar dispute.

Allowing both possibilities, as Coote does, is an acceptable solution, since the context of this col. supports both options. The eschatological conflict seems to be indicated by mention of "sword," "famine," and "plague" (line 1), the "forty years" (lines 7-8), and the word *mwᶜd*, which is sometimes used to refer to the end-time (e.g., 1QS 3:18; 4:18, 20; 1QM 1:8; 3:7). On the other hand, real times of specific conflict or penance may be referred to by the phrases "those who return to the Law" (lines 2-3) or "the traps of Belial" (lines 10-11).

the traps of Belial (*pḥy blyᶜl*). This is the only occurrence in the pesharim of the name Belial. In biblical Hebrew the noun *bĕlîyaᶜal*, the etymology of which is quite contested (see B. Otzen, "Bᵉlîjaᶜal," *TWAT* 1. 654-58), means "wickedness" or "destruction." In QL the wickedness is often personified, and Belial appears as Satan, the Angel of Malevolence (1QM 13:11), who has a powerful dominion (1QS 2:5; 4QFlor 1-2 i 8), and an army (1QM 1:1, 13; 4:2; 15:3; 18:3). He will be unleashed against Israel for a certain time (CD 4:13; 8:2), but he will ultimately be destroyed (1QM 1:5; 11:8; 13:2; 18:1). Belial is described as the moving force behind the wicked enemies in Israel's history (CD 5:18). The "traps of Belial" mentioned here may be compared to a passage in the Damascus Document (CD 4:14-18), where Isa 24:17 is interpreted (*pšrw*) as a reference to the three nets (*mṣwdwt*) of Belial, namely, fornication (*znwt*), riches (*hwn*), and profanation of the Temple (*ṭmʾ hmqdš*). See further P. von der Osten-Sacken, *Gott und Belial* (SUNT 6; Göttingen: Vandenhoeck & Ruprecht, 1969); H. W. Huppenbauer, "Belial in den Qumrantexten," *TZ* 15 (1959) 81-89.

they will delight in all .[ ].y *of the land* (*ytᶜngw* [*b*]*kwl* .[ ].*y* *hʾrṣ*). The reading of this clause is uncertain, and what is preserved could be interpreted in two ways. (1) The words following *ytᶜngw* could be taken as the subject of the verb, "all . . . of the land will delight . . . ." This is the way Allegro reads the clause, but he does not attempt to restore the missing subject (*kwl b*[ ]*y*). Carmignac, too, interprets the clause this way, and he suggests restoring as the subject either [*ywrš*]*y*, "those who take possession of," or [*ywšb*]*y*, "those who inhabit" ("Notes," 521). Similarly, Strugnell reads *kwl yw*[*r*]*šy* (followed by Pardee and Coote). (2) The subject of *ytᶜngw* could still be *ᶜdt hʾbywnym* of line 10, and the words that follow could be read as the object of the verb. The latter syntax is paralleled below in 1-10 ii 20, where there is no change of subject following *wʾḥr*. I agree with Stegemann in this interpretation of the clause and adopt his reading [*b*]*kwl* (*pace* Strugnell), which fills an otherwise abnormally large space between words ("Pešer Psalm 37," 248-49 and nn. 51-52). For the next word Stegemann makes no restoration in his transcription, but in a note he suggests *ᶜ*[*dn*]*y*, "the pleasures of." But the letter partially preserved before the break cannot be an *ᶜ*; judging from the photographs in *Qumrân Cave 4*, I think the possibilities are *b*, *k*, *m*, and *p*. If a word meaning some legitimate pleasure is restored here, then the Qumran commentator would be describing the eschatological triumph of the Qumran community, the rewards of the righteous, but if a word designating some sinful pleasure is restored, the author must be referring to an apostasy within the community; see further the note on the next phrase.

and they will grow fat in all tᶜ . . [ ] *of flesh* (*whtdšnw bkwl tᶜ* . .[ ] *bśr*). The only word in this clause that can be read with certainty is *bśr* in line 12. The frg. on which the verb is visible should be placed a little farther to the right, joining the larger frg. at the bottom of the final *ṣ* of *hʾrṣ*. This makes possible reading *bkwl* after the verb, parallel to the preceding phrase. The letters of the verb are faint, but the best reading is probably Allegro's suggestion, *whtdšnw,* "and they will grow fat," although this verb is unattested in the hithpael in biblical or Qumran Hebrew. Carmignac's suggestion, *wht*[*ḥ*]*śkw,* which he translates "et se preserveront" ("Notes," 521), does not fit the visible traces of letters as well as Allegro's reading.

The last word in the line cannot be read with certainty from any of the published photographs because of a fold in the skin (cf. *pḥy* in line 10). Only the *t* and the ᶜ are clear. It is almost certain that the word should be a noun in construct with *bśr.* In the preliminary publication Allegro read *tᶜnyt,* cf. line 10, but in the *editio princeps* he gives *tᶜnwg,* "comfort," "luxury." Neither of these readings is compatible with what is visible on the photograph, where the third letter does not look like a *n.* Only the *t* and the ᶜ are transcribed by Stegemann ("Pešer Psalm 37," 248) and Pardee ("Restudy," 164). Carmignac suggests *tᶜbwt,* "abominations," ("Notes," 521), and Stegemann mentions as a possibility the pl. masc. form *tᶜby* ("Pešer Psalm 37," 249, n. 55), but there is no such masc. substantive attested in Qumran Hebrew. Moreover, nowhere else in the Qumran writings is the noun *tôᶜēbâ* spelled defectively.

Even though there are relatively few possibilities, it is difficult to choose when the context is so unclear. In line 10 it is evident that the congregation of the poor ones, namely, the Qumran community, will be saved from all the traps of Belial, and it is assumed that the subject of *ytᶜngw* in line 11 is still the congregation of the poor ones. If a noun denoting some legitimate pleasure is restored in the preceding phrase, then this phrase could be filled in similarly, e.g., with a noun like *tᶜlh* "healing," but the form *tᶜlt* does not fit the visible traces of letters. As in the preceding phrase, if a noun referring to some sinful pleasure is restored, then the Qumran commentator must be saying that the members of the Qumran community are going to be unfaithful and turn to worldly delights. The latter is possible, since there does seem to be evidence of division within the sect; see below, lines 14-15; 1-10 iii 12; 1-10 iv 18-19, and see further J. Murphy-O'Connor, "The Essenes and their History," 233-38.

The pesher ends with the word *bśr* at the beginning of line 12, and the rest of the line is blank.

1-10 ii 13-14 (Allegro's 1-2 ii 12-13) The citation of Ps 37:12-13 presents the following variants from the MT:

(1) *yhwh* (MT: ᵓ*dny*). The addition here of 4Q*183* frg. 3 (see *Qumrân Cave 4,* pl. XXVI), suggested to Strugnell by P. W. Skehan, gives the first three letters of *yhwh,* and Strugnell regards the join as certain (see

"Notes," 259 and pl. IIIa). The tetragrammaton is written in paleo-Hebrew script; see the note above on 1-10 i 19-20.

(2) *b*ʾ (MT: *yb*ʾ). The form in the Qumran text could be read either as the qal perf. or as the qal part.

1-10 ii 14-16 (Allegro's 1-2 ii 13-15) *the ruthless ones of the covenant who are in the house of Judah* (*ʿryṣy hbryt ʾšr bbyt yhwdh*). In the phrase *ʿryṣy hbryt, hbryt* can be interpreted either as an objective genitive, "those who are ruthless toward the covenant," or as a subjective genitive, "those of the covenant who are ruthless." Stegemann ("Pešer Psalm 37," 259, n. 138) followed by Pardee ("Restudy," 167; he translates it "the ones who do frightful things to the covenant") prefers the first interpretation, and he thinks that the phrase refers to enemies of the Qumran community within Judaism. This is based on his view that the phrase *byt yhwdh* designates the whole of Judaism and not only the Qumran group. The latter point, however, is open to question. While it is true that there are several instances where "Judah" refers to the land of Palestine (e.g., 1QM 12:13 = 19:5) or to all of Judaism (e.g., CD 6:5), there are also clear examples of "Judah" as a designation for the Qumran community, e.g., 1QpHab 8:1; 4QpNah 3-4 iii 4. Moreover, the allegorical scheme Ephraim = the Pharisees, Manasseh = the Sadducees, and Judah = the Essenes is presented in 4QpNah 3-4 ii 2, 8; 3-4 iii 4-5, 9; 3-4 iv 1, 3-4, 5, 6. The fact that Ephraim and Manasseh appear in the very next pesher section in this text (1-10 ii 18-20) indicates that the same scheme is probably operative here and that *byt yhwdh* refers specifically to the Qumran community. See further J. Amoussine, "Éphraim et Manassé dans le péshèr de Nahum," *RevQ* 4 (1963-64) 389-96, but cf. J. Murphy-O'Connor, "The Essenes and their History," 220-21, 240-41.

Among the pesharim the word *ʿryṣ* occurs as here in the phrase *ʿryṣy hbryt* (below in 1-10 iii [12]; 1QpHab 2:[6]), in the phrase *ʿryṣy gwym* (below in 1-10 ii 20; 1-10 iv 10), and in a broken text (below in 1-10 iv 1), cf. 1QH 1:[39]; 2:11, 21. The meaning of the root *ʿrṣ* is "to quiver or tremble with fright." I favor understanding the phrase *ʿryṣy hbryt* as a subjective genitive, referring to a violent faction within the Qumran community. That internal strife and sometimes schism occurred within the congregation is supported by 1QpHab 2:[3], which almost certainly speaks of the "traitors to the new covenant," see also the House of Absalom in 1QpHab 5:9. In this pesher "the ruthless ones of the covenant" would be members of the larger Qumran community (the house of Judah) who were opposed to "those who observe the Law" in the council of the community, a smaller group within the whole congregation.

those who observe the Law (*ʿwśy htwrh*), cf. below 1-10 ii 23 and

1QpHab 7:10-11 (*ʾnšy hʾmt ʿwśy htwrh*), 8:1 (*kwl ʿwśy htwrh bbyt yhwdh*), 12:4-5 (*ptʾy yhwdh ʿwśh htwrh*).

the council of the community (*ʿṣt hyḥd*). See the note above on 1QpHab 12:4.

1-10 ii 16 (Allegro's 1-2 ii 15) *into their power* (*bydm*), literally, "into their hand." This is probably the correct reading, but only the *b* and the *m* are fairly certain from the photo.

1-10 ii 16-17 (Allegro's 1-2 ii 15-16) The citation of Ps 37:14-15 presents the following variants from the MT:

(1) *wydrwkw* (MT: *wdrkw*). The impf. form found in 4QpPs[a] preserves the long *o* vowel after the second radical, reflecting a penultimate accent; see the note above on 1QpHab 4:6.

(2) *lpyl* (MT: *lhpyl*). The form in 4QpPs[a] is the hiph. inf. cs. with the *h* elided; see the note above on 1QpHab 3:1.

(3) *wlṭbwḥ* (MT: *lṭbwḥ*).

(4) *wqštwtyhm* (MT: *wqštwtm*).

1-10 ii 18-20 (Allegro's 1-2 ii 17-19) *the wicked ones of Ephraim and Manasseh* (*ršʿy ʾprym wmnšh*). This probably refers to the Pharisees and Sadducees respectively. For a survey of various other proposed identifications, see Pardee, "Restudy," 179-80. Elsewhere in the pesharim, the "city of Ephraim" is identified with the Seekers-After-Smooth-Things (=the Pharisees) in 4QpNah 3-4 ii 2, and Ephraim is said to "lead astray" in 4QpNah 3-4 ii 8; cf. 4QpNah 3-4 iii 5; 3-4 iv 5. In 4QpHos[b] 2:2-3 is a passage that seems to be just the opposite of this one. Here, Ephraim and Manasseh will seek to lay their hands on the Priest, while in 4QpHos[b] it is the last priest who will smite Ephraim. See the note above on 4QpHos[b] 2:3.

on the priest (*bkwhn*). This certainly refers to a priestly leader of the Qumran community, and the impf. verb *ybqšw* in line 18 indicates a future confrontation, cf. the "last priest" in the related passage in 4QpHos[b] 2:3. There is nothing in the text to indicate that the reference is to an eschatological return of the Teacher of Righteousness. See further Pardee, "Restudy," 180-81.

and on his partisans (*wbʾnšy ʿṣtw*). See the note above on 1QpHab 12:4.

the time of testing (*ʿt hmṣrp*), literally, "the time of the crucible." The word *mṣrp* occurs twice in biblical Hebrew meaning "melting pot" (Prov 17:3; 27:21) and the noun does not occur in Mishnaic Hebrew. Elsewhere in the Qumran writings it appears in 1QS 1:17; 8:4; 1QM 17:1, 9; 1QH 5:16; etc. P. Wernberg-Møller (*The Manual of Discipline: Translated and Annotated with an Introduction* [STDJ 1; Leiden: Brill, 1957] 49, n. 42) translates the noun in 1QS 1:17 and 8:4 as "affliction," relating it to the Syriac root *ṣrp,* "to afflict." Yadin, however, understands the noun in 1QM as the biblical Hebrew melting pot or crucible. He remarks that the word "is frequent in the DSS as a symbol for the testing of the Sons of Light in the 'epoch of Belial'" (*The Scroll of the War of the Sons of Light against the Sons of Darkness: Edited with Commentary and Introduction* [Oxford: University Press, 1962] 339). Although Stegemann asserts that the noun in the Qumran documents does not always refer to the trial of the end-time and that such a translation of this text is unsupported ("Pešer Psalm 37," 260, n. 143), the present context is probably eschatological as indicated by the impf. verbs *ybqšw, ypdm,* and *yntnw,* and reference to the Priest, who may be the same as the "last priest" of 4QpHos[b] 2:3.

but afterwards (*wʾḥr kn* or possibly *wʾḥr*[*y*] *kn*). In the preliminary publication Allegro transcribed *wʾḥr*[ ], and in *Qumrân Cave 4* he supplies *wʾḥr*[*y*] *kn* (followed by Lohse and Pardee). Though there is room for a letter after the *r,* no trace is visible on the photograph in the *editio princeps.* However, a letter could be obscured by the break in the skin, since the spot is right at the juncture of two frgs. Both phrases are thus far unparalleled in QL. In the light of biblical Hebrew one might expect the phrase *ʾḥry kn,* which is frequent, but Stegemann ("Pešer Psalm 37," 250, n. 65) notes three places where the phrase *ʾḥr kn* occurs, Lev 14:36; Deut 21:13; and 1 Sam 10:5.

1-10 ii 22-27 (Allegro's 1-2 ii 21-26) Although these lines were included in the photograph presented in the preliminary publication, Allegro did not offer a transcription or translation of them there.

everyone who observes the Law ([*kwl*] *ʿwśh htwrh*) The participle *ʿwśh* appears to be the sing. masc. and perhaps a sing. substantive is to be restored at the end of line 22. The same phrase *ʿwśh htwrh* occurs in 1QpHab 12:4-5, but in that text the form *ʿwśh* is probably a scribal error for the plural *ʿwśy.*

1-10 ii 24 (Allegro's 1-2 ii 23) *for evil* (*lrʿwt*). Without the immediate context, it is impossible to tell for certain whether the last word in this pesher is the pl. of the substantive *rāʿâ* or the inf. cs. of the verb *rʿh,* "to graze." Given the broader context of the conflict between the righteous and the wicked, I prefer the former; see further Carmignac, "Notes," 522; *Les Textes,* 2. 123, n. 28.

The citation of Ps 37:17 presents the following variant from the MT: *ʾzrwʿ*[*wt*] (MT: *zrwʿwt*). In biblical Hebrew both *ʾezrôaʿ* and *zĕrôaʿ* mean "arm," but the former occurs only in Jer 32:21 and Job 31:22. Carmignac describes the form with the initial ʾ as an Aramaizing form ("Notes," 522). It is also possible that the initial ʾ is a dittography of the ʾ at the end of the preceding word (*kyʾ*).

1-10 ii 25 (Allegro's 1-2 ii 24) Allegro continues the citation, restoring 37:18 in this line followed by the introductory phrase of the pesher, but this is too long for one line. Strugnell shortens line 25 a little by suggesting that the words *yhwh* and *ywd*ᶜ were transposed. But there is no need to alter the form of the biblical text. Rather, I restore a short pesher in lines 25-26 and the text of 37:18-19a in lines 26-27.

1-10 ii 26 (Allegro's 1-2 ii 25) *his bidding* (*rṣwn*[*w*]). The reading is not certain, but is better than Stegemann's suggestion, *bṣdy*[*qym*] ("Pešer Psalm 37," 250-51) or Carmignac's reading, *bqwm*[or *mqwm*[("Notes," 523). Pardee suggests restoring *bny* at the end of the preceding line, making the phrase *bny rṣwn,* "the children of his good pleasure" (see further J. A. Fitzmyer, "'Peace upon earth among men of his good will' [Lk 2:14]," *Essays on the Semitic Background of the New Testament* SBLSBS 5; Missoula: Society of Biblical Literature and Scholars Press, 1974] 101-104). It is impossible to know what preceded this word in the interpretation of Ps 37:17, but I suggest the phrase [*l*ᶜ*śwt* ᵓ*t*] *rṣwn*[*w*] in the light of 1-10 i [21], see also 1-10 ii 5 (ᶜ*wśy rṣwnw*).

Fragments 1-10, Column iii

1-10 iii 1-2 The col. opens in the midst of a commentary on Ps 37:18-19a, which was restored at the end of col. ii.

those who return to the wilderness (*šābê hammidbār*), literally, "the returnees of the wilderness." This phrase is translated similarly by Burrows, Carmignac, and Pardee, cf. *šby yś*[*r*ᵓ*l*] restored below in 1-10 iv 24; 4QpHosᵃ 1:16-17; 4QpIsaᶜ 6-7 ii 15. Others translate with Allegro "the penitents of the wilderness" (e.g., Vermes and Maier) or "the converts of the desert" (Dupont-Sommer). Some translations reflect the double meaning of the Hebrew *šwb,* "to return" and "to repent," e.g., "die Umkehrer der Wüste" (Bardtke, similarly Lohse). Stegemann ("Pešer Psalm 37," 260-61, n. 150) translates "die zur Wüste umkehren," and he understands the phrase as a figurative designation for the Qumran community insofar as they have turned away from the wilderness of sin and have turned to the Teacher of Righteousness. Van der Woude's reading of the form as *šōbê,* the qal participle of *šbh,* "de ballingen van de woestijn," is unlikely. See the note above on 4QpHosᵃ 1:16-17 and see further Pardee ("Restudy," 182-83), who thinks that a double meaning was probably intended by the Qumran author.

in safety (*byšw*[ᶜ]*h*). This is suggested by Strugnell in the light of 1QM 1:5. Allegro reads *byšrh,* "in uprightness" (so Pardee, van der Woude). The word cannot be read with certainty from any of the published photographs; only the first two letters are clear. The substantive *yišrâ* is not attested in Qumran or later Hebrew, and it occurs only once in biblical Hebrew in 1 Kgs 3:6. The noun *yšw*ᶜ*h* on the other hand, is used frequently in QL not only to describe the acts of God for his people (e.g., 1QS 11:12) but also to describe the eschatological state of the chosen ones (e.g., 1QM 1:5). Moreover, frg. 3 should be moved a little to the left, since more space is needed in line 2 where the restoration of the biblical text is almost certain. This improves the vertical alignment of the text and gives enough room to accommodate the extra letter in *yšwʿh.*

all the inheritance of Adam (*kwl nḥlt ʾdm*), cf. *nḥlt kwl hgdwl*[*ym*], "the inheritance of all the great ones," below in 1-10 iii 10. It is not certain whether this phrase should be translated "inheritance of Adam" (so van der Woude, Carmignac, Vermes, Pardee, and Stegemann) or "inheritance of humanity." Elsewhere in the pesharim the noun *ʾdm* is attested only in 4QpIsa^{c} 6-7 ii 8, but the context is lost. Compare the phrase *kbwd ʾdm* in 1QS 4:23; 1QH 17:15; CD 3:20, where the word is generally interpreted as the proper name Adam. See further Stegemann, "Pešer Psalm 37," 262, n. 153.

1-10 iii 2-3 The citation of Ps 37:19b-20a presents the following variant from the MT: *rʿb* (MT: *rʿbwn*). Both words mean "hunger," but the form *rĕʿābôn* in the MT occurs only here and in Gen 42:19, 33.

1-10 iii 3-5 *time of affliction* (or *fasting*) (*mwʿd h*[*tʿ*]*nyt*). I follow Strugnell's reading, though only the smallest traces of the *h* and the *n* are visible before and after the break. For the preliminary publication Allegro did not have frg. 3, but he suggested restoring *tʿnyt* after *mwʿd,* corresponding to his preliminary reading of 1-10 ii 10 (his 1-2 ii 9). In the *editio princeps,* however, he restores *mwʿd h*[*tʿ*]*wt,* "the season of error," corresponding to his revised reading of 1-10 ii 10. Stegemann ("Pešer Psalm 37," 262, n. 157) does not think that *tʿnyt* makes sense in apposition to *rʿb.* Although he offers no restoration, he indicates that some expression of eschatological distress is to be supplied. In view of the parallel above in 1-10 ii 10, however, the restoration of *htʿnyt* is probably justified. For the double translation "affliction" or "fasting," see the note above on 1-10 ii 9-12.

all who do not go out from there to be with the congregation of his chosen ones (*kwl ʾšr lwʾ yṣʾ*[*w mšm*] *lhywt* [ʿ]*m ʿdt bḥyrw*). At the end of line 4 Allegro reads *yṣʾ*[*w . . .*] *lhywt* ʿ[*m*], but he does not fill in the lacuna. The reading is not certain; after the break only the *l* is clear, probably followed by a *h* and a *y.* Carmignac ("Notes," 523) thinks he can see the tops of the letters of the word *yhwdh,* "Judah," which would give a text parallel to CD 6:5-6. He translates the phrase "tous ceux qui ne [seront] pas sortis [du pays de Juda]" (similarly van der Woude, Dupont-Sommer, Vermes, Stegemann). But the reading *yhwdh* does not accurately reflect the traces of letters that are visible on the photograph in *Qumrân Cave 4;* nor is there room to restore the word at the end of the line. I follow Strugnell, who, at the suggestion of P. W. Skehan, restores *yṣʾ* [*w mšm*] *lhywtʿm.*

For the translation of *bḥyrw* as "his chosen ones," see the note above on 1QpHab 5:4.

1-10 iii 5a Allegro places this interlinear insertion, the citation of Ps 37:20b-c and the beginning of the pesher, after *bḥyrw* in line 5. Strugnell explains that the commentary probably began with *pšr*[*w* *ˁl* *ˁdt bḥyrw*]. Thus, the line was omitted through homoioteleuton. If this suggestion is correct, it indicates that the manuscript is a copy. The addition is written in a different hand, which Strugnell describes as "semi-cursive" and later than the script of the rest of the document. The tetragrammaton here is written regularly in square script in contrast to other places in this document, where it is written in paleo-Hebrew script; see the note above on 1-10 i 19-20.

The citation of Ps 37:20b-c presents the following variants from the MT, which actually create a text with a sense opposite to that of the MT:

(1) *wʾwhby,* "those who love" (MT: *wĕʾōyĕbê,* "the enemies of").

(1) *kwrym* (MT: *kārîm*). The reading of the MT could be the plural of *kār,* "pasture," or *kār,* "lamb." There are problems with the MT in this verse, which are complicated by the variants in the Qumran citation. As it stands in the MT, the phrase *kîqar kārîm,* "like the splendor of pastures" is awkward and unclear. M. Dahood (*Psalms I: 1-50. Introduction, Translation, and Notes* [AB 16; Garden City, NY: Doubleday, 1966] 226) translates the phrase "like the burning of the hollows," taking *kîqar* from a root *yqr/qrh,* "to burn" (he makes reference to Job 30:17, 30; Prov 29:8) and *kārîm* from *krh,* "to dig" (he makes reference to Num 33:32; Ps 65:14). He concludes that the psalmist is here describing a grass fire whose smoke vanishes quickly. In the text as it appears in 4QpPs[a], the form *kwrym* is puzzling. It looks like the pl. of *kwr,* "furnace," a substantive that occurs several times in the Qumran writings (e.g., 1QH 3:8, 10, 12; 5:16; CD 20:3). It would make sense here if the preceding word *kîqar* were taken, as Dahood does, from a root meaning "to burn." Then the text would be translated "those who love Yahweh are like the burning of furnaces." But in the light of the pesher on this phrase, which mentions "sheep" (*ṣwn*) and "flocks" (*ˁdryhm*), I am inclined to agree with Allegro ("Newly-Discovered Fragment," 74, n. 4a) and Stegemann ("Pešer Psalm 37," 263, n. 159) that the Qumran commentator probably understood *kwrym* as "sheep" or "pastures" rather than as "furnaces" or as a form of *krh,* "to dig." Further, the pesher speaks of "chiefs" and "princes," which suggests that *kyqr* is to be connected with *yĕqār,* "splendor" or "precious things," rather than with the root *yqr/qrh,* "to burn."

At the end of the line I restore *pšr*[*w ˁl ˁdt bḥyrw*] to be continued by *ʾšr yhyw* in line 5, as suggested by Strugnell.

1-10 iii 5-6 The end of line 5 is restored in the light of Gen 46:32, cf. CD

13:9; 19:8 (similarly Dupont-Sommer, Gaster, Habermann, and van der Woude). The commentary ends with the first three words of line 6 and the rest of the line is blank.

1-10 iii 7 The citation of Ps 37:20d presents the following variants from the MT:

(1) *kᶜšn* (MT: *bᶜšn*).

(2) *kwlw* (MT: *klw* [second]). The form of the MT, *kālû,* is a repetition of the first verb, "they are consumed," but the form in 4QpPsa must be the substantive *kwl* with the 3rd pers. sing. masc. sf., *kûllô,* "all of it." Within the citation, the antecedent of the suffix could be "smoke" in verse 20d or "splendor" in verse 20c or, as it is interpreted here, "they" collectively (so Allegro and Stegemann ["Pešer Psalm 37," 264, n. 166], who makes reference to 1QpHab 3:8). Pardee translates the form adverbially "completely" ("Restudy," 168).

1-10 iii 7-8 *the interpretation ‹of it›* (*pšr‹w› ᶜl*). The introductory formula is surely to be read as *pšr‹w› ᶜl*. Between *pšr* and *ᶜl* there is a space, but no *w* is visible on the photograph. From his examination of other photographs, Strugnell is certain that the *w* was omitted rather than obscured through damage to the skin. Therefore it should be supplied in the transcription as an editorial correction (*pšr‹w›*) rather than a restoration, as Allegro does (*pšr*[*w*]).

the wicked princes (*śry hr*[*š*]*ᶜh*). Compare the overthrow of the "prince of the kingdom of wickedness," *śr mmšlt ršᶜh,* in 1QM 17:5-6.

who oppress (*ʾšr hwnw*). The reading is probable but not absolutely certain. The form *hwnw* is here taken to be the hiph. perf. 3rd pers. pl. of *ynh,* but this is the only attestation thus far in QL of the verb *ynh.*

who will perish like smoke that is lost in the wind (*ʾšr ywbdw kᶜšn hʾwb*[*d brw*]*ḥ*). The pesher compares the demise of the wicked to the image of smoke being blown away by the wind. The exact Hebrew words that the Qumran author chose for his description are not known. The only clear letters on the photograph in *Qumrân Cave 4* are *hʾw* (or *hʾy*), followed by one stroke before the break and a trace of a *ḥ* after the break. In the preliminary publication Allegro noted that it was possible to see a *w* (or a *y*) before the last *ḥ,* and it has been generally accepted that the word to be restored here is *brwḥ,* "in (*or* by) the wind." But there have been various suggestions for what might have preceded this. Allegro first read the letter before the break as *r,* supplying *hʾw*[*r,* "a flame" (similarly Bardtke, Burrows). Subsequently Carmignac (followed by Maier) interpreted the visible stroke as a *d,* suggesting *hʾw*[*d,* "un tison" ("À propos d'une restitution," 431). This is also the reading of Allegro in the *editio princeps,* but it is unclear whether he took the suggestion from Carmignac or came to the reconstruction independently. Based on other photographs, Strugnell would read either *h'wz.*[or *h'wn.*[, but he offers no restoration. Following this, Pardee notes the appropriateness of *h'wzl,* the qal part. of *'zl,* "to disappear," but he acknowledges that the upper tip of the *l* is not visible but almost certainly would be if this were the correct reading ("Restudy," 84). I restore *h'wb[d,* "that perishes," as suggested by Stegemann ("Pešer Psalm 37," 252-53, 264, n. 169) following Dupont-Sommer.

From line 8 to the bottom of the col. the left hand portion of the frg. is so damaged that it is extremely difficult to read from the photograph in *Qumrân Cave 4.* I rely on the transcriptions of those who have seen the frgs. themselves or other photographs.

1-10 iii 8-9 The citation of Ps 37:21-22 presents the following variants from the MT:

(1) *mbwrk*[*w*] (MT: *mbrkyw*). The form in 4QpPs^a is restored in the light of the defectively written suffix of *wmqwllw* (with the second *w* written above the line), where the MT has *wmqwllw.* Both are orthographic variants.

(2) The form *yšrw* is restored rather than *yyršw* as in the MT in the light of the same variant above in 1-10 ii 4.

1-10 iii 10-13 *the congregation of the poor ones* (*ʿdt h'bywnym*), see 1-10 i [21].

theirs is the inheritance ('[*šr lh*]*m nḥlt*), cf. Matt 5:5. I adopt Strugnell's restoration of the first lacuna in line 10. Allegro transcribes only *h*[. . .]*m*.

After the word *kwl* in line 10, Allegro transcribes *h*[.].*l*[. Stegemann gives *kwl t*[*b*]*l*[, "die ganze W[el]t," which fits the context but is too short for the space. Similarly, Strugnell suggests *nḥlt kwl htbl,* but he offers no justification for the use of the article with *tbl,* which always occurs in biblical Hebrew without it and so too elsewhere in Qumran Hebrew. Pardee moves in a different direction with *kwl h*[*ʿw*]*l*[*h 'šr*], "all iniquity" ("Restudy," 165, 168, 185). Though I do not agree with this interpretation, Pardee gives a good analysis of the various possibilities of substantives that might be construed with *nḥlt.* In addition to those he mentions, another possibility is *hgmwlm,* "their due," see below 1-10 iv 9 and 1QpHab 12:3. However, there is no reason why a noun must be restored here. One might suggest *hgwlym,* "those who went into exile," *hgwml* or *hgwmlym,* "the one(s) who dealt wickedly," cf. 1QpHab 12:3, *hmšlmym,* "those who repay," or *hmšwlmym,* "those who are repaid," cf. the verb *šlm* above in the citation of Ps 37:21; 1-10 iv 9; 1QpHab 12:2. I tentatively restore *hgdwlym,* "the great ones," in the light of 4QpNah 3-4 i 5, where it probably refers to the nobles allied with the Lion of Wrath in Jerusalem.

The restoration of the very end of the line depends on how the above phrase is reconstructed. I supply *ʾšr* as an introduction to the rest of the pesher, but it is left untranslated as above in 1-2 ii 8.

and on his holy mountain (*[wbh]r qwdšw*). This is suggested by Carmignac (*Les Textes,* 2. 124-25; so also Maier, Strugnell, Pardee) in the light of Ezek 20:40, where the phrase *bĕhar qodšî* is juxtaposed with *bĕhar mĕrôm yiśrāʾēl,* the same phrase that occurs above in this pesher. Allegro's first suggestion, *wʿm qwdšw,* "and his holy people" ("Newly-Discovered Fragment," 71; followed by Bardtke, Burrows) fills the space better than his restoration in the *editio princeps, wbqwdšw,* "and on his holy place" (so Stegemann, "Pešer Psalm 37," 264, 265, and n. 175), but Carmignac's suggestion is preferred.

The next part of the pesher—from the end of line 11 through line 13—has a structure like that of 4QpIsa[a] 7-10 iii 6-13 (Allegro's 8-10:2-9); see also 1QpHab 12:3-5, 7-9, with a phrase of the citation repeated and then interpreted with a brief figurative identification. See further Part II, p. 238.

and those who are cursed by him (*w[mqwl]lw*). I follow Allegro in reading the defectively written suffix, where the MT has *wmqwllyw,* cf. above line 9 and *bḥyrw* in 1-10 ii 5.

the ruthless ones of the covenant (*ʿryṣy hb[ryt]*). See above 1-10 ii 14, and cf. *ʿryṣy gwʾym* in 1-10 ii 20; 1-10 iv 10.

the wicked ones of Israel (*[r]šʿy yśrʾl*). This is restored by Allegro. Strugnell (followed by Pardee) suggests *p]wšy yśrʾl,* "the simple ones of Israel," which he thinks would fill the space better. But this phrase is thus far unparalleled in the Qumran writings, while *ršʿy yśrʾl* can be compared with *ršʿy ʿmw* (1QpHab 5:5), *ršʿy ʿmym* (1QH 5:17), *ršʿy gwym* (4QpNah 3-4 i 1), *ršʿy ʾprym wmnšh* (above 1-10 ii 18), *ršʿy ʾprym* (4QpNah 3-4 iv 5), and *ršʿy mnšh* (4QpNah 3-4 iv 1).

The pesher ends with the first word of line 13, and the rest of the line is blank.

1-10 iii 14-15 The citation of Ps 37:23-24 begins with the word *kyʾ,* which is not in the MT. It is impossible to tell whether this word is to be understood as part of the citation, or whether it is an introductory word, cf. possibly *whwʾh* in 4QpIsa[c] 4, 6-7 i 7 (Allegro's 4-7 i 4).

and he delights in his way (*[wd]rkw yḥpṣ*). I follow Strugnell's restoration of these words, though he indicates that he is able to read the *d* of *[w]drkw.* Allegro reads *kwn]nw bkwl drkw yḥpṣ,* "in all his ways does he delight." (In the preliminary publication he read *[w]kwl [d]rkw yḥpṣ.*) I agree with Strugnell and Stegemann that *bkwl* is impossible. It is an unattested variant from the MT and makes the line too long; moreover, there is no trace of a *l* on the photograph where it would be expected (*pace* Allegro, "Newly-Discovered Fragment," 74).

for if he should charge (*ky*ʾ *y*[*pw*]*l*). For this translation, see M. Dahood, *Psalms I: 1-50,* 231.

At the end of the line I follow Allegro's transcription in the *editio princeps,* but Strugnell (followed by Pardee) reads *yp*[*w*]*l* [*lw*ʾ].

1-10 iii 15-17 *the Priest, the Teacher of Righteousness* (*hkwhn mwrh h*[*ṣdq*]). This pesher provides two facts about the Teacher of Righteousness: (1) he was a priest, cf. 1QpHab 2:8; (2) he was the founder or "builder" of the community. See further Pardee, "Restudy," 186-87.

whom God chose ([ʾ*šr b*]*ḥr bw*). Here I follow Strugnell, who, at the suggestion of P. W. Skehan, restores [*b*]*ḥr* (followed by Pardee). This verb is very frequently construed with the preposition *b,* while such a construction with *dbr,* meaning "to command," as restored by Allegro, would be awkward.

as the pillar (*l*ʿ*mwd*). This form is generally taken as the qal inf. cs. of ʿ*md* (*la*ʿ*ămôd*), "to take a stand," which is certainly possible. I suggest the noun ʿ*ammûd,* "column," "pillar," which is attested in 1QM 5:10. This noun is not used figuratively in biblical Hebrew, but such an image is not inconsistent with the picture of the Qumran community as the Temple of God. See above, p. 126.

for he established him (*(k*[*y*ʾ]*hkynw*). Allegro transcribes *w*[ʾ*šr*] *hkynw,* which is possible. Strugnell supplies instead *l*ʿ*mwd l*[*pnyw ky*ʾ] *hkynw,* "to stand before him, for he established him" (followed by Pardee). I disagree with Strugnell on the number of spaces in the lacuna and prefer a shorter reconstruction. Moreover, *ky*ʾ appears three times in the biblical text in lines 14-15. For a similar use of *ky*ʾ*,* see above 1-10 i 27; 1-10 ii 3.

the congregation of his chosen ones in truth (ʿ*dt* [*bḥyrw b*ʾ*mt*]). There are many ways in which the end of line 16 could be restored. In the preliminary publication Allegro suggested simply ʿ*dt bḥyrw* ("Newly-Discovered Fragment," 71, 75). Other suggestions include ʿ*dt h*ʾ*mt,* "a congregation of truth" (Dupont-Sommer), ʿ*dt h*ʾ*bywnym,* "the congregation of the poor ones" (Pardee). Also possible would be ʿ*dt qwdš,* "a congregation of holiness." The present restoration is suggested in the light of 1-10 ii 5 and *l*ʾ*mt* in line 17; cf. 4QpIsa^{d} 1:3. Compare the description of the Wicked Priest in 1QpHab 10:10; he established "a congregation with deceit" (*wlqym* ʿ*dh bšqr*).

his way is straight ([*wdr*]*kw yšr*). Since the context is uncertain, it is not clear whether the form *yšr* is to be read adjectivally, *yāšār,* or whether it is a defectively written form of the verb *yšr,* e.g., the qal impf. *yišar,* "his way is straight." For defective spelling of the impf. of verbs with initial *y,* see above 1-10 ii 4, 9; 1-10 iii 11.

to the truth (*l*ʾ*mt*). Allegro reads *l*ʾ*mtw,* "to his truth," but Strugnell does not think that it is possible to read a *w* at the end of the form. The reading cannot be judged with certainty from the photograph in *Qumrân Cave 4*.

1-10 iii 17-18 The citation of Ps 37:25-26 presents the following variant from the MT: *wgm* (MT: *gm*).

1-10 iii 18-20 Only a few words of this pesher are preserved, but it seems to have focussed on the Teacher of Righteousness.

1-10 iii 21-27 These lines are completely lost, but they almost certainly contained the text of Ps 37:27 and a commentary. The citation of Ps 37:28 probably began at the end of line 27 and continued into the first line of col. iv.

Fragments 1-10, Column iv

The width of this col. can be determined from the restoration of Ps 37:32-33 in line 7, which makes the col. about one and one-third times as wide as the first three cols.

1-10 iv 1 Allegro has probably miscalculated the position of frg. 7; consequently, the first three lines of his transcription do not reflect the true width of the col. This forces him to restore an emended version of the last phrases of Ps 37:28. When frgs. 3, 7, and 8 are moved apart, however, there is room to restore the full text of Ps 37:28 continued from line 27 of col. iii. I follow the restoration proposed by Strugnell at the suggestion of P. W. Skehan (except for the word *nšmdw*, for which see below).

they are preserved (*nšmrw*). This is read in agreement with the MT. Allegro (followed by Strugnell and Pardee) reads *nšmdw*, "they will be destroyed," reflecting the Greek ἐκδιωχθήσονται. The reading is not certain, but compare the *r*'s in *wzrᶜ* immediately following, in *ᶜryṣy* at the end of the line, and in *htwrh* in line 2 with the *d*'s in *tdbr* in line 3, *dbrw* in line 4, and *hgyd* in line 5.

1-10 iv 1-2 For the short pesher on Ps 37:28 I make the following suggestions: (1) restoring the introductory formula *pšrw hmh* to fill out line 1, see 1-10 ii 4-5 (so also Pardee); (2) *ᶜryṣy hbryt,* see 1-10 ii 14; 1-10 iii [12]; (3) *ʾšr ykrtw,* see 1-10 iii 12; (4) *mʾsw ʾt htwrh,* see 1QpHab 1:11; 5:11; 4QpIsaᶜ 23 ii 14a. A similar proposal is that of Pardee ("Restudy," 165, 169, 187): *pšrw*] *hmh ᶜryṣy* / [*hbryt bbyt yhwdh ʾšr lwʾ ᶜśw*] *htwrh,* "these are the ones who do frightful things to the covenant in the house of Judah, who do not carry out the law."

In the citation of Ps 37:29 the defective spelling of *yršw* is restored rather than *yyršw* as in the MT in the light of 1-10 ii 4, 9; 1-10 iii 11.

1-10 iv 3 To be restored at the beginning of line 3 is a short pesher that probably identifies *ṣdqym* of Ps 37:29 with the Qumran community. It may refer either to their "taking possession of the land" or to their "living upon it forever." The partial restoration offered here is made in light of 1-10 iii 1. Pardee ("Restudy," 165) suggests [*pšrw* *ʿl* *ḥṣdyqym hywšry* [*sic*] *hʾrṣ*] *bʾlp* [*dwr,* "Its interpretation concerns the just who shall possess the earth for 1000 generations."

1-10 iv 3-4 *wisdom* ([*ḥ*]*wkmh*). In the citation of Ps 37:30-31, just after the break in line 3, I read with Strugnell *ḥ*]*wkmh* (so also Pardee), which conforms better to the usual Qumran orthography than *ḥkmh,* as read by Allegro, see *ḥwkmh* in 4QpIsa[a] 7-10 iii 16 (Allegro's 8-10:12).

In the continuation of the citation in line 4, I follow Strugnell's suggestion of restoring the impf. form *tmʿwd* (mistakenly printed *tʿmwd* in "Notes," 216), which preserves the long vowel after the second radical, and in giving the full writing of *ʾlwhyw* and *ʾšwryw* (so also Pardee).

his feet never slip ([*lwʾ* *tmʿwd* *ʾšwryw*]). See M. Dahood, *Psalms I: 1-50,* 231.

1-10 iv 4-6 Allegro gives the beginning of the pesher on Ps 37:30-31 as *pšrw* *ʿl*] *hʾmt* *ʾšr dbr,* "Its interpretation concerns] the truth which [. . .] spoke. . . ." Strugnell's suggestion is too long for the line: *pšrw* *ʿl hkwhn hnqrʾ bšm* (or *ʿl šm*)] *hʾmt,* "The interpretation of it concerns the Priest who was called by the name of truth" (cf. 1QpHab 8:9). Pardee proposes *pšrw* *ʿl hʾwhb*] *hʾmt* *ʾšr dbr,* "Its interpretation concerns the one who loves] the truth, who speaks. . . ." The reading of the last word in the line is not certain owing to a fold or a break in the skin. It is possible that the verb could be read as the pl. *dbrw,* in which case I might suggest *pšrw* *ʿl ʾnšy*] *hʾmt* *ʾšr dbrw,* "the interpretation of it concerns the men of truth who spoke," cf. 1QpHab 7:10; 1QH 14:2.

1-10 iv 7 *nor will he let him be condemned as guilty* ([*w*]*l*[*wʾ* *y*]*ršyʿnw*). Though it was not indicated by Allegro, there is a trace of a letter visible in this line before *yršyʿnw,* probably the *l* of *wlwʾ*.

. . . *when he comes to trial* ({{*w*}}*bhšpṭw*). Before *bhšpṭw* a *w* has been erased but is still partially visible, though it was not indicated by Allegro. Stegemann's suggestion ("Pešer Psalm 37," 254, n. 99) that the *w* was an error of dittography is possible.

1-10 iv 8-10 *who lay in ambush* (*ʾšr* *ṣ*[*ph*]). I restore the qal perf. of *ṣph* rather than the participle as suggested by Allegro. In the preliminary publication Allegro had *ʾšr* *š*[*lḥ* *ʾl,* "who sent to. . . ."

for the Teacher of Righteousness ([*lmwr*]*h* *hṣd*[*q*]). In the light of similar descriptions of the aggressiveness of the Wicked Priest against the Teacher of Righteousness, e.g., 1QpHab 8:16—9:2; 9:9-12; 11:5-8, 12-16; 12:2-6, this restoration is justified. It can be made by moving frgs. 5 and 6 a little farther apart. This also makes possible a better restoration of line 9; see below.

and sought to murder him (*[wybqš l]hmytw*). I restore the impf. of *bqš* rather than the participle (*wmbqš*) as suggested by Allegro.

At the end of line 8 a trace of the last letter of the word before *whtwrh* is visible on the photograph in *Qumrân Cave 4.* Allegro reads it as a *t* (followed by Stegemann). Carmignac ("Notes," 524) suggests reading *q* and restoring perhaps *(h)ṣd]q,* "la justice." Strugnell proposes *hḥw]q,* "the precept" (followed by Pardee), but he notes that the letter could also be *w.* It looks to me more like a final *n.*

After *whtwrh* at the end of the line, Carmignac ("Notes," 524) thinks he can read *ʿ[l]* (followed by Stegemann), but according to Strugnell the stroke that is visible is not part of a letter but is one of the marks of ruling. Moreover, it would be syntactically difficult to read a preposition between *whtwrh* and *ʾšr* in line 9.

but God will not abandon him into his hand (*wʾl lwʾ yʿ[zbnw bydw]*). Strugnell indicates that he can make out an additional letter, giving either *yʿw[zbnw* or *yʿz[wbnw,* but it is impossible to judge from the photograph in *Qumrân Cave 4.* I follow the restoration proposed by Allegro in the preliminary publication (*yʿ[zbnw bydw]*). In the *editio princeps,* because of his placement of frg. 6, he is forced to supply simply *yʿ[zbnw]*. However, if frgs. 5 and 6 are separated as was suggested above, there is room to restore the phrase as it is in the citation of Ps 37:33 in line 7 above.

when he comes to trial (*[b]hšpṭw*). This is Allegro's reading, and it is preferable to *špkm,* "he has shed," suggested as a possibility by Dupont-Sommer (*Essene Writings,* 272, n. 2).

God will pay him his due (*wl[w y]šlm [ʾl ʾt] gmwlw*). I follow the restoration of the second lacuna that was suggested by Allegro in the preliminary publication (*[ʾl ʾt] gmwlw*), which is better both in terms of space and in terms of syntax than *[ʾl g]mwlw,* as he gives in the *editio princeps.*

to wreak vengeance upon him (*lʿśwt bw [nqmwt]*). After *bw* Allegro restores *mšpṭ* (followed by Pardee), but I prefer *nqmwt,* as suggested by Strugnell, cf. 1QpHab 9:2.

1-10 iv 10-12 *wait for Yahweh* (*[qwh ʾl y]hwh*). The verb form *qawwēh* is restored in agreement with the MT, but cf. the spelling of *qwʾy,* "those who wait," in 1-10 ii 4.

you will gloat (*tr[ʾh]*), or possibly "you will exult." For this translation of the verb *rʾh* with the preposition *b,* see e.g., Obad 12; Ps 22:18.

Restoration of the beginning of this pesher depends on how the last visible word of line 11 (*wʿm*) and the first word of line 12 (*bḥyrw*) are interpreted. There is a break in the skin at the word *wʿm,* and it is impossible to tell from the published photographs if this is the last word in the line. It is so interpreted by most commentators, who translate *wʿm bḥyrw* either "and with his elect" (so Allegro), taking *wʿm* as the preposition *ʿim,* in which case the subject of the plural verb *yśmḥw* would have to be the same as the subject of *yrʾw* restored in line 11, or "and the people of his elect," i.e., "his chosen people" (so Stegemann), taking *wʿm* as the substantive *ʿam*, in which case this phrase would probably be the subject of the verb *yśmḥw*. In both of these cases what should be restored at the beginning of the interpretation in line 11 is a designation of the Qumran community; Stegemann suggests *ʿdt hʾbywnym*, "the congregation of the poor ones" ("Pešer Psalm 37," 254).

The interpretation of *wʿm . . . bḥyrw* followed here is that proposed by Pardee ("Restudy," 166, 169, 188), who takes *wʿm* as the preposition *ʿim* but not as the last word of the line. He restores *ʿdt* after the preposition at the end of line 11; thus, "and with the congregation of his chosen ones" (see 1-10 ii 5; 1-10 iii 5). (Pardee, however, translates *bḥyrw* as the sing. noun with the sing. sf., but I think it is better to understand *bḥyrw* as the defectively written pl. noun with the sing. sf., see the note above on 1-10 ii 5.) Since this phrase as restored designates the Qumran community, a different group should probably be indicated at the beginning of the pesher, and I supply *hdwr hʾḥrwn*, "the last generation," see 1QpHab 2:7; 7:2. Pardee suggests *pšrw ʿl ʿwśy hṣdq*, "Its interpretation concerns those who carry out what is right." Whatever group is restored here would, together with "the congregation of his chosen ones," form the compound subject of *yśmḥw*.

wickedness (*ršʿh*), cf. 1-10 i 24. This word might also be translated "wicked ones" (so Stegemann), cf. *kwl hršʿh* in 1-10 ii 7.

Strugnell calls attention to what seems to be a trace of a letter just before the break in line 12, which could indicate that there was a word following *ʾmt*. In view of this observation Pardee restores [*mdwr ldwr*], "forever" ("Restudy," 166). But the stroke could also be part of one of the letters in line 11. The second half of line 12 is blank.

1-10 iv 13-14 The Hebrew of Ps 37:35-36 is obscure. The text is restored here according to the MT, and the following variants from the MT are preserved:

(1) [*w*]*ʾʿbwr*, 1st pers. sing. (MT: *wyʿbr*, 3rd pers. sing.).

(2) *ʿl m*[*qw*]*mw* is not in the MT.

Carmignac's suggestion (*Les Textes*, 2. 126) that the first words of Ps 37:35 be restored according to the LXX, *ršʿ ʿlyṣ*, "l'impie brutal s'elevant," is impossible, since *ršʿ ʿryṣ* is clear. Moreover, if the next phrase were *wmtʿlh kʾzry hlbnwn*, "towering like the cedars of Lebanon," as in the LXX, I should expect to find Lebanon mentioned or identified figuratively in the pesher on this verse, cf. 1QpHab 12:3; 4QpIsa[a] 7-10 iii 3-13 (Allegro's 8-10:3-9); 4QpNah 1-2 ii 7.

and he displays himself (*wmtʿ*[*rh*]). I follow Stegemann's reading in agreement with the MT ("Pešer Psalm 37," 254) rather than *mtʿ[rh]* as read by Allegro (followed by Pardee).

like a native tree of luxuriant growth (?) (*kʾzrḥ rʿnn*). Allegro restores this phrase in agreement with the MT, but he translates it according to the Septuagint "like the cedars of Lebanon" (ὡς τὰς κέδρους τοῦ Λιβάνου).

and I passed by before his place. But lo! He was not there (*[w]ʾʿbwr ʿl m[qw]mw wh[nh ʾyn]nw*). This is suggested by Strugnell; Allegro reads *ʾʿbwr ʿl p[nyw whnh]*.

1-10 iv 14-16 On the photograph in *Qumrân Cave 4,* line 14 is illegible from *hkzb* to *lšbyt.* I follow Allegro's transcription for this and the next line.

the Man of the Lie (*[ʾ]yš hkzb*). See 1-10 i 26; 1QpHab 2:1-2; 5:11.

In the second half of line 15 Strugnell reads *lʿśwt[m]mnw mšpṭ* (followed by Pardee, who translates "so as to execute judgment against him" ["Restudy," 169]).

1-10 iv 16-17 The beginning of line 17 is illegible on the photograph in *Qumrân Cave 4;* the only clear letter is *h.* This brief pesher probably focussed on the Teacher of Righteousness.

1-10 iv 17-18 The citation of Ps 37:37-38 presents the following variant from the MT: *yḥd wʾḥryt* (MT: *yḥdw ʾḥryt*).

1-10 iv 18-19 *the ruthless ones of the covenant* (*[ʿryṣy hbryt]*). This is restored in the light of 1-10 iii 12-13 above.

the congregation of the community (*ʿdt hyḥd*). This phrase does not occur elsewhere in the pesharim; the only attestation of it thus far elsewhere in QL is in 1QSa 2:21.

1-10 iv 19-20 The citation of Ps 37:39-40 presents the following variants from the MT:

(1) *wyhlṭm,* "and he saves them" (MT: *wyplṭm* [first], "and he brings them to safety").

(2) *wyplṭm* (MT: *ypltm* [second]).

Allegro's transcription of the word *wt[šw]t[* in line 19 does not reflect the text as it appears in the photograph in the *editio princeps,* where the line is completely broken off after *wt[ ].*

1-10 iv 20-21 This pesher ends the commentary on Psalm 37. It probably referred to the eschatological deliverance envisioned by the Qumran community. Line 22 is blank and line 23 begins a commentary on Psalm 45.

1-10 iv 23 The commentary on Psalm 45 opens with the superscription or title of the psalm followed by an interpretation, rather than with the first line of the poem. Compare 3QpIsa 1, where the text begins similarly with the title of the book of Isaiah; see also the restoration of the beginning of 1QpHab.

1-10 iv 23-24 Just after the first break in line 23, Strugnell transcribes [*šwš*]*nym,* but I can see traces only of the *y* and the *m* on the photograph in *Qumrân Cave 4.* These are the only letters of the citation of Ps 45:1 that are preserved, so it is impossible to tell how the Qumran author read the citation. Allegro translates the restored text *šyr ydydwt* as "a song of lots," apparently taking *ydydwt* as a form of the verb *ydd,* "to cast a lot upon." This is tempting since the lot (*gwrl*) is a significant concept in the writings of the Qumran sect; see the note above on 4QpIsa[d] 1:8.

the seven divisions of the returnees of Israel (*šbᶜ mḥlqwt šby yś*[*rʾl*]). See the note above on 1-10 iii 1-2.

1-10 iv 25 Allegro transcribes nothing at the beginning of this line, but there are traces of two letters visible on the photograph in *Qumrân Cave 4.* I transcribe *ʾw*[*mr*], but Strugnell suggests [*ʾ*]*wm*[*r*]. At the end of the lacuna, before *qwdš,* Allegro restores *rw*]*ḥ,* "spirit," but this is doubtful. The visible traces look more like strokes of two letters than one (*ḥ*).

1-10 iv 26 Both Allegro and Strugnell note the uncertainty of the placement of frg. 9. The only words that can be tentatively read on the frg. are *spry* and *ᶜl mwrh,* and these words give no clue to where the frg. belongs. The only indication is that the bottom margin of a col. is visible. If frg. 9 were removed from this position, Strugnell would continue the citation of Ps 45:2b that begins in line 26 through Ps 45:3a in line 27. But this would probably not leave enough room after the citation for the beginning of the pesher.

Fragments 11-12

These two frgs. show the top margin of a col. Strugnell thinks that they are closely connected to the previous text and that they might preserve part of the commentary on Ps 45:2, which would be the top of col. v.

11:2 *the chosen ones of Israel* (*bḥyr*[*y*] *yśrʾl*), see 4QpIsa[e] 6:[1]. The word transcribed as *bḥyry* by Allegro is illegible on the photograph in *Qumrân Cave 4.*

12:1 *with the lip of* (*bšpt*). The occurrence of *špt,* "lip," here might support Strugnell's suggestion that these frgs. belong to the commentary on Ps 45:2; see *lšwny,* "my tongue," above in line 26 (Ps 45:2b).

12:2 There is a trace of a letter visible beneath the *p* of *bšpt* in line 1. It is probably the upper tip of a *l,* but it was not transcribed by Allegro.

Fragment 13

Strugnell suggests a possible connection between frg. 13 and 4Q*172* frg. 10 (see the Appendix below), but this cannot be verified from the photographs in *Qumrân Cave 4.*

13:3-4 The citation of Ps 60:8-9 is restored with the full writing of *bqwdšw, ʾᶜlwzh, rwʾšy.* If the restoration of these biblical verses is correct, the following variant from the MT should be noted: *ᵓmddh* (MT: *ᵓmdd*), parallel to the other two impf. forms *ᵓᶜlwzh* and *ᵓḥlqh*.

I restore the biblical text and commentary in these lines following Allegro's suggestion, but this is not entirely satisfactory. These verses would probably have been favored by the Qumran commentators because of the mention of Ephraim, Manasseh, and Judah. I should then expect the pesher to identify these names in some way with the Pharisees, the Sadducees, and the Essenes respectively. The problem with the present arrangement is that it ends the citation after verse 9b, thus excluding from this lemma the phrase *yĕhûdâ mĕḥōqĕqî,* "Judah is my scepter." It seems most unlikely that the interpreter would have separated this last phrase from the rest of the verse, but there is not enough room to include it according to the transcription given by Allegro.

4QpPs^b (4Q*173*)

Editio princeps: "Commentary on Psalms (B)" (J. M. Allegro), *Qumrân Cave 4,* Vol. I, pp. 51-53 and pl. XVIII.

Secondary literature: J. Strugnell, "Notes," 219-20.

Allegro designates as 4QpPs^b five small frgs. He identifies frgs. 1-3 with parts of Psalm 127, but too little of the supposed biblical text is preserved to verify this identification. In identifying frg. 4 with Psalm 129, Allegro is probably correct. The last two verses are partially preserved, and the letters visible in line 3 are probably part of a commentary. Frg. 5, however, does not belong with the other four. J. Strugnell regards the script of frg. 5 as at least a half-century later than that of the other frgs. He points out further that there is no indication that the frg. belongs to the literary genre of the pesher. For this reason it is included in the appendix; see below, p. 266.

The only clues to the content of the interpretation are the mention of the Teacher of Righteousness (1:4; 2:2) and the priest at the end of time (1:5). The commentary may have had an eschatological thrust.

4QpPs^b: Translation

Fragment 1

1.].[
2.]ᵓ*lk*.[
3. w]ho seek[
4. the hid]den things of the Teacher of Righteousness[

5. the prie]st at the end of ti[me
6.] (*vacat*) [
7. those who] take possession of the inheritance[

Fragment 2

1.] The interpretation of the mat[ter
2. the Tea]cher of Righteous[ness

Fragment 3

1.] . . the man[
2.]who will be *q* [
3.]they will not be ashamed[

Fragment 4

1. [WITH WHICH] THE HARVESTER DID [NOT] FILL HIS PALM, NOR [(DID) THE ONE WHO GATHERS EARS OF GRAIN (FILL) HIS POUCH, AND THOSE WHO PASS BY DO NOT SAY] Ps 129:7-8
2. ["THE BLESSING OF YA]HWEH BE UPO[N YO]U! [WE] BL[ESS YOU IN THE NAME OF YAHWEH"]
3. [ ].*šᶜ*[ ]*l*[ ]

4QpPsᵇ: Notes

1:2-3 Allegro restores the text of Ps 127:2-3 on the basis of his reading]ʾ*lk*.[in line 2, which he takes as *šwʾ lkm,* the first two words of Ps 127:2, and *ywršy hnḥlh* in line 7, which he interprets as a commentary on Ps 127:3a (*hnh nḥlt yhwh bnym,* "Behold, sons are an inheritance from Yahweh"). This is far from a certain identification. Even if it is possible to restore Ps 127:2 in lines 2-3 of the frg., there is no room for 127:3 before line 7, which is supposedly the interpretation of that verse.

1:4 *the hidden things of* ([*ns*]*trwt*). Allegro's restoration ᶜ]*trwt,* "the supplications of," is possible, but the noun *ᶜtr* is not attested elsewhere in QL. If *ns*]*trwt* is accepted (the niph. part. is preferable to Allegro's alternative suggestion of the pl. substantive *strwt*), it is noteworthy, since this is the only attestation of the word thus far among the pesher texts. The participle *nstrwt* (e.g., 1QS 5:11; 1QH 17:9; CD 3:14) along with *rz,* "mystery" (e.g., 1QpHab 7:5, 8, 14) and *swd,* "secret" (e.g., 1QS 4:6; 1QH 5:26), are the words used at Qumran to indicate "mysteries" (see further R. E. Brown, "The Pre-Christian Semitic Concept of 'Mystery,'" *CBQ* 20 [1958] 436-43). The "mystery" of the prophetic writings and the "pesher" are complementary concepts (see 1QpHab 7:4-5 and see further Part II, p. 237.

1:5 *the priest at the end of time* ([*hkw*]*hn lʾḥryt hq*[*ṣ*]). The restoration is not certain. The phrase *lʾḥryt hqṣ* is elsewhere unattested in QL, but cf. *hqṣ hʾḥrwn* (1QpHab 7:7, 12; similarly 1QS 4:16-17), *lʾḥryt hymym,* which is frequent, *kwhm hʾḥrwn* (4QpHos[b] 2:3), and *kwnhy yrwšlm hʾḥrwnym* (1QpHab 9:4-5). See further the note on 4QpHos[b] 2:3.

1:7 It is unclear how many words are preserved in this line and where the break or breaks between words occur. Strugnell rejects Allegro's reading of the first word in favor of]*wršp,* but he does not comment on what this form would mean, nor does he suggest what letter is to follow the *p,* which is not written in the final form. Allegro's reading of the line is preferred here, but the identification of frg. remains uncertain.

2:1 Allegro restores Ps 127:3b at the beginning of the line based on his reading]*pšrw hpr*[*y,* but the reading is uncertain, and this calls the placement of the frg. into question. I follow Strugnell, who reads *pšr* rather than *pšrw.* The first letter of the next word is clearly *h,* but the second letter cannot be read with certainty. However, it cannot be *d,* so the formula *pšr hdbr* is excluded. Strugnell suggests reading either *hṭ*[or *hpt*[*gm*]; the latter is restored. See the note above on 4QpIsa[a] 2-6 ii 26, where the formula [*pšr h*]*ptgm lʾḥryt hymym* is restored.

3:1 Allegro reads ʾ]*šry hgbr*[and restores Ps 127:5a, but only traces of the first word are visible on the photograph in *Qumrân Cave 4.*

3:3 On the photograph in the *editio princeps* the only certain letters seem to be *l* and *šw.* Allegro, however, is able to read *lwʾ ybwšw k*[*y* (=Ps 127:5b?), and Strugnell apparently does not object.

4:1 *his pouch* ([*ḥṣnw*]), i.e., "the bosom of his garment." The MT has *ḥiṣĕnô,* while 11QPs[a] has *ḥwṣnw.* It is impossible to tell how this text should be restored. Again, for *wlʾ ʾmrw* of the MT, 11QPs[a] has *šlwʾ ʾmrw.*

4:2 The apparent citation of Ps 129:7-8 presents the following variant from the MT: *ʿlykm* (MT: *ʾlykm*). 11QPs[a] also reads *ʿlykm.*

4:3 Allegro's reading,]*ršʿ*[, is possible. A form of *yšʿ,* "to help," in the context of blessing might also be suggested.

Allegro should have transcribed the *l,* on top of which is clearly visible beneath the *b* of line 2.

PART II

THE LITERARY GENRE

Introduction

From the preceding presentation of the texts a composite picture of the pesharim emerges made up of what the texts themselves say about pesher interpretation and of what can be observed as characteristic of the pesher texts. Both of these factors must be taken into account in an attempt to describe the literary genre of the pesharim.

From the texts themselves[1] it is learned that the Qumran commentators believed (1) that the words of the books that they were interpreting were full of mysteries revealed by God ("and God told Habakkuk to write down the things that are going to come upon the last generation, but the fulfillment of the end-time he did not make known to him" [1QpHab 7:4]); (2) that the mysteries hidden in the biblical books referred to history, specifically to the history of their community ("the words of his servants the prophets, by whose hand God enumerated all that is going to come upon his people and upon his congregation" [1QpHab 2:9-10]); (3) that the interpretation of these mysteries was revealed to the Teacher of Righteousness and to selected interpreters who followed him ("the interpretation of it concerns the Teacher of Righteousness to whom God made known all the mysteries of his servants the prophets" [1QpHab 7:4-5]; "when they hear all that is going to come upon the last generation from the mouth of the priest into whose heart God put understanding to interpret all the words of his servants the prophets" [1QpHab 2:7-10]). Thus, the picture that emerges from the texts themselves is that the pesher is an interpretation made known by God to a selected interpreter of a mystery revealed by God to the biblical prophet concerning history.[2]

[1]This is if the author of the Habakkuk pesher can be taken as representative of the interpretative tradition that lies behind the pesharim.

[2]I use the word "revealed" in the sense that it is used in these texts, namely, that mysteries and their interpretations were made known by God to prophets and interpreters. I do not intend the word as it is used here to carry with it any dogmatic connotations. These texts do not give any clues as to how the Qumran interpreters characterized or experienced this revelation. On this point, see further O. Betz (*Offenbarung und Schriftforschung in der Qumran-*

Complementing this description is the picture that is drawn by the observations that modern commentators can make about these texts—observations about the word *pēšer,* the structure of the texts, the use of formulas, the modes of interpretation, and the content of the interpretation-sections.

The Word *Pēšer*

All of the texts presented in Part I use the word *pēšer,* and it is this word by which the texts are identified and described.[3] The object of this word study is not to give an exhaustive tabulation of all the occurrences of the word but to situate the term etymologically by examining significant examples and to arrive at a translation that will reflect the correct meaning of the word and thereby illuminate the character of these documents.

There is disagreement about the etymology of the word *pēšer;* involved in the conflicting opinions are four consonant groups, *pṭr, pšr, ptr,* and *pṯr.*

pṭr

The first of these groups can be dealt with briefly. It is mentioned here only because it has been mistakenly related etymologically to the root *ptr.*[4] However, *pṭr* is a common Semitic root (Akkadian *paṭāru,* Hebrew *pāṭar,* Aramaic *pĕṭar*) meaning "separate," "set free," "loosen." It is well-attested in biblical Hebrew, Mishnaic Hebrew, and later Aramaic. Though similar in some shades of meaning to *ptr* and *pšr,* the root *pṭr* should not be connected etymologically with either *ptr* or *pšr.*

sekte [WUNT 6; Tübingen: Mohr-Siebeck, 1960]), who investigates in detail the meaning of revelation for the sect as it is expressed in the Qumran documents.

[3]Short word studies, usually limited to descriptions of the use of *pēšer* and related terms in the Bible, are included by several authors in introductory remarks to the pesharim, e.g., O. Betz, *Offenbarung und Schriftforschung in der Qumransekte,* 77-80; F. F. Bruce, *Biblical Exegesis in the Qumran Texts* (Grand Rapids: Eerdmans, 1959) 7-10. For more extensive word studies, see, e.g., G. Dautzenberg, *Urchristliche Prophetie: Ihre Erforschung, ihre Voraussetzungen im Judentum und ihre Struktur im ersten Korintherbrief* (BWANT 104; Stuttgart: Kohlhammer, 1975) 43-64; I. Rabinowitz, "*Pêsher/Pittârôn:* Its Biblical Meaning and its Significance in the Qumran Literature," *RevQ* 8 (1973) 219-32; A. Leo Oppenheim, *The Interpretation of Dreams in the Ancient Near East. With a Translation of an Assyrian Dream-Book* (Transactions of the American Philosophical Society, Volume 46, Part 3; Philadelphia: American Philosophical Society, 1956) 217-25. Oppenheim's work is especially important, as will be seen, for understanding the term *pēšer* in the context of dream-interpretation, and I shall return to the article by Rabinowitz in the discussion of the translation of the word *pēšer.*

[4]E.g., KB, under the root *ptr.*

pšr

The root *pšr,* from which the Hebrew *pēšer* is derived, is a common Semitic root attested in Akkadian, Aramaic, Hebrew, and Arabic, meaning "loosen," "dissolve."

In Akkadian[5] the root appears with this meaning as early as the old Babylonian period (the first half of the second millennium B.C.) as a verb *pašāru* and in substantive formations such as *pišru, pāšertu, pišertu,* etc. The verb is used in the simple conjugation with several meanings developed from the basic definition "loosen," e.g., "release (prisoners)," "settle (a dispute)," "loose (an oath or curse)," and "report or explain (dreams)." Similarly in the intensive conjugation the verb is used meaning "unravel (thread)," "loosen (an evil spell)," "interpret (dreams, especially by magic)." Less frequently the verb appears in the reflexive and causative conjugations. The noun *pišru,* the same segolate formation as the Hebrew *pēšer,* means "interpretation," "solution," and is also used to refer to a magic wand for the magician (*iṣ pišri*).

The use of the Akkadian *pašāru* to refer to the interpretation of dreams has been discussed by A. Leo Oppenheim, who describes the different but interrelated facets of meaning of the root: (1) It can refer to the reporting of a dream to another person, in which case the subject is the dreaming person, and the activity is "translating" the symbols of the dream into language. (2) It can refer to the "interpreting" of an enigmatic dream by another person, in which case the subject is the person to whom the dreamer presents the dream, and the activity is discerning the symbolic import of the dream. The "interpretation," however, is not an exposition but is the revelation of the message of the deity addressed to the dreaming person concerning the future. The "interpretation" is carried out for therapeutic reasons, and this overlaps the next point. (3) It can refer to the process of dispelling or removing the evil consequences or omens of a dream by magic means. In this sense *pašāru* is a technical term designating a therapeutic-magic process.[6]

In Akkadian, then, the basic meaning "loosen" is extended to "explain," "interpret." Beginning in the Middle Babylonian period, i.e., from the second half of the second millennium B.C. and continuing on, connotations of magic are prominent, especially with reference to interpreting dreams by magic and loosing curses or oaths.

[5]For further references in detail, see W. von Soden, *Akkadisches Handwörterbuch* (Wiesbaden: Harrassowitz, 1969) 2. 842-43 under the word *pašāru;* p. 844 under *pāšertu;* and p. 868 under *pišertu* and *pišru.*

[6]*Dream Interpretation,* 217-25.

In nonbiblical documents of the Official Aramaic period (700-200 B.C.), the verb *pšr* is attested in an Aramaic text described as an account or an inventory, but the meaning is uncertain (*AP* 63.14).[7]

In the biblical period, the root *pšr* appears in Hebrew only late as a noun *pēšer* in Qoh 8:1, *mî kĕheḥākām ûmî yôdēaʿ pēšer dābār,* "who is like the wise one, and who knows the interpretation of a word/thing?" Compare the Greek τίς οἶδε σοφοὺς, καὶ τίς οἶδε λύσιν [*pšr*] ῥήματος, with the Greek translation λύσιν reflecting the root meaning "loosen." The fem. form of the segolate *pišrâ* (cf. Akkadian *pišertu*) occurs in Ben Sira 38:14 in a discourse on the role of the physician, *ky gm hwʾ ʾl yʿtyr ʾšr yṣlḥ lw pšrh wrpʾwt lmʿn mḥyh,* "for he too will pray to God that *pšrh* will avail him, and healing in order to preserve life."[8] In the RSV, the word *pšrh* is translated "diagonsis," presumably understood as an interpretation of symptoms.[9] However, if the root meaning of a therapeutic dispelling of evil omens or consequences can be applied to illness as it is to dreams, the passage might be translated "that a release will benefit him and healing to preserve life." Compare the Greek καὶ γὰρ αὐτοὶ κυρίου δεηθήσονται, ἵνα εὐοδώσῃ αὐτοῖς ἀνάπαυσιν [*pšrh*] καὶ ἴασιν χάριν ἐμβιώσεως, "for they too will pray to the Lord that ἀνάπαυσιν [*pšrh*] will be good for them and healing for the maintenance of life." The Greek ἀνάπαυσις may reflect an extended meaning of the basic definition of the root *pšr,* "loosen," similar to the translation of the Hebrew verse, "that relief will be good for them."[10]

In biblical Aramaic, the root *pšr* appears both as a verb, meaning "interpret," and as a noun, meaning "interpretation." In Daniel it is used in connection with the interpretation of dreams (frequently in chaps. 2 and 4) and in connection with the explanation of the mysterious message on the wall at Belshazzar's feast (chap. 5). I shall return to these occurrences below.

[7]A. Cowley, *Aramaic Papyri of the Fifth Century B.C.* (Oxford: Clarendon, 1923) 167-68. The form is the haphel perf. 3rd pers. masc. sing. *hpšr,* which Cowley thinks may be similar in meaning to a use of the hiph. of *pšr* in Mishnaic Hebrew, i.e., "make a covenant," "make an agreement."

[8]This verse is preserved in Hebrew in manuscript B of the Ben Sira fragments from the Cairo Geniza. Fragments of the Hebrew text of Ben Sira have been discovered at Qumran and Masada, but none preserves this portion of the text.

[9]See, e.g., H. L. Strack (*Die Sprüche Jesus', des Sohnes Sirachs. Der jüngst gefundene hebräische Text mit Anmerkung und Wörterbuch* [Schriften des Institutum Judaicum in Berlin 31; Leipzig: A. Deichert'sche Verlagsbuchhandlung (Georg Böhme), 1903] 69), who translates "Deutung," "Diagnose." R. Smend translates similarly "die Deutung der Krankheit" (*Die Weisheit des Jesus Sirach. Hebräisch und Deutsch* [Berlin: Georg Reimer, 1906] 65).

[10]Or it may have arisen through a misreading of ΑΝΑΛΥΣΙΝ in an uncial manuscript (ΑΝΑΑΥΣΙΝ), subsequently altered to ΑΝΑΠΑΥΣΙΝ for the sense. See G. Dautzenberg, *Urchristliche Prophetie,* 55.

Slightly later, in the Hebrew of the Qumran documents, the root *pšr* appears both as a verb and as a noun. The verb is rare; the only certain occurrences that have thus far come to light are the qal inf. cs. *lpšwr* in 1QpHab 2:8 referring to the interpretation of the words of the prophets, and the qal impf. *ypšwr* in 4QEnoch Giants^b ii:14, 23 (restored).[11] In the latter text, both occurrences concern the interpretation of dreams. The qal impv. *pšwr* is restored by J. T. Milik in 1Q*22* 1:3.

Thus far in the Qumran texts the noun *pēšer* is found with only one exception as part of a stereotyped formula introducing the interpretation of a biblical text. The exception is 1Q*30,* a fragmentary text that Milik describes with hesitation as part of a liturgical document.[12] But even this text is connected with biblical material. In frg. 1, after the mention of "the books in five parts" ([*s*]*prym hwmšym*[, line 4), and "the rest more than/about four" (]*wywtr* ʿ*l* ʾ*rb*ʿ*t*[, line 5), the text preserved in line 6 is]*wpšryhm lpy*[, "and their interpretations according to." Here the noun *pēšer* may refer to some distinct works, possibly written commentaries. Elsewhere, however, the word is part of the formulas that have been seen in the texts in Part I, and it is always singular.

In later Aramaic,[13] the verb *pšr* occurs in the simple and intensive conjugations meaning "melt," "be broken (of a charm)" (e.g., *b. Sanh.* 67b); "solve a riddle or interpret a dream" (*Tg. Onq.* Gen 40:16; 41:12; *b. Ber.* 56a). Two noun formations appear: *pāšar* (or *paššar*), "interpreter," in *Tg. Onq.* Gen 40:8; and *pěšar,* "interpretation," in *Tg. Jer. II* Gen 40:8[14] and *Tg. Qoh* 8:1 (where the Hebrew word is *pēšer*).

In Mishnaic Hebrew the root *pšr* appears only as a verb, preserving the original meaning "loosen," "dissolve." A root *pšr,* which may be a different word, occurs meaning "be tepid" (*b. Ber.* 16b), "temper" (*b. Šabb.* 40b).

In summary, the common Semitic root *pšr* appears in Akkadian and throughout the Hebrew and Aramaic of the biblical and post-biblical periods with the basic meaning "loosen." The extended meaning "interpret"

[11]J. T. Milik, "Turfan et Qumran: Livre des Géants juif et manichéen," *Tradition und Glaube: Das frühe Christentum in seiner Umwelt. Festgabe für Karl Georg Kuhn zum 65. Geburtstag* (ed. G. Jeremias *et al.;* Göttingen: Vandenhoeck & Ruprecht, 1971) 122.

[12]Qumran Cave I (DJD 1; Oxford: Clarendon, 1955) 132.

[13]For more references and further detail on the roots occurring in later Aramaic and Mishnaic Hebrew, see M. Jastrow, *A Dictionary of the Targumim, the Talmud Babli and Yerushalmi, and the Midrashic Literature* (New York: Pardes, 1950) pp. 1248-49, 1255-56, under the roots *pšr, ptr.* etc.

[14]The Hebrew of Gen 40:8 is *ûpōtēr* ʾ*ēn* ʾ*ōtô,* "and there was no one to interpret it (a dream)." To render the word *pōtēr, Tg. Onq.* uses the equivalent expression *pāšar,* while *Tg. Jer. II* uses the noun formation *pěšar.*

appears already in Akkadian, where it refers especially to the interpretation of dreams by magic. In biblical Hebrew only noun formations occur: in Qoh 8:1 meaning "interpretation," and in Ben Sira 38:14 probably preserving the root meaning "loosen." In neither is there any reference to dreams, but the latter may have some of the force of the magical dispelling of evil omens. In roughly the same period in the Aramaic of Daniel the root *pšr* is used both as a verb and as a noun specifically with reference to interpreting dreams and also a mysterious text or inscription. Here, too, there is the connection with magic and the occult, which began in the Babylonian period, as evidenced by the following: the task of interpreting dreams normally fell to the magicians, the enchanters, the sorcerers (Dan 2:2); Daniel is called the chief of the magicians (4:6); the mystery (*rāzâ*) of the dream and the interpretation were revealed to Daniel in a vision of the night (2:19). It is clear, however, that the notion of interpreting dreams by magic has been theologized; the interpretation is revealed by God.

Slightly later in Qumran Hebrew, the word appears mainly in formulas introducing the interpretation of biblical texts. There is no mention of magic; the *rāz* or mystery concealed in the prophetic text, which is the object of interpretation, can be unfolded only by the revelation of God (1QpHab 2:8-10; 7:4-5).

In Mishnaic Hebrew, there is no attestation of a meaning "interpret," while in the Aramaic of the same period and later the meaning "interpret (dreams)" is well-attested. As is the case with Daniel and the Qumran writings, the idea of interpretation by divine revelation prevails.[15]

ptr and pṯr

The word picture is not complete without a consideration of the consonant group *ptr,* which is used in Hebrew and Aramaic meaning "interpret."[16]

[15]See further, M. Gertner, "Terms of Scriptural Interpretation: A Study in Hebrew Semantics," *BSO(A)S* [University of London] 25 (1962) 1-27.

[16]This same consonant group *ptr* appears as a substantive in Akkadian and Aramaic meaning "table," but this is not connected with the meaning "interpret." In a papyrus list of names and accounts that Cowley dates possibly to 300 B.C., the noun *ptwrʾ* occurs. Cowley identifies this with hesitation as the "table of a money-changer" (*AP* 83.21 and pp. 202-203). The same substantive meaning "table" seems to be attested late in the Middle Aramaic period (A.D. 165) in an inscription from Hatra; see *An Aramaic Handbook* (ed. F. Rosenthal; Wiesbaden: Harrassowitz, 1967) Part I/1, p. 46. In Uruk, a cuneiform document dated to the fifth-fourth century B.C., the substantive is vocalized *pa-tu-ú-ri* and *pa-tu-ú-ru;* see J. J. Koopmans, *Aramäisches Chrestomathie* (Leiden: Nederlands Instituut Voor Het Nabije Oosten, 1962) II. Teil, No. 56, p. 47. A masc. substantive *ptr* is attested in a Punic inscription, but the meaning is unknown; see C. G. Jean and J. Hoftijzer, *Dictionnaire des inscriptions semitiques de l'ouest* (Leiden: Brill, 1965) p. 240 under the root *ptr.* Other meanings that

The earliest attestation of *ptr*, "interpret," is in biblical Hebrew in Genesis 40 and 41. Deriving from the Elohist source, this section is part of the story of Joseph in Egypt and describes Joseph interpreting Pharaoh's dreams. Here *ptr*, both as a verb and in the noun form *pittārôn*, "interpretation," is used in the same way as is *pšr* in Akkadian and Aramaic. In Mishnaic Hebrew, where the root *pšr* is not attested with the meaning "interpret," *ptr* does occur both as a verb and in the noun form *pitrôn*, referring to the interpretation of dreams (e.g., *b. Ber.* 55b).

Oddly enough, *ptr* meaning "interpret" appears in late Aramaic alongside *pšr* as a verb (e.g., *Tg. Jer II* Gen 40:12, 18) and in the noun formations *pĕtār* and *pitrônaʾ*, and the latter is used specifically with reference to the interpretation of dreams in *Tg. Jer. II* Gen 40:12, 18.

From the above, it is apparent that *pšr* and *ptr* overlap in the meaning "interpret." For this reason *ptr* is sometimes mistakenly described as the Hebrew cognate of the Aramaic *pšr*, supposedly derived from the Akkadian *pašāru*. Although the common proto-Semitic root *pšr* could account for both Hebrew and Aramaic *pšr*, there is no common Semitic root that could at the same time yield Hebrew *ptr* and Aramaic *pšr*. The only root that could in any way account for both Hebrew/Aramaic *pšr* and Hebrew/Aramaic *ptr* would be *pṯr* (with the dental spirant *ṯ*. Such a common Semitic root would come into Hebrew as *pšr*, Aramaic as *ptr* (old Aramaic *pšr*), and Akkadian as *pšr*. There is no attestation of a root *pṯr* in Arabic or Ugaritic, but when the evidence of Hebrew (*pšr*), Akkadian (*pšr*), and Aramaic (*ptr*) is taken together, it shows that Hebrew *pšr* and Aramaic *ptr* could have been derived from a proto-Semitic root **pṯr* meaning something like "interpret." But how then can the opposite use of Hebrew *ptr* and Aramaic *pšr* meaning "interpret" be explained?

In Genesis 40 and 41, interpretation of dreams is indicated in Hebrew by *ptr* rather than by *pšr*, a root that was well-attested in Akkadian with reference to dream interpretation. However, in Akkadian the root *pšr* was overlaid with connotations of magic and the occult. This nuance might have rendered the word offensive or even idolatrous to the Hebrews. The originator of the stories in Genesis 40 and 41 may have avoided the word for this reason and may have borrowed directly from Aramaic a similar root *ptr*. The root *pšr* meaning "interpret" does not appear in Hebrew until Qoheleth, Ben Sira, and Qumran writings. In these instances it is frequently regarded as an Aramaic loanword,[17] but exactly the opposite

appear for this consonant group in Akkadian are "sword," "club? (weapon)," "some kind of flower," "an uncultivated tract of land." Such a diverse set of meanings indicates that there is no common Semitic root *ptr*.

[17]E.g., KB under the word *pēšer;* E. Osswald, "Zur Hermeneutik des Habakuk-Kommen-

may be the case. If Akkadian *pšr,* Hebrew *pšr,* and Aramaic *ptr* point to a proto-Semitic root **p̲tr,* then the use of *pšr* in Aramaic may be a direct borrowing from Akkadian in the Babylonian period or from Hebrew at a later time.

This survey of the significant uses of and etymological questions about the root *pšr* brings up the problem of translating the term *pēšer* in the Qumran texts. The translation "interpretation" is not ideal, since it can connote scholarly exegetical activity of the modern type, especially in a biblical context. But the English word "interpretation" does not have to imply this, and I do not think that it gives rise to the degree of misunderstanding that I. Rabinowitz asserts or that most modern commentators use the word "interpretation" with reference to the pesharim to mean a type of exegesis or exposition, "the achievement and transmission to others of an intellectual understanding of something."[18] Rabinowitz's starting point is the dream interpretation in the OT. Analyzing the use of the root *ptr* in Genesis 40 and 41, he concludes that the word carries these connotations: (1) The interpretation "consists of a determination and disclosure of a dream's *presage* or *prognostic.*" (2) The word "may denote not merely the dreamed, though as yet unfulfilled or unrealized, presage of some event or circumstance, but *the presage thought of as fulfilled or realized, the reality presaged* by the dream."[19] He translates both the verb and the noun as "presage," denoting both "presage of reality and realized presage."[20] He finds that this translation is also suitable for the use of *pšr* in Daniel and in the Qumran documents.

Although Rabinowitz's study has situated the term *pēšer* in the proper context to draw out its meaning, I am not willing to go along with his translation of the word *pēšer* as "presage." After all, to use his example of Gen 40:5, is his translation "each dreamed according to the reality presaged by his dream" a significant improvement in English over "each dreamed the

tars," *ZAW* 68 (1956) 253; G. Vermes, "A propos des Commentaires bibliques découverts à Qumrân," *RHPR* 35 (1955) 98. I. Rabinowitz describes *pittārôn* and *pātar* as "closely related phonetic variants and synonyms" of *pēšer* and *pěšar* (*"Pêsher/Pittârôn,"* 220). He further suggests that *ptr* came into classical Hebrew and thence into subsequent Hebrew and Jewish Aramaic through an earlier Aramaic borrowing from the Akkadian *pšr,* and that Aramaic/Hebrew *pšr* is the result of a later taking over the Akkadian root as such (p. 220). But the "phonetic variation" Hebrew *ptr*/Aramaic *pšr* cannot be traced to Akkadian *pšr.* As was pointed out above, Hebrew *ptr* may have been borrowed directly from Aramaic *ptr,* and Aramaic *pšr* may have been borrowed directly from either the Akkadian or the Hebrew *pšr,* but all three roots—Akkadian *pšr,* Hebrew *pšr,* and Aramaic *ptr*—may point to a proto-Semitic root **p̲tr.*

[18]*"Pêsher/Pittârôn,"* 225.

[19]*"Pêsher/Pittârôn,"* 221. The italics are his.

[20]*"Pêsher/Pittârôn,"* 222.

likeness of the interpretation of his dream?"[21] Moreover, the translation of *pēšer* as "presage" does not bring out the root meaning "loosen." Rather than emphasizing the "foretelling" aspect of the word, it seems to me better to stress the nuances of the unravelling of mysteries or the "translating" of symbols, and so I retain the translation "interpretation" with this in mind. Other translations of the word *pēšer* include "meaning" (Brownlee, Milik, Burrows, Elliger, and similarly Stegemann) and "explication" (Dupont-Sommer, Vermes).

Before moving on from this word study, mention should be made of the complementary concept of *rāz*, the mystery that is interpreted. The word *rāz* is a Persian loan-word that does not occur in biblical Hebrew but is found in biblical Aramaic in Dan 2:18, 19, 27, 28, 29, 30, 47 (twice); 4:6 (English 4:9). The concept of mystery expressed by the term *rāz* developed out of the idea of the ancient prophets' being introduced in their visions into the heavenly assembly and there learning the secret divine plans for cosmic history.[22]

In the pesharim[23] the word refers to the mystery concerning the things that are going to come, which were hidden in the prophetic writings (1QpHab 7:4-5), not made known fully to the prophet. Corresponding to this hidden *rāz* or mystery was the *pēšer* or interpretation, which was also revealed by God to a selected interpreter. The mystery could not be unravelled or solved by human wisdom; the interpretation was made known by God.

Structure of the Pesharim

The pesharim presented in Part I follow the same basic pattern: citation, section by section of a single biblical book, with each lemma followed by an interpretation. The only apparent exception to the use of a single book is 4QpIsa^{c}, where there are indications that there may have been citations

[21]"*Pêsher/Pittârôn,*" 221-22. Another important feature of Rabinowitz's study is his treatment of the pesher formulas. See below, pp. 243-44.

[22]In later Hebrew the word is attested meaning "secret" and also "strength" or "foundation," and similarly in later Aramaic, it means "secret." See further R. E. Brown, "The Pre-Christian Semitic Concept of 'Mystery,'" *CBQ* 20 (1958) 417-43; "The Semitic Background of the New Testament *Mysterion,*" *Bib* 39 (1958) 426-48; 40 (1959) 70-87; in a slightly revised form *The Semitic Background of the Term "Mystery" in the New Testament* (Facet Books, Biblical Series 21; Philadelphia: Fortress, 1968).

[23]See also J. M. Casciaro Ramírez, "El tema del 'Misterio' divino en la 'Regla de la Comunidad' de Qumran," *Scripta Theologica* 7 (1975) 481-97; "Los 'Himnos' de Qumrān y el 'Misterio' paulino," *Scripta Theologica* 8 (1976) 9-56; "El 'Misterio' divino en los escritos posteriores de Qumrān," *Scripta Theologica* 8 (1976) 445-75.

from Jeremiah and Zechariah (though the text is fragmentary), and there are allusions to passages from Hosea and Zechariah.[24] Even though many of the texts are not well-preserved, it is virtually certain that—with rare exceptions—each commentary followed the individual biblical book continuously. Again, 4QpIsa^{c} is one exception. There are places where verses or whole sections of Isaiah are skipped, and the omissions seem to be deliberate.[25] In 4QpHos^{a} there could be two places where one colon of the biblical text is lacking (4QpHos^{a} 1:7-8 = Hos 2:8a, c; 4QpHos^{a} 1:15 cites Hos 2:9b, but there is no citation of 2:9a), but since the text is fragmentary this is not certain.

The documents generally follow the verse divisions known from the MT. The citations vary in length from one-fourth verse to five verses, but most of the lemmas are from one-half to two verses long. In 4QpIsa^{a} the citations tend to be a little longer, with three to five verses quoted at a time. The length of the interpretation-sections varies from as little as one-half line to as much as nine and one-half lines (1QpHab 2:1-10), but most of the interpretations are about two to three lines long.[26]

Within the basic framework of a lemma followed by an interpretation, some of the texts repeat part of the citation (1QpHab, 4QpIsa^{a} and possibly also 4QpIsa^{e} and 4QpHos^{b}). This repetition may conclude the interpretation (being followed immediately by the next lemma, e.g., 1QpHab 3:2-3, 13-14), or it may be followed by another pesher section (e.g., 1QpHab 5:6-7; 6:2-5; 7:3-5; 9:2-7; 10:1-5; 12:6-10; 4QpIsa^{a} 2-6 ii [6-9]; 7-10 iii [6-8], [10-11], [11-13], 26-29; 4QpIsa^{c} 6-7 ii [7-8], [15-17]. Sometimes there is a series of these repetitions between the main citations (e.g., 1QpHab 6:2-8; 4QpIsa^{a} 7-10 iii 6-13) or possibly a second repetition of a portion of the lemma (4QpIsa^{a} 7-10 iii 10-11).

The commentaries are not divided into section or chapters, though some of the documents show fairly regular patterns of spacing or indentation: (1) A few units of space may be left between the end of the lemma and the pesher within a line (1QpHab, 4QpIsa^{e}, 4QpHos^{b}, 4QpNah). (2) Conversely, a few units may be left between the end of a pesher and the begin-

[24]See above, p. 95.

[25]See above, p. 95.

[26]Since the width of the cols. is not uniform among the various documents or even within a single text, this indicates only the relative length of the interpretations. The width of the cols. in some of the pesharim is not certain and must be conjectured from probable restorations. In several of the texts (1QpMic, 1QpZeph, 4QpIsa^{a,b,c,d}) the width of the cols. is about 50 units, i.e., letters and spaces. But 1QpHab has narrower cols., averaging 35-40 units, and some of the documents have much wider cols., e.g., 4QpIsa^{e}, 63 units, and 4QpNah, 70-80 units. There is sometimes variation within a single text, e.g., 4QpPs^{a} has three cols. that are 45-50 units in width and one col. of 65-70 units.

ning of the next lemma within a line (4QpNah). (3) The rest of a line may be left blank after the last word of a citation, with the pesher beginning at the margin of the next line (1QpHab, 4QpHos^a, 4QpNah). (4) Conversely, the rest of a line in which a pesher ends may be left blank, with the next lemma beginning at the margin of the next line (4QpHos^{a,b} 4QpPs^a). (5) A citation that begins a new line may be indented (3QpIsa, 4QpIsa^a). (6) A whole line may be left blank (*vacat*) (4QpIsa^a, 4QpHos^a, 4QpPs^a). Analysis of the spacing patterns can sometimes aid in restoring the text.

Finally, two of the texts (1QpHab and 4QpIsa^c) have various signs or marks in the margins of some of the columns. I mention this here in my observations on the basic form of the pesharim, though I have been unable to discern any structural significance for these marks.

Formulas in the Pesharim

In this section the formulas that are used to introduce citations and/or interpretations are examined with a view to understanding how and where they are used and how they are constructed.[27]

I. Formulas introducing interpretations of the biblical text

  A. Formulas using the word *pšr*[28]

    1. *pšr hdbr* ("the interpretation of the passage")[29]

      a. *pšr hdbr* + *ʿl* + substantive [to which the interpretation refers] ("the interpretation of the passage concerns *x*,"

[27]The lists include some doubtful readings and some formulas that are partially or completely restored with fair certainty; these references appear in brackets. The major publications and photographs should be consulted to determine the strength of individual readings. For specific discussions of the formulas that occur in 1QpHab, see K. Elliger, *Studien zum Habakuk-Kommentar,* 123-29. See also B. M. Metzger, "The Formulas Introducing Quotations of Scripture in the New Testament and the Mishnah," *JBL* 70 (1951) 297-307; F. L. Horton, "Formulas of Introduction in the Qumran Literature," *RevQ* 7 (1969-71) 505-14; J. A. Fitzmyer, "The Use of Explicit Old Testament Quotations in Qumran Literature and in the New Testament," *Essays on the Semitic Background of the New Testament* (SBLSBS 5; Missoula: Society of Biblical Literature and Scholars Press, 1974) 3-58.

[28]Fragmentary passages that preserve part of the word *pšr* or part of the formula but are of virtually no use in analyzing the formulas in this section include 1QpHab 3:15; 4:14; 10:15; 1QpMic 10:2; 17-18:5; 1QpZeph 4; 1QpPs 4:2; 4QpIsa^c 22:1; 29:3; 4QpIsa^e 6:6; 4QpHos^b 7-8:1; 10, 26:2; 11-13:9; 16:1; 19:1; 4QpNah 3-4 ii 11; 3-4 iv 7; 4QpPs^a 1-10 iv 16; 4QpPs^b 1:2; 4QpUnid 1:3; 14:1.

The basic structure of the formulas using the word *pšr* is a nominal sentence with *pšr hdbr* ("the interpretation of the passage") or *pšrw* ("the interpretation of it") as the subject and one of several constructions as the predicate. The initial nominal sentence of the interpretation may be continued by one or more verbal clauses or full sentences.

[29]I translate *dbr* as "passage" (so also Milik, Brownlee, Allegro). Other possibilities include "word" (Dupont-Sommer), "saying" (Burrows), or "matter."

literally, "the interpretation of the passage [is] concerning *x*")[30]

i. + *ʾšr*[31] + verb:[32] 1QpHab 8:[16]; 10:9; 12:2-3,[33] 12-13; 4QpIsa^e 1-2:[3]

ii. + ?: 1QpHab 9:[16] (*ʾšr* preserved); 4QpIsa^c 6-7 ii 4; 4QpPs^a 1-10 iii [18-19]

b. *pšr hdbr* + *ʾšr* + verb[34] ("the interpretation of the passage [is] that . . ."): 1QpHab 5:3; 4QpIsa^b 1:2

c. *pšr hdbr lʾḥryt hymym* ("the interpretation of the passage with regard to the end of days")

i. + *ʿl* + substantive + *ʾšr:*[35] 4QpIsa^c 23 ii [10-11]

ii. + *l*[36] + substantive: 4QpIsa^b 2:1

iii. + ?: 4QpIsa^c 6-7 ii [14]; 4QpIsa^e 5:[2]

2. *pšrw*

a. *pšrw ʿl* ("the interpretation of it concerns," literally, "the interpretation of it [is] concerning")[37]

[30]In this structure, the predicate of the nominal sentence is a prepositional phrase—*ʿl* and its object—modified by relative clause(s) following *ʾšr*. One text that is best placed here, although it does not conform exactly to any of the formulas listed, is 1QpHab 2:1-10. This is an interpretation of Hab 1:5. I restore the opening formula as *pšr hdbr ʿl*. This is followed by a substantive. Then, instead of a relative clause beginning with *ʾšr,* there is a clause beginning with *ky*. This clause apparently serves the same function as the usual *ʾšr*-clause, i.e., describing the action of the subject of the interpretation. Next there is a second section of the interpretation beginning with *wʿl,* which seems to be a shortened introductory formula. This is followed by a substantive and another descriptive clause beginning with *ky*. Finally, there is a third section of the interpretation introduced by the words *wkn pšr hdbr* [*ʿl*] ("and likewise, the interpretation of the passage concerns"), followed by a substantive. In this instance, instead of a clause beginning with *ʾšr* or *ky* the description begins with the personal pronoun *hmh*. The subject of each of the three parts of the interpretation is the "traitors" (*bwgdym*): first, those in the time of the Teacher of Righteousness; second, those in the new covenant; third, those at the end of days.

[31]The translation of the relative sign *ʾšr* in these formulas must always be determined from context. In some cases it is better left untranslated, as is also the *ʾšr* in the parallel formula *pšr hdbr lʾḥryt hymym* (I A 1 c i).

[32]The substantive to which the interpretation refers may be the subject of the verb (e.g., 1QpHab 8:[16]; 10:9; 4QpIsa^e 1-2:[3]) or the object (1QpHab 12:12-13).

[33]See the note in Part I on 1QpHab 12:2-6.

[34]Here the predicate of the basic nominal sentence is a noun clause introduced by the relative sign *ʾšr,* and in 1QpHab 5:3 the subject of the noun clause follows the verb.

[35]This is a nominal sentence of the same type as *pšr hdbr ʿl* + substantive + *ʾšr* above; see note 30.

[36]I take the preposition *l* here to be equivalent to *ʿl* ("concerning") in the preceding formula. This meaning for *l* is attested in biblical Hebrew and seems to be used in other formulas in the pesharim, e.g., 4QpIsa^a 2-6 ii [26]; 4QpIsa^c 6-7 ii 8, 17. See below I A 2 e.

[37]This is a nominal sentence of the same type as *pšr hdbr ʿl* and *pšr hdbr lʾḥryt hymym ʿl* above.

i. + substantive + ʾšr + verb:[38] 1QpHab 3:[9-10]; 4:5, [10-11]; 5:9-10; 6:10; 7:4, 10-11; 8:8-9; 9:4-5, 9-10; 11:4-5, 12; 13:1-2; 4QpHos^{b} 2:[3]; 4QpNah 3-4 i [2]; 3-4 ii 4-5; 3-4 iii 3, [6-7]; 3-4 iv 3; 4QpPs^{a} 1-10 i [26]; 1-10 ii 2-3, 7-8, 9-10, 14-15, 18, [22-23]; 1-10 iii 5a-5, 7, [15-16]; 1-10 iv [8], [11]

ii. + substantive + ʾšr + personal pronoun + participle:[39] 1QpHab 2:[12]

iii. + substantive + ʾšr + nominal sentence: 1QpHab 3:4; 4QpPs^{a} 1-10 iii [10]

iv. + substantive + ?: 1QpMic 10:[4]; 1QpPs 9:[1]; 4QpIsa^{d} 1:4, 7; 4QpNah 3-4 i [6-7]; 3-4 iv 5; 4QpPs^{a} 1-10 iv [14], [27]

b. *pšrw ʾšr* ("the interpretation of it [is] that . . . .")[40]

i. + verb:[41] 1QpHab 4:1-2; 5:7; 7:7, 15; 4QpHos^{a} 2:[2-3], 12; 4QpHos^{b} 11-13:[4]; 4QpPs^{a} 1-10 iii [3]

ii. + ?: 4QpIsa^{a} 7-10 iii 27; 4QpHos^{a} 2:[15-16][42]

iii. + personal pronoun + participle:[43] 1QpHab 6:[3-4], 6

c. *pšrw* + substantive + personal pronoun ("the interpretation of it: *x*, he/she/it/they [is/are] . . ."[44] 1QpHab

[38]This is the most frequent introductory formula in the pesharim. In its construction it corresponds to *pšr hdbr* + *ʿl* + substantive + *ʾšr* + verb (I A 1 a i). It introduces interpretations of one or more clauses and/or sentences, and it occurs with the following syntactical variations: (1) The substantive (predicate of the nominal sentence beginning with *pšrw*) may be the subject of an active verb in the relative clause, or its condition may be described by a passive verb (1QpHab 3:9-10; 4:5, [10-11] (with intervening phrase); 6:10; 8:8-9; 9:4-5; 11:4-5; 13:1-2; 4QpHos^{b} 2:[3]; 4QpPs^{a} 1-10 i [26]; 1-10 ii 2-3, 7-8 (with intervening clause), 18, [22-23]; 1-10 iii 5a-5, 7; 1-10 iv [8], [11]. (2) The substantive may be a compound (1QpHab 5:9-10) or two substantives in apposition (1QpHab 7:10-11; 4QpNah 3-4 i [2]). (3) The substantive may be the object or indirect object of the verb and another subject may be expressed (1QpHab 7:4; 8:1-2; 9:9-10 [with intervening phrase]; 4QpPs^{a} 1-10 iii [15-16]). (4) The substantive may be described by a relative clause beginning with *ʾšr,* with another subject of the verb expressed (1QpHab 11:12; 4QpNah 3-4 ii 4-5; 3-4 iii 3, [6-7]; 3-4 iv 3 [with intervening phrase]).

[39]The participle acts as a finite verb (see GKC §116 f).

[40]This formula corresponds to *pšr hdbr ʾšr* above (I A 1 b).

[41]The subject of the verb may be expressed (1QpHab 7:7) or understood from a preceding interpretation (1QpHab 4:1-2; 5:7; 7:15 [?]; 4QpHos^{a} 2:[2-3] [?]; 4QpHos^{b} 11-13:[4]). The subject is understood as God in 4QpHos^{a} 2:12; 4QpPs^{a} 1-10 iii [3].

[42]In this text as restored the subject is understood, and the direct object precedes the verb following *ʾšr.*

[43]The subject of the predicate clause is expressed by the personal pronoun used demonstratively, referring to the preceding interpretation, and the part. functions as a finite verb. Cf. the uses of the personal pronoun in the formulas below.

[44]The introductory word *pšrw* is almost like a heading to be followed by a colon. The substantive to which the interpretation refers stands as a pendant nominative followed by a

1:[13]; 12:7-10; 1QpPs 9:[3]; 4QpNah 1-2 ii [1-2], [4a, 5a], [5-7]; 3-4 i [10]—3-4 ii 1; 3-4 iii 9

d. *pšrw* + personal pronoun + substantive ("the interpretation of it: he/she/it/they . . ."):[45] 1QpHab 10:3; 4QpNah 3-4 ii 2; 3-4 iv [1]; 4QpPs^a 1-10 ii 4-5; 1-10 iv [1-2] (?), [3] (?)

e. *pšrw l* ("the interpretation of it concerns," literally, "[is] concerning . . ."): 4QpIsa^c 6-7 ii 8, 17[46]

3. *pšr hptgm lʾḥryt hymym + l* ("the interpretation of the matter with regard to the end of days concerns," literally, "[is] concerning . . ."): 4QpIsa^a 2-6 ii [26][47]

B. Formulas without the word *pšr*

1. *ʾlh hm* + substantive + *ʾšr*: 4QpIsa^b 2:6-7[48]

2. personal pronoun + substantive + *ʾšr:* 4QpIsa^a 7-10 iii [7], 9, [10], [12];[49] 4QpIsa^b 2:10[50]

C. Formulaic phrases within interpretations

1. *kyʾ hmh*: 1QpHab 9:7[51]

nominal sentence with the personal pronoun as the subject, e.g., 1QpHab 12:7 *pšrw hqryh hyʾ yrwšlm,* "the interpretation of it: the town, it is Jerusalem." (For the sake of a smoother English translation, I sometimes translate these interpretations as simple sentences, e.g., "the interpretation of it: the 'town' is Jerusalem.") In this construction there may be a single nominal sentence (as seemingly in 4QpNah 1-2 ii [4a, 5a]), but in the other instances noted above the first nominal sentence is continued by another (*w* + substantive + personal pronoun, etc.), thus identifying two or more subjects of interpretation and setting up a metaphorical commentary. When there is a difference in gender and number between the predicate of the personal pronoun in the nominal sentence and the pendant nominative to which it refers, the personal pronoun usually agrees in form with its own predicate (see e.g., 1QpHab 12:7-10; 4QpNah 3-4 i [10]).

[45]Following *pšrw,* which again functions almost as an introductory heading, the structure of these interpretations is a nominal sentence with the personal pronoun as the subject.

[46]See the notes in Part I on 4QpIsa^c 6-7 ii 8, 17, and note 36 above.

[47]See the note in Part I on 4QpIsa^a 2-6 ii [26], and note 36 above.

[48]The text reads *ʾlh hm ʾnšy hlṣwn ʾšr byrwšlym,* "these are the Scoffers who are in Jerusalem." The structure is a nominal sentence, with the demonstrative *ʾlh* as the subject, strengthened by the personal pronoun *hm.* See GKC §136 d, and see the note in Part I on 4QpIsa^b 2:6-7.

[49]As col. iii of frgs. 7-10 in 4QpIsa^a is restored, these instances all introduce brief interpretations of second citations of the biblical text.

[50]This text is not absolutely certain, since *hyʾ* is the first word preserved in the line, but the restoration of the biblical text at the beginning of the line and the occurrence of a similar formula in 2:6-7 support this reconstruction.

[51]The text is *kyʾ hmh ytr hʿmym,* "for they are the remainder of the peoples." This nominal sentence could be taken simply as the concluding remark to the pesher, but it is separated from the rest of the interpretation by several units of space.

2. *ky*ʾ + substantive (from the biblical text) + personal pronoun + substantive: 1QpHab 12:3-4[52]

II. Formulas introducing lemmas
  A. Formulas apparently introducing a lemma for the first time[53]
    1. *wʾšr:* 4QpHos^b 10, 26:1
    2. Formulas using the root *ktb*[54]
      a. *kʾšr ktwb* ("as it it written"): 4QpIsa^c 1:[4]; 2:[6]; 4, 6-7 i [4]; 6-7 ii 18; 8-10:[8] (?); 47:[2] (?)
      b. *wʾšr ktwb* ("and as for what is written"): 4QpIsa^e 1-2:2; 6:[2]; 8:[2]
  B. Formulas introducing repetitions of citations[55]
    1. *kyʾ hwʾ ʾšr ʾmr* ("for this is what it says:")
      a. + repetition + new lemma: 1QpHab 3:2-3, [13-14]
      b. + repetition + interpretation: 1QpHab 5:6-7
    2. *wʾšr ʾmr* ("and as for what it says" or "and when it says")[56]
      a. + repetition + interpretation: 1QpHab 6:2-3; 7:3-4; 9:2-4; 10:1-3; 12:6-7; and possibly 4QpIsa^a 2-6 ii [6-8]
      b. + ?: 4QpIsa^b 1:3; [4-5]; 4QpIsa^c 6-7 ii 7; 22:[4]; 24:[2] (*ʾšr ʾmr*)

With minor differences, these formulas are interpreted by most modern scholars in much the same way as they are analyzed here. A different approach is that of I. Rabinowitz.[57] It was noted above that Rabinowitz favors the translation "presage" for the word *pēšer*. In line with this he

[52]This formula sets up a figurative interpretation similar to I A 2 c. The first substantive is taken from the lemma, and the second substantive is the figurative identification.

[53]It is rare that an initial citation is introduced in these documents. The apparent occurrence in 4QpHos^b is doubtful. In 4QpIsa^e only one of the instances of the formula is certain (1-2:2), but this may not introduce an *initial* citation. The other occurrences of such formulas appear in 4QpIsa^c, a text that departs in several ways, as has been seen, from the practices observed in the other commentaries, and in 4QpIsa^e, which also shows other variations in formulas.

[54]For formulas in other Qumran documents that introduce explicit citations of Scripture using the root *ktb*, see J. A. Fitzmyer, "The Use of Explicit Old Testament Quotations," 7-10.

[55]There is one place where a repetition of a portion of the lemma occurs with no introductory phrase: 1QpHab 6:5-6 (and possibly also 1QpHab 4:[13-14]).

[56]This formula introduces the repetition of part of the lemma and seems always to be followed by another interpretation. I interpret the formula + repetition + interpretation as one sentence, i.e., "and as for what it says . . . , the interpretation of it is . . . ." Cf. the use of the formula *kyʾ hwʾ ʾšr ʾmr*, which may conclude an interpretation, being followed immediately by a new lemma, or may be followed by an interpretation-section. I take the subject of the verb *ʾmr* to be "it" with Scripture understood. See further M. Burrows, "The Meaning of *ʾšr ʾmr* in DSH," *VT* (1952) 255-60.

[57]"*Pêsher/Pittârôn,*" 226-30; see above, pp. 236-37.

translates the preposition *ʿl* literally as "upon," and he takes the object of the preposition as "the person or group *upon* whom, or the epoch upon which, the *pēsher* (=the presaged reality of the cited Scriptural words) has already come or is expected to come."[58] He understands the relative clauses beginning with *ʾšr* as the presaged reality, e.g., his translation of 1QpHab 6:10-12: "Its presage is upon (*pšrw ʿl*) the Kittiʾim: that (*ʾšr*) they kill many with the sword, lads old men and elders, women and little children, and have no mercy upon fruit of womb."[59] With this translation, Rabinowitz does not present a substantive difference in the understanding of the pesher formula but rather a different nuance. He emphasizes the prophetic omen drawn out of the biblical text. The principal difficulty that I have with his translation is with the English usage. Is it correct to say that a presage is "upon" someone or something?

Modes of Interpretation in the Pesharim

This section examines the ways in which the Qumran commentators expressed the prophetic meaning of the biblical text.[60] The main area of interest here is not the historical or theological content of the interpretation-sections but how the pesher grows out of the biblical text, how it illuminates the mystery of the prophetic words.

I observe four categories of interpretation. These categories are not mutually exclusive, and many of the pesher sections could fit into more than one of these groups: (1) The pesher may follow the action, ideas, and words of the lemma closely, developing a similar description in a different context.[61] (2) The pesher may grow out of one or more key words, roots, or ideas, developing the interpretation from these isolated elements apart from the action or description of the lemma.[62] (3) The pesher may consist

[58]"*Pêsher/Pittrârôn,*" 226.

[59]"*Pêsher/Pittrârôn,*" 227.

[60]In some of the texts, so little of the interpretation is preserved that they are of minimal use here. I concentrate on 1QpHab, 4QpIsa[a,d], 4QpHos[a], 4QpNah, and 4QpPs[a]. I have not attempted an exhaustive classification of all the interpretation-sections, but I point out some examples of the main types of interpretation and interpretative techniques. In the examples listed in this section, I have not indicated those texts that are partially restored, since the texts that I have chosen for purposes of illustration are all fairly certain.

[61]Examples include 1QpHab 2:10-16; 2:16—3:2; 3:2-6, 6-14; 3:17—4:3; 4:3-9; 5:8-12; 6:8-12; 7:9-14; 9:3-7; 10:5-13; 10:14—11:2; 11:2-8, 8-17; 4QpIsa[a] 7-10 iii 15-29 (?); 4QpNah 3-4 i 4-6; 3-4 ii 3-6, 7-10; 3-4 iv 1-4; 4QpPs[a] 1-10 ii 1-4, 5-8, 9-12, 13-16, 16-20; 1-10 iii 2-5, 7-8; 1-10 iv 7-10, 10-12, 19-21.

[62]In these examples the key root, word or words, or idea is indicated in parentheses: 1QpHab 1:10-11 (*twrh*); 4:9-13 (*ʿbr*); 6:2-5 (*zbḥ*); 6:5-8 (*ḥlq, mʾkl*); 7:5-8 (*qṣ*); 8:3-13 (*hwn,*

of metaphorical identifications of figures or things named in the lemma, with or without a description or elaboration of action.[63] (4) There are instances in which the pesher seems to be only loosely related to the lemma.[64]

Within these general forms, the pesher is often drawn out or developed by means of one or more of the following techniques: use of synonyms for words in the lemma;[65] use of the same roots as in the lemma, appearing in the same or different grammatical forms;[66] plays on words in the lemma;[67] changing the order of letters of words in the lemma;[68] use of a different textual tradition;[69] and referring back to an earlier lemma or anticipating a following lemma.[70]

bgd, qbṣ); 12:10-14 (*psl*); 12:15—13:4 (*ʾbn, ʿṣ*); 4QpIsa[d] 1:1-3 (*ysd, spyr*); 1:3-6 (*šmš*); 4QpHos[a] 2:14-17 (*mwʿd*); 4QpNah 3-4 iv 4-6 (idea of drinking and drunkenness).

[63]Examples include 1QpHab 1:12-13; 11:17—12:6; 12:7-10; 4QpIsa[a] 7-10 iii 6-13; 4QpNah 1-2 ii 3-4; 3-4 i 8—3-4 ii 1; 3-4 iii 8-9, 10-11; 3-4 iii 12—3-4 iv 1; 4QpPs[a] 1-10 ii 4-5; 1-10 iii 12-13; 1-10 iii 27—1-10 iv 2.

[64]For example, 1QpHab 9:8-12; 4QpIsa[a] 2-6 ii 21-29; 4QpIsa[d] 1:6-8; 4QpHos[a] 2:1-6; 4QpNah 3-4 iii 5-8.

[65]This is frequent in the pesharim. In the following examples the first word in parentheses is from the lemma, and the second is the synonym from the pesher: 1QpHab 5:6-8 (*rʿ / ršʿh*); 4QpNah 3-4 i 4-6 (*ʾry / kpyr*); 3-4 ii 3-6 (*ḥnyt / ḥrb*); 4QpPs[a] 1-10 ii 9-12 (*ʿnwym / ʿdt hʾbywnym*); 1-10 iv 17-19 (*šmd / ʾbd*).

[66]This is the most common technique of interpretation found in the pesharim. There is no need to list examples, since instances are so frequent.

[67]This is related to the preceding technique, since some of the word-plays involve the same root with different meanings, e.g., 1QpHab 8:6-13: *mšl* in the citation of Hab 2:6 means "a taunt," and in the pesher it means "to rule"; 4QpPs[a] 1-10 iv 13-16: *bqš* in Ps 37:36 means "to look for," and in the pesher it means "to attempt." Another type of word-play that appears in the pesharim is the use of similar roots, e.g., 1QpHab 5:2-3, where the verb *ykl,* "to be able," occurs in the citation of Hab 1:13, and the verb *klh,* "to exterminate," appears in the pesher; 1QpHab 7:3-5, where the verb *rwṣ,* "to run," occurs in the citation of Hab 2:2b, and the substantive *rz,* "mystery," appears in the pesher.

[68]This technique is not as frequent as the preceding ones; examples include 1QpHab 1:5-6, where the biblical text of Hab 1:3a has *ʿml,* "trouble," and the fragmentary pesher includes the word *mʿl,* "unfaithfulness"; 4QpHos[b] 2:2-3, where the restored citation of Hos 5:14a contains the substantive *šḥl,* "young lion," and in the pesher the verb *šlḥ,* "to stretch out," occurs.

[69]For example, 1QpHab 4:9-13, where the Qumran citation of Hab 1:11 has *wyśm,* "and he makes," while the MT has *wĕʾāšēm,* "and a guilty one," and the substantive *ʾšm[tm],* "their guilt," appears in the pesher; 1QpHab 11:8-16, where the Qumran citation of Hab 2:16 has the verb *whrʿl,* "to cause to stumble" (the suggested emendation in *BHS,* cf. the Greek διασαλεύθητι καὶ σείσθητι, while the MT has *wĕhēʿārēl,* "be uncircumcised," and the phrase *lwʾ ml ʾt ʿwrlt lbw,* "he did not circumcise the foreskin of his heart," appears in the pesher.

[70]Instances where part of the pesher refers not to the immediately preceding lemma but to an earlier citation include 1QpHab 5:9-12 (commentary on Hab 1:13b), which contains the phrase *btwkḥt mwrh hṣdq,* "at the rebuke of the Teacher of Righteousness," probably referring back to *mwkyḥw,* "his reprover," of Hab 1:12 (for *hwkyḥ,* "chastisement," of the MT).

To illustrate these techniques, the following texts will be treated briefly: 1QpHab 1:16—2:10; 11:2-8; 4QpNah 3-4 i 8—3-4 ii 1; and 4QpPsa 1-10 i 25—1-10 ii 1.

1QpHab 1:16—2:10

This section presents the text of Hab 1:5 and commentary. The general category into which the pesher can be placed is (2) above, i.e., development of the interpretation from one or more key words in the lemma. The key words in this text are the substantive *bwgdym,*[71] "traitors," and the verb *ʾmn,* "to believe." The context of the verse in Habakkuk is Yahweh's answer to the prophetic complaint (1:2-4): Yahweh will perform a "work," raising up the Chaldeans to act out divine judgment, and none will believe that the Chaldeans are Yahweh's instrument of intervening in history. This verse is interpreted in three different contexts. First, the traitors are described as those who allied themselves with the Wicked Priest against the Teacher of Righteousness in the early days of the community; they did not believe the Teacher of Righteousness. Second, the traitors are those of the new covenant who are unfaithful. Here there is a play on the verb *ʾmn,* which can mean "to believe" and "to be faithful." Finally, the traitors are those in the end-time who will not believe the words of "the Priest" concerning the eschatological events.

1QpHab 11:2-8

These lines contain the citation and interpretation of Hab 2:15. This section can be placed in category (1) above, since it develops the interpretation describing action similar to that presented in the lemma. In Habakkuk, the verse is a curse against the ruthless conquerors. In the Qumran commentary, the verse is interpreted in the context of the conflict between the Wicked Priest and the Teacher of Righteousness in the early days of the community. The pesher employs the following techniques: (1) The idea of drinking (MT: *mašqēh*) and drunkenness (MT: *šakkēr*) is related to the verb *blʿ,* "to swallow up," in the interpretation. (2) The biblical phrase

Conversely, there are places where part of the pesher seems to be based on a following lemma, e.g., in 1QpHab 10:5 (commentary on Hab 2:10b) the substantive *ʾš,* "fire," occurs, anticipating the *ʾš* in the next lemma, Hab 2:12-13; in 4QpNah 1-2 ii 9 (commentary on Nah 1:4b), the phrase [*wkw*]*l ywšby tbl,* "and all the inhabitants of the world," is almost certainly restored, anticipating the phrase *tbl wkwl ywšby bh* in the next lemma, Nah 1:5; in 4QpNah 3-4 iii 1 (commentary on Nah 3:5), the substantive *šqwṣ,* "filth," appears, anticipating the next lemma, Nah 3:6-7a.

[71]The noun *bwgdym,* the emendation suggested in *BHS,* is restored rather than *bgwym,* "among the nations," as in the MT on the basis of the pesher. The other restored portions of the pesher are almost certain; see the notes in Part I on 1QpHab 1:16—2:10.

msph hmtw,[72] "mixing in his poison," is developed in the pesher as the "poisonous vexation" (*kʿs hmtw*) of the Wicked Priest. There is certainly a play on the word *hmt,* which can mean "poison" and also "wrath." This is reflected in *kʿs,* "vexation." There may be a further play on this word in the pesher in the phrase *ʾbyt glwtw,* "in his place of exile," since the biblical Hebrew word *ḥămāt,* the place name Hamath, is pictured as a place of exile, e.g., in Isa 11:11. (3) For the reading of the MT, *lĕmaʿan habbîṭ ʿal mĕʿôrêhem,* "in order to gaze on their nakedness," the lemma in the Qumran text reads *lmʿn hbṭ ʾl mwʿdyhm,* "in order to gaze on their feasts."[73] The noun *mwʿd* is taken up in the pesher in the phrase *wbqṣ mwʿd,* "at the end of the feast" (which is then identified with the Day of Atonement) and is reflected in *bywm ṣwm,* "on the fast day," and *šbt mnwḥtm,* "their sabbath repose." Further, there is a play on the consonants *m,* ʿ, and *d.* The root *mʿd* means "to totter," "to stumble," and this meaning is reflected in the pesher in the form *lkšylm,* "to make them stumble."

4QpNah 3-4 i 8—3-4 ii 1

This citation and interpretation of Nah 2:14 is an example of category (3), the metaphorical identification of figures and things named in the lemma. The biblical verse is part of the description of the downfall of Nineveh. Mentioned in the verse are *rwbkh,* "your abundance," *kpyrykh,* "your lions" (or "your villages"), *ṭrph,* "its prey," and *mlʾkykh,* "your messengers."[74] In the pesher, these nouns are repeated and identified with figures apparently contemporary with the Qumran author: the "abundance" is the army of the Lion of Wrath; "his lions" are his great ones; "his prey" is the stolen wealth and booty; and "his messengers" are his envoys.

4QpPs^a 1-10 i 25—1-10 ii 1

These lines contain the citation and interpretation of Ps 37:7, and the pesher can be placed in category (2), with the interpretation growing out of a key word. The key word in the biblical text is *maṣlîaḥ,* "the one who makes (his way) prosperous." In the pesher, the order of three of the consonants (*m, ṣ,* and *l*) of this word is changed to give a new word, *mlyṣ,* "the interpreter." The interpretation is then built around the figure of the *mlyṣ dʿt,* "the Interpreter of Knowledge," independent of the action described in the lemma.

[72]The MT has *ḥămātĕkā.*

[73]On this variant, see the note in Part I on 1QpHab 11:2-3.

[74]The MT has *rikbâ,* "her chariots," *kpyryk, ṭrpk,* and *mlʾkkh;* see the note in Part I on 4QpNah 3-4 i 9-10.

Content of the Pesharim

The Qumran interpretations of the prophetic texts deal with history: the past history of the community[75] and the events of the last days,[76] in which the Qumran authors believed that their congregation was living.[77]

For the Qumran authors, hidden in the mysteries of the prophetic words were the meaning of the emergence of their community and all of Yahweh's plans for the judgment of the wicked and the deliverance of the righteous, and the content of the interpretations of the prophetic writings was the revealed pesher of that mystery.

To sum up: (1) The pesher texts themselves purport to be interpretations made known by God to selected Qumran commentators of mysteries revealed by God to the biblical writers. (2) It is observed that the pesharim are a group of sectarian writings that present, section by section, continuous commentaries on biblical books, namely, prophets and psalms.[78] The interpretations and sometimes the citations are introduced by formulas, several of which use the word *pēšer.* The interpretations refer the

[75]The passages that refer to the past history of the community generally use the perfect tense. Important sections include 1QpHab 1:12; 2:1-3; 5:9-12; 7:4-5; 8:8-13; 8:16—9:2; 9:9-12; 10:9-13; 11:4-8, 12-15; 12:2-6, 7-10; 4QpHos^a 2:12-14; 4QpNah 3-4 i 1, 2-4, 5-6, 6-8, 10-12; 4QpPs^a 1-10 i 26-27; 1-10 iii 15-17; 1-10 iv 8-10. Fragmentary passages that probably refer to the history of the sect include 4QpIsa^e 1-2:3; 4QpHos^a 2:2-6; 4QpPs^a 1-10 iii 18-19; 1-10 iv 14-15, 27.

[76]The passages that refer to the events of the last days generally use the imperfect tense. Important sections include 1QpHab 2:12-15; 2:17—3:1; 3:4-6, 9-13; 4:1-3, 5-9; 6:1-2, 3-8, 10-12; 7:7-8, 10-14; 8:1-3; 9:4-7; 10:3-5; 12:12-14; 13:1-4; 4QpIsa^a 2-6 ii 26-29; 7-10 iii 7-9, 12-13, 22-26, 27-29; 4QpIsa^b 2:1-2; 4QpHos^b 2:3; 4QpNah 1-2 ii 3-5a, 5-9; 3-4 ii 4-6, 8-10; 3-4 iii 3-5, 6-9; 3-4 iv 1, 3-4; 4QpPs^a 1-10 ii 1, 2-4, 7-8, 9-12, 14-16, 18-20; 1-10 iii 1-2, 3-5, 5a-6, 7-8, 10-11, 12-13; 1-10 iv 20-21. Fragmentary passages include 1QpMic 17-18:5-6; 4QpIsa^a 2-6 ii 8-9, 17-19; 4QpIsa^c 6-7 ii 14-15; 13:4; 23 ii 10-13; 4QpHos^a 1:10-12; 4QpNah 3-4 iv 5-6, 7-8; 4QpPs^a 1-10 iv 1-2, 3, 11-12.

[77]The pesharim contain many allusions that are important for reconstructing the history of the Qumran community, but this evidence is still the subject of much scholarly discussion. Some specific observations are included in the notes in Part I where they are necessary for understanding the text or the restorations; see further the survey in the general introduction.

[78]This may indicate that the Psalms were taken to be prophetic. The same supposition is found in the NT in Peter's Pentecost speech in Acts 2:30. With reference to David, Peter says, "Being therefore a prophet," (προφήτης οὖν ὑπάρχων). There is no reference in the OT to David as a prophet, though it appears in later Jewish and Christian tradition. It is found in Qumran literature explicitly stated in 11QPs^a 27:2-11, where an enumeration of David's compositions concludes with the statment "all these he spoke through prophecy." This explicit statement and the implicit support of it in the existence of pesharim on the Psalms are the earliest instances of the tradition of David as a prophet. See further J. A. Fitzmyer, S.J., "David, 'Being Therefore a Prophet . . .' (Acts 2:30)," *CBQ* 34 (1972) 332-39.

biblical citations to the history of the sect—past, present, or future—and use modes of interpretation such as metaphor, plays on words, developments of key words or key ideas in the biblical text.

The Pesharim and Some Other Interpretative Writings

In attempting to identify the literary genre of the pesharim, most modern commentators have compared these texts with other interpretative writings, including other Qumran documents,[79] with rabbinic midrashic and targumic writings,[80] with Jewish apocalyptic works, especially the book of Daniel, with writings outside the Jewish tradition, e.g., the Egyptian Demotic Chronicle,[81] and with other specific writings such as the gnostic Pistis-Sophia[82] and the New Testament.[83] The degree to which any of these comparisons illuminates the pesharim depends on the significance and the nature of the elements that are compared, but most of these studies

[79]O. Betz (*Offenbarung und Schriftforschung,* esp. pp. 40-41) looks at the pesher texts in the light of the attitude toward Scripture revealed mainly in 1QS and CD. He observes that whereas the "searching of the Torah" (Torahforschung) referred mostly to determining the precise meaning of regulations, pesher interpretation referred to the correct understanding of history. The interpretation of the prophetic message carried as much weight as the disclosure of hidden things in the Torah, and the interpreter of the prophetic message, in the view of the sect, often understood the meaning of the prophetic words better than the prophet himself (p. 82).

[80]I shall return to the question of midrash below. For comparisons with targumic writings, see W. H. Brownlee, "The Habakkuk Midrash and the Targum of Jonathan," *JJS* 7 (1956) 169-86; R. P. Gordon, "The Targum to the Minor Prophets and the Dead Sea Texts: Textual and Exegetical Notes," *RevQ* 8 (1974) 425-29; N. Wieder, "The Habakkuk Scroll and the Targum," *JJS* 4 (1953) 14-18; G. Vermes, "A propos des Commentaires bibliques découverts à Qumrân," *RHPR* 35 (1955) 95-102; "The Symbolical Interpretation of *Lebanon* in the Targums: The Origin and Development of an Exegetical Tradition," *JTS* 9 (1958) 1-12; C. Rabin, "Notes on the Habakkuk Scroll and the Zadokite Documents," *VT* 5 (1955) 148-62.

[81]F. Daumas, "Littérature prophétique et exégétique égyptienne et commentaires esséniens," *À la rencontre de Dieu: Mémorial Albert Gelin* (Bibliothèque de la faculté catholique de théologie de Lyon 8; Le Puy: Éditions Xavier Mappus, 1961) 203-21; John J. Collins, "Jewish Apocalyptic against its Hellenistic Near Eastern Environment," *BASOR* 220 (1975) 28, 30-33.

[82]J. Carmignac, "Le genre littéraire du 'péshèr' dans la Pistis-Sophia," *RevQ* 4 (1963-64) 497-522.

[83]E.g., K. Stendahl, *The School of St. Matthew and its use of the Old Testament* (2nd ed.; Philadelphia: Fortress, 1968) 183-202; B. Gärtner, "The Habakkuk Commentary (DSH) and the Gospel of Matthew," *ST* 8 (1954) 1-24; R. Longenecker, *Biblical Exegesis in the Apostolic Period* (Grand Rapids: Eerdmans, 1975); G. Dautzenberg, *Urchristliche Prophetie: Ihre Erforschung, ihre Voraussetzungen im Judentum und ihre Struktur im ersten Korintherbrief* (BWANT 104; Stuttgart: Kohlhammer, 1975).

have focussed on one or more of the external features that are observed in the pesharim and in other writings.

The original editor of the Habakkuk commentary, William H. Brownlee, compared the pesharim with rabbinic midrash and characterized them as a new type of midrash, the midrash pesher, related to but different from the midrash halakah and midrash haggadah.[84] Following Brownlee's study, there has been considerable debate about whether the Qumran pesharim should be described as midrash.

The biblical Hebrew word *midraš* is a miqtal noun type from the root *drš,* which means "to seek with care," "to inquire of." The noun form occurs only very late in biblical Hebrew in 2 Chr 13:22 (*midraš hannābîʾ ʿiddô*) and 24:27 (*midraš sēper hammĕlākîm*), both of which seem to refer to some sort of written commentary (cf. Ben Sira 51:23). The noun appears in Qumran Hebrew meaning "study" or "inquiry" in 1QS 6:24; 8:15, 26. There are two places where it probably means "interpretation" (CD 20:6 and 4QFlor 1-2 i 14). If "midrash" is defined literally and broadly according to the meaning of the root as "searching into" or "inquiring into," then a pesher might possibly be called a midrash.[85]

[84]This was proposed in a mimeographed paper, referred to by K. Stendahl (*School of St. Matthew,* 184). Brownlee made a detailed examination of the interpretation in 1QpHab for the purpose of showing that the Qumran exposition of Scripture is "essentially midrashic" ("Biblical Interpretation Among the Sectaries of the Dead Sea Scrolls," *BA* 14 [1951] 54-76). He set out thirteen features that he referred to as "hermeneutical principles or presuppositions," which he believed could be found in 1QpHab. The first two principles—that everything the ancient prophet wrote has a veiled, eschatological meaning, and that the meaning is often to be ascertained through a forced or abnormal construction of the biblical text—are the presuppositions, and the remaining eleven principles are amplifications of the second. Some of the techniques, such as the use of textual or orthographic peculiarities (no. 3), use of textual variants (no. 4), analogical application (no. 5), allegorical application (no. 6), double meaning of words (no. 7), use of synonyms (no. 8), rearrangement of letters in a word (no. 9), and substitution of similar letters (no. 10) are to be found in 1QpHab and in the other pesharim, but it is doubtful that these techniques can be assumed to be essentially or exclusively midrashic. The last three principles—word-splitting (no. 11), interpretation of words or parts of words as abbreviations (no. 12), and the use of other passages of Scripture (no. 13)—are questionable. Many of the problems of this approach can be traced to the confusion of the two areas of evidence—what the texts purport to be and what can be observed about the texts. Brownlee's first principle hints at one of the things that can be learned from the texts themselves, but all the rest of his techniques involve observable features of these documents. See further K. Elliger's critique of Brownlee's hermeneutical principles (*Studien zum Habakuk-Kommentar,* 157-64).

[85]Among those who have applied the term "midrash" to the pesharim with this or similar qualification are J. von der Ploeg (*Bijbelverklarung te Qumrân* [Mededelingen der Koninklijke Nederlandse Akademie van Wetenschappen, Letterkunde Nieuwe Reeks, Deel 23, No. 8; Amsterdam: North-Holland, 1960] 209) and J. T. Milik, who uses the term generically as a

The problem is that the word "midrash" usually calls to mind the rabbinic process of oral and written biblical interpretation, as well as works emanating from that tradition of interpretation with their many exegetical techniques. It is this application of the term midrash to the pesharim that is the subject of controversy.[86] The discussion is further complicated by the fact that there is so much ambiguity and disagreement about the origin, nature, development, and extent of midrash that one cannot simply assume that there is a commonly-accepted definition of midrash on which to base comparisons.[87] Any attempt to relate these two types of interpretation

simple synonym for commentary ("Fragments d'un midrash de Michée dans les manuscrits de Qumrân," *RB* 59 [1952] 413).

[86]Most of those who classify the Qumran pesharim as midrash are aware of the differences between the two types of literature, but they find parallels and similar features: A. Finkel ("The Pesher of Dreams and Scriptures," *RevQ* 4 [1963-64] 357-70) attempts to shed light on the pesher method by examining parallels in rabbinic dream interpretation, and he thinks that the interpretations introduced by the formula *pšr hdbr* are similar to some old Tannaitic homilies introduced by the formula *pāṭar qĕrā*ʾ. M. P. Miller ("Targum, Midrash and the Use of the Old Testament in the New Testament," *JSJ* 2 [1971] 29-82) concludes that in terms of methods and techniques the pesharim belong to the category of midrash, but that in terms of structure they are closer to the targums. I. L. Seeligmann ("The Epoch-Making Discovery of Hebrew Scrolls in the Judean Desert," *BO* 6 [1949] 1-8 and "Voraussetzungen der Midrasch-exegese," *Congress Volume: Copenhagen 1953* [VTSup 1; Leiden: Brill, 1953] 150-81) feels that the pesharim must be called midrash because of their modernization or actualization of Scripture. See also L. H. Silbermann ("Unriddling the Riddle. A Study in the Structure and Language of the Habakkuk Pesher," *RevQ* 3 [1961-62] 323-64), M. R. Lehmann ("Midrashic Parallels to Selected Qumran Texts," *RevQ* 3 [1961-62] 545-51), and E. Slomovic ("Toward an Understanding of the Exegesis of the Dead Sea Scrolls," *RevQ* 7 [1969] 3-15.

There are those who argue against comparing the two types of literature: F. Maass ("Von den Ursprüngen der rabbinischen Schriftauslegung," *ZTK* 52 [1955] 153-54) says that no similar formulas appear in the Tannaitic exegetical literature. J. Neusner ("Types and Forms in Ancient Jewish Literature: Some Comparisons," *HR* 11 [1971-72] 367) points out that one cannot reconstruct an equivalent Pharisaic sequential commentary on a single chapter of Scripture, let alone a whole book. Similar opinions are expressed by C. Rabin ("Notes on the Habakkuk Scroll," 148), F. M. Cross (*Ancient Library,* 218), and M. Burrows ("Prophecy and the Prophets at Qumran," *Israel's Prophetic Heritage: Essays in Honor of James Muilenberg* [ed. B. W. Anderson and W. Harrelson; New York: Harper & Brothers, 1962] 227).

[87]In recent years midrash has been defined very broadly by R. Bloch ("Midrash," *DBSup* 5 [ed. L. Pirot *et al.;* Paris: Letouzey et Ané, 1957] cols. 1263-81). She describes midrash as "un genre édifiant et explicatif étroitement rattaché à l'Écriture, dans lequel la part de l'amplification est réelle mais secondaire et reste toujours subordonée à la fin religieuse essentielle, qui est de mettre en valeur plus plainement l'oeuvre de Dieu, la Parole de Dieu" (col. 1263). On the basis of this definition, she includes under the heading of midrash—besides the rabbinic works known by that name—several biblical passages (including prophetic writings, wisdom literature, and psalms), some elements of the apocalyptic writings (including *Jubilees* and *Testaments of the Twelve Patriarchs*), targumic literature, some NT passages, and 1QpHab. Bloch's study occasioned other attempts to clarify the definition and extent of midrash; see especially A. G. Wright, "The Literary Genre Midrash," *CBQ* 28 (1966) 105-38;

should evolve in the context of a treatment of the history of biblical interpretation and reflection[88] and should not grow out of isolated parallels.

When the pesharim and certain midrashic writings are compared, their respective historical contexts are often neglected. Seeking to illuminate the pesharim, all of which were written before A.D. 70, by pointing to allegedly similar elements in rabbinic midrashic writings dating from the second century A.D. on is taking the cart before the horse. This is not to deny that some of the presuppositions and techniques that are observed in rabbinic midrashic material may be found in works that are much earlier than the rabbinic writings—even in the biblical books themselves—but rather to warn that the results of isolated comparisons may be anachronistic and misleading. From this perspective, the term "midrash" is neither a useful nor an informative term by which to characterize the pesharim. But the greatest difficulty is that comparisons in terms of so-called exegetical techniques, i.e., the modes of interpretation that are observed by modern commentators, obscures the important fact that the Qumran commentaries present themselves as the unfolding of the content of mysteries revealed to selected interpreters. The question, then, should be: Do the midrashic writings purport to be revealed interpretations of revealed mysteries referring to history?

A more fruitful area of comparison grew out of the observation that the root *pšr* and the word *rāz* are used in the Qumran biblical interpretations (in Hebrew) and in Daniel (in Aramaic) in similar contexts. The relationship of some of the features of Daniel to elements of the pesharim and other Qumran texts is beginning to be explored in depth, but it is a very complicated area of study.[89] Involved in it are not only all of the

417-57; and in book form *The Literary Genre Midrash* (Staten Island, NY: Alba House, 1967); and a review of Wright's book by R. Le Déaut, "A propos d'une définition du midrash," *Bib* 50 (1969) 395-413 (an English translation appeared as "Apropos a Definition of Midrash," *Int* 25 [1971] 259-82).

[88]Some work along these lines has been done. See e.g., G. Vermes, "The Qumran Interpretation of Scripture in Its Historical Setting," ALUOS 6 (1966-1968) (ed. J. Macdonald; Leiden: Brill, 1969) 85-97, also in *Post-Biblical Jewish Studies* (SJLA 8; Leiden: Brill, 1975) 37-49; "Bible and Midrash: Early Old Testament Exegesis," *Post-Biblical Jewish Studies,* 59-91; *Scripture and Tradition in Judaism: Haggadic Studies* (SPB 4; Leiden: Brill, 1961); S. Lowy, "Some Aspects of Normative and Sectarian Interpretation of the Scriptures (The Contribution of the Judean Scrolls towards Systematization)," ALUOS 6 (1966-1968), 98-163; D. Patte, *Early Jewish Hermeneutic in Palestine* (SBLDS 22; Missoula: Scholars Press, 1975).

[89]In his exhaustive study of the Habakkuk commentary, K. Elliger called attention to the verbal similarity and concluded that "HK steht in der Methode der Auslegung dem Buche Daniel näher als der rabbinischen Literatur" (*Studien zum Habakuk-Kommentar,* 164). He suggested that the relationship between 1QpHab and Daniel would be a productive area of

See now Trever's theory of Daniel in Brownlee Festschr.

questions that are still unanswered about the book of Daniel and about the individual Qumran texts, but also all of the problems and obscurities connected with the vast arena of apocalyptic literature.[90] In the limited context of this study it must suffice to call attention to some of the more significant considerations.

The first point is that the time of the final redaction of Daniel may not be too far removed from the time of composition of some of the Qumran scrolls. Even though there is debate about the unity and authorship of the book of Daniel, it is generally agreed that the final redaction of the present book of Daniel is from Maccabean times.[91] It is more difficult to determine the time of composition of the Qumran documents. Specialists in paleography can fix the approximate relative date that an individual document was written, but that does not tell when the work originated. It does, however, indicate the latest possible date of composition. On paleographic grounds, F. M. Cross places the writing of the various scrolls between 200 B.C. and A.D. 70, noting that some biblical manuscripts are early but that all extant copies of the sectarian works should be placed in the Hasmonean (150-30 B.C.) and Herodian periods (30 B.C.—A.D. 70).[92] These broad dates are supported by the archeological evidence, which confirms

inquiry (p. 157). Following Elliger's recommendation, this has been studied by A. Mertens (*Das Buch Daniel im Lichte der Texte vom Toten Meer* [SBM 12; Stuttgart: Katholisches Bibelwerk; Würzburg: Echter Verlag, 1971]). His examination of word usage in Daniel and in the Qumran writings, along with angelology, methods of interpretation, and eschatological beliefs, led him to suggest that there was a connection between the Maccabean redactor of Daniel and the community of the Dead Sea scrolls. See also. A. Szörényi, "Das Buch Daniel, ein kanonisierter Pescher?" *Volume du Congrès. Genève 1965* (VTSup 15; Leiden: Brill, 1966) 278-94; H. P. Müller, "Mantische Weisheit und Apokalyptik," *Congress Volume. Uppsala 1971* (VTSup 22; Leiden: Brill, 1972) 268-93; "Märchen, Legende und Enderwartung. Zum Verständnis des Buches Daniel," *VT* 26 (1976) 338-50; I. Willi-Plein, "Das Geheimnis der Apokalyptik," *VT* 27 (1977) 62-81; John J. Collins, "Jewish Apocalyptic," 30-32; "The Court-Tales in Daniel and the Development of Apocalyptic," *JBL* 94 (1975) 218-34; *The Apocalyptic Vision of the Book of Daniel* (HSM 16; Missoula: Scholars Press, 1977); G. Dautzenberg, *Urchristliche Prophetie,* 44-53.

[90]See below, pp. 256-59.

[91]The basic questions concerning the background, character, and unity of the book of Daniel are treated, for example, in the commentaries of J. A. Montgomery (*A Critical and Exegetical Commentary on the Book of Daniel* [ICC; Edinburgh: Clark, 1927]); A. Bentzen (*Daniel* [2d ed.; HAT 19; Tübingen: Mohr-Siebeck, 1952); O. Plöger (*Das Buch Daniel* [KAT 18; Gütersloh: Mohn, 1965]). See also the summary of the diverging scholarly opinions in A. Mertens, *Das Buch Daniel,* 13-19.

[92]*Ancient Library,* 119. Cross suggests that in the case of the commentaries the date of writing very probably indicates the date of composition, since there is, he feels, strong reason to believe that these writings are autographs (p. 114). But see my remarks on this question above, pp. 3-4.

that the Essene community flourished at Qumran at least from the time of the reign of John Hyrcanus I (135-104 B.C.) until 31 B.C. when a fire and an earthquake damaged the settlement. After a period of diminished activity during the reign of Herod the Great, there was a major rebuilding, and the community again prospered until A.D. 68.[93]

Also important for determining the dates of composition of the scrolls is the internal evidence, especially the historical allusions. Here I narrow the consideration to the pesharim, but as has been seen, the problems of identifying the historical subjects are complex.[94] To make the point here, however, it need be stated only that the clearest historical allusions in the commentaries are to events in the Hasmonean period, though references to the days when the community was led by the Teacher of Righteousness probably refer to earlier years. Thus, the pesharim preserved material from about 150 B.C. on and were all composed before A.D. 70. The earliest stratum of tradition, then, might be relatively close to the time of the final redaction of Daniel.

As was said above, the comparison of the pesharim and the book of Daniel was suggested by the fact that the root *pšr* and the word *rāz* are used in both Daniel and the Qumran biblical commentaries.[95] The interpretations in the book of Daniel provide other points of comparison on the level of what can be observed about the texts. There is one place where a formulaic introductory phrase that is reminiscent of the formulas in the pesharim appears. When Daniel interprets the writing on the wall at Belshazzar's feast, he says *dĕnâ pĕšar millĕtāʾ*, "this is the interpretation of the matter" (5:26).

Some of the same modes of interpretation that were observed in the pesharim can be found in Daniel. The interpretation of Nebuchadrezzar's dream in Dan 2:36-45 is similar to the pesharim that follow the action of the lemma and develop metaphorical interpretations.[96] The parts of the image that Nebuchadrezzar saw in his dream are of different metals, and these metals are given figurative explanations as the succeeding kingdoms that would come to power. The action of the dream, that the limbs of the image would be broken in pieces by a stone cut by no human hand, is echoed in the interpretation, where the downfall of the kingdoms before

[93]The archeological facts can be found in the basic introductions to and collections of the Dead Sea scrolls. See also J. T. Milik, *Ten Years,* 49-56; E.-M. Laperrousaz, *Qoumrân. L'établissement essénien des bords de la Mer Morte. Histoire et archéologie du site* (Paris: Picard, 1976).

[94]See above, pp. 5-9.

[95]The uses of the root *pšr* and the word *rāz* were summarized in the word-study section; see above, pp. 230-37.

[96]Categories (1) and (3) as described on pp. 244-45.

Yahweh is described. Similarly in Nebuchadrezzar's dream in Daniel 4, the image of the tree is metaphorically identified with Nebuchadrezzar, and the content of the dream is explained in the context of Nebuchadrezzar's reign. Finally, the interpretation of the mysterious writing on the wall at Belshazzar's feast (Dan 5:24-28) involves plays on the three words that are inscribed. The three monetary values, *mnʾ, tql,* and *prs,* are interpreted as three verbs of corresponding consonantal roots, "he counted," "he weighed," and "he divided." It can be said, therefore, that the mystery of the dreams in Daniel, the *rāz,* is illuminated in some of the same ways that the Qumran commentators drew out the *rāz* of the prophetic words.[97]

Just as the content of the interpretations in the pesharim refers to the clarification of past history, the present and future circumstances of the community and the world, or eschatological events, so too the interpretations in Daniel refer to history.[98] In the explanation of Nebuchadrezzar's dream (2:31-45), four world empires are symbolized by different metals: Babylon, Media, Persia, and Greece. The interpretation thus encompasses the past, present, and future historical situation, culminating in the end-time, the triumph of the kingdom of God. In the interpretation of Nebuchadrezzar's next dream (4:20-26), the subject is the impending downfall of the king i.e., the immediate future, and the interpretation of the cryptic inscription at Belshazzar's feast (5:24-29) is similar. So it is clear that the interpretations in the book of Daniel seek to illuminate the meaning of past and present events, to predict the future, and to press toward the eschatological cataclysm and deliverance.

Now that these similarities have been observed, it should be asked: Do the interpretations in the book of Daniel purport to be revealed interpretations of revealed mysteries in the same way as the pesharim? Indeed, the book of Daniel tells that the *rāz,* i.e., the hidden mystery (in a dream, vision, or mysterious writing) was sent by God, and its interpretation was revealed by God to a chosen interpreter ("Then the mystery [*rāzâ*] was revealed by God to Daniel in a vision of the night" [2:19]; "no wise men, enchanters, magicians, or astrologers can show to the king the mystery . . . , but there is a God in heaven who reveals mysteries" [2:27-28]). Thus the interpretations of mysteries[99] in Daniel show similarities to the pesharim

[97]See further A. Mertens, *Das Buch Daniel,* 114-41.

[98]The book of Daniel purports to deal with the history of the time of Jehoiakim, king of Judah, and Nebuchadrezzar, king of Babylon, i.e., the late seventh and early sixth centuries B.C. (Dan 1:1). It is not crucial in this connection that the actual date of the various parts of Daniel be determined (see John J. Collins, *Apocalyptic Vision,* 8-11, 27-59); the point is that the interpretations refer to history.

[99]Consideration can also include the reinterpretation in Dan 9:24-27 of the prophecy of the seventy years in Jer 25:11-12 (cf. 29:10). Though the root *pšr* is not used here, this is an

not only in terms of the use of the root *pšr* and the word *rāz* and other observable features such as modes of interpretation and content of the interpretations, but also in the understanding expressed in both types of interpretation, that *pšr* refers to the interpretation made known by God to a selected interpreter of a mystery revealed by God.[100]

The existence of such significant similarities between the type of interpretation found in the book of Daniel and that observed in the pesharim calls for the field of comparison to be widened to illuminate further the character and background of this type of interpretation. A broader comparison should begin with the fact that Daniel is an eschatologically-oriented work, specifically an apocalyptic work, i.e., it exhibits a particular type of eschatological belief. Entering the area of apocalyptic, the present work can only roughly sketch the importance of studying the pesharim in such ever-widening circles of tradition, the directions that current studies are taking, and significant points for further consideration.

Among the characteristic features of the apocalyptic outlook are reinterpretation of national history and destiny, revelation of divine mysteries in dreams and visions that were often expressed in cosmic imagery and fantastic symbolism, determinism, and expectation of a messianic deliverer and a time of cataclysm and judgment. The apocalyptic visionaries looked for a decisive, imminent divine intervention in history, the final struggle between the kingdom of God and its enemy.[101]

example of a contemporizing application of a prophetic text. See further G. Dautzenberg, *Urchristliche Prophetie,* 52-53; O. Eissfeldt, *Old Testament Introduction,* 150; E. Osswald, "Zur Hermeneutik des Habakuk-Kommentars," *ZAW* 68 (1956) 246-53; P. Grelot, "Soixante-dix semaines d'années," *Bib* 50 (1969) 169-86. Again, the visions in Daniel 7 and 8 are interpreted with reference to eschatological events, though the root *pšr* is not used (see John J. Collins, *Apocalyptic Vision,* 78).

[100]See further John J. Collins, *Apocalyptic Vision,* 74-78.

[101]Writings on the literary genre of apocalyptic abound, and they continue to appear at a rapid pace as the character of apocalyptic is investigated and as specific texts that are described as apocalyptic writings are examined. See, for example, the surveys of J. Barr ("Jewish Apocalyptic in Recent Scholarly Study," *BJRL* 58 [1975] 9-35) and J. Coppens ("L'Apocalyptique. Son dossier. Ses critères. Ses éléments constitutifs. Sa portée néotestamentaire," *ETL* 53 [1977] 1-23). Recent general works include D. S. Russell, *The Method and Message of Jewish Apocalyptic: 200 B.C. — A.D. 100* (Philadelphia: Westminster, 1964); P. von der Osten-Sacken, *Die Apokalyptik in ihrem Verhältnis zu Prophetie und Weisheit* (Theologische Existenz heute 157; Munich: Kaiser, 1969); K. Koch, *The Rediscovery of Apocalyptic* (tr. by M. Kohl; SBT 22; London: SCM, 1972); W. Schmithals, *The Apocalyptic Movement. Introduction and Interpretation* (tr. by J. E. Steely; Nashville: Abingdon, 1975); H. H. Rowley, *The Relevance of Apocalyptic. A Study of Jewish and Christian Apocalypses from Daniel to the Revelation* (2nd ed.; London: Lutterworth, 1961). See also the special issue on apocalyptic literature, *CBQ* (Vol. 30, No. 3, July, 1977), and the works listed above in n. 89.

Apocalypticism is indeed a well-attested feature of the Qumran writings. Not only have there been found copies of Daniel and of pseudepigraphical apocalyptic works (e.g., 1QDan^{a,b}; 1QHenGiants; 2QJub^{a,b}; 3QJub), but there are also sectarian documents that are apocalyptic in character (e.g., 1QM, 1QMyst; 1QSa; 4QPrNab).[102] Among the prominent Qumran beliefs that can be associated with apocalyptic are messianic expectation (e.g., in 1QS), belief in angels and demons (e.g., 11QMelch), and expectation of an imminent eschatological battle (e.g., 1QM).

In the pesharim some of the same apocalyptic elements are found. The most evident motif is the expectation of the end, which permeates all the commentaries (e.g., 1QpHab 2:5-9; 7:7-8, 10-14; 4QpIsa^{a} 2-6 ii 26; 4QpIsa^{b} 2:1-2). There is mention of an eschatological battle (4QpPs^{a} 1-10 ii 7-8) and judgment (1QpHab 5:3-6; 12:2-10; 13:1-4; 4QpNah 1-2 ii 3-5), and possibly one reference to messianic expectation (4QpIsa^{a} 7-10 iii 2-26). The fantastic imagery, angelology, and mythology are absent from these documents, but many of the same presuppositions, beliefs, and modes of expression can be found in the Qumran biblical commentaries and Jewish apocalyptic writings, especially Daniel.

Further study of other Jewish apocalyptic works could give additional insight into the climate of thought that may have influenced the Qumran writers. For example, the book of Enoch is filled with dreams and visions, especially chaps. 83-90. In 83:1-9 the first dream-vision, concerning the destruction of the earth, is revealed to Enoch, who recounts it to his grandfather, who "interprets" it and exhorts Enoch to prayer to ward off the apocalyptic destruction. This calls to mind the idea of a therapeutic magic "interpretation" of a dream to dispel evil omens and consequences that is attested in the Akkadian use of the verb *pašāru*.[103] The second dream-vision (chaps. 85-90) revealed to Enoch portrays in fantastic symbolism the whole history of the world up to the final judgment and establishment of a messianic kingdom.[104]

[102]For references to the major publications, see J. A. Fitzmyer, *The Dead Sea Scrolls: Major Publications and Tools for Study* (2d ed.; SBLSBS 8; Missoula: Scholars Press, 1977). See also the list of apocalyptic Qumran documents in D. S. Russell, *Method and Message,* 39.

[103]See above, p. 231.

[104]For further comparison of the concepts of dreams, prophecy, and interpretation in apocalyptic works and in the Qumran writings, see, e.g., G. Dautzenberg, *Urchristliche Prophetie,* 43-121; D. S. Russell, *Method and Message,* 36-48; G. Vermes, "A propos des Commentaires bibliques découverts à Qumrân," *RHPR* 35 (1955) 97-100; B. J. Roberts, "Some Observations on the Damascus Document and the Dead Sea Scrolls," *BJRL* 34 (1952) 368-84; D. Patte, *Early Jewish Hermeneutic in Palestine* (SBLDS 22; Missoula: Scholars Press, 1975) 139-308, esp. pp. 159-75, 181-204; E. Osswald, "Zur Hermeneutik," 247-55.

Those who study the pesharim in the widening context of Jewish apocalyptic eventually must reckon with the fact that apocalypticism was not restricted to the Jewish writings. It can be found throughout the ancient Near East, growing in reaction to the loss of political independence and the Hellenistic levelling of national identities.[105] One way that the ever-growing mass of information about apocalyptic literature in the ancient Near East can be sorted out is by taking a "history-of-religions" approach to a particular problem. This has been done by John J. Collins, who studied Jewish apocalyptic in the broader context of the ancient Near East. He includes Daniel and the Qumran pesharim as examples of "prophecy by interpretation," which was found throughout the literature of the Hellenistic era.[106] He confirms that interpretation of scripture so as to produce an eschatological prophecy was not peculiar to Judaism, and he names the Egyptian Demotic Chronicle as a parallel to the Qumran pesharim.[107]

The so-called Demotic Chronicle is a fragmentary papyrus from the early Ptolemaic period that presents an obscure oracle concerned with the re-establishment of the native monarchy and an interpretation of the oracle in terms of Egyptian history. Citations from the oracle are presented, each followed by an interpretation. These interpretations are sometimes introduced by a formulaic expression that is translated "this is," and the interpretations refer to national history, sometimes by means of metaphorical or figurative equations. Thus, similarities can be observed between the Demotic Chronicle and the Qumran pesharim. Moreover, the former Egyptian work seems to have been considered in some way revelatory.[108]

[105]See John J. Collins, "Jewish Apocalyptic against its Hellenistic Near Eastern Environment," *BASOR* 220 (1975) 27-36.

[106]According to Collins ("Jewish Apocalyptic," 32-33), "prophecy by interpretation" differs from biblical prophecy by its suggestion of determinism and by the fact that it involves the interpretation of mysterious realities hidden in Scripture, dreams, and other phenomena, rather than a direct transmission of the word of God as in prophetic revelation. He explains further that the "objective of this type of prophecy is not to change the course of events but to understand and adapt" (p. 33). See his additional comments in *Apocalyptic Vision,* 74-88; and also A. Szörényi ("Das Buch Daniel, ein kanonisierter Pescher?" *Volume du Congrès. Genève 1965* [VTSup 15; Leiden: Brill, 1966] 282), who suggests that Daniel is the product of a literary *Gattung* that was then commonly known.

[107]"Jewish Apocalyptic," 32, noting that the similarity between the Demotic Chronicle and the pesharim had been the subject of a study by F. Daumas (see above, n. 81). For the text of the Demotic Chronicle, see *Die sogenannte Demotische Chronik des Pap. 215 der Bibliothèque Nationale zu Paris* (ed. W. Spiegelberg; Leipzig: J. C. Hinrichs'sche Buchhandlung, 1914).

[108]F. Daumas, "Littérature prophétique et exégétique égyptienne," 207; S. K. Eddy, *The King is Dead: Studies in the Near Eastern Resistance to Hellenism 334-31 B.C.* (Lincoln: University of Nebraska, 1961) 291; W. Spiegelberg, *Die sogenannte Demotische Chronik,* 5-6.

Other interpretive traditions will have to be examined in order to fill in the picture of the pesharim. It was pointed out above in the survey about the word *pēšer* that the root *pšr* appears in Akkadian referring to the interpretation of dreams, and John J. Collins calls attention to an interpretation in the Persian Bahman Yasht that is reminiscent of Daniel 2.[109]

The aim of this type of "history-of-religions" approach would not be to seek out a direct literary dependence of the Qumran pesharim on other documents that might be considered, but to achieve a better understanding of all the various interpretative writings and traditions that may share a common heritage.

Conclusion

The substance of this study has been the presentation of the continuous pesharim of Qumran literature, and its main contributions are those that set the stage for future work: corrections and improvements in reading the Hebrew texts, restoration of some lacunas, a more precise delineation of the structure of the documents, a description of the basic characteristics of the pesher interpretation, and an introduction to the background of these documents within a larger context.

Thus, the pesharim begin to come into focus as "companions" to the biblical text, unravelling section by section the mysteries that were believed to be contained in the biblical text. According to the Qumran commentators, both the mysteries and their interpretations were revealed by God—the mystery to the prophetic author and the interpretation to the Teacher of Righteousness and to selected interpreters who followed him in the sect's tradition of biblical interpretation. The pesharim are sectarian documents, and all of the hidden mysteries are interpreted in terms of the history, life, and beliefs of the Qumran community.

[109]"Jewish Apocalyptic," 32; see above 252-56 and A. Leo Oppenheim, *The Interpretation of Dreams in the Ancient Near East With a Translation of the Assyrian Dream-Book* (Transactions of the American Philosophical Society 46/3; Philadelphia: American Philosophical Society, 1956), esp. pp. 217-25. In this connection it is significant that the interpretation of dreams in Daniel are set in the Babylonian kingdom, and John J. Collins suggests that there is material in the court-tales in chaps. 1-6, especially in chap. 2, that might go back to a Babylonian prophecy (see "The Court-Tales in Daniel and the Development of Apocalyptic," *JBL* 94 [1975] 224; *Apocalyptic Vision,* 31-32, 36-46). The "Babylonian connection" is intriguing, too, in the light of J. Murphy-O'Connor's thesis that the origin of the Qumran community is to be traced to Babylon (see "The Essenes and their History," *RB* 81 [1974] 219-223).

APPENDIX

3QpIsa (3Q*4*)

Editio princeps: "Commentaire d'Isaïe" (M. Baillet), *Les 'petite grottes,'* pp. 95-96 and pl. XVIII, no. 4.

Preliminary publication: R. de Vaux, "Exploration de la région de Qumrân: Rapport préliminaire," *RB* 60 (1953) 555-57 and pl. XXIV b.

Secondary translations: H. Bardtke, *Die Handschriftenfunde,* 108; J. Carmignac, *Les Textes,* 2. 65-66.

This single frg. is described by R. de Vaux and M. Baillet as a commentary on Isaiah, a judgment based on the fact that a portion of the biblical text is followed by a section that does not come from the biblical text as it is in the MT and is therefore assumed to be part of an interpretation. While this identification could be correct, it should be noted that no introductory formula for the interpretation is preserved. For this reason it is placed here in the appendix.

Both de Vaux and Baillet regard this text as a different type of commentary from that of 1QpHab. De Vaux remarks that the interpretation does not seem to apply the prophetic words to contemporary events, but seems to be a simple gloss on the biblical text. Baillet terms this commentary "more literal" than the type represented by 1QpHab. These judgments should be revised in view of the number of Qumran commentaries that have now come to light. A frequent motif in the pesharim is "the end of days," and the mention of "the day of judgment" in line 6 of 3QpIsa could indicate that this text exemplifies an eschatological interpretation.

3QpIsa: Translation

1. THE VISION OF ISAIAH, THE SON OF A[MOZ, WHICH HE SAW CONCERNING JUDAH AND JERUSALEM, IN THE DAYS OF UZZIAH] Isa 1:1
2. AND JOTHAM, AHAZ AND [HEZEKIAH, THE KINGS OF JUDAH. The interpretation of it concerns all the things that are going to come, which
3. [I]sa[iah] prophesied con[cerning Judah and Jerusalem . . .]

4. to [Uzzia]h, king of Ju[dah. HEAR, O HEAVENS, AND GIVE EAR, O EARTH, FOR YAHWEH HAS SPOKEN.] 1:2a
5. (*vacat?*) [ ]
6. [the d]ay of judgmen[t . . .]
7. [ ]*l*[ ]*hw*[ ]

3QpIsa: Notes

1:1-2 The apparent citation of Isa 1:1 presents the following variants from the MT:

(a) *yšᶜyh* (MT: *yšyᶜhw*). 3QpIsa gives the form of the name Isaiah that is reflected in the Greek 'Hσαΐας. The usual form of the name in 1QIsa[a] is also *yšᶜyh;* however, at 1:1 and at 38:21 1QIsa[a] has *yšyᶜhw*. The name *ᶜzyh* is restored similarly, cf. the Greek 'Oζίου in Isa 1:1 (nom.: 'Oζίας), while the form of the MT is *ᶜzyhw*.

(b) *wyrwšlym* is restored rather than *wyrwšlm* as in the MT, cf. 1QIsa[a] I:1. On the spelling of the name Jerusalem in the pesharim, see the note on 1QpHab 9:4.

(c) *wywtm* (MT: *ywtm*). In 3QpIsa the names of the kings are grouped in pairs as in the Greek. Thus, Baillet restores *wyḥzqyh* rather than *yḥzqyhw* as in the MT.

A commentary might have begun in line 2, continuing to line 4. Line 2 is tentatively restored in the light of 1QpHab 2:10; 7:1.

4QpMic (4Q*168*)

Editio princeps: "Commentary on Micah (?)" (J. M. Allegro), *Qumrân Cave 4,* Vol. I, p. 36 and pl. XII.

Secondary translation: [The text listed as 4QpMic by J. Carmignac (*Les Textes,* 2. 82-84) is actually the translation of 1QpMic.]

Secondary literature: J. Strugnell, "Notes," 204, 258, and pl. II d.

Allegro places four frgs. under the title 4QpMic, noting that the script is similar to that of 4QpHos[b] (4Q*167*) and that possibly these two documents originally formed part of a pesher on the whole of the Minor Prophets. J. Strugnell, however, thinks that 4QpMic and 4QpHos[b] actually come from the same hand; consequently, the small frgs. of these two texts are very difficult to identify. According to Strugnell, the frgs. that belong to 4QpMic have not darkened as much as those of 4QpHos[b]. He suggests that 4QpMic frg. 2 be added to 4QpHos[b] (see above, 4QpHos[b] frgs. 15, 33) and that 4QpHos[b] frgs. 9 and 36 be placed with 4QpMic. Though it is impossible to verify the correctness of this suggestion from the photograph in *Qumrân Cave 4,* I have no reason to reject it.

Allegro transcribes the four frgs. separately; Strugnell, however, was able to join frg. 3 to frg. 1 to give the beginning of line 2 (see Strugnell's pl. II d, p. 258). The restoration of the biblical text in frgs. 1, 3 is not certain. The length of the lines seems to be about fifty units. Strugnell's arrangement of the lines is followed here, but line 1 seems a little long. Another problem, noted by Allegro, is that the biblical text of Mic 4:11b-12a, which is to be restored between *h'w]mrym* (line 5) and *ʿṣtw* (line 6), is too long for the apparent line length of this document.

There seems to be nothing at all preserved of any commentary on the biblical text; indeed, there is no indication that this text is in fact a pesher. Perhaps that is the reason for Allegro's hesitation in the title for the frgs.

4QpMic: Translation

Fragments 1, 3

1. [WHICH BELONGS TO THE DAUGHTER OF JERUSA]L[E]M. [NOW WHY ARE YOU SHOUTING? IS YOUR KING NO LONGER AMONG YOU? OR HAS YOUR COUNSELOR PERISHED?] Mic 4:8c-12
2. FOR [CONTRACTIONS] HAVE [S]EIZED YOU [LIKE A WOMAN GIVING BIRTH. WRITHE AND PUSH, O DAUGHTER OF ZION, LIKE A WOMAN GIVING BIRTH, FOR]
3. NOW YOU WILL GO OUT FROM THE CIT[Y AND LIVE IN THE OPEN COUNTRY, AND YOU WILL GO TO BABYLON. THERE YOU WILL BE DELIVERED. THERE]
4. [Y]AHWEH [WILL REDEE]M YOU FROM [THE HAND OF YOUR ENEMIES. NOW MANY NATIONS ARE GATHERED AGAINST YOU]
5. [SA]YING, "LET HER [BE POLLUTED AND LET OUR EYES GAZE UPON ZION," BUT THEY DO NOT KNOW THE THOUGHTS OF]
6. [YAHWEH, NOR ARE THEY ABLE TO DISCERN] HIS PLAN. [FOR HE HAS COLLECTED THEM LIKE SHEAVES TO THE THRESHING FLOOR . . .]

Fragment 2: see 4QpHos^b frgs. 15, 33.

Fragment 4

].*ṣym* [

4QpHos^b frg. 9

]*'t yš* [

4QpHos^b frg. 36

]*yš* [

4QpMic: Notes

1, 3:1 Strugnell's suggestion of *yrwš*]*l* [*y*]*m* rather than *yrwšlm* as in the MT brings the text into accord with the usual Qumran spelling of the name Jerusalem and is better in terms of space; see the note above on 1QpHab 9:4.

1, 3:2 The apparent citation of Mic 4:9 presents the following variant from the MT: *hḥzyqkh* (MT: *hḥzyqk*). The form of 4QpMic gives not only the suffix with the final vowel letter *h* as opposed to the MT, but also the masc. sf., where the MT form is vocalized as the fem., *heḥĕzîqēk*. It is uncertain whether the final vowel letter was used elsewhere in suffixes in this document, but the phrase [*yg*ʾ]*lk* [*y*]*hwh* in line 4 (=Mic 4:10d) apparently agrees with the MT. There is not enough room for a final *h* to be restored. (The letter *k* is mutilated, and it is impossible to tell whether it was written in the final form.)

and push ([*wgḥy*]). This form is take to be the qal impv. 2nd pers. sing. fem of *ngḥ*.

Fragment 4

I follow Strugnell; Allegro reads]*nym*.

4QpUnid (4Q*172*)

Editio princeps: "Commentaries on Unidentified Texts" (J. M. Allegro), *Qumrân Cave 4,* Vol. I, pp. 50-51 and pl. XVIII.

Secondary literature: J. Strugnell, "Notes," 218-19.

4QpUnid is the title given by Allegro to this group of fourteen frgs. that may be from pesher documents but for which no certain identification is possible. The frgs. have been placed together because of their similar physical appearance and the similarity of the script, which Allegro regards as reminiscent of 4QpIsa[a], 4QpHos[a,b], and 4QpPs[a]. I agree with J. Strugnell, however, that 4QpHos[b] should be excluded from this group.

On the basis of physical appearance, Strugnell questions the inclusion of frgs. 4 and 5 under this heading, and he suggests that frgs. 9, 11, and 13 may belong to 4QpPs[a]. In addition, he actually places frg. 10 with 4QpPs[a] frg. 13. To these suggestions I add the tentative proposal that frg. 1 might also be connected with 4QpPs[a]. This suggestion is based on the occurrence of the word *r*ʿ*b,* "famine," in 4QpUnid 1:2 and in 4QpPs[a] 1-10 ii 1; 1-10 iii 2, 4, and on the fact that the formula restored in 4QpUnid 1:3, i.e., *pšrw*+ *hw*ʾ*h*/*hy*ʾ*h*+noun, occurs also in 4QpPs[a] 1-10 ii 4-5 and is partially restored in 1-10 iv 1 and 1-10 iv 23. See also 1QpHab 10:3 and 4QpNah 3-4 ii 2; 3-4 iii [11]; 3-4 iv 1, and see further Part II, p. 242.

There is too little preserved on any of the frgs. to determine the character or content of the texts. In 1:2 the formula *wʾšr ʾmr* might possibly be restored, and a second citation of some biblical text would be expected to follow (see Part II, p. 243). In the next line a commentary might be introduced by the formula *pšrw* + *hyʾh* + noun. In 7:1 there might be a reference to the Teacher of Righteousness, and in frg. 14 the word *pšr* is preserved.

For Allegro's suggestions of possible identifications of the individual frgs. biblical citations, allusions, and cross references to other Qumran documents, see *Qumrân Cave 4,* 50-51.

4QpUnid: Translation

Fragment 1

1. he s]aid, "All[
2.]in the time of famine, and when [it says
3. The inter]pretation of it: it is the righteousne[ss
4.]they will gather *ʾt ṣ*.[
5.]*ḥṭ*[

Fragment 2

1.] . . . which *hʾw*.[
2.]fastened like a garment upon *hʾ*[
3.].*w*]

Fragment 3

1.]*kwt* in the hand of[
2.]the increase of his kingdom[

Fragment 4

1.]*kn* and they will feed (?) with them[
2. all the men of]iniquity have fled[
3.]Gomorrah was insolent[
4.]burning, and also *k*.[
5.]their heart [
6.].with me *bḥ*[

Fragment 5

1.]*ṣ* days .[
2.]*h* in it *hbš*[
3.]all *bh*[

Fragment 6

1.]*ym* [
2.]deceit *wm*[
3.].[

Fragment 7

1.]the Teacher of [Righteousness
2.]*š* all[

Fragment 8

1.]to sav[e
2.]*d*[

Fragment 9

1.]their return[
2.]roaring lions[
3.]*dm* [

Fragment 10

]deceit (?) [

Fragment 11

] *ʾt*[

Fragment 12

]all[

Fragment 13

]*dʿh* [

Fragment 14

1.] (The) interpretation[
2.]concerning[

4QpUnid: Notes

1:3 Strugnell's reading is followed, although *ḥṣdq*[*h*] cannot be read with certainty from the photograph in *Qumrân Cave 4.* Allegro reads *pš*]*rw hyʾh hṣ*. .[.

1:5 Allegro indicates only traces of letters, while Strugnell suggests]*ḥr*[.

2:3 Allegro's transcription does not indicate the probable space after the *w*.

4:1 I follow Strugnell; Allegro reads]*bhywtw ʿmm*[, "when he is with them." Another possible translation for the present reading is "and their people will feed."

4:2 *men of evil* ([*ʾnšy*] *ḥʿwl*). See 1QS 5:2, 10; 9:17.

4:4 Strugnell suggests a possible connection of this line with Hos 7:2-6.

4:6 I follow Strugnell; Allegro reads] . .*yty b*.[.

5:1 I follow Strugnell; the trace of a letter at the end is either *w* or *y*. Allegro reads]. *nymym ʾ*[.

5:3 Here I agree with Allegro; Strugnell questions the division into two words, but compare the spacing in lines 1 and 2.

9:2-3 Strugnell may be correct in identifying frg. 9 with Psalm 104. He restores Ps 104:21-23 in this way in lines 2-3:

2. *hkpyrym*]*šwʾgym*[*lṭrp wg* . . .
3. *yṣʾ ʾdm*[ ]*l*[*pwʿlw* . . .

9:3 Allegro reads]*d*.[.

Fragment 11. Allegro reads]*ʾt*[.

Fragment 12. Allegro's transcription does not indicate the space after the *h*.

4QpPs^b (4Q*173*) Fragment 5

Editio princeps: "Commentary on Psalms (B)" (J. M. Allegro), *Qumrân Cave 4,* Vol. I, pp. 51-53 and pl. XVIII.

Secondary literature: J. Strugnell "Notes," 219-20.

Allegro included five frgs. under the title 4QpPs^b, but frg. 5 does not belong with the other four. There is no evidence that it is part of a pesher, and J. Strugnell observes that the script is at least a half-century later than the Herodian script of the other frgs. of 4Q*173*.

4QpPs^b fragment 5: Translation

1.]*brw m.* .[
2.]the house of stumbling[
3.].*t* the altar *y*.[
4. THIS IS] THE GATE TO GOD; THE RIGHT[EOUS WILL ENTER INTO IT   Ps 118:20 (?)
5.]desolate places *wḥry*.[
6.]*l* to Jacob[

4QpPs^b fragment 5: Notes

5:1 The first visible trace of a letter could also be *k* or *p,* and the second could be *d* as well as *r*.

5:3 The first letter of the word after *mzbḥ* could be *w* or *y*.

5:4 Allegro notes that *lʾl* is written in a cryptic form, with the ʾ in the form of a reversed Greek minuscule alpha.

This line seems to be a quotation of or an allusion to Ps 118:20.

5:5 Confusion of *w* and *y* makes certain reading of the last word impossible.

BIBLIOGRAPHY

Albright, William F., "A Catalogue of Early Hebrew Lyric Poems (Psalm LXVIII)," *HUCA* 23 (1950-51) 1-39.

Allegro, John Marco, "Addendum to Professor Millar Burrow's [*sic*] Note on the Ascent from Accho in 4QpIsa[a]," *VT* 7 (1957) 183.

_______, "Further Light on the History of the Qumran Sect," *JBL* 75 (1956) 89-95 and 4 pls.

_______, "Further Messianic References in Qumran Literature," *JBL* 75 (1956) 174-87 and 4 pls.

_______, "More Isaiah Commentaries from Qumran's Fourth Cave," *JBL* 77 (1958) 215-21.

_______, "More Unpublished Pieces of a Qumran Commentary on Nahum (4Q pNah)," *JSS* 7 (1962) 304-308 and 3 pls.

_______, "A Newly-Discovered Fragment of a Commentary on Psalm XXXVII from Qumrân," *PEQ* 86 (1954) 69-75.

_______, *The People of the Dead Sea Scrolls in Text and Pictures* (Garden City, NY: Doubleday, 1958).

_______, "A Recently Discovered Fragment of a Commentary on Hosea from Qumran's Fourth Cave," *JBL* 78 (1959) 142-47.

_______, "*Thrakidan,* the 'Lion of Wrath' and Alexander Jannaeus," *PEQ* 91 (1959) 47-51.

_______(ed.), *Qumrân Cave 4: I (4Q158-4Q186)* (DJD 5; Oxford: Clarendon, 1968).

Amoussine, Joseph D., "A propos de l'interprétation de 4 Q 161 (fragments 5-6 et 8)," *RevQ* 8 (1974) 381-92.

_______, "Bemerkungen zu den Qumran-Kommentaren," *Bibel und Qumran: Beiträge zur Erforschung der Beziehungen zwischen Bibel- und Qumranwissenschaft: Hans Bardtke zum 22.9.1966* (ed. S. Wagner; Berlin: Evangelische Haupt-Bibelgesellschaft, 1968) 9-19.

_______, "Éphraïm et Manassé dans le Péshèr de Nahum (4 Q p Nahum)," *RevQ* 4 (1963-64) 389-96.

_______, "Observatiunculae qumraneae," *RevQ* 7 (1969-71) 533-52.

Atkinson, K. M. T., "The Historical Setting of the Habakkuk Commentary," *JSS* 4 (1959) 238-63.

Audet, J.-P., *La Didachè: Instructions des Apôtres* (EBib; Paris: Gabalda, Librairie Lecoffre, 1958).

Avigad, Nachman, "The Palaeography of the Dead Sea Scrolls and Related Documents," *Aspects of the Dead Sea Scrolls* (ed. C. Rabin and Y. Yadin; Scripta Hierosolymitana 4; 2d ed.; Jerusalem: Magnes Press, Hebrew University, 1965) 56-87.

Baer, Yitzhak, *"Pšr ḥbqwq wtqwptw* [Pesher Habakkuk and its Period]," *Zion* 34 (1969) 1-42.

Baillet, M., J. T. Milik, and R. de Vaux (eds.), *Les 'petites grottes' de Qumrân: Exploration de la falaise: Les grottes 2Q, 3Q, 5Q, 6Q, 7Q à 10Q, Le rouleau de cuivre* (DJD 3; Oxford: Clarendon, 1962).

Bardtke, Hans, *Die Handschriftenfunde am Toten Meer: Die Sekte von Qumrān* (Berlin: Evangelische Haupt-Bibelgesellschaft, 1958).

———, *Hebräische Konsonantentexte aus biblischem und ausserbiblischem Schriftum für Übungszwecke ausgewählt* (Leipzig: Harrassowitz, 1954).

———, "Literaturbericht über Qumrān. X. Teil: Der Lehrer der Gerechtigkeit und die Geschichte der Qumrāngemeinde," *TRu* 41 (1976) 97-140.

———, "Neue Funde und Forschungen am Toten Meer," *Die Zeichnen der Zeit* 10 (1956) 448-55.

Barthélemy, J.-D., O.P., "Notes en marge de publications récentes sur les manuscrits de Qumran," *RB* 59 (1952) 187-218.

———, and J. T. Milik *et al.* (eds.), *Qumran Cave I* (DJD 1; Oxford: Clarendon, 1955).

Baumgarten, Joseph M., "Does *TLH* in the Temple Scroll Refer to Crucifixion?" *JBL* 91 (1972) 472-81.

———, "The Duodecimal Courts of Qumran, Revelation, and the Sanhedrin," *JBL* 95 (1976) 59-78.

Benoit, P., J. T. Milik, and R. de Vaux (eds.), *Le grottes de Murabbaᶜat* (DJD 2; Oxford: Clarendon, 1961).

———, *et al.,* "Le travail d'édition des fragments manuscrits de Qumrân," *RB* 63 (1956) 49-67. An English translation of this article appeared as "Editing the Manuscript Fragments from Qumran," *BA* 19 (1956) 75-96.

Betz, Otto, *Offenbarung und Schriftforschung in der Qumransekte* (WUNT 6: Tübingen: Mohr-Siebeck, 1960).

Birnbaum, S. A., "The Date of the Habakkuk Cave Scroll," *JBL* 68 (1949) 161-68.

Bloch, Renée, "Midrash," *Dictionnaire de la Bible* (ed. F. G. Vigoroux); *Supplément 5* (ed. L. Pirot, A. Robert, and H. Cazelles; Paris: Letouzey et Ané, 1957) cols. 1263-81.

Boccaccio, P., and G. Berardi, *Pšr Ḥbqwq: Interpretatio Habacuc 1QpHab* (3d ed.; Fano: Pontificium Seminarium Picenum, 1955; Rome: Pontificium Institutum Biblicum, 1958).

Bosshard, Martin, "Bemerkungen zum Text von Habakuk I 8," *VT* 19 (1969) 480-82.

Brown, J. R., "Pesher in the Habakkuk Scroll," *ExpTim* 66 (1954-55) 125.

Brown, Raymond E., "The Pre-Christian Semitic Concept of 'Mystery,'" *CBQ* 20 (1958) 417-43.

_______, "The Semitic Background of the New Testament *Mysterion,*" *Bib* 39 (1958) 426-48; 40 (1959) 70-87. These articles appeared in a slightly revised form as *The Semitic Background of the Term "Mystery" in the New Testament* (Facet Books, Biblical Series 21; Philadelphia: Fortress, 1968).

Brownlee, William H., "Biblical Interpretation among the Sectaries of the Dead Sea Scrolls," *BA* 14 (1951) 54-76.

_______, "The Composition of Habakkuk," *Hommages à André Dupont-Sommer* (ed. A. Caquot and M. Philonenko; Paris: Librairie D'Amérique et D'Orient Adrien-Maisonneuve, 1971) 255-75.

_______, "Emendations of the Dead Sea Manual of Discipline and Some Notes Concerning the Habakkuk Midrash," *JQR* 45 (1954-55) 141-58, 198-218.

_______, "Further Corrections of the Translation of the Habakkuk Scroll," *BASOR* 116 (1949) 14-16.

_______, "Further Light on Habakkuk," *BASOR* 114 (1949) 9-10.

_______, "The Habakkuk Midrash and the Targum of Jonathan," *JJS* 7 (1956) 169-86.

_______, "The Historical Allusions of the Dead Sea Habakkuk Midrash," *BASOR* 126 (1952) 10-20.

_______, "The Jerusalem Habakkuk Scroll," *BASOR* 112 (1948) 8-18.

_______, *The Meaning of the Qumrân Scrolls for the Bible with Special Attention to the Book of Isaiah* (New York: Oxford University, 1964).

_______, "Messianic Motifs of Qumran and the New Testament," *NTS* 3 (1956-57) 12-30, 195-210.

_______, "The Original Height of the Dead Sea Habakkuk Scroll," *BASOR* 118 (1950) 7-9.

_______, "The Placarded Revelation of Habakkuk," *JBL* 82 (1963) 319-25.

_______, *The Text of Habakkuk in the Ancient Commentary from Qumran* (JBL Monograph Series 11; Philadelphia: Society of Biblical Literature and Exegesis, 1959).

Bruce, F. F., *Biblical Exegesis in the Qumran Texts* (Grand Rapids: Eerdmans, 1959).

_______, "The Dead Sea Habakkuk Scroll," *ALUOS* 1 (1958-59) 5-24.

Burgmann, H., "Gerichtsherr und Generalankläger: Jonathan und Simon," *RevQ* 9 (1977) 3-72.

Burrows, Millar, "The Ascent from Acco in 4Q p Isa^{a}," *VT* 7 (1957) 104-105.

_______, *The Dead Sea Scrolls* (New York: Viking, 1955).

_______, "The Meaning of *ʾšr ʾmr* in *DSH,*" *VT* 2 (1952) 255-60.

_______, *More Light on the Dead Sea Scrolls* (New York: Viking, 1958).

_______, "Prophecy and the Prophets at Qumrân," *Israel's Prophetic Heritage: Essays in Honor of James Muilenberg* (ed. B. W. Anderson and W. Harrelson; New York: Harper & Brothers, 1962) 223-32.

———, (ed.), with the assistance of John C. Trever and William H. Brownlee, *The Dead Sea Scrolls of St. Mark's Monastery, Volume I: The Isaiah Manuscript and the Habakkuk Commentary* (New Haven: American Schools of Oriental Research, 1950).

Bush, F. W., "Evidence from Milḥama and the Masoretic Text for a Penultimate Accent in Hebrew Verbal Forms," *RevQ* 2 (1959-60) 501-14.

Cantera Ortiz de Urbina, Jesús, *El Comentario de Habacuc de Qumran* (Textos y estudios del Seminario Filológico Cardenal Cisneros 3; Madrid: Consejo Superior de Investigaciones Científicas, 1960).

Carmignac, Jean, "A propos d'une restitution dans le Commentaire du Psaume 37," *RevQ* 1 (1958-59) 431.

———, "Les citations de l'Ancien Testament, et spécialement des Poèmes du Serviteur, dans les Hymnes de Qumrân," *RevQ* 2 (1959-60) 357-94.

———, *Le docteur de justice et Jésus-Christ* (Paris: Orante, 1957). This book appeared in English as *Christ and the Teacher of Righteousness: The Evidence of the Dead Sea Scrolls* (tr. K. G. Pedley; Baltimore: Helicon, 1962).

———, "Le document de Qumran sur Melkisédeq," *RevQ* 7 (1969-71) 343-78.

———, "Le genre littéraire du 'péshèr' dans la Pistis-Sophia," *RevQ* 4 (1963-64) 497-522.

———, "Notes sur les Peshârîm," *RevQ* 3 (1961-62) 505-38.

———, "Vestiges d'un Pésher de Malachie (?)," *RevQ* 4 (1963-64) 97-100.

———, É. Cothenet, and H. Lignée, *Les Textes de Qumrân traduits et annotés. Volume II* (Autour de la Bible; Paris: Letouzey et Ané, 1963).

Carreira das Neves, Joaquim, "Qumran: Exegese Histórica e Teologia de Salvação," *Didaskalia* 1 (1971) 65-105.

Casciaro Ramírez, J. M., "Los 'Himnos' de Qumrān y el 'Misterio' Paulino," *Scripta Theologica* 8 (1976) 9-56.

———, "El 'Misterio divino en los escritos posteriores de Qumrān," *Scripta Theologica* 8 (1976) 445-75.

———, "El tema del 'Misterio' divino en la 'Regla de la Comunidad' de Quman," *Scripta Theologica* 7 (1975) 481-97.

Cathcart, Kevin J., *Nahum in the Light of Northwest Semitic* (BibOr 26; Rome: Biblical Institute, 1973).

Collins, John J., "Apocalyptic Eschatology as the Transcendence of Death," *CBQ* 36 (1974) 21-43.

———, *The Apocalyptic Vision of the Book of Daniel* (HSM 16; Missoula: Scholars Press, 1977).

———, "The Court-Tales in Daniel and the Development of Apocalyptic," *JBL* 94 (1975) 218-34.

———, "Jewish Apocalyptic against its Hellenistic Near Eastern Environment," *BASOR* 220 (1975) 27-36.

_______, *The Sibylline Oracles of Egyptian Judaism* (SBLDS 13; Missoula: Scholars Press, 1974).

Coote, Robert B., "'MWᶜD HTᶜNYT' in 4 Q 171 (Pesher Psalm 37), fragments 1-2, col. II, line 9," *RevQ* 8 (1972) 81-86.

Cross, Frank Moore, *The Ancient Library of Qumran and Modern Biblical Studies* (rev. ed.; Anchor Books; Garden City, NY: Doubleday, 1961).

_______, D. N. Freedman, and J. A. Sanders (eds.), *Scrolls from Qumran Cave I: The Great Isaiah Scroll, The Order of the Community, The* Pesher *to Habakkuk* (from the photographs by John C. Trever; Jerusalem: Albright Institute of Archaeological Research and the Shrine of the Book, 1972). This is an edition of color photographs; an edition of black-and-white photographs appeared under the same title in 1974.

Dagut, M. B., "The Habakkuk Scroll and Pompey's Capture of Jerusalem," *Bib* 32 (1951) 542-48.

Dahood, Mitchell, S.J., "Hebrew Lexicography: A Review of W. Baumgartner's *Lexikon,* Volume II," *Or* 45 (1976) 327-65.

_______, *Psalms I: 1-50. Introduction, Translation, and Notes* (AB 16; Garden City, NY: Doubleday, 1966).

_______, *Psalms II: 51-100. Introduction, Translation, and Notes* (AB 17; Garden City, NY: Doubleday, 1968).

Daumas, François, "Littérature prophétique et exégétique égyptienne et commentaires esséniens," *À la rencontre de Dieu: Mémorial Albert Gelin* (Bibliothèque de la faculté catholique de théologie de Lyon 8; Le Puy: Xavier Mappus, 1961).

Dautzenberg, Gerhard, *Urchristliche Prophetie: Ihre Erforschung, ihre Voraussetzungen im Judentum und ihre Struktur im ersten Korintherbrief* (BWANT 104; Stuttgart: Kohlhammer, 1975).

Delcor, M., "Des diverses manières d'écrire le tétragramme sacré dans les anciens documents hébraïques," *RHR* 147 (1955) 145-73.

_______, *Les manuscrits de la Mer Morte: Essai sur le Midrash d'Habacuc* (LD 7; Paris: Cerf, 1951).

_______, "Le Midrash d'Habacuc," *RB* 58 (1951) 521-48.

_______, "Où en est le problème du Midrash d'Habacuc," *RHR* 142 (1952) 129-46.

Detaye, Cyrille, "Le cadre historique du Midrash d'Habacuc," *ETL* 30 (1954) 323-43.

Díez-Macho, Alexandro, "El texto bíblico del comentario de Habacuc de Qumran," *Lex tua veritas: Festschrift für Hubert Junker zur Vollendung des siebzigsten Lebensjahres am 8. August 1961* (ed. H. Gross and F. Mussner; Trier: Paulinus-Verlag, 1961) 59-64.

Díez Merino, Luis, "La crucifixión en la antigua literatura judía (Período intertestamental)," *Estudios Eclesiásticos* 51 (1976) 5-27.

_______, "El suplicio de la Cruz en la literatura judía intertestamental," *SBFLA* 26 (1976) 31-120.

Drazin, Nathan, "What can 'Betalmud' prove?" *JQR* 54 (1963-64) 333.

Driver, G. R., "Hebrew Notes," *VT* 1 (1951) 241-50.

_______, "Linguistic and Textual Problems: Minor Prophets," *JTS* 39 (1938) 154-66, 260-73, 393-405.

Dupont, Jacques, "Les 'simples' (*petâyim*) dans la Bible et à Qumrân: A propos de *nēpioi* de Mt. 11,25; Lc 10,21," *Studi sull'Oriente e la Bibbia offerti al P. Giovanni Rinaldi nel 60° compleanno da allievi, colleghi, amici* (Genoa: Studio e Vita, 1967) 329-36.

Dupont-Sommer, André, *Aperçus préliminaires sur les manuscrits de la mer Morte* (L'Orient ancien illustré 4; Paris: Maisonneuve, 1950). This work appeared in English as *The Dead Sea Scrolls: A Preliminary Survey* (tr. E. M. Rowley; Oxford: Blackwell, 1952).

_______, "Le commentaire d'Habacuc découvert près de la mer Morte," *CRAIBL* (1950) 196-98.

_______, "Le 'Commentaire d'Habacuc' découvert près de la Mer Morte: Traduction et notes," *RHR* 137 (1950) 129-71.

_______, "Le Commentaire de Nahum découvert près de la Mer Morte (4Q p Nah): Traduction et notes," *Sem* 13 (1963) 55-88.

_______, *Les écrits esséniens découverts près de la mer Morte* (Bibliothèque historique; 3d. ed.; Paris: Payot, 1964). An English translation of the second revised and enlarged edition of this work (1960) appeared as *The Essene Writings from Qumran* (tr. G. Vermes; Gloucester, MA: Peter Smith, 1973).

_______, "'*Élus de Dieu*' et '*Élu de Dieu*' dans le Commentaire d'Habacuc," *Proceedings of the Twenty-Second Congress of Orientalists Held in Istanbul, September 15th to 22nd, 1951* (ed. Z. V. Togan; Istanbul: Osman Yalcin Matbaasi, 1953). *Volume II: Communications* (Leiden: Brill, 1957) 568-72.

_______, "Encore sur le mot *ʾbwt* dans *DSH* xi 6," *VT* 2 (1952) 276-78.

_______, "Les Esséniens (X): Les commentaires bibliques," *Évidences* 9 (1957) No. 65, pp. 19-28.

_______, "Lumières nouvelles sur l'arrière-plan historique des écrits de Qoumran," *E. L. Sukenik Memorial Volume (1889-1953)* (ed. N. Avigad, M. Avi-Yonah, H. Z. Hirschberg, B. Mazar; Eretz-Israel 8; Jerusalem: Israel Exploration Society, 1967) 25-36.

_______, "Le Maître de Justice ful-il mis à mort?" *VT* 1 (1951) 200-15.

_______, "New Light on the Historical Background of the Qumran Writings," *Dead Sea Scrolls Research: A Symposium* (Jerusalem: The Shrine of the Book Fund, 1965).

_______, *Nouveaux aperçus sur les manuscrits de la mer Morte* (L'Orient ancien illustré 5; Paris: Maisonneuve, 1953). An English translation of this work appeared as *The Jewish Sect of Qumran and the Essenes: New Studies on the Dead Sea Scrolls* (tr. R. D. Barnett; London: Valentine, Mitchell & Co., 1954).

_______, "Observations nouvelles sur l'expression 'suspendu vivant sur le bois' dans le Commentaire de Nahum (4Q pNah II 8) à la lumière du Rouleau du Temple (11Q Temple Scroll LXIV 6-13)," *CRAIBL* (1972) 709-20.

———, *Observations sur le commentaire d'Habacuc découvert près de la mer Morte: Communication lue devant l'Académie des Inscriptions et Belles-Lettres le 26 mai 1950* (Paris: Maisonneuve, 1950).

———, "Observations sur le Commentaire de Nahum découvert près de la mer Morte," *CRAIBL* (1963) 242-43.

———, "Observations sur le Commentaire de Nahum découvert près de la mer Morte," *Journal des Savants* (October-December 1963) 201-27.

———, "Quelques remarques sur le Commentaire d'Habacuc à propos d'un livre récent," *VT* 5 (1955) 113-29.

———, "Résumé des cours de 1963-64: Hébreu et Araméen," *Annuaire du Collège de France* 64 (1964-65) 309-24.

———, "Résumé des cours de 1968-69: Hébreu et Araméen," *Annuaire du Collège de France* 69 (1969-70) 383-405.

———, "Résumé des cours de 1969-70: Hébreu et Araméen," *Annuaire du Collège de France* 70 (1970-71) 399-414.

———, "Résumé des cours de 1970-71: Hébreu et Araméen," *Annuaire du Collège de France* 71 (1971-72) 375-96.

Eddy, Samuel K., *The King is Dead. Studies in the Near Eastern Resistance to Hellenism* (Lincoln: University of Nebraska, 1961).

Eissfeldt, Otto, "Die Menetekel-Inschrift und ihre Deutung," *ZAW* 63 (1951) 105-14.

———, "Zahl und Art der in den Rollen enthaltenen Schriftwerke: Ihre Entstehungszeit und ihre religionsgeschichtliche Einordnung," *TLZ* 74 (1949) 95-98.

Elliger, Karl, *Studien zum Habakuk-Kommentar vom Toten Meer* (BHT 15; Tübingen: Mohr-Siebeck, 1953).

Étiemble, G., "Sur le commentaire au Commentaire d'Habacuc," *Les Temps Modernes* 6 (1950-51) 1284-92.

Finkel, Asher, "The Pesher of Dreams and Scriptures," *RevQ* 4 (1963-64) 357-70.

Fitzmyer, Joseph A., S.J., *The Aramaic Inscriptions of Sefîre* (BibOr 19; Rome: Pontifical Biblical Institute, 1967).

———, "A Bibliographical Aid to the Study of the Qumran Cave IV Texts 158-186," *CBQ* 31 (1969) 59-71.

———, "Crucifixion in Ancient Palestine, Qumran Literature, and the New Testament," *CBQ* 40 (1978) 493-513.

———, "David, 'Being Therefore a Prophet . . .' (Acts 2:30)," *CBQ* 34 (1972) 332-39.

———, *The Dead Sea Scrolls: Major Publications and Tools for Study* (SBLSBS 8; Missoula: Society of Biblical Literature and Scholars Press, 1975, 1977).

———, *Essays on the Semitic Background of the New Testament* (SBLSBS 5; Missoula: Society of Biblical Literature and Scholars Press, 1974).

———, "The Use of Explicit Old Testament Quotations in Qumran Literature and in the New Testament," *Essays on the Semitic Background of the New Tes-*

tament (SBLSBS 5; Missoula: Society of Biblical Literature and Scholars Press, 1974) 3-58.

_______, review of *Qumrân Cave 4* (ed. John Marco Allegro; DJD 5; Oxford: Clarendon, 1968) *CBQ* 31 (1969) 235-38.

Flusser, David, *"Pšr yšᶜyhw wrᶜywn šnym ᶜśr hšlyḥym brʾšyt hnṣrwt* [The *Pesher* of Isaiah and the Twelve Apostles]," *E. L. Sukenik Memorial Volume (1889-1953)* (ed. N. Avigad, M. Avi-Yonah, H. Z. Hirschberg, B. Mazar; Eretz-Israel 8; Jerusalem: Israel Exploration Society, 1967) 52-62.

_______, "Qumran und die Zwölf," *Initiation: Contributions to the Theme of the Study-Conference of the International Association for the History of Religions Held at Strasburg, September 17th to 22nd 1964* (ed. C. J. Bleeker; Studies in the History of Religions (Supplements to *Numen*) 10; Leiden: Brill 1965) 134-46.

Freedman, David Noel, "The 'House of Absalom' in the Habakkuk Scroll," *BASOR* 114 (1949) 11-12.

_______, "The Massoretic Text and the Qumran Scrolls: A Study in Orthography," *Textus* 2 (1962) 87-102.

Fujita, Shozo, "The Metaphor of Plant in Jewish Literature of the Intertestamental Period," *JSJ* 7 (1976) 30-45.

Gärtner, Bertil, "The Habakkuk Commentary (DSH) and the Gospel of Matthew," *ST* 8 (1954) 1-24.

_______, *The Temple and the Community in Qumran and the New Testament: A Comparative Study in the Temple Symbolism of the Qumran Texts and the New Testament* (SNTSMS 1; Cambridge University Press, 1965).

Gaster, Theodor H., *The Dead Sea Scriptures In English Translation With Introduction and Notes* (rev. and enlarged ed.; Anchor Books; Garden City, NY: Doubleday, 1964).

Gertner, M., "Terms of Scriptural Interpretation: A Study in Hebrew Semantics," *BSO(A)S* [University of London] 25 (1962) 1-27.

Glanzman, George S., "Sectarian Psalms from the Dead Sea," *TS* 13 (1952) 487-524.

Goossens, Roger, "Les Kittim du Commentaire d'Habacuc," *La nouvelle Clio* 4 (1952) 137-70.

Gordon, Robert P., "The Targum to the Minor Prophets and the Dead Sea Texts: Textual and Exegetical Notes," *RevQ* 8 (1974) 425-29.

Goshen-Gottstein, M. H., "Linguistic Structure and Tradition in the Qumran Documents," *Aspects of the Dead Sea Scrolls* (ed. C. Rabin and Y. Yadin; Scripta Hierosolymitana 4; Jerusalem: Magnes Press, Hebrew University, 1965) 101-37.

_______, "Philologische Miszellen zu den Qumrantexten," *RevQ* 2 (1959-60) 43-51.

_______, "Studies in the Language of the Dead Sea Scrolls," *JJS* 4 (1953) 104-107.

_______, *Text and Language in Bible and Qumran* (Jerusalem: Orient, 1960).

Grelot, P., "Soixante-dix semaines d'années," *Bib* 50 (1969) 169-86.

Habermann, Abraham M., *ᶜEdah we-ᶜeduth. Three Scrolls from the Judaean Desert: The Legacy of a Community. Edited with Vocalization, Introduction, Notes and Indices* (Jerusalem: Maḥbaroth Le-Sifruth, 1952).

_______, *Megilloth Midbar Yehuda: The Scrolls from the Judean Desert* (Jerusalem: Machbaroth Lesifruth, 1959).

Harris, John G., *The Qumran Commentary on Habakkuk* (Contemporary Studies in Theology 9; London: Mowbray, 1966).

Hoenig, Sidney B., "BeTalmud and Talmud," *JQR* 54 (1963-64) 334-39.

_______, "Dorshé Ḥalakot in the Pesher Nahum Scrolls," *JBL* 83 (1964) 119-38.

_______, "The New Qumran Pesher on Azazel," *JQR* 56 (1965-66) 248-53.

_______, "The Pesher Nahum 'Talmud,'" *JBL* 86 (1967) 441-45.

_______, "Qumran Pesher on 'Taanit,'" *JQR* 57 (1966-67) 71-73.

_______, "What is the Explanation for the Term 'BᵉTalmud' in the Scrolls?" *JQR* 53 (1962-63) 274-76.

Horton, Fred L., "Formulas of introduction in the Qumran literature," *RevQ* 7 (1969-71) 505-14.

Howard, G., "The Tetragram and the New Testament," *JBL* 96 (1977) 63-83.

Huppenbauer, H.-W., "Enderwartung und Lehrer der Gerechtigkeit im Habakuk-Kommentar," *TZ* [Basel] 20 (1964) 81-86.

_______, "Gerichtshaus und Gerichtstag im Habakuk-Kommentar von Qumran," *TZ* [Basel] 17 (1961) 281-82.

Iwry, Samuel, "Was there a Migration to Damascus? The Problem of *šby yśrʾl,*" *W. F. Albright Volume* (ed. A. Malamat; Eretz-Israel 9; Jerusalem: Israel Exploration Society, 1969) 80-88.

Jongeling, B., "Les formes qṭwl dans l'hébreu des manuscrits de Qumrân," *RevQ* 1 (1958-59) 483-94.

Kaddari, M. Z., "The Root *tkn* in the Qumran Texts," *RevQ* 5 (1964-66) 219-24.

Keck, Leander E., "The Poor among the Saints in Jewish Christianity and Qumran," *ZNW* 57 (1966) 54-78.

_______, "The Poor among the Saints in the New Testament," *ZNW* 56 (1965) 100-29.

Kutscher, E. Y., *The Language and Linguistic Background of the Isaiah Scroll* (*1QIsaᵃ*) (STDJ 6; Leiden: Brill, 1974).

Lambert, G., "Le Maître de Justice et la Communauté de l'Alliance," *NRT* 74 (1952) 259-97.

Land, F. A. W. van 't and A. S. van der Woude, *De Habakuk-Rol van ᶜAin Fašḥa: Tekst en Vertaling* (Semietische Teksten met Vertaling 1; Assen: Van Gorcum, 1954).

_______, and A. S. van der Woude, "De Habakukrol van ᶜAin Feschka," *Vox Theologica* 23 (1952-53) 41-49.

Lane, William R., "A New Commentary Structure in 4Q Florilegium," *JBL* 78 (1959) 343-46.

_______, "Pešer style as a reconstruction tool in 4Q Pešer Isaiah *b*," *RevQ* 2 (1959-60) 281-83.

Laridon, V., "De commentario hebraico in librum Habacuc recens invento," *Collationes Brugenses* 48 (1952) 147-53, 178-81, 225-30, 253-59.

Leahy, Thomas, S.J., "Studies in the Syntax of 1QS," *Bib* 41 (1960) 135-57.

Le Déaut, Roger, "À propos d'une définition du midrash," *Bib* 50 (1969) 395-413. An English translation of this article appeared as "Apropos a Definition of Midrash," *Int* 25 (1971) 259-82.

_______, "La tradition juive ancienne et l'exégèse chrétienne primitive," *RHPR* 51 (1971) 31-50.

Lehmann, Manfred R., "Midrashic Parallels to selected Qumran Texts," *RevQ* 3 (1961-62) 545-55.

_______, "*1 Q Genesis Apocryphon* in the light of the Targumim and Midrashim," *RevQ* 1 (1958-59) 249-63.

_______, "Talmudic Material relating to the Dead Sea Scrolls," *RevQ* 1 (1958-59) 391-404.

Lehman, O. H., "Materials Concerning the Dating of the Dead Sea Scrolls: I: Habakkuk," *PEQ* 83 (1951) 32-54.

Leibel, Daniel, *"Hᶜrwt ʾḥdwt l 'pšr nḥwm'* [Some Remarks on the 'Commentary on the Book of Nahum']," *Tarbiz* 27 (1957-58) 12-16.

Licht, Jacob, *"Dpym nwspym lpšr nḥwm* [Additional Leaves of the Pesher Nahum]," *Molad* 19 (1961) 454-58.

_______, *Mgylt hhwdywt mmgylwt mdbr yhwdh* [*The Thanksgiving Scroll: A Scroll from the Wilderness of Judea*] (Jerusalem: Bialik Institute, 1957).

Lohse, Eduard (ed.), *Die Texte aus Qumran. Hebräisch und Deutsch mit masoretischer Punktation: Übersetzung, Einführung und Anmerkungen* (2d ed.; Munich: Kösel-Verlag, 1971).

Longenecker, Richard, *Biblical Exegesis in the Apostolic Period* (Grand Rapids: Eerdmans, 1975).

Lowy, Simeon, "Some Aspects of Normative and Sectarian Interpretation of the Scriptures (The Contribution of the Judean Scrolls towards Systematization)," *ALUOS* 6 (1966-68) 98-163.

Maass, Fritz, "Von den Ursprüngen der rabbinischen Schriftauslegung," *ZTK* 52 (1955) 129-61.

Maier, Johann, *Die Texte von Totem Meer,* 2 vols. (Munich: Reinhardt 1960).

_______, "Weitere Stücke zum Nahumkommentar aus der Höhle 4 von Qumran," *Judaica* 18 (1962) 215-50.

Mansoor, Menahem, "Some Linguistic Aspects of the Qumran Texts," *JSS* 3 (1958) 40-54.

Martin, Malachi, *The Scribal Character of the Dead Sea Scrolls,* 2 vols. (Bibliothèque du *Muséon* 44; Louvain: Publications Universitaires, Institut Orientaliste, 1958).

Mejía, J., "Posibles contactos entre los manuscritos de Qumran y los Libros de los Macabeos," *RevQ* 1 (1958) 51-72.

Mertens, Alfred, *Das Buch Daniel im Lichte der Texte vom Totem Meer* (SBM 12; Würzburg: Echter Verlag; Stuttgart: Katholisches Bibelwerk, 1971).

Metzger, Bruce M., "The Formulas Introducing Quotations of Scripture in the MT and the Mishnah," *JBL* 70 (1951) 297-307.

Meyer, Rudolf, "Bemerkungen zu den hebräischen Aussprachetraditionen von Chirbet Qumrān," *ZAW* 70 (1958) 39-48.

_______, "Der gegenwärtige Stand der Erforschung der in Palästina neu gefundenen hebräischen Handschriften: 14. Zur Sprache von ᶜAin Feschcha," *TLZ* 75 (1950) 721-26.

_______, "Zur Geschichte des hebräischen Verbums," *VT* 3 (1953) 225-35.

Michaud, Henri, "Un passage contesté d'un des rouleaux de la mer Morte," *VT* 2 (1952) 83-85.

Michel, Albert, *Le maître de justice d'après les documents de la Mer Morte, la littérature apocryphe et rabbinique* (Avignon: Maison Aubanel Père, 1954).

Michelini Tocci, Franco, *I manoscritti del Mar Morto: Introduzione, traduzione e commento* (Biblioteca di cultura moderna 631; Bari: Editori Laterza, 1967).

Milik, J. T., "Fragments d'un midrash de Michée dans les manuscrits de Qumrân," *RB* 59 (1952) 412-18.

_______, "Milkî-ṣedeq et Milkî-rešaᶜ dans les anciens écrits juifs et chrétiens," *JJS* 23 (1972) 95-144.

_______, *Ten Years of Discovery in the Wilderness of Judaea* (tr. J. Strugnell; SBT 26; London: SCM, 1959).

_______, "Turfan et Qumran: Livre des Géants juif et manichéen," *Tradition und Glaube. Das frühe Christentum in seiner Umwelt. Festgabe für Karl Georg Kuhn zum 65. Geburtstag* (ed. G. Jeremias, H.-W. Kuhn, and H. Stegemann; Göttingen: Vandenhoeck & Ruprecht, 1971) 117-27.

Miller, Merrill P., "Targum, Midrash and the Use of the Old Testament in the New Testament," *JSJ* 2 (1971) 29-82.

Molin, Georg, "Der Habakukkommentar von ᶜEn Fešḫa in der alttestamentlichen Wissenschaft," *TZ* [Basel] 8 (1952) 340-57.

_______, *Die Söhne des Lichtes: Zeit und Stellung der Handschriften von Totem Meer* (Vienna: Verlag Herold, 1954).

Moraldi, Luigi, *I manoscritti de Qumrān* (Classici delle religioni, La religione ebraica; Turin: Unione tipografico — Editrice Torinese, 1971).

Moriarity, Frederick L., "The Habakkuk Scroll and a Controversy," *TS* 13 (1952) 228-53.

Müller, Hans-Peter, "Mantische Weisheit und Apokalyptik," *Congress Volume. Uppsala 1971* (VTSup 22; Leiden: Brill, 1972) 268-93.

———, "Märchen, Legende und Enderwartung. Zum Verständnis des Buches Daniel," *VT* 26 (1976) 338-50.

Murphy, Roland E., "*Bśr* in the Qumrân Literature and *sarks* in the Epistle to the Romans," *Sacra Pagina: Miscellanea biblica congressus internationalis catholici de re biblica* (ed. J. Coppens, A. Descamps, and É. Massaux, BETL 12-13; Paris: Gabalda, Librairie Lecoffre, 1959; Gembloux: Duculot, 1959) 2. 60-76.

———, "GBR and GBWRH in the Qumran Writings," *Lex tua veritas: Festschrift für Hebert Junker zur Vollendung des siebzigsten Lebensjahres am 8. August 1961* (ed. H. Gross and F. Mussner; Trier: Paulinus-Verlag, 1961) 137-43.

Murphy-O'Connor, Jerome, O.P., "Demetrius I and the Teacher of Righteousness," *RB* 83 (1976) 400-20.

———, "The Essenes and their History," *RB* 81 (1974) 215-44.

Neusner, Jacob, "Types and Forms in Ancient Jewish Literature: Some Comparisons," *HR* 11 (1971-72) 354-90.

Nickelsberg, G. W. E., "Simon—A Priest With a Reputation for Faithfulness," *BASOR* 223 (1976) 67-68.

Obermann, Julina, "Calendaric Elements in the Dead Sea Scrolls," *JBL* 75 (1956) 285-97.

Oppenheim, A. Leo, *The Interpretation of Dreams in the Ancient Near East. With a Translation of an Assyrian Dream-Book* (Transactions of the American Philosophical Society Held at Philadelphia for Promoting Useful Knowledge, New Series 46/3; Philadelphia: American Philosophical Society, 1956).

Osswald, Eva, "Zur Hermeneutik des Habakuk-Kommentars," *ZAW* 68 (1956) 243-56.

Pardee, Dennis, "A Restudy of the Commentary on Psalm 37 from Qumran Cave 4 (Discoveries in the Judaean Desert of Jordan, vol. v, n° 171)," *RevQ* 8 (1973) 163-94.

Patte, Daniel, *Early Jewish Hermeneutic in Palestine* (SBLDS 22; Missoula: Scholars Press, 1975).

Ploeg, J. P. M. van der, *Bijbelverklaring te Qumrân* (Mededelingen der Koninklijke Nederlandse Akademie van Wetenschappen, afd. Letterkunde, Nieuwe Reeks 23/8; Amsterdam: North Holland, 1960) 207-29.

———, "Le Rouleau d'Habacuc de la grotte de ᶜAin Fešḫa," *BO* 8 (1951) 2-11.

———, "L'usage du parfait et de l'imparfait comme moyen de datation dans le commentaire d'Habacuc," *Les manuscrits de la mer Morte: Colloque de Strasbourg 25-27 mai 1955* (Bibliothèque des Centres d'Études supérieures spécialisés; Paris: Presses Universitaires de France, 1957) 25-35.

Rabin, C., "The Historical Background of Qumran Hebrew," *Aspects of the Dead Sea Scrolls* (ed. C. Rabin and Y. Yadin; Scripta Hierosolymitana 4; 2d ed.; Jerusalem: Magnes Press, Hebrew University, 1965) 144-61.

———, "Notes on the Habakkuk Scroll and the Zadokite Documents," *VT* 5 (1955) 148-62.

Rabinowitz, I., "The Existence of a Hitherto Unknown Interpretation of Psalm 107 Among the Dead Sea Scrolls," *BA* 14 (1951) 50-52.

________, "The Guides of Righteousness," *VT* 8 (1958) 391-404.

________, "The Second and Third Columns of the Habakkuk Interpretation-Scroll," *JBL* 69 (1950) 31-49.

________, "*Pêsher/Pittârôn.* Its Biblical Meaning and its Significance in the Qumran Literature," *RevQ* 8 (1973) 219-32.

________, "Sequence and Dates of the Extra-Biblical Dead Sea Scroll Texts and 'Damascus Fragments,'" *VT* 3 (1953) 175-85.

Ratzaby, Y., "Remarks Concerning the Distinction Between *Waw* and *Yodh* in the Habakkuk Scroll," *JQR* 41 (1950-51) 155-57.

Reider, J., "The Dead Sea Scrolls," *JQR* 41 (1950-51) 59-70.

Ringgren, Helmer, *The Faith of Qumran: Theology of the Dead Sea Scrolls* (tr. E. T. Sander; Philadelphia: Fortress, 1963).

Roberts, B. J., "Some Observations on the Damascus Document and the Dead Sea Scrolls," *BJRL* 34 (1951-52) 366-87.

Rosenthal, Judah M., "Biblical Exegesis of 4QpIs," *JQR* 60 (1969-70) 27-36.

Rost, Leonhard, "Der gegenwärtige Stand der Erforschung der in Palästina neu gefundenen hebräischen Handschriften: 12. Bemerkungen zum neuen Habakkuk-text," *TLZ* 75 (1950) 477-82.

Roth, Cecil, "The Era of the Habakkuk Commentary," *VT* 11 (1961) 451-55.

________, "The Subject Matter of Qumran Exegesis," *VT* 10 (1960) 51-68.

Rowley, H. H., "4QpNahum and the Teacher of Righteousness," *JBL* 75 (1956) 188-93.

________, "The Kittim and the Dead Sea Scrolls," *PEQ* 88 (1956) 92-109.

Sanders, J. A., "Habakkuk in Qumran, Paul, and the Old Testament," *JR* 39 (1959) 232-44.

Schoeps, H.-J., "Beobachtungen zum Verständnis des Habakukkommentars von Qumran," *RevQ* 2 (1959-60) 75-80.

________. "Der Habakuk-Kommentar von ᶜAin Feshkha, ein Dokument der Hasmonäischen Spätzeit," *ZAW* 63 (1951) 249-58.

Schreiden, Jacques, *Les énigmes des manuscrits de la mer Morte* (Wetteren: Éditions Cultura, 1961).

Schubert, Kurt, "Die jüdischen und judenchristlichen Sekten im Lichte des Handschriftenfundes von ᶜEn Fešcha," *ZKT* 74 (1952) 1-62.

Seeligman, Isaac Leo, "The Epoch-Making Discovery of Hebrew Scrolls in the Judean Desert," *BO* 6 (1949) 1-8.

________, "Voraussetzungen der Midraschexegese," *Congress Volume: Copenhagen 1953* (VTSup 1; Leiden: Brill, 1953) 150-81.

Segal, M. H., *A Grammar of Mishnaic Hebrew* (Oxford: Clarendon, 1958).

_______, "The Habakkuk 'Commentary' and the Damascus Fragments (A Historical Study)," *JBL* 70 (1951) 131-47.

Segert, Stanislav, "Zur Habakuk-Rolle aus dem Funde vom Toten Meer," *ArOr* 21 (1953) 218-39; 22 (1954) 99-113, 444-59; 23 (1955) 178-83, 364-73, 575-619.

Siegel, Jonathan P., "The Employment of Palaeo-Hebrew Characters for the Divine Names at Qumran in the Light of Tannaitic Sources," *HUCA* 42 (1971) 159-72.

Silberman, Lou H., "Unriddling the Riddle: A Study in the Structure and Language of the Habakkuk Pesher (1 Q p Hab.)," *RevQ* 3 (1961-62) 323-64.

Skehan, Patrick W., "A New Translation of Qumrân Texts," *CBQ* 25 (1963) 119-23.

Sjöberg, Erik, "The Restoration of Col. II of the Habakkuk Commentary of the Dead Sea Scrolls," *ST* 4 (1950) 120-28.

Slomovic, Elieser, "Toward an Understanding of the Exegesis in the Dead Sea Scrolls," *RevQ* 7 (1969-71) 3-15.

Southwell, P. J. M., "A Note on Habakkuk ii. 4," *JTS,* New Series 19 (1968) 614-17.

Sparks, H. F. D., "The Symbolical Interpretation of *Lebanon* in the Fathers," *JTS* New Series 10 (1959) 264-79.

Spiegelberg, Wilhelm, *Die sogenannte demotische Chronik des Pap. 215 der Bibliothèque Nationale zu Paris, nebst den auf der Rückseite des Papyrus stehenden Texten* (Demotische Studien 7; Leipzig. J. C. Hinrichs, 1914).

Stauffer, Ethelbert, "Der gegenwärtige Stand der Erforschung der in Palästina neu gefundenen hebräischen Handschriften: 19. Zur Frühdatierung des Habakukmidrasch," *TLZ* 76 (1951) 667-74.

Stegemann, Hartmut, "Der Pešer Psalm 37 aus Höhle 4 von Qumran (4QpPs37)," *RevQ* 4 (1963-64) 235-70.

_______, "Weitere Stücke von 4 Q p Psalm 37, von 4 Q Patriarchal Blessings und Hinweis auf eine unedierte Handscrhift aus Höhle 4 Q mit Exzerpten aus dem Deuteronomium," *RevQ* 6 (1967-69) 193-227.

Stendahl, Krister, *The School of St. Matthew and its use of the Old Testament* (2d ed.; Philadelphia: Fortress, 1968).

Stenzel, Meinrad, "Habakkuk II 15-16," *VT* 3 (1953) 97-99.

Stern, S. M., "Notes on the New Manuscript Find," *JBL* 69 (1950) 18-30.

Strugnell, John, "Notes en marge du volume V des 'Discoveries in the Judaean Desert of Jordan,'" *RevQ* 7 (1969-71) 163-276.

Sutcliffe, E. F., *The Monks of Qumran as Depicted in the Dead Sea Scrolls with Translations in English* (Westminster, MD: Newman, 1960).

Szörenyi, Andreas, "Das Buch Daniel, ein kanonisierter Pescher?" *Volume du Congrès. Genève 1965* (VTSup 15; Leiden: Brill, 1966) 278-94.

Talmon, S., "Aspects of the Textual Transmission of the Bible in the Light of Qumran Manuscripts," *Textus* 4 (1964) 95-132.

_______, "Notes on the Habakkuk Scroll," *VT* 1 (1951) 33-37.

_______, "Yom Hakkippurim in the Habakkuk Scroll," *Bib* 32 (1951) 549-63.

Tångberg, K. A., "A Note on *pištî* in Hosea II 7, 11," *VT* 27 (1977) 222-24.

Trever, John C., "A Paleographic Study of the Jerusalem Scrolls," *BASOR* 113 (1949) 6-23.

_______, "Preliminary Observations on the Jerusalem Scrolls," *BASOR* 111 (1948) 3-16.

_______, "The Qumran Covenanters and Their Use of Scripture," *The Personalist* 39 (1958) 127-38.

Vaux, Roland de, "Exploration de la région de Qumrân: Rapport préliminaire," *RB* 60 (1953) 540-61.

Vermes, Geza, "A propos des Commentaires bibliques découverts à Qumrân," *RHPR* 35 (1955) 95-102.

_______, "'Car le Liban, c'est le conseil de la communauté': Note sur Pésher d'Habacuc 12,3-4," *Mélanges bibliques rédigés en l'honneur de André Robert* (Travaux de l'Institut Catholique de Paris 4; Paris: Bloud & Gay, n.d.) 316-25.

_______, *The Dead Sea Scrolls in English* (rev. ed.; Pelican Books; Baltimore: Penguin Books, 1968).

_______, *Discovery in the Judean Desert* (New York: Desclee, 1956).

_______, *Les manuscrits du désert de Juda* (Tournai: Desclée, 1953).

_______, "The Qumran Interpretation of Scripture in Its Historical Setting," *ALUOS* 6 (1966-68) 85-97.

_______, *Scripture and Tradition in Judaism: Haggadic Studies* (SPB 4; Leiden: Brill, 1961).

_______, "The Symbolical Interpretation of *Lebanon* in the Targums: The Origin and Development of an Exegetical Tradition," *JTS* 9 (1958) 1-12.

Vincent, Albert, *Les manuscrits hébreux du désert de Juda* (Textes pour l'histoire sacrée; Paris: Fayard, 1955).

Vogt, E., "Fragmentum Ps 37 ex Qumran," *Bib* 36 (1955) 263-64.

_______, "Prima nomina historica in Qumrân (4QpNah)," *Bib* 37 (1956) 530-32.

Wacholder, B. Z., "A Qumran Attack on the Oral Exegesis? The Phrase *ʾšr btlmwd šqrm* in 4 Q Pesher Nahum," *RevQ* 5 (1964-66) 575-78.

Walter, Norman, "The Renderings of *rāṣôn,*" *JBL* 81 (1962) 182-84.

Weis, P. R., "The Date of the Habakkuk Scroll," *JQR* 41 (1950-51) 125-54.

Weiss, Raphael, "A Comparison Between the Massoretic and the Qumran Texts of Nahum III, 1-11," *RevQ* 4 (1963-64) 433-49.

_______, "Fragments of a Midrash on Genesis from Qumran Cave 4," *Textus* 7 (1969) 132-34.

_______, "*Hʿrwt ldpym hnwspym mpšr nḥwm* [Notes on the Additional Columns of the Pešer of Nahum]," *Beth Mikra* 2 (1962-63) 57-63.

_______, *"K᾽wrh (pšr nḥwm b', w')* [*K᾽wrh* (Pesher Nahum 2.6)]," *Beth Mikra* 3 (1963-64) 156.

Wernberg-Møller, P., "A Note on *zwr* 'to stink,'" *VT* 4 (1954) 322-25.

_______, "The Noun of the *Qᵉṭol* class in the Massoretic Text," *RevQ* 2 (1959-60) 448-50.

Whitley, Charles F., "A Note on Habakkuk 2:15," *JQR* 66 (1975-76) 143-47.

Wieder, N., "The Dead Sea Scrolls Type of Biblical Exegesis among the Karaites," *Between East and West: Essays Dedicated to the Memory of Bela Horovitz* (ed. A. Altmann; London: East and West Library, 1958) 75-106.

_______, "The Habakkuk Scroll and the Targum," *JJS* 4 (1953) 14-18.

_______, "The term *qṣ* in the Dead Sea Scrolls and in Hebrew Liturgical Poetry," *JJS* 5 (1964) 22-31.

Wilcox, M., "'Upon the Tree'—Deut 21:22-23 in the New Testament," *JBL* 96 (1977) 85-99.

Williamson, H. G. M., "The translation of 1 Q p Hab V, 10," *RevQ* 9 (1977) 263-65.

Willi-Plein, I., "Das Geheimnis der Apokalyptik," *VT* 27 (1977) 62-81.

Worrell, John, *"ᶜṣh:* 'Counsel' or 'council' at Qumran?" *VT* 20 (1970) 65-74.

Woude, A. S. van der, *Bijbelcommentaren en Bijbelse verhalen* (Die Handschriften van de Dode Zee in Nederlandse Vertaling; Amsterdam: Proost en Brandt, 1958).

_______, "Het Habakkuk-commentaar von ᶜAin Faschka," *Vox Theologica* 24 (1953-54) 47-54.

_______, *Die messianischen Vorstellungen der Gemeinde von Qumrân* (Assen: Van Gorcum; G. A. Hak & Dr. J. J. Prakke, n.d.).

Wright, Addison G., "The Literary Genre Midrash," *CBQ* 28 (1966) 105-38, 417-57.

_______, *The Literary Genre Midrash* (Staten Island, NY: Alba House, 1967).

Yadin, Y., *The Message of the Scrolls* (London: Weidenfeld and Nicolson, 1957).

_______, *Hmgylwt hgnwzwt mmdbr yhwdh* [*The Hidden Scrolls from the Judaean Desert*] (Jerusalem: Schocken, 1958).

_______, "Pesher Nahum (4Q pNahum) Reconsidered," *IEJ* 21 (1971) 1-12 and pl. I.

_______, "Recent Developments in Dead Sea Scrolls Research," *Studies in the Dead Sea Scrolls: Lectures delivered at the third Annual Conference (1957) in memory of E. L. Sukenik* (ed. J. Liver; Jerusalem: Israel Society for Biblical Research, 1957) 40-54.

_______, "Some Notes on Commentaries on Genesis xlix and Isaiah, from Qumran Cave 4," *IEJ* 7 (1957) 66-68.

_______, "Some Notes on the Newly Published *Pesharim* of Isaiah," *IEJ* 9 (1959) 39-42.

Zeitlin, Solomon, "Asher Betalmud," *JQR* 54 (1963-64) 340-41.

_______, "'A Commentary on the Book of Habakkuk': Important Discovery or Hoax?" *JQR* 39 (1948-49) 235-47.

_______, "The Dead Sea Scrolls: A Travesty on Scholarship," *JQR* 47 (1956-57) 1-36.

_______, "Dreams and Their Interpretation from the Biblical Period to the Tannaitic Time: An Historical Study," *JQR* 66 (1975-76) 1-18.

_______, "The Expression BeTalmud in the Scrolls Militates Against the Views of the Protagonists of their Antiquity," *JQR* 54 (1963-64) 89-98.

_______, "The Word BeTalmud and the Method of Congruity of Words," *JQR* 58 (1967-68) 78-80.

INDEX

This index of Hebrew words lists all the words in the pesharim as these texts are presented here. It does not provide references to the body of the monograph, but it can serve as an index to the whole work insofar as the translation and notes for the lines indicated can be consulted for comments on the word or topic indexed. The interests of space have dictated some features of this index that should be noted. With rare exceptions the words are presented in the dictionary form of biblical Hebrew (unvocalized), so that the texts themselves must be examined to check the form and the spelling that occur in each instance in the Qumran documents. The short definition that follows each Hebrew entry is intended only to distinguish the root or word-formation being indexed. Neither does this definition convey the full range of meaning of the individual word, nor does it necessarily provide a translation of the word in the text studied here. References that are set off in italics occur in citations of the biblical text within a pesher document. This does not mean that the word as it appears in the Qumran writing corresponds in every instance to the form that appears in the Masoretic Text but only that the word occurs in a section that is quoting the prophetic text. Finally, square brackets indicate words that have been partially or completely restored, and the Hebrew text must be examined to judge the strength of the restoration.

ʾbd ("to perish"): 1QpHab 2:13; 6:10; 4QpIsa^{a} 2-6 ii [8]; 4QpNah 1-2 ii 8; 3-4 i [11]; 3-4 ii 9; 3-4 iii 7; 3-4 iv [4]; 4QpPs^{a} 1-10 ii 1; 1-10 iii *3*, 4, 8, [8], 18; 4QpMic *1, 3:[1]*
ʾbh ("to want"): 4QpIsa^{c} *23 ii 4*
ʾbywn ("poor"): 1QpHab 12:3, 6, 10; 4QpIsa^{c} *8-10:13; 18-19:[2];* 4QpIsa^{e} *6:[6];* 4QpPs^{a} 1-10 i [21]; 1-10 ii 10, *16;* 1-10 iii 10
ʾbyr ("bull"): 1QpPs *9:[3]*
ʾbyt = *ʾl byt:* 1QpHab 11:6
ʾbk ("to whirl up"): 4QpIsa^{c} *4, 6-7 i [17]*
ʾbl ("mourning"): 4QpHos^{a} 2:17
ʾbn ("stone"): 1QpHab *9:[15];* 10:1; *12:[15];* 13:2; 4QpIsa^{c} 12:5; 4QpIsa^{d} 1:3 (bis), *[6];* 4QpIsa^{e} *3:[1]*
ʾbq ("dust"): 4QpNah *1-2 ii [1]*
ʾbrhm ("Abraham"): 4QpIsa^{c} *18-19:[5]*
ʾbšlwm ("Absalom"): 1QpHab 5:9
ʾgm ("grieved"): 4QpIsa^{c} *11 ii [2]*
ʾgmwn ("reed"): 4QpIsa^{c} *4, 6-7 i [8]*
ʾdwn ("lord"): 1QpMic *1-5:[1], [2];* 14:1; 4QpIsa^{a} *2-6 ii [2], [10]; 7-10 iii [1];* 4QpIsa^{c} *2:[2]; 4, 6-7 i [11]; 6-7 ii [1], 19, 21; 23 ii 8, [16];* 4QpIsa^{e} *11:[3]*
ʾdm ("humanity" or "Adam"): 1QpHab *5:12; 9:8; 12:1;* 4QpIsa^{c} 6-7 ii 8, [17]; *18-19:2, [3];* 31:2; 4QpHos^{b} *7-8:[1];* 4QpPs^{a} 1-10 iii 2
ʾdmh ("ground"): 4QpIsa^{c} *22:[4]*
ʾdyr ("mighty"): 4QpIsa^{a} *7-10 iii [3], 6, [11]*
ʾhb ("to love"): 4QpHos^{a} *2:[10], [19];* 4QpPs^{a} 1-10 i [23]; *1-10 iii 5a, [27]*
ʾwyl ("fool"): 4QpIsa^{c} *11 ii [2]*
ʾwly ("perhaps"): 4QpHos^{b} *11-13:[7]*
ʾwn ("harm," "trouble"): 1QpHab *1:[5];* 4QpIsa^{c} *18-19:3;* 4QpIsa^{e} *6:[3]*
ʾwpn ("wheel"): 4QpNah *3-4 ii 3*
ʾwr ("to give light"): 4QpIsa^{d} 1:5
ʾwr ("light"): 1QpMic 22:2; 4QpIsa^{b} *3:[2];* 4QpIsa^{d} 1:6; 4QpPs^{a} *1-10 i [20]*
ʾwrym ("Urim"): 4QpIsa^{d} 1:5
ʾwt ("sign"): 1QpHab 6:4
ʾz ("then"): 1QpHab *4:9;* 4QpIsa^{c} *8-10:2;* 4QpHos^{a} *1:[16]*
ʾzwr ("waistcloth"): 4QpIsa^{a} *7-10 iii [20]* (bis)
ʾzn ("to listen to"): 3QpIsa [4]
ʾzn ("ear"): 4QpIsa^{a} *7-10 iii [18], 27;* 4QpIsa^{c} *23 ii 18*
ʾzrwʿ ("arm"): 4QpPs^{a} *1-10 ii [24]*
ʾzrḥ ("native"): 4QPs^{a} *1-10 iv [13]*
ʾḥ ("brother"): 4QpIsa^{c} *4, 6-7 i [18]*
ʾḥʾb ("Ahab"): 1QpMic *17-18:[4]*
ʾḥd ("one"): 4QpIsa^{a} 7-10 iii 29; 4QpIsa^{c} *4,*

1:[1], [2]
ʾmr (“word”): 4QpIsa^{e} *6:[5];* 4QpPs^{a} 1-10 i 26
ʾmrh (“word”): 4QpIsa^{b} *2:7*
ʾmt (“truth”): 1QpHab 7:10, 12; 8:9; 1QpPs 2:[1]; 4QpIsa^{a} 2-6 ii 9; 4QpIsa^{c} *6-7 ii 12;* 4QpPs^{a} 1-10 iii [16], 17; 1-10 iv 4, 12
ʾn (“where,” “when”): 1QpHab *1:[1]*
ʾnw (“we”): 4QpIsa^{c} *11 ii 4*
ʾny (“I”): 4QpPs^{a} *1-10 iv [25]*
ʾnky (“I”): 4QpHos^{a} *2:1;* 4QpHos^{b} *2:2*
ʾntykws (“Antiochus”): 4QpNah 3-4 i 3
ʾsp (“to gather”): 1QpHab *3:[14]; 8:5;* 4QpIsa^{e} *11:[5];* 4QpHos^{a} 1:12 4QpMic *1, 3:[4];* 4QpUnid 1:[4]
ʾp (“also”): 1QpHab *8:3; 11:3;* 4QpNah 3-4 ii 6
ʾp (“nose,” “anger”): 1QpHab 3:12, 13; 1QpZeph *1:3, [4];* 4QpIsa^{a} *2-6 ii [12];* 4QpIsa^{b} *2:8, [10];* 4QpIsa^{c} *4, 6-7 i [7], [13], 21;* 4QpNah *1-2 ii 11;* 4QpPs^{a} *1-10 ii 1*
ʾpwʾ (“then”): 4QpIsa^{c} *11 ii [4]*
ʾpyq (“streambed”): 4QpIsa^{c} *2:3*
ʾpl (“darkness”): 4QpIsa^{c} *18-19:1*
ʾps (“to be at an end”): 4QpIsa^{c} *18-19:[2]*
ʾprym (“Ephraim”): 4QpIsa^{c} *4, 6-7 i 20, [20];* 4QpHos^{b} *2:[2],* 3; *5-6:[3]; 10, 26:[1];* 4QpNah 3-4 i [12]; 3-4 ii 2, 8; 3-4 iii 5; 3-4 iv [5]; 4QpPs^{a} 1-10 i [24]; 1-10 ii 18; *13:[4]*
ʾqdḥ (“precious stone”): 4QpIsa^{d} *1:[6]*
ʾrbʿ (“forty”): 4QpPs^{a} 1-10 ii 8
ʾrg (“to weave”): 4QpIsa^{c} *11 ii 1*
ʾrz (“cedar”): 4QpIsa^{c} *8-10:2,* [3]
ʾrḥh (“caravan”): 4QpIsa^{e} *5:[4]*
ʾry (“lion”): 4QpNah *3-4 i 1* (bis), *4*
ʾrk (“to be long”): 1QpHab 7:7
ʾrm (“Aram”): 4QpIsa^{c} *4, 6-7 i [6]*
ʾrṣ (“earth,” “land”): 1QpHab *2:[16];* 3:1, 10; 4:[13]; 6:8; *9:8; 10:14; 12:1, 7,* 9; *13:1,* 4; 1QpMic *1-5:[3];* 23: [2]; 1QpZeph *1:[1], [2],* 5; 4QpIsa^{a} *2-6 ii [3],* 9; *7-10 iii [19]* (bis); 4QpIsa^{b} 2:1, 2; *3:[2];* 4QpIsa^{c} *2:[4]; 4, 6-7 i [18]; 6-7 ii [19]; 8-10:5;* 31:[5]; 4QpIsa^{e} *1-2:4; 5:[4];* 4QpHos^{b} 2:[6]; 4QpNah 1-2 ii 2, [4], *10; 3-4 i [9];* 4QpPs^{a} *1-10 ii 4,* 8, *9,* 11; *1-10 iii 9; 1-10 iv [2],* [3], *11;* 3QpIsa *[4]*
ʾš (“fire”): 1QpHab 10:5, *7,* 13; 1QpMic *1-5:[4];* 1QpZeph *1:[1];* 4QpIsa^{c} *4, 6-7 i [16], [18];* 4QpNah *1-2 ii [11]*
ʾšh (“woman”): 1QpHab 6:11; 4QpNah 3-4 iv 4
ʾšwr (“Asshur”): 4QpIsa^{a} *2-6 ii [11];* 4QpIsa^{c} *2:[2]; 6-7 ii [2];* 40:1; 4QpIsa^{e} *11:[4]*
ʾšm (“to become guilty”): 1QpHab 5:5; 4QpHos^{b} *2:[5]*
ʾšmh (“guilt”): 1QpHab 4:[11]; 8:12; 4QpNah 3-4 ii 6 (bis); 3-4 iii 4
ʾšr (“to lead”): 4QpIsa^{c} *4, 6-7 i [10]* (bis)
ʾšr (relative sign): 1QpHab *1:[1],* [2], [4], [5], [6], 11; 2:6, 8, [9], [12]; 3:2, 4, 9, 13, [15]; 4:1, 5, 11; 5:3, 5, 6, 7, 10, 11; 6:2, 3, 6, 10; 7:3, 4, 7, 8, 11, 13, 15; 8:1, *4,* 8, 9, 11, 16; 9:2, 5, 9, [11], 16; 10:1, 3, 9, 13, [15]; 11:1, 4, 12; 12:3, 5, 6 (bis), 8, 9, 13; 13:2; 1QpMic 6:[4]; 10:4, 6; 15:[2]; 1QpZeph 1:[5]; 1QpPs 3:5; 9:[2]; 4QpIsa^{a} 2-6 ii [6]; 7-10 iii [7], [10], 12, 26, 27, 28; 4QpIsa^{b} *1:1,* 2, 3, 4, {{4}}*;* 2:7 (bis), 10; 3:[6]; 4QpIsa^{c} 1:[2], [4]; 2:[6]; 4, 6-7 i [4]; 6-7 ii 7, [15], 18; 8-10:4, [8]; 12:[5], [8]; *15-16:3, [4]; 18-19:[4];* 21:4; 22:2, [4]; 23 ii 11; 24:2; 25:8; 28:2; 47:[2]; 4QpIsa^{d} 1:[2], [4]; 4QpIsa^{e} 1-2:2, [3]; *5:[1];* 6:2; 8:1, [2]; 9:2; *11:[3];* 4QpHos^{a} 1:[8], [16]; 2:3, 4, 12, 13, 15, *18, [18];* 4QpHos^{b} 2:3, *5;* 10, 26:1; 10a, 4, 18, 24:5, 6; 11-13:[4], [5]; 16:1; 18:2; 19:4; 4QpNah 1-2 ii 2, [3], 5a; 3-4 i [1], *1,* 2, [5], 5, 7, [10], [11], 11 (bis); 3-4 ii 1, 2, 5, 8; 3-4 iii 3, 7, *10;* 3-4 iv 3, 6; 4QpZeph 1-2:[3]; 4QpPs^{a} 1-10 i [21], 26; 1-10 ii 3, 8, 10, 14 (bis), 15, 18, 23; 1-10 iii 1, [3], 4, 5, 7, 8, [10] (bis), 12, [15], [19]; 1-10 iv [2], 4, 8, 9, 11 [14], [18], [24], [27]; 4QpPs^{b} 1:[3]; 3:2; 3QpIsa *[1],* [2]; 4QpUnid 1:2; 2:1
ʾšr (“step”): 4QpPs^{a} *1-10 iv [4]*
ʾšry (“blessed”): 4QpIsa^{c} *23 ii 9*
ʾt (“you”): 4QpNah *3-4 iv [4], [6]*
ʾt (accusative particle): 1QpHab *1:12;* 2:4, 7, 8, 9, *10;* 3:1, 10, [11]; 4:13; 5:3, 4, 5, 11; 6:1, 6 (bis); 7:1, 2, 4; 8:10; 10:3, 13, *14;* 11:13; 12:2, 8; 13:2 (bis), 3, 4; 1QpMic *17-18:[4];* 1QpZeph *1:[2];* 1QpPs 8:3; 11:2; 4QpIsa^{a} 7-10 iii [8], [22], [23]; 4QpIsa^{b} *2:3, 7* (bis); 4QpIsa^{c} *2:2, [2]* (bis); *4, 6-7 i [6], [11]* (bis), *[20], 20; 6-7 ii [1];* 14:7; *15-16:1, [1], [2], [3]; 18-19:[4], [6]; 21:[8];* 23 ii [14], *[17]; 25:7;* 4QpIsa^{d} 1:2; 4QpIsa^{e} 1-

bynh ("insight"): 1QpHab 2:[8]; 4QpIsa^{a} *7-10 iii 16*
byt ("house"): 1QpHab 4:11; 5:9; 8:1, 2; *9:12, 14;* 10:3; 11:6; 1QpMic *1-5:[5]; 17-18:[4],* 6; 20-21:[2]; 1QpPs *3:[3];* 4QpIsa^{c} *6-7 ii 11 18-19:[4];* 4QpHos^{b} *2:[3]; 10, 26:[1];* 4QpNah 3-4 iv 1; 4QpZeph *1-2:[1], [4];* 4QpPs^{a} 1-10 ii 14; 4QpPs^{b} 5:2
byt ʾbšlwm ("House of Absalom"): 1QpHab 5:9
byt plg ("House of Peleg"): 4QpNah 3-4 iv 1
bkh ("to weep"): 4QpIsa^{c} *23 ii [15]* (bis); 29:1
bkwrym ("first fruits"): 4QpNah *3-4 iv [9]*
bky ("weeping"): 4QpIsa^{e} *4:2*
bkr ("first-born"): 4QpIsa^{c} *8-10:[13]*
bly ("without"): 4QpIsa^{b} *2:4, 5;* 4QpHos^{b} *11-13:[6]*
blyʿl ("Belial"): 4QpPs^{a} 1-10 ii 11
blʿ ("to swallow up"): 1QpHab *5:8;* 11:5, 7, 15; 4QpIsa^{c} 1:3; *4, 6-7 i [10];* 4QpHos^{b} *11-13:7; [7]*
bmh ("high place"): 1QpMic 1-5:[3]; *10:3*
bn ("son"): 4QpIsa^{a} 2-6 ii 5; 4QpIsa^{c} *11 ii [3], 4; 21:[9];* 22:3 4QpIsa^{e} *5:[1];* 4QpHos^{b}11-13:2; 4QpPs^{a} *1-10 iv [23];* 3QpIsa *1*
bnh ("to build"): 1QpHab *10:6,* 10; 4QpHos^{b} *15, 33, 4Q168 frg. 2, col. ii:[1];* 4QpZeph *1-2:[4];* 4QpPs^{a} 1-10 iii 16
bʿbwr ("for the sake of"): 1QpHab 8:2, 10; 9:11; 10:11, 12
bʿh ("to ask"): 4QpIsa^{e} *5:[3]* (bis)
bʿl ("Baal"): 4QpHos^{a} *2:[2]*
bʿlh ("witch"): 4QpNah *3-4 ii 7*
bʿr ("to burn"): 4QpIsa^{c} *4, 6-7 i [16];* 4QpNah *3-4 i [9];* 4QpUnid 4:4
bʿr ("to graze"): 4QpIsa^{b} *1:[1]*
bʿr ("to be stupid"): 4QpIsa^{c} *11 ii [3]*
bṣʿ ("to make a profit"): 1QpHab *9:12;* 4QpIsa^{c} *6-7 ii 1*
bṣʿ ("profit"): 1QpHab 9:5, *12*
bṣr ("gold ore"): 1QpPs *9:[3]*
bqʿ ("to split"): 1QpMic *1-5:[3]*
bqʿh ("valley-plain"): 4QpIsa^{a} 2-6 ii 27
bqr ("morning"): 4QpIsa^{b} *2:2;* 4QpIsa^{e} *5:[3]*
bqrb ("in the midst"): 4QpIsa^{a} *2-6 ii [3];* 4QpIsa^{c} *6-7 ii [19]*
bqš ("to seek"): 4QpIsa^{c} 13:[5]; 4QpHos^{b} *2:5;* 4QpNah 3-4 i 2; *3-4 iii 6; 3-4 iv [6];* 4QpPs^{a} 1-10 ii 18; *1-10 iii 18; 1-10 iv 7,* [8], *[13],* [14]; 4QpPs^{b} 1:3
brʾ ("to create"): 4QpNah 1-2 ii [2]
brwš ("cypress"): 4QpIsa^{c} *8-10:[1],* 3
brzl ("iron"): 4QpIsa^{a} *7-10 iii [3], 6, 10*
brḥ ("to flee"): 1QpPs 1; 4QpIsa^{a} 7-10 iii 13; 4QpUnid 4:2
brḥ ("fugitive"): 4QpIsa^{e} *4:[1]*
bryʾ ("fat"): 1QpHab *5:[16]; 6:5*
bryt ("covenant"): 1QpHab 2:[3], 4, [6], [14]; 4QpHos^{b} *7-8:1;* 4QpPs^{a} 1-10 ii 14; 1-10 iii [12]; 1-10 iv [2], [18]
brk ("to bless"): 1QpPs *8:2,* 3; 4QpPs^{a} *1-10 iii [9];* 4QpPs^{b} *4:[2]*
brkh ("blessing"): 4QpPs^{a} *1-10 iii [18];* 4QpPs^{b} *4:[2]*
brq ("lightning"): 4QpNah *3-4 ii 4*
bśr ("flesh"): 1QpHab 9:2; 4QpIsa^{c} *4, 6-7 i [20];* 4QpNah 3-4 ii 6; 4QpPs^{a} 1-10 ii 12
bšn ("Bashan"): 4QpNah *1-2 ii [5],* [5]
bšt ("shame"): 1QpHab *9:13;* 4QpIsa^{c} *21:[13]*
bt ("daughter"): 4QpIsa^{c} *2-6 ii 23, 25;* 4QpMic *1, 3:[1], [2]*
bth ("desert"?): 4QpIsa^{b} *1:[2]*

gʾwt ("ascent"): 4QpIsa^{c} *4, 6-7 i [17]*
gʾl ("to redeem"): 4QpMic *1, 3:[4]*
gbwl ("boundary"): 4QpIsa^{a} 2-6 ii 29; 4QpNah 5:2 (?)
gbwr ("manly"): 1QpHab 2:12; 4QpIsa^{a} *7-10 iii [2],* 8, 9; 4QpIsa^{c} *6-7 ii [12];* 4QpNah 3-4 iii [11]; 3-4 iv 4
gbwrh ("strength"): 4QpIsa^{a} *7-10 iii [16],* [23]; 4QpIsa^{c} *23 ii 4*
gbym ("Gebim"): 4QpIsa^{a} *2-6 ii 24*
gbʿ ("Gibea"): 4QpIsa^{a} *2-6 ii 22*
gbʿh ("Gibeah"): 4QpIsa^{a} *2-6 ii [22]*
gbʿh ("hill"): 4QpIsa^{a} *2-6 ii 25;* 4QpIsa^{c} *23 ii 8;* 4QpIsa^{e} *1-2:[4];* 4QpNah *1-2 ii [9]*
gbr ("to excell"): 1QpHab 11:12
gbr ("young man"): 1QpHab *8:3;* 4QpPs^{a} *1-10 iii [14];* 4QpPs^{b} 3:1
gdwd ("raiding party"): 4QpIsa^{c} *23 ii [14];* 4QpNah 3-4 i 10
gdwl ("great"): 4QpIsa^{a} 7-10 iii 12; 4QpNah 3-4 i 5, 11; 3-4 iii [9]; *3-4 iv [2];* 4QpPs^{a} 1-10 iii [10]
gdyh ("bank"): 4QpIsa^{c} *2:[3]*
gdl ("bravado"): 4QpIsa^{c} *6-7 ii [2]*
gdʿ ("to cut off"): 4QpIsa^{a} *7-10 iii [2], 9*

ḥbqwq (''Habakkuk''): 1QpHab *1:[1],* [2]; 7:1
ḥbr (''company''): 4QpIsa^{c} *23 ii [14]*
ḥg (''festival''): 4QpHos^{a} *2:[15]*
ḥdd (''to be quick''): 1QpHab 3:6
ḥdš (''new''): 1QpHab 2:3
ḥdš (''new moon''): 4QpHos^{a} *2:[15]*
ḥwbh (''condemnation'' ?): 4QpIsa^{b} 2:1
ḥwh (''to bow down''): 1QpHab 12:13
ḥwṭ (''thread''): 1QpHab *9:14; 10:2*
ḥwl (''sand''): 1QpHab *3:[14];* 4QpIsa^{a} *2-6 ii [1], [7];* 4QpIsa^{c} *6-7 ii [13], [16]*
ḥwmh (''wall''): 4QpNah *3-4 iii 10*
ḥwṣ (''street''): 4QpIsa^{b} *2:9;* 4QpNah *3-4 iv 2*
ḥwr (''to grow pale''): 4QpIsa^{c} *11 ii [1]; 18-19:[5]*
ḥwrh (''cave'' ?): 4QpNah *3-4 i 6*
ḥwrnym (''Horonaim''): 4QpIsa^{e} *4:[2]*
ḥwš (''to hurry''): 1QpHab *3:8*
ḥzh (''to see''): 1QpHab *1:[1];* 4QpIsa^{c} *15-16:[2];* 3QpIsa *[1];* 4QpMic *1, 3:[5]*
ḥzwn (''vision''): 1QpHab *6:[15]; 7:5;* 3QpIsa *1*
ḥzwt (''vision''): 4QpIsa^{c} *15-16:[2]*
ḥzq (''to be strong''): 4QpNah 3-4 iii 8, [9]; *5:[3];* 4QpMic *1, 3:[2]*
ḥṭʾ (''to sin''): 4QpIsa^{c} *18-19:[3]*
ḥḥʾt (''sin''): 1QpMic *1-5:[5];* 4QpIsa^{c} *21:[10], [11]*
ḥṭr (''rod''): 4QpIsa^{a} *7-10 iii [15]*
ḥy (''living''): 4QpNah 3-4 i 7, 8
ḥydh (''riddle''): 1QpHab *8:6*
ḥyh (''to live''): 1QpHab *7:[17];* 4QpPs^{a} 1-10 iii 1, 3
ḥyh (''animals''): 1QpPs *9:[2],* 3; 4QpHos^{a} *2:[19]*
ḥyl (''writhe''): 4QpPs^{a} *1-10 i 25;* 4QpMic *1, 3:[2]*
ḥyl (''army''): 1QpHab 9:7; 4QpIsa^{a} 1 i 28; 4QpNah 3-4 i 10; *3-4 iii 10,* [11]; 4QpZeph *1-2:[1], [3]*
ḥyl (''labor pains''): 4QpMic *1, 3:[2]*
ḥkh (''to wait for''): 1QpHab *7:9;* 4QpIsa^{c} *23 ii 8, 9, 14*
ḥkh (''fishhook''): 1QpHab *5:[13]*
ḥkm (''wise''): 4QpIsa^{c} *11 ii [2], [3], [4]*
ḥkmh (''wisdom''): 4QpIsa^{a} *7-10 iii 16;* 4QpPs^{a} *1-10 iv [3]*
ḥlh (''to become ill''): 4QpIsa^{a} *2-6 ii [22]*
ḥlyl (''flute''): 4QpIsa^{b} *2:3*
ḥll (''to profane''): 1QpHab 2:[4]
ḥll (''slain''): 4QpNah *3-4 ii 4,* 6
ḥlp (''to pass by''): 1QpHab *4:9;* 4QpIsa^{c} *2:[3]*
ḥlṣym (''loins''): 4QpIsa^{a} *7-10 iii [20]*
ḥlq (''to divide''): 1QpHab 6:6; 1QpPs *3:[3],* 5; 4QpPs^{a} *13:[3]*
ḥlq (''smoothness''): 4QpIsa^{c} 23 ii 10; 4QpNah 1-2 ii [7]; 3-4 i 2, 7; 3-4 ii 2, 4; 3-4 iii 3, 7
ḥlq (''share of booty''): 1QpHab *5:15; 6:5*
ḥmh (''heat,'' ''anger''): 1QpHab 3:12; *11:3, 6, 14;* 4QpNah *1-2 ii [11];* 4QpPs^{a} *1-10 ii 1*
ḥml (''to feel compassion''): 1QpHab *6:9;* 4QpIsa^{c} *4, 6-7 i [19]*
ḥms (''violence''): 1QpHab *1:[4],* [5], *[7]; 3:8;* 8:11; *9:8; 11:[17]; 12:1, 7,* 9
ḥmr (''clay''): 4QpIsa^{c} *17:[1]*
ḥmš (''five''): 4QpIsa^{c} *23 ii 7*
ḥmt (''Hamath''): 4QpIsa^{e} *11:[4]*
ḥn (''charm''): 4QpNah *3-4 ii 7*
ḥnwn (''gracious''): 4QpPs^{a} *1-10 iii 9*
ḥnyt (''spear''): 4QpNah *3-4 ii 4*
ḥnn (''to be gracious''): 4QpIsa^{c} *23 ii [8], [15]* (bis); 4QpPs^{a} *1-10 iii 18*
ḥns (''Hanes''): 4QpIsa^{c} *21:14*
ḥnp (''to be defiled''): 4QpMic *1, 3:[5]*
ḥnp (''estranged from God''): 4QpIsa^{c} *4, 6-7 i [12]*
ḥnp (''godlessness''): 4QpIsa^{e} *6:[3]*
ḥnq (''to strangle''): 4QpNah *3-4 i 4*
ḥsd (''faithfulness''): 1QpPs 2:2
ḥsh (''to seek refuge''): 4QpIsa^{c} *21:[12];* 4QpPs^{a} *1-10 iv [20]*
ḥswt (''refuge''): 4QpIsa^{c} *21:[13]*
ḥsyd (''one who is faithful''): 4QpPs^{a} *1-10 iv [1]*
ḥsr (''to diminish''): 4QpIsa^{e} *6:[4]*
ḥpṣ (''to delight''): 4QpPs^{a} *1-10 iii 14*
ḥpṣ (''joy''): 4QpHos^{b} *11-13:[8]*
ḥṣy (''half''): 4QpPs^{a} 13:5
ḥṣyr (''grass''): 4QpPs^{a} *1-10 i [13]*
ḥṣn (''bosom of garment''): 4QpPs^{b} *4:[1]*
ḥq (''statute''): 1QpHab 2:15; 8:10, 17; 1QpMic *17-18:[3];* 1QpZeph *1:[2a];* 4QpIsa^{b} *2:5;* 4QpIsa^{c} 6-7 ii 5; 4QpHos^{b} 7-8:2
ḥqq (''to decree''): 1QpHab 7:13
ḥrb (''to dry up''): 1QpHab 6:8; 4QpNah *1-2 ii [4],* [6]

ywm hkpwrym ("Day of Atonement"): 1QpHab 11:7
ywn ("Greece"): 4QpNah 3-4 i 2, 3
ywtm ("Jotham"): 3QpIsa *2*
yḥd ("to join"): 4QpIsa^{c} *4, 6-7 i 21*
yḥd ("community"): 1QpHab 12:4; 1QpMic 10:6; 4QpIsa^{d} 1:2, [4]; 4QpIsa^{e} 9:[3]; 4QpPs^{a} 1-10 ii 15; *1-10 iv 18,* 19; 11:1
yyn ("wine"): 1QpMic *17-18:[3];* 4QpIsa^{b} *2:2, 3*
ykḥ ("to reproach"): 1QpHab *5:1;* 4QpIsa^{a} *7-10 iii [18]* (bis), *27;* 4QpIsa^{c} *18-19:[3]*
ykl ("to be able"): 1QpHab *5:2;* 4QpIsa^{c} *15-16:[4]*
yld ("to give birth"): 1QpZeph *1:[2a];* 4QpMic *1, 3:[2]* (bis)
yld ("child"): 4QpIsa^{c} *18-19:[5]*
ym ("sea"): 1QpHab 3:11; *5:12;* 6:2; *10:15;* 11:2; 4QpIsa^{a} *2-6 ii [1], [7], [14];* 4QpIsa^{b} *3:[2];* 4QpIsa^{c} *6-7 ii [13], [16];* 4QpIsa^{e} *11:[5];* 4QpNah *1-2 ii 3* (bis); *3-4 iii 10*
ymyn ("right side"): 1QpHab *11:10;* 4QpIsa^{c} *4, 6-7 i [19]*
ymn ("to turn to the right"): 4QpIsa^{c} *23 ii [19]*
ynh ("to oppress"): 4QpPs^{a} 1-10 iii 7
ysd ("to lay the foundation"): 1QpHab *5:1;* 4QpIsa^{d} *1:1,* 2
ysp ("to add"): 1QpHab *5:14;* 6:1; 8:12; 11:15; 1QpMic 10:5; 4QpIsa^{c} *6-7 ii [10]; 18-19:[1]; 21:[10];* 4QpIsa^{e} *11:[3];* 4QpNah 3-4 iii 7
y^{c}l ("to help"): 1QpHab 12:10; 4QpIsa^{c} *21:[15]* (bis)
y^{c}p ("to become tired"): 1QpHab *10:8*
y^{c}ṣ ("to plan"): 1QpHab *9:13;* 4QpIsa^{c} *8-10:[4], [6]; 11 ii [2];* 4QpIsa^{e} *6:5;* 4QpMic *1, 3:[1]*
y^{c}qb ("Jacob"): 1QpMic *1-5:[4]; 10:[2];* 4QpIsa^{c} *6-7 ii 11, [12]; 18-19:[4], 5, [6];* 4QpPs^{b} 5:6
y^{c}r ("wood"): 4QpIsa^{a} *7-10 iii [3], [6], [10];* 4QpIsa^{c} *4, 6-7 i [17]; 6-7 ii [7];* 4QpIsa^{e} *5:4;* 4QpHos^{a} *2:19*
yp^{c} ("to shine"): 1QpHab 11:7
yṣʾ ("to go out"): 1QpHab *1:[11], 14; 3:3;* 1QpMic *1-5:[2];* 12:3; 4QpIsa^{a} *7-10 iii [15],* 29; 4QpIsa^{c} *8-10:[12];* 4QpPs^{a} *1-10 i [20];* 1-10 iii [4]; 4QpMic *1, 3:3*
yṣb ("to take one's stand"): 1QpHab *6:13*
yṣhr ("olive oil"): 4QpHos^{a} *2:[2]*
yṣr ("to fashion"): 1QpHab *12:10, 11,* 13; 4QpIsa^{c} *17:[1]*
yṣr ("what is made"): 1QpHab *12:11*
yṣt ("to set on fire"): 4QpIsa^{c} *4, 6-7 i 16*
yqr ("glory"): 4QpPs^{a} *1-10 iii 5a* (?)
yrʾ ("to fear"): 1QpHab *3:3;* 4QpIsa^{a} 2-6 ii [11]; 4QpIsa^{c} *6-7 ii [21]*
yrʾh ("fear"): 4QpIsa^{a} *7-10 iii [17]* (bis)
yrd ("to go down"): 1QpMic *1-5:[3];* 4QpIsa^{b} *2:6;* 4QpIsa^{c} *21:[11]; 25:[5];* 4QpIsa^{e} *3:[1]*
yrh ("to throw"): 4QpNah *3-4 iv 2*
yrh ("to teach"): 1QpHab *12:[16];* 4QpIsa^{a} 7-10 iii 28
yrwšlm ("Jerusalem"): 1QpHab 9:4; 12:7; 1QpMic *10:[4]; 11:[3];* 1QpPs *9:[1],* 2; 4QpIsa^{a} *2-6 ii 25,* 29; 4QpIsa^{b} 2:7, 10 4QpIsa^{c} *6-7 ii [1];* 23 ii 11, *[15];* 4QpIsa^{e} 1-2:2; 4QpNah 3-4 i [1], 2, [3], [10], 11; 3QpIsa *[1],* [3]; 4QpMic *1, 3:[1]*
yrmyh ("Jeremiah"): 4QpIsa^{c} 1:[4]
yr^{c} ("to tremble"): 4QpIsa^{e} *4:[1]*
yrq ("green plant"): 4QpPs^{a} *1-10 i [14]*
yrš ("to take possession"): 1QpHab *2:[17]; 3:2;* 4QpIsa^{c} 31:4; 4QpPs^{a} *1-10 ii 4, 9; 1-10 iii [9],* 11; *1-10 iv [2],* [3], *10;* 4QpPs^{b} 1:[7]
yrš ("to press grapes"): 1QpMic *17-18:[3]*
yśrʾl ("Israel"): 1QpHab 8:10; 1QpMic *1-5:[5];* 4QpIsa^{a} 1 i [27]; *2-6 ii [1], [7];* 7-10 iii 7, [13], [23]; 4QpIsa^{b} *2:8;* 4QpIsa^{c} *4, 6-7 i [6], [8];* 6-7 ii 7, *[10], [12], [13],* [15], *[16]; 18-19:[2]; 23 ii 3; 25:7;* 4QpIsa^{d} 1:1, 7; 4QpIsa^{e} *5:[1];* 6:1; *11:[5];* 4QpHos^{a} 1:[17]; 4QpHos^{b} [9]; *10, 26:[1], 2; 11-13:[3], [7]; 15, 33, 4Q168 frg. 2, col. ii:[1];* 20:[2]; 4QpNah 3-4 i 8, 12; 3-4 iii 3, [5]; 3-4 iv [3]; 5:[2]; 4QpPs^{a} 1-10 iii [11], 12; 1-10 iv [24]; 11:2
yšb ("to dwell"): 1QpHab 4:8; *9:8; 12:1;* 1QpMic *17-18:[5];* 1QpZeph *1:[2],* [5]; 4QpIsa^{a} *2-6 ii [11], [24];* 4QpIsa^{c} *6-7 ii [21]; 23 ii [15]* 4QpIsa^{e} *5:[4];* 4QpNah 1-2 ii 9, *[10]; 3-4 iii [8];* 4QpZeph *1-2:[4]*
yšw^{c}h ("safety"): 4QpPs^{a} 1-10 iii [1]
yšy ("Jesse"): 4QpIsa^{a} *7-10 iii 15*
yš^{c} ("to save"): 1QpHab *1:[4];* 4QpIsa^{a} 7-10 iii [22]; 4QpIsa^{c} *23 ii [3];* 4QpHos^{a} 2:14; 4QpPs^{a} *1-10 iv [20],* 21; 4QpUnid 8:[1]
yš^{c}yh ("Isaiah"): 3QpIsa *1,* [3]

4QpIsa^{d} 2:1; 4QpIsa^{e} *6:[2], 3;* 4QpHos^{a} *1:[8],* 9; *2:[1], 11,* 14; 4QpHos^{b} *2:[1],* 7; *11-13:[3];* 16:[3]; 28; 4QpNah 3-4 i [3], *10;* 3-4 ii 1, *3,* 5; 3-4 iii 7, 8; 4QpZeph *1-2:[1], 1,* 2, *[4];* 4QpPs^{a} 1-10 i 27; 1-10 ii 3, 8, 15, 23, *[27];* 1-10 iii 4, *8, [14], 17; 1-10 iv [1], [4], [7]* (bis), 9 (bis), *13;* 4QpPs^{b} 3:3; *4:[1]* (bis); 4QpMic *1, 3:[5], [6]*

lʾm ("people"): 1QpHab *10:8*

lb ("heart"): 1QpHab 2:[8]; 8:10; 11:13; 4QpIsa^{a} 7-10 iii [8]; 4QpIsa^{c} 23 ii 13; 4QpIsa^{e} *4:[1]; 6:[3];* 4QpPs^{a} *1-10 ii 17; 1-10 iv [4], [24];* 4QpUnid 4:5

lbb ("heart"): 4QpIsa^{c} *6-7 ii 2;* 4QpHos^{a} 1:[9]

lbyʾ ("female lion"): 4QpNah *3-4 i 4*

lbnwn ("Lebanon"): 1QpHab *11:[17];* 12:3; 4QpIsa^{a} *7-10 iii [3], 6, 11;* 4QpIsa^{c} *8-10:2,* [3]; 21:2; 4QpNah *1-2 ii 5,* 7, [7]

lhb ("flame," "sword"): 4QpNah *3-4 ii 3*

lwb ("Libyans"): 4QpNah *3-4 iii [12]*

lwh ("to join"): 4QpNah 3-4 ii 9; 3-4 iii 5; 3-4 iv 1

lwh ("to borrow"): 4QpPs^{a} *1-10 iii 8, 18*

lwz ("to be lost to one's sight"): 4QpHos^{a} 1:5

lwḥ ("tablet"): 1QpHab *6:15*

lwḥyt ("Luhith"): 4QpIsa^{a} *4:[1]*

lḥm ("to fight"): 4QpIsa^{a} 2-6 ii 27

lḥm ("bread"): 4QpIsa^{c} *22:4; 23 ii [16];* 4QpIsa^{e} *5:[4],* 6; 4QpPs^{a} *1-10 iii [18]*

lḥṣ ("oppression"): 4QpIsa^{c} *23 ii [16]*

lyl ("night"): 4QpIsa^{e} *5:[3]*

lylh ("night"): 4QpIsa^{e} *5:[3]* (bis); 4QpHos^{b} 3:2

lyn ("to stay the night"): 4QpIsa^{e} *5:4*

lyšh ("Laishah"): 4QpIsa^{a} *2-6 ii [23]*

lkd ("to capture"): 1QpHab *4:4*

lkn ("therefore"): 4QpIsa^{a} *2-6 ii 10;* 4QpIsa^{b} *2:4, 5;* 4QpIsa^{c} *2:[2]; 6-7 ii 21; 18-19:4; 23 ii 8* (bis); 58; 4QpHos^{a} *1:[7]; 2:8*

lmh ("why?"): 1QpHab *1:[5]; 5:8;* 4QpMic *1, 3:[1]*

lmʿn ("in order that"; see also mʿn): 1QpHab *6:15; 7:3; 11:3,* 14; 1QpMic *17-18:[4];* 4QpIsa^{c} *21:10;* 4QpPs^{a} 1-10 i 27

lʿg ("to ridicule"): 1QpHab 4:2

lʿg ("derision"): 1QpHab 4:6

lpny ("before"; see also *l, pnh*): 1QpPs 9:2; 4QpHos^{b} 15, 33, 4Q*168* frg. 2, col. ii:[5]; 4QpNah *1-2 ii [10]*

lṣ ("scoffer"): 4QpIsa^{c} *18-19:[2]*

lṣwn ("bragging"): 4QpIsa^{b} 2:6, 10

lqḥ ("to take"): 1QpHab 8:12; 4QpHos^{a} *2:8*

lšwn ("tongue"): 4QpNah 3-4 ii 8, 10; 4QpPs^{a} *1-10 iv 3, 26,* 27

mʾd ("very"): 4QpIsa^{c} *25:[6]*

mʾznym ("balance"): 4QpIsa^{e} *1-2:[4]*

mʾḥry ("behind"; see also *ʾḥr*): 4QpIsa^{c} *23 ii [18]*

mʾkl ("food"): 1QpHab *5:[16]; 6:5,* 7

mʾklt ("food"): 4QpIsa^{c} *4, 6-7 i [18]*

mʾn ("to refuse"): 4QpPs^{a} 1-10 ii 3

mʾs ("to reject"): 1QpHab 1:11; 5:11; 4QpIsa^{b} *2:7;* 4QpIsa^{c} *23 ii 14a;* 4QpPs^{a} 1-10 iv [2]

mbly ("without"; see also *bly*): 4QpIsa^{b} *2:4*

mbṣr ("fortress"): 1QpHab *4:4,* 6; 4QpNah *3-4 iv [8]; 5:[3]*

mgwg ("Magog"): 4QpIsa^{a} 7-10 iii 25

mgmh ("totality" ?): 1QpHab *3:8, [14]*

mgrwn ("Migron"): 4QpIsa^{a} *2-6 ii [21]*

mdbr ("wilderness"): 4QpIsa^{a} 2-6 ii 18; 4QpPs^{a} 1-10 iii 1

mdd ("to measure"): 4QpIsa^{e} *1-2:[3];* 4QpPs^{a} *13:4*

mdwn ("quarrel"): 1QpHab *1:[7]*

mdwr ("dwelling place" ?): 4QpNah 3-4 i 1

mdyn ("Midian"): 4QpIsa^{a} *2-6 ii [13]*

mdmnh ("Madmenah"): 4QpIsa^{a} *2-6 ii 24*

mdšh ("something downtrodden"): 4QpIsa^{e} *5:[1]*

mh ("what?"): 1QpHab *1:[5]; 5:8; 6:13, 14; 12:10;* 1QpMic *10:[2], 3;* 4QpIsa^{e} *5:3, [3];* 4QpHos^{b} *5-6:[3], 3*

mhh ("to delay"): 1QpHab *7:9*

mhyr ("skilled"): 4QpPs^{a} 1-10 iv [27]

mhr ("to hurry"): 1QpHab *2:11*

mhrh ("quickly"): 4QpPs^{a} *1-10 i [14]*

mhtlh ("deceit"): 4QpUnid 10 (?)

mwʾb ("Moab"): 4QpIsa^{e} *4:[1]*

mwg ("to melt"): 4QpNah *1-2 ii [9]*

mwʿd ("appointed time"): 1QpHab *7:6; 11:3,* 6; 4QpHos^{a} *2:[8], 15,* [16], 16; 4QpPs^{a} 1-10 ii 10; 1-10 iii 3

mwʿl ("infidelity" ?): 4QpHos^{a} 1:9

mwʿṣh ("advice"): 1QpMic *17-18:4*

mwrʾ ("fear"): 1QpHab 6:5

mwrd ("slope"): 1QpMic *1-5:[4]*

mwrh ("teacher"): 1QpHab 1:13; 2:2; 5:10; 7:4; 8:3; 9:9; 11:5; 1QpMic 10:[4];

4QpIsa^{c} *4, 6-7 i [9];* 21:6; *23 ii [17]* (bis); 46:3 (?); 4QpIsa^{e} 1-2:[3]; 4QpHos^{b} 5-6:2; 4QpPs^{a} 1-10 iii 15, [19]; 1-10 iv [8], 27; 4QpPs^{b} 1:4; 2:[2]; 4QpUnid 7:1

mwrh hṣdq ("Teacher of Righteousness"): 1QpHab 1:13; 2:2; 5:10; 7:4; 8:3; 9:9-10; 11:5; 1QpMic 10:[4]; 4QpIsa^{e} 1-2:[3]; 4QpPs^{a} 1-10 iii [15], [19]; 1-10 iv [8], [27]; 4QpPs^{b} 1:4; 2:[2]; 4QpUnid 7:[1]

mwš ("to cease"): 4QpNah *3-4 ii 3,* 5

mwt ("to die"): 1QpHab *4:[17];* 4QpIsa^{a} *7-10 iii [20];* 4QpIsa^{b} *2:4;* 4QpIsa^{c} 5:1; *8-10:[14];* 4QpPs^{a} *1-10 iv [7],* [8]

mwt ("death"): 1QpHab *8:4;* 4QpIsa^{c} *8-10:[11]*

mzbḥ ("altar"): 4QpPs^{b} 5:3

mzwr ("boil"): 4QpHos^{b} *2:1*

mzmh ("evil plan"): 4QpPs^{a} *1-10 i 26*

mzʿr ("few"): 4QpIsa^{a} *2-6 ii [12]*

mzrḥ ("east"): 4QpNah 3-4 ii 12

mḥlh ("sickness"): 1QpHab 9:1

mḥlqt ("division"): 4QpPs^{a} 1-10 iv 24

mḥmd ("precious thing"): 4QpIsa^{c} 32:2

mḥšbh ("design"): 1QpHab 3:5; 4QpMic *1, 3:[5]*

mṭh ("staff"): 4QpIsa^{a} *2-6 ii [11], [14]*

mṭh ("stretching"): 4QpIsa^{c} *2:4*

mṭyp hkzb ("the One who Spouts the Lie"): 1QpHab 10:9; 10:[17]—11:1 (?)

my ("who?"): 4QpIsa^{c} *8-10:[6], [7]; 17:[1], 1;* 4QpIsa^{e} *1-2:[3];* 4QpNah *1-2 ii [10]* (bis); *3-4 iii 6*

mym ("water"): 1QpHab *10:14;* 11:1; 1QpMic *1-5:[4];* 4QpIsa^{c} *2:2; 23 ii [16];* 36:3; 4QpIsa^{e} *1-2:[3]; 5:[4];* 4QpNah *3-4 iii 10* (bis)

myšwr ("level ground," "fairness"): 1QpHab 3:1; 4QpIsa^{a} *7-10 iii [19]*

mkʾb ("pain"): 1QpHab 11:5

mkmrt ("fishnet"): 1QpHab *5:[14], [15]; 6:3*

mkmš ("Michmash"): 4QpIsa^{a} *2-6 ii [21]*

mkr ("to sell"): 4QpNah *3-4 ii 7* (?)

mkšwl ("offense," "stumbling"): 4QpPs^{b} 5:2

mlʾ ("to fill"): 1QpHab *10:14;* 4QpNah *3-4 i [6];* 4QpPs^{b} *4:1*

mlʾ ("full"): 4QpNah *3-4 ii 1*

mlʾ ("what fills"): 4QpIsa^{c} *2:4*

mlʾk ("messenger"): 4QpIsa^{c} *21:[14];* 4QpNah *3-4 i [10];* 3-4 ii 1

mlwn ("lodging for the night"): 4QpIsa^{a} *2-6 ii 22*

mlḥmh ("battle"): 1QpHab 2:13; 6:4; 4QpIsa^{a} 7-10 iii 11; 4QpIsa^{c} 25:3; 4QpIsa^{e} *5:[5];* 4QpNah 3-4 i [5]; 3-4 iii [11]

mlṭ ("to escape"): 4QpIsa^{a} 2-6 ii [9]; 4QpPs^{a} *1-10 iv 20*

mlyṣ ("interpreter"): 1QpHab *8:6;* 4QpPs^{a} 1-10 i 27

mlk ("to rule"): 4QpIsa^{e} 9:2

mlk ("king"): 1QpHab *3:[17];* 4:2; 1QpPs *3:3; 9:[1];* 4QpIsa^{c} *2:[2]; 6-7 ii 2;* 8-10:1, *11; 11 ii [4];* 25:1; 30:[5]; 4QpIsa^{e} 8:[1]; 4QpNah 3-4 i 2, 3; 3-4 ii [9]; 4QpPs^{a} *1-10 iv [25];* 3QpIsa *[2],* 4; 4QpMic *1, 3:[1]*

mlkwt ("dominion"): 4QpNah 3-4 iv 3; 4QpUnid 3:2

mll ("to dry up"): 4QpPs^{a} *1-10 i [14]*

mll ("to circumcise"): 1QpHab 11:13

mlpny ("before"; see also *mn, l, pnh*): 1QpHab 4:12; *13:1;* 1QpPs frg. 1; 4QpIsa^{a} 7-10 iii [13]; 4QpNah 1-2 ii 8, *[10];* 3-4 i [6]

mlpnym ("formerly"; see also *mn, l, pnh*): 4QpNah 3-4 i 8

mmlkh ("kingdom"): 4QpNah *3-4 ii 11*

mmšlh ("dominion"): 1QpHab 2:13; 4QpNah 1-2 ii 5a; 3-4 ii 4

mn ("from"): 1QpHab 2:2, 7; *3:3, 6, 7, 7* (?), 10, 11; 4:12, *[16]; 5:2, 6, 9;* 7:11; 8:2; 9:5, *8, 13, 15* (bis); 10:4, *7, 11:9,* 12; *12:1, 6; 13:1,* 4; 1QpMic *1-5:[2]* (bis), *4;* 10:6; 12:2; 1QpPs frg. 1; *9:[1];* 4QpIsa^{a} *2-6 ii [11], [15]* (ter), 18, 19, 27; 7-10 iii 13, *[15], 15,* 29; 4QpIsa^{b} 2:1, *4;* 4QpIsa^{c} *4, 6-7 i [6]* (bis), *[8]; 8-10:2,* 8, *[12]; 18-19:1* (bis), *21:[10]; 23 ii 6* (bis), *[18];* 4QpIsa^{d} 1:6; 4QpIsa^{e} *5:[1], 3* (bis), *[3], [5a], [5], 5a, 5; 11:[4]* (sex.), *4, [5];* 4QpHos^{a} 1:11, *[16];* 2:6, *9, 10, 11,* 14; 4QpHos^{b} *2:[1],* [6]; *11-13:[3];* 4QpNah 1-2 ii 4, 8, *[9], 10* (bis), *[11];* 3-4 i 3, [6], 8, *[9];* 3-4 ii 5 (bis), *7,* [10]; *3-4 iii 2, 5, 6; 3-4 iv 7; 1-10 ii 1,* 3, 10, 20, *22;* 1-10 iii [4], *14,* 19, *[19], 20,* 21; 4QpMic *1, 3:3, [4]*

mnwḥh ("rest"): 1QpHab 11:6, 8

mny ("from"): 4QpNah *3-4 iii 8*

mnšh ("Manasseh"): 4QpIsa^{c} *4, 6-7 i [20], [21];* 4QpNah 3-4 iii 9 (bis), [9]; 3-4 iv [1], 1, 3, 6; 4QpPs^{a} 1-10 ii 18; *13:[4],* [5]

ms ("forced service"): 1QpHab 6:7

[9], 10
nʾṣ ("to reject"): 4QpIsab *2:8*
nb ("Nob"): 4QpIsaa *2-6 ii [24]*
nbʾ ("to prophesy"): 1QpHab 1:[2]; 3QpIsa 3
nbṭ ("to look at"): 1QpHab *1:5, [16]; 5:2, 8; 11:3;* 4QpIsab *2:4; 3:[2]*
nbyʾ ("prophet"): 1QpHab *1:[1];* 2:9; 7:5, 8; 4QpIsac *4, 6-7 i [9]; 15-16:[1];* 4QpHosa 2:5
nbl ("to wither"): 4QpPsa *1-10 i [14]*
nbl ("to treat disdainfully"): 4QpNah *3-4 iii [1]*
nbl ("fool"): 4QpIsae *6:[2], [3]*
nbl ("harp"): 4QpIsab *2:3*
nblh ("stupidity"): 4QpIsac *4, 6-7 i [12];* 26:2; 4QpIsae *6:[3]*
nblh ("corpse"): 4QpIsab *2:9*
nblwt ("genitals"): 4QpHosa *2:10*
ngd ("before"): 1QpHab *1:[7];* 4QpHosb 1:2
ngd ("to report"): 4QpIsac *11 ii [4];* 4QpIsae *5:[2];* 4QpPsa 1-10 iv 5
ngwʿ ("injury" ?): 1QpHab 9:1
ngʿ ("to touch"): 1QpMic *11:[3];* 4QpIsac *2:[4]; 21:14*
ngʿ ("plague"): 1QpHab 9:11
ngr ("to pour out"): 1QpMic *1-5:[4]*
ndb ("to volunteer'): 1QpMic 10:5
ndd ("to flee"): 1QpPs *3:[3]* (bis); 4QpIsaa *2-6 ii [24];* 4QpIsae *5:[5], 5a;* 4QpNah *3-4 iii 2,* 5
ndh ("pollution"): 1QpHab 8:13; 4QpNah 3-4 iii 1
ndḥ ("to scatter"): 4QpIsae *11:[5]*
ndyb ("noble"): 4QpIsae *6:[2]*
nhm ("to groan"): 4QpIsab *3:[1]*
nhmh ("groaning"): 4QpIsab *3:[2]*
nhr ("river"): 4QpIsac *2:2;* 4QpNah 1-2 ii [4a], *[4]*
nwh ("to express sympathy"): 4QpNah *3-4 iii 6*
nwh ("to be comely"): 1QpHab *8:4*
nwh ("abode"): 1QpPs *3:[3]*
nwḥ ("to settle"): 4QpIsaa *7-10 iii [15]*
nws ("to flee") 4QpIsaa *2-6 ii [23];* 4QpIsac *23 ii 5* (bis), *7;* 4QpNah 3-4 i [6]
nwp ("to wield"): 4QpIsaa *2-6 ii [25]*
nzr ("crown"): 4QpIsaa 7-10 iii 24
nḥlh ("inheritance"): 4QpPsa *1-10 ii [26];* 1-10 iii 1, 10; 1-10 iv 12; 4QpPsb 1:7
nḥm ("to comfort"): 4QpNah *3-4 iii 6*
nḥr ("to blow"): 4QpIsac 56
nḥš ("serpent"): 4QpIsac *8-10:12*
nḥt ("rest"): 4QpIsac *23 ii [3]*
nṭh ("to stretch out"): 4QpIsab *2:8, [10];* 4QpIsac *4, 6-7 i [13]; 8-10:[5], [6]; 18-19:[4]*
nṭp ("to drip"): 1QpHab 10:9, [17]
nṭš ("to abandon"): 4QpIsae *5:5*
nynwh ("Nineveh"): 4QpNah *3-4 iii 6*
nkh ("to strike"): 1QpHab 3:1; 4QpIsaa *2-6 ii [11], [13], [19];* 4QpIsab *2:8;* 4QpIsac *6-7 ii [11]; 8-10:[12];* 4QpIsae *6:[4];* 4QpHosa 2:12; 4QpHosb 2:3; 4QpNah 3-4 i 5
nkl ("cunning"): 1QpHab 3:5
nkr ("to recognize"): 1QpPs 3:2
nmr ("leopard"): 1QpHab *3:6*
ns ("standard"): 4QpIsac *23 ii 8;* 4QpIsae *11:[5]*
nsk ("to pour out"): 4QpIsac *21:[10]*
nʿr ("youth"): 1QpHab 6:11; 4QpIsac *6-7 ii [3], [7];* 4QpPsa *1-10 iii [17]*
npl ("to fall"): 4QpIsaa *7-10 iii [3], [7]* (bis), *[12];* 4QpNah 3-4 ii 6, 10; 4QpPsa *1-10 ii 16; 1-10 iii [14]*
npṣ ("pelting rain"): 4QpIsac 25:[3]
npš ("throat," "breath"): 1QpHab *7:[15]; 8:4;* 9:11, *[14]; 10:2;* 4QpIsab *2:5;* 4QpIsac 5:1; *11 ii [2];* 14:7; 4QpIsae *4:[1]; 6:[4]*
nṣ ("blossoms"): 1QpZeph *1:2a*
nṣḥ ("to supervise"): 4QpPsa *1-10 iv 23*
nṣḥ ("victory"): 1QpHab *1:[11]*
nṣl ("to rescue"): 1QpHab 8:2; *9:13;* 12:14; 1QpMic 10:[6]; 4QpIsab *3:1;* 4QpHosa *2:9, 11;* 4QpPsa 1-10 ii 10; 1-10 iv [21]; 4QpMic *1, 3:[3]*
nṣr ("shoot"): 4QpIsaa *7-10 iii 15*
nqmh ("vengeance"): 1QpHab 9:2; 4QpPsa 1-10 iv [10]
nqp ("to cut down"): 4QpIsaa *7-10 iii [2], [6], 10*
nqp ("to surround"): 1QpHab 4:7
nśʾ ("to raise"): 1QpHab *1:[7]; 8:6;* 4QpIsaa *2-6 ii [11], [14];* 4QpIsac *4, 6-7 i [9];* 4QpIsae *11:3, [5];* 4QpNah *1-2 ii [10]*
nśyʾ ("chief"): 4QpIsaa 2-6 ii 19
nšk ("to borrow"): 1QpHab *8:[14]*
nšp ("twilight"): 4QpIsab *2:2*
nšr ("eagle"): 1QpHab *3:8,* 11
ntybh ("path"): 4QpHosa *1:7*

ʿy ("ruin"): 1QpMic *10:8*

ʿylwl ("child" ?): 4QpNah *3-4 iv 2,* 4

ʿylm ("Elam"): 4QpIsa^{e} *11:[4]*

ʿyn ("eye"): 1QpHab *5:1, 6,* 7; 4QpIsa^{a} *7-10 iii [17], [27];* 4QpIsa^{b} 1:6; 4QpIsa^{c} *6-7 ii [2];* 4QpIsa^{c} *15-16:[1]; 18-19:[1]; 23 ii [17];* 4QpIsa^{d} 1:1; 4QpHos^{a} *2:10,* 13; 4QpMic *1, 3:[5]*

ʿyr ("city"): 1QpHab 3:1; *10:5,* 10; 12:9; 4QpIsa^{a} 2-6 ii 28; 4QpHos^{b} *15, 33, 4Q168 frg. 2, col. ii:[2];* 4QpNah 3-4 i [4]; *3-4 ii 1;* 3-4 ii 2, 9, 12; 3-4 iii [9]; *3-4 iv 7,* 8

ʿyt ("Aiath"): 4QpIsa^{a} *2-6 ii 21*

ʿkw ("Acco"): 4QpIsa^{a} 2-6 ii 27

ʿl ("upon," "concerning"): 1QpHab 1:[2] (bis), 3, 4, [6] (bis), *10, [14];* 2:[1], 3, [5], [7], 10, [10], 12, 16, [17]; 3:4 (bis), 9, [15]; 4:2 (bis), 5 (bis), 6, [10]; 5:9, 11, *[14], 14; 6:2,* 7, *8,* 10, 11, *12, 13, [14], 15;* 7:1, 2, 4, 7, 10, 12, 15; 8:1, *6, 7,* 8, 9, 12, 16; 9:4, 9, 12; 10:9, *15;* 11:4, *10, 11,* 12, [15]; 12:2, 3, *11,* 12; 13:1; 1QpMic *1-5:[3],* [5]; 10:2, [4], 5; 17-18:5; 1QpZeph *1:[3], [4],* [5]; 1QpPs *9:[1],* 1; 4QpIsa^{a} *2-6 ii [12]* (bis), *[13], [14], [15]* (bis), [19]; *7-10 iii 15,* [22], 28; 4QpIsa^{b} *2:8* (bis); *3:[1];* 4QpIsa^{c} 1:4; *2:[2], 3* (bis); 4, 6-7 i [5], *10, [11], [19]* (bis), *[21]; 6-7 ii [1], [2],* 4, *[11]* (bis); 8-10:1, *3,* [5], *[5],* 10; 13:4; *15-16:[1], [4]; 21:[11], [15]; 23 ii 5* (quater), *7, 8,* 10, 20; *25:5, [5], 6, [6];* 4QpIsa^{d} 1:4, 7; 4QpIsa^{e} 1-2:[3]; 6:6; 4QpHos^{a} 2:13; 4QpHos^{b} 2:[3]; 5-6:2; 17:1; 4QpNah 1-2 ii 4; 3-4 i [1], [2], [5], 5, 6, 8; 3-4 ii 4, [8], *11; 3-4 iii 1,* 3, 4, 5, [6]; 3-4 iv 1, *2,* 3, 5, [7]; 4QpZeph 1-2:[4]; 4QpPs^{a} *1-10 i [19]* (bis), [21], 26; 1-10 ii 2, *7,* 7, *9,* 9, *[13],* 14, 18, 19, [22], [25], [27]; 1-10 iii [5a], [5], 7, 10, 15, 19; *1-10 iv 2,* [4], 8, [11], *13,* 14 (bis), [16], [18], *23,* 27; 4QpPs^{b} *4:[2];* 3QpIsa *[1],* [2], [3]; 4QpMic *1, 3:[4];* 4QpUnid 2:2

ʿl ("yoke"): 1QpHab 6:6; 4QpIsa^{a} *2-6 ii [15]* (bis)

ʿlh ("to go up"): 1QpHab *5:13;* 10:4; 4QpIsa^{a} 2-6 ii 27; 4QpIsa^{b} *1:[2], 3;* 4QpIsa^{c} *2:[2], [3]; 8-10:[2];* 4QpIsa^{e} *4:2;* 4QpNah *3-4 ii 3*

ʿlz ("exult"): 4QpPs^{a} *13:[3]*

ʿlyz ("exultant"): 4QpIsa^{b} *2:6*

ʿlm ("to be hidden"): 4QpNah *3-4 iv 5*

ʿlmh ("young woman"): 1QpPs *8:[2]*

ʿm ("people"): 1QpHab 2:10; 3:6, 11, [13]; 4:3, 6, 7, 14; 5:3, 5; 6:7; *8:5,* 12, *15,* [17]; *9:4,* 5, 7, *14; 10:2,* 4, *7;* 1QpMic *11:3;* 1QpPs *9:[3];* 4QpIsa^{a} *2-6 ii [1],* 6, *[6], [11], [18];* 7-10 iii 26; 4QpIsa^{b} *2:4, 8;* 4QpIsa^{c} *4, 6-7 i [10], [18];* 6-7 ii 5, *13, [16], [21]; 21:[15]; 23 ii 15;* 27:2; 4QpIsa^{d} 1:[2]; 4QpIsa^{e} 5:6; *11:[3];* 4QpHos^{b} 11-13:4; 4QpNah 3-4 ii 9; 4QpPs^{a} 1-10 iii [5], 7

ʿm ("with"): 1QpHab 2:1; 3:6, 13; 6:1; 9:6; *10:7;* 4QpIsa^{a} 7-10 iii 29; 4QpIsa^{c} *2:[4];* 4QpNah 1-2 ii 5a; 3-4 ii 9; *3-4 iv 9;* 4QpPs^{a} 1-10 iii [4]; *1-10 iv 11;* 4QpUnid 4:1

ʿmd ("to stand"): 1QpHab *6:12;* 8:9; 4QpIsa^{a} *2-6 ii [24];* 7-10 iii 22; 4QpNah *1-2 ii [10];* 4QpNah 3-4 i 3

ʿmwd ("pillar" ?): 4QpPs^{a} 1-10 iii 16

ʿmyr ("cut grain"): 4QpMic *1, 3:[6]*

ʿml ("tribulation"): 1QpHab *1:[5]; 5:2;* 8:2; 10:12

ʿmm ("to be black"): 4QpIsa^{c} *4, 6-7 i [17]* (?)

ʿmnw ʾl ("Immanuel"): 4QpIsa^{c} *2:[4]* (?)

ʿmq ("valley"): 1QpMic *1-5:[3];* 4QpHos^{b} 1:1; 4QpPs^{a} *13:[4]*

ʿmr ("to gather grain"): 4QpPs^{b} *4:[1]*

ʿmrh ("Gomorrah"): 4QpUnid 4:3

ʿmry ("Omri"): 1QpMic *17-18:[3]*

ʿng ("to take delight in"): 4QpPs^{a} *1-10 ii 9,* 11; 1-10 iii 11

ʿnh ("to answer"): 1QpHab *6:14, 9:[15];* 4QpIsa^{a} *2-6 ii [23];* 4QpIsa^{c} *23 ii [16]*

ʿnh ("to humble"): 1QpHab 9:10

ʿnw ("humble"): 4QpIsa^{a} 7-10 iii 7, *[19];* 4QpIsa^{c} *18-19:[1]; 21:7;* 4QpIsa^{e} *6:[5];* 7:[2]; 4QpPs^{a} *1-10 ii 9*

ʿny ("poor"): 4QpPs^{a} *1-10 ii 16*

ʿnn ("cloud"): 4QpNah *1-2 ii 1,* [2]

ʿntwt ("Anathoth"): 4QpIsa^{a} *2-6 ii [23]*

ʿpl ("to have audacity"): 1QpHab *7:14*

ʿpr ("dirt"): 1QpHab *4:4;* 4QpIsa^{e} *1-2:[4]*

ʿṣ ("tree," "wood"): 1QpHab *9:15;* 10:1; *12:15;* 13:2; 4QpIsa^{c} *6-7 ii [7];* 4QpNah 3-4 i 8

ʿṣb ("idol"): 1QpHab 13:3

ʿṣh ("counsel," "council"): 1QpHab 3:5; 4:11; 5:10, 12; 9:10; 12:4; 1QpMic 10:6; 4QpIsa^{a} *7-10 iii [16];* 4QpIsa^{c} *8-10:[4]; 11 ii [3]; 21:[9];* 4QpIsa^{d} 1:2, [4]; 4QpNah 1-2 ii [8]; 3-4 i 2, 5, [11]; 3-4 ii 6, 9; 3-4 iii 7, 8;

3:4, [9], [15]; 4:1, 5, 10, 14; 5:3, 7, 9, [16]; 6:3, 6, 10; 7:4, 7, 10, 15; 8:1, 8, [16]; 9:4, 9, [16]; 10:3, 9, 15; 11:4, 12; 12:2, 7, 12; 13:1; 1QpMic 1-5:[5]; 10:2, [4]; 17-18:[5]; 1QpZeph 1:4; 1QpPs 3:[3] (?); 4:2; 9:1, 3; 4QpIsa^{a} 2-6 ii [17], [26]; 7-10 iii [22], 27; 4QpIsa^{b} 1:2; 2:1; 4QpIsa^{c} 6-7 ii 4, 8, 14, 17; 13:[4]; 22:1; 23 ii 10; 29:3; 4QpIsa^{d} 1:[1], 4, 7; 4QpIsa^{e} 1-2:3; 4:[2]; 5:2; 6:6; 4QpHos^{a} 1:[8], [16]; 2:[2], 12, 15; 4QpHos^{b} 2:[1], [3], [6]; 7-8:[1]; 10, 26:[2]; 11-13;[4], [5], [9]; 16:[1]; 17:[1]; 19:[1]; 4QpNah 1-2 ii [1], [3], [4a], [5]; 3-4 i [1], [2], [5], 6, [10]; 3-4 ii 2, 4, [8], 11; 3-4 iii 3, 6, 9, [11]; 3-4 iv 1, 3, 5, [7]; 4QpZeph 1-2:[1], [3], 4; 4QpPs^{a} 1-10 i [14], [21], [26]; 1-10 ii 2, 4, 7, 9, 14, 18, [22], [25], [27]; 1-10 iii 3, [5a], 7, 10, 15, [18]; 1-10 iv [1], [3], [4], 8, [11], [14], 16, [18], [20], [23], [25], [27]; 13:[5]; 4QpPs^{b} 2:1; 3QpIsa [2]; 4QpUnid 1:[3]; 14:1

pšt ("flax"): 4QpHos^{a} *2:9*

ptgm ("decree," "matter"): 4QpIsa^{a} 2-6 ii [26]; 7-10 iii [22]; 4QpPs^{b} 2:[1]

ptḥ ("to open"): 4QpPs^{a} *1-10 ii 16*

pty ("simple person"): 1QpHab 12:4; 1QpMic 10:[3]; 7:[3]; 20-21:[1]; 4QpNah 3-4 iii 5, [7]

ptrws ("Pathros"): 4QpIsa^{e} *11:[4]*

ṣʾn ("small cattle"): 4QpIsa^{c} *21:7;* 4QpPs^{a} 1-10 iii 6

ṣbʾ ("army"): 1QpHab *10:7;* 1QpPs *3:3;* 4QpIsa^{a} *2-6 ii [3];* [11], *[13]; 7-10 iii [1];* 4QpIsa^{c} *4, 6-7 i 17; 6-7 ii [19], [21]; 8-10:6;* 4QpIsa^{e} *5:[1];* 4QpNah *3-4 i [9]; 3-4 ii [10]*

ṣbr ("to pile up"): 1QpHab *4:4*

ṣdwq ("Zadok"): 4QpIsa^{c} 22:3

ṣdyq ("righteous"): 1QpHab *1:12,* [13]; *5:9; 7:[17];* 4QpIsa^{c} *18-19:[4];* 4QpPs^{a} *1-10 ii 13, 22, [24]; 1-10 iii 9, [17]; 1-10 iv [2], [3], 7, [19];* 4QpPs^{b} *5:[4]*

ṣdq ("righteousness"): 1QpHab 1:13; 5:10; 7:4; 8:3; 9:10; 11:5; 1QpMic 10:4; 4QpIsa^{a} *7-10 iii [18], [20];* 4QpIsa^{e} 1-2:[3] (bis); 4QpPs^{a} *1-10 i [20];* 1-10 iii [15], [19]; 1-10 iv [8], [27]; 4QpPs^{b} 1:4; 2:[2]; 4QpUnid 7:[1]

ṣdqh ("righteousness"): 1QpHab 2:2; 4QpIsa^{a} *2-6 ii [2], [7], [18];* 4QpUnid 1:[3]

ṣhl ("to shout"): 4QpIsa^{a} *2-6 ii [23]*

ṣhrym ("noonday"): 4QpPs^{a} *1-10 i [20]*

ṣwʾr ("neck"): 4QpIsa^{a} *2-6 ii [15];* 4QpIsa^{c} *2:[4]*

ṣwh ("to order"): 4QpIsa^{c} 12:8

ṣwm ("fast"): 1QpHab 11:8

ṣwʿr ("Zoar"): 4QpIsa^{e} *4:[1]*

ṣwr ("rock"): 1QpHab *5:1;* 4QpIsa^{a} *2-6 ii [13];* 4QpNah *1-2 ii [11]*

ṣḥh ("parched"): 4QpIsa^{b} *2:5*

ṣywn ("Zion"): 4QpIsa^{a} *2-6 ii [11], 25;* 4QpIsa^{c} *6-7 ii [1];* 4QpIsa^{c} *23 ii 15;* 4QpMic *1, 3:[2], [5]*

ṣyr ("messenger"): 4QpNah 3-4 ii 1

ṣl ("shadow"): 4QpIsa^{c} *21:12, 13*

ṣlḥ ("to be successful"): 4QpPs^{a} *1-10 i 25*

ṣmʾ ("thirst"): 4QpIsa^{b} *2:5*

ṣmʾ ("thirsty"): 4QpIsa^{e} *5:[4]; 6:[4]*

ṣmʾh ("thirst"): 1QpHab 11:14

ṣmḥ ("shoot"): 4QpIsa^{a} 7-10 iii [22]; 4QpHos^{b} *11-13:[6]*

ṣmr ("wool"): 4QpHos^{a} *2:9*

ṣʿn ("Zoan"): 4QpIsa^{c} *11 ii [2]; 21:[14]*

ṣph ("to lie in wait"): 1QpHab *6:13;* 4QpPs^{a} *1-10 iv 7,* [8]

ṣpʿ ("viper"): 4QpIsa^{c} *8-10:[13]*

ṣr ("distress"): 1QpHab 5:6; 4QpIsa^{b} *3:[2];* 4QpIsa^{c} *23 ii [16];* 4QpHos^{b} *2:5*

ṣrh ("distress"): 4QpHos^{a} 2:14; 4QpPs^{a} *1-10 iv [19]*

qbl ("to accept"): 4QpPs^{a} 1-10 ii 10

qbṣ ("to gather"): 1QpHab *8:5,* 11, 9:5; 4QpNah 3-4 i [11]; 4QpPs^{a} 13:6; 4QpMic *1, 3:[6]*

qdwš ("holy"): 4QpIsa^{b} *2:7;* 4QpIsa^{c} *6-7 ii [11]; 18-19:[2], [6]; 23 ii 3; 25:[7]*

qdym ("east wind"): 1QpHab *3:9, [14]*

qdm ("to meet"): 4QpIsa^{e} *5:[5]*

qdm ("front," "ancient"): 1QpHab *4:[16];* 4QpIsa^{c} *4, 6-7 i [6]; 11 ii [4]*

qdš ("to be holy"): 4QpIsa^{c} *18-19:6, [6]*

qdš ("a holy thing"): 1QpHab 2:4; *4:[17]; 12:[17];* 1QpMic *1-5:[2];* 1QpPs 8:[3]; 4QpIsa^{a} 7-10 iii [24]; 4QpIsa^{c} 60:3; 4QpPs^{a} 1-10 iii 8, 11; 1-10 iv 25; *13:[3]*

qwh ("to wait for"): 4QpPs^{a} *1-10 ii 4; 1-10 iv [10]*

qwl ("voice"): 4QpIsa *2-6 ii 23;* 4QpIsa^{c} *23 ii [15];* 4QpNah *3-4 i [10];* 3-4 ii 1, *3* (bis)

qwm ("to rise"): 1QpHab *2:10; 8:13;* 10:10; 4QpNah *1-2 ii [11]*

rmh ("height"): 4QpPs^{a} 1-10 iv 15
rmh ("Ramah"): 4QpIsa^{a} *2-6 ii [22]*
rms ("to trample"): 4QpNah 3-4 i 3
rmś ("reptiles"): 1QpHab *5:13*
rʿ ("evil"): 1QpHab *5:2, 7;* 9:2, *12, 13;* 4QpIsa^{e} *6:[5];* 4QpNah 3-4 iii 3; 4QpPs^{a} *1-10 ii 2*
rʿ ("shout"): 4QpMic *1, 3:[1]*
rʿ ("friend"): 1QpHab 4:12; *11:2*
rʿb ("to be hungry"): 4QpIsa^{c} *4, 6-7 i [19]*
rʿb ("famine"): 1QpHab 2:[13]; 4QpIsa^{b} 2:1, *4;* 4QpIsa^{c} *8-10:[14];* 4QpHos^{a} 2:12; 4QpPs^{a} 1-10 ii 1; *1-10 iii 2,* 3, 4; 4QpUnid 1:2
rʿb ("hungry"): 4QpIsa^{e} *6:[4]*
rʿh ("to graze," "to shepherd"): 4QpIsa^{c} *8-10:[13];* 4QpIsa^{e} *1-2:[2]* (bis); 4QpPs^{a} 1-10 iii [5]
rʿh ("evil"): 4QpPs^{a} 1-10 ii 2, 24, *[27]*
rʿl ("to stagger"): 1QpHab *11:9*
rʿnn ("luxuriant"): 4QpPs^{a} *1-10 iv [13]*
rʿʿ ("to do evil"): 1QpHab 3:5; 4QpIsa^{c} *4, 6-7 i [12];* 4QpZeph *1-2:1;* 4QpPs^{a} *1-10 ii 2*
rʿš ("to quake"): 4QpNah *1-2 ii [9]*
rʿš ("clatter"): 4QpNah *3-4 ii 3*
rph ("to become slack," "to forsake"): 1QpHab 7:11; 4QpPs^{a} *1-10 ii 1*
rps (also *rpś*, "to muddy by trampling"): 1QpPs *9:[3]*
rṣh ("to be pleased"): 1QpHab 7:16; 4QpHos^{a} 1:4; 4QpHos^{b} 16:3
rṣwn ("what is acceptable"): 4QpPs^{a} 1-10 i 21; 1-10 ii 5, [26]
rqd ("to dance"): 4QpNah *3-4 ii 3*
rqmh ("variegated colors"): 4QpIsa^{a} 7-10 iii [24]
ršʿ ("to be guilty"): 1QpHab 9:11; 10:5; 4QpPs^{a} *1-10 iv [7],* [9]
ršʿ ("wrong," "guilt"): 4QpNah 3-4 i 1
ršʿ ("guilty," "wicked"): 1QpHab *1:[12];* [13] (bis); 2:[14]; 5:5, *9;* 8:8; 9:[9]; 11:4; 12:2, 8; 13:4; 4QpIsa^{a} *7-10 iii [20];* 4QpIsa^{c} 30:3; 4QpHos^{b} 10, 26:[3]; 4QpNah 3-4 iv [1], 5; 4QpPs^{a} *1-10 ii 5,* [9], *13, 16,* 18, *22, [24]; 1-10 iii 2, 8,* [12]; *1-10 iv [1], 7,* 8, *11, 13, [18], 20,* [21]
ršʿh ("guilt," "wickedness"): 1QpHab 5:8; 9:1; 4QpIsa^{c} *4, 6-7 i [16];* 4QpNah 1-2 ii 6; 4QpPs^{a} 1-10 i 24; 1-10 ii 7; 1-10 iii [7]; 1-10 iv 11

rtq ("to be bound"): 4QpNah *3-4 iv [2]*
śʾt ("dignity"): 1QpHab *3:3*
śbʿ ("to be satiated"): 1QpHab *8:4; 11:8;* 4QpHos^{a} 2:[3]; 4QpPs^{a} *1-10 iii [2]*
śbʿh ("satiation"): 1QpHab 3:12
śdh ("field"): 1QpMic *10:8;* 4QpHos^{a} *2:[19];* 4QpMic *1, 3:[3]*
śwk ("hedge"): 4QpHos^{a} *1:[7]*
śḥq ("laugh"): 1QpHab *4:4,* 6; 4QpPs^{a} *1-10 ii 13*
śym ("to put," "to make"): 1QpHab *4:9, [13]; 5:1; 9:12; 10:[8];* 4QpIsa^{a} 7-10 iii [25]; 4QpIsa^{d} *1:[3];* 4QpHos^{a} *2:19;* 4QpNah *3-4 iii 1*
śkr ("wages" ?): 4QpIsa^{c} *11 ii 2*
śmʾl ("left side"): 4QpIsa^{c} *4, 6-7 i 19*
śmʾl ("to turn to the left"): 4QpIsa^{c} *23 ii [19]*
śmḥ ("to rejoice"): 1QpHab *5:14;* 4QpIsa^{c} *4, 6-7 i [11]; 8-10:[2], [11];* 4QpPs^{a} 1-10 iv 12
śmḥh ("joy"): 4QpIsa^{c} *18-19:[2];* 4QpHos^{a} 2:[17]
śnʾ ("hate"): 4QpNah 3-4 iii 4
śʿyr ("Seir"): 1QpMic 12:2; 4QpIsa^{e} *5:3*
śʿrh ("gale"): 4QpNah *1-2 ii [1],* [1]
śph ("lip"): 4QpIsa^{a} *7-10 iii [19];* 4QpNah 3-4 ii 8; 4QpPs^{a} 12:1
śr ("chief"): 1QpHab 4:3; 4QpIsa^{c} *11 ii [2]; 21:[14];* 4QpNah 3-4 ii 9; 4QpPs^{a} 1-10 iii 5, 7
śrp ("flying serpent"): 4QpIsa^{c} *8-10:[13]*
š (relative particle): 4QpPs^{b} *4:[1]*
šʾg ("to roar"): 4QpUnid 9:2
šʾwl ("Sheol"): 1QpHab *8:4;* 4QpIsa^{b} *2:5*
šʾwl ("Saul"): 4QpIsa^{a} *2-6 ii [23]*
šʾwn ("uproar"): 4QpIsa^{b} *2:6*
šʾl ("to ask"): 4QpIsa^{c} *21:[11]*
šʾr ("to be left over"): 4QpIsa^{e} *11:[4]*
šʾr ("remainder"): 4QpIsa^{a} *2-6 ii [1], [7];* 4QpIsa^{c} *6-7 ii [7], [10], [12]* (bis), *[13], [16];* 4QpIsa^{e} *11:[3]*
šʾryt ("rest"): 4QpIsa^{c} *8-10:[14]*
šbb ("to chop to splinters" ?): 4QpHos^{b} *11-13:[3], [5]*
šbṭ ("rod," "tribe"): 4QpIsa^{a} *2-6 ii [11],* [19]; *7-10 iii [19],* [25]; 4QpIsa^{c} *8-10:12;* 4QpIsa^{d} 1:7; 4QpPs^{a} 13:5
šby ("captives"): 1QpHab 3:14; 4QpNah 3-4 ii 5; *3-4 iv [1],* 4
šbʿ ("seven"): 4QpPs^{a} 1-10 iv 23

šnʿr ("Shinar"): 4QpIsa^{e} *11:[4]*

šʿh ("to look"): 4QpIsa^{c} *25:[6]*

šʿl ("hollow hand"): 4QpIsa^{e} 1-2:[3]

šʿn ("to lean on"): 4QpIsa^{c} *6-7 ii [11]* (bis); *25:[5];* 4QpHos^{a} 2:13

šʿr ("gate"): 1QpMic *11:3;* 4QpIsa^{c} *18-19:[3];* 4QpIsa^{d} *1:[6];* 4QpPs^{b} *5:4*

šʿrwry ("horrible thing"): 1QpHab 9:1; 4QpHos^{b} *10, 26:[1]*

špṭ ("to judge"): 1QpHab 10:5; 12:5; 4QpIsa^{a} 7-10 iii [8], *[18], 18, 26, [27], 28;* 4QpPs^{a} *1-10 iv 7,* [9]

špl ("to be low"): 4QpIsa^{a} 7:2; *7-10 iii [2];* 4QpNah 3-4 iv 3

šqd ("to lie in wait for"): 4QpIsa^{c} *18-19:3*

šqh ("to give drink"): 1QpHab *11:2*

šqwṣ ("abomination"): 4QpNah 3-4 iii [1], *1*

šqṭ ("to be quiet"): 4QpIsa^{c} *23 ii [4]*

šql ("to weigh"): 4QpIsa^{e} *1-2:4*

šqr ("lie"): 1QpHab 10:10, 12; *12:11;* 4QpIsa^{c} *4, 6-7 i [9];* 4QpIsa^{e} *6:[5];* 4QpNah 3-4 ii [2], 8; 4QpPs^{a} 1-10 i 27; 4QpUnid 6:2

šrqh ("whistling"): 1QpMic *17-18:[5]*

šrš ("root"): 4QpIsa^{a} *7-10 iii [15];* 4QpIsa^{c} *8-10:[12], [14]*

šth ("to drink"): 1QpHab *11:9;* 4QpMic *17-18:3*

štwt ("weavers" ?): 4QpIsa^{c} *11 ii [1]*

tʾnh ("fig"): 4QpHos^{a} *2:[18];* 4QpNah *3-4 iv 9*

tbwʿh ("produce"): 4QpIsa^{c} *22:[4]*

tbl ("world"): 4QpNah 1-2 ii 9, *[10]*

tblyt ("annihilation"): 4QpIsa^{a} *2-6 ii [13]*

thw ("wasteland," "nothingness"): 4QpIsa^{b} *1:[2];* 4QpIsa^{c} *18-19:[4]*

twḥlt ("expectation"): 1QpHab 1:[2]

twk ("midst"): 1QpHab 5:12; 10:4, 5; 1QpPs *8:[2];* 4QpIsa^{d} 1:[2], 3; 4QpNah 3-4 iii 5; 4QpPs^{a} 1-10 iii 6; 1-10 iv 19

twkḥt ("reproach," "objection"): 1QpHab 5:4, 10; *6:14*

twʿbh ("abominable thing"): 1QpHab 8:[13]; 12:8; 4QpNah 3-4 iii 1

twʿh ("perversion"): 4QpIsa^{e} *6:4*

twrh ("law"): 1QpHab *1:10,* 11; 5:12; 7:11; 8:1; 12:5; 1QpMic 10:[6]; 4QpIsa^{b} *2:7;* 4QpIsa^{c} 2:5; 23 ii 12, *14a;* 4QpIsa^{e} 1-2:3; 6:7; 4QpPs^{a} 1-10 ii 3, 15, 23; 1-10 iv 2, *[4],* 8; 11:1

tḥlh ("beginning"): 1QpHab 8:9; 4QpIsa^{e} 9:1

tḥt ("beneath"): 1QpMic *1-5:[3]*

tymʾ ("Tema"): 4QpIsa^{e} *5:[4]*

tyrwš ("wine"): 4QpHos^{a} *2:[1], 8*

tkwnh ("fixed place"): 1QpHab 7:13

tkn ("to determine the measure"): 4QpIsa^{e} *1-2:[4];* 4QpUnid 2:2 (?)

tlh ("to hang"): 4QpNah 3-4 i 7, 8

tlmwd ("teaching" ?): 4QpNah 3-4 ii 8

tm ("completeness"): 4QpIsa^{c} 14:1

tm ("blameless"): 4QpPs^{a} *1-10 iv [16]*

tmh ("to be stunned"): 1QpHab *1:[17]* (bis)

tmhwn ("confusion"): 4QpHos^{a} 1:8

tmyd ("continuance"): 1QpHab *6:8*

tmym ("blameless"): 4QpPs^{a} *1-10 ii [26]*

tmym ("Thummim"): 4QpIsa^{d} 1:5

tmm ("to be finished"): 4QpNah 1-2 ii 5a; 4QpPs^{a} 1-10 ii 8

tʿh ("to go astray"): 1QpHab 10:9; 1QpMic 11:[1]; 4QpIsa^{c} *4, 6-7 i [10];* 4QpHos^{a} 2:5; 4QpNah 3-4 ii 8 (bis); 3-4 iii 5, 7; 4QpPs^{a} 1-10 i 23, 26

tʿnyt ("affliction"): 4QpPs^{a} 1-10 ii 10; 1-10 iii [3]

tʿʿ ("to make fun of"): 1QpHab 4:3

tp ("timbrel"): 4QpIsa^{b} *2:3;* 4QpIsa^{c} 25:2

tpʾrt ("beauty"): 4QpIsa^{c} *6-7 ii [2];* 1QpPs 3:[4]

tpp ("to drum"): 1QpPs *8:[2]*

tpś ("to capture," "to be overlaid"): 1QpHab 4:7; *12:[16];* 4QpHos^{b} 16:2

trbwt ("increase"): 4QpUnid 3:2

trdmh ("deep sleep"): 4QpIsa^{c} *15-16:[1]*

trn ("flagstaff"): 4QpIsa^{c} *23 ii 7*

tšwʿh ("salvation"): 4QpPs^{a} *1-10 iv [19]*